The Institute of Direct and Digital Marketing (IDM) is Europe's leading body for the professional development of direct, data and digital marketers. We offer a range of training courses and bespoke training solutions, internationally respected qualifi cations, membership, events and conferences. Our programme refl ects the very latest developments in our fast-moving profession. More than 10,000 marketing professionals hold an internationally respected IDM qualifi cation and over 62,000 marketers have attended an IDM open course. IDM members gain privileged access to a wealth of knowledge-based services and a network of over 4,000 fellow marketing professionals.

www.theidm.com

DIRECT AND DIGITAL MARKETING IN PRACTICE

2ND EDITION

**BRIAN THOMAS &
MATTHEW HOUSDEN**

Bloomsbury Information
An imprint of Bloomsbury Publishing Plc

B L O O M S B U R Y
LONDON • NEW DELHI • NEW YORK • SYDNEY

Bloomsbury Information

An imprint of Bloomsbury Publishing Plc

50 Bedford Square
London
WC1B 3DP
UK

1385 Broadway
New York
NY 10018
USA

www.bloomsbury.com

BLOOMSBURY and the Diana logo are trademarks of Bloomsbury Publishing Plc

First published in 2011 by A&C Black Business Information and Development
Reprinted by Bloomsbury Information 2015

British Library Cataloguing-in-Publication Data

A catalogue record for this book is available from the British Library.

ISBN: 978-1-4081-2752-0

Library of Congress Cataloging-in-Publication Data

Dunn, Marilyn.

Belief and Religion in Barbarian Europe c. 350 - 700/

Marilyn Dunn.

pages cm.

Includes bibliographical references and index.

ISBN 978-1-4411-3160-7 (hardcover) - ISBN 978-1-4411-6532-9 (paperback) -
ISBN 978-1-4411-0023-8 (ebook(pdf)) ISBN 978-1-4411-2382-4 (ebook(epub))

1. Christianity and other religions - Germanic. 2. Germanic Peoples - Religion. 3. Conversion - Christianity - History. 4. Europe - Church history. 5. Europe - Church history - 600-1500. 6. Paganism - Europe - History. I Title.

BR128.G4D86 2014

274'.02-dc23

Series: Business on a Shoestring, 1234567X, volume 6

Typeset by Jones Ltd, London
Printed and bound in Great Britain

CONTENTS

ACKNOWLEDGEMENTS

There are two kinds of supporters I want to acknowledge: those who helped and advised me when I was learning the business, and those who helped me in writing this book.

The greatest influence on my business career was undoubtedly the late Peter Donoghue. Peter introduced me to direct marketing and the power of segmentation and targeting thirty years ago. He also taught me about marketing in the wider sense and generally how business works.

Peter also introduced me to Graeme McCorkell, years ago I was a Marketing Director and Graeme was my advertising agent. Graeme filled in the gaps that Peter left and taught me, in a very practical way, how to make advertising work.

There are many people with whom I have worked running marketing departments and agencies. I could list dozens but the two from whom I learned the most were Drayton Bird and Stewart Pearson.

In the eight years since this book was first published there have been huge changes, mainly relating to the Internet, and so I have been learning avidly again from the many young web wizards I am lucky enough to know.

I also want to thank my two co-authors Matthew Housden and Professor Derek Holder, without whom I would have only half a book, and the entirely unflappable Ellen Grace of A & C Black, who remained calm and pleasant through many traumatic moments.

Brian Thomas

I often give the following advice to students; find something you enjoy, find someone who is great at it and learn as much from them as you can. In this regard I would like to thank Brian Thomas and Professor Derek Holder who also happen to be my co-authors.

I have been lucky to be involved with the IDM for many years since Professor Alan Tapp introduced me. My thanks go to him and the team there, especially those in qualifications.

I would also like to thank delegates and students at the IDM and at Greenwich University whom I have been lucky enough to meet and who continually inspire me with their dedication and enthusiasm whilst studying and their skill in implementing what they have learned in practice.

As the cause of many of Brian's "traumatic moments" I would particularly like to thank the team at A & C Black especially Ellen Grace for her professionalism, forbearance and charm.

Finally my thanks and love to Kook Magoon, Lemon Drop, Wilbur Woo and to Groyne, without whom none of this would have happened.

Matthew Housden

CHAPTER 1
THE NEW DISCIPLINE OF DIRECT AND DIGITAL MARKETING

by Professor Derek Holder, Founder and Managing Director
of the Institute of Direct Marketing (IDM)

IN THIS CHAPTER

We will introduce the new discipline of direct and digital marketing and discuss the following points:

- What do we mean by direct marketing?
- From mass marketing to digital marketing
- Direct marketing: three applications
- Firms that deal direct
- Multi-channel marketing
- Direct marketing and Pareto's Principle
- Principles of direct and digital marketing (TICC)
- Ten ways in which digital marketing is different
- Data: the direct and digital marketer's information system
- Data, CRM and eCRM
- Limitations of the customer information system
- Summary

Lester Wunderman first coined the term 'direct marketing' in 1961, but experienced marketing practitioners are still arguing about what direct marketing really stands for. From those early days we have seen the rise of new (or enhanced) methodologies bearing descriptions such as 'database marketing' 'relationship marketing' 'interactive marketing' and 'customer relationship marketing'.

In this chapter we attempt to set the record straight and discuss the essential similarities and differences between direct marketing and these newcomers.

We look at the origins of direct marketing, its adoption by multi-channel users and how its disciplines underpin all that has followed its inception. We discuss the four basic principles of direct marketing: Targeting, Interaction, Control and Continuity (TICC).

Finally, we introduce the direct, data and digital marketer's information system, establishing its context within the company-wide information system.

WHAT DO WE MEAN BY DIRECT MARKETING?

The origins of what came to be called direct marketing lie in the mail-order business: the classic examples in the USA were the Sears Roebuck and Montgomery Ward catalogues, which can be traced back to the 1880s. Later it came to include telephone marketing, magazine subscription selling, continuity book and music publishing, and other direct-to-consumer methods over and above catalogue-based mail order. As late as the 1980s Stan Rapp, a US direct marketing pioneer, was still defining direct marketing as a means of distribution – not a definition that would be widely accepted today.

There must be as many definitions of direct marketing as there are writers on the subject. Rather than adding to them, here are three which you may find helpful:

'Direct marketing is a collection of methodologies for communicating a message to individuals with a view to obtaining a measurable, cost-effective response.'

Federation of Direct and Interactive Marketing Association

'Direct marketing is the process in which individual customers' responses and transactions are recorded…and the data used to inform the targeting, execution and control of actions…that are designed to start, develop and prolong profitable customer relationships.'

Graeme McCorkell, Direct and Database Marketing

'Direct marketing is the accountable practice of building and harnessing customer data and insight to target, execute and control the creation and delivery of superior customer value across all interactive channels to start and prolong profitable customer relationships.'

Holder and McCarthy, The Institute of Direct Marketing, 2009

The first lesson from these definitions is that direct marketing is a collection of methodologies or a *process*.

The second lesson is that the primary job of direct marketing – as indeed of all marketing – is to convey a *message*, a message which is intended to provoke a response.

The last definition, by Holder and McCarthy, is the most contemporary as it talks about creating customer value, which is recognised today as the overriding purpose of a business. It further includes 'interactive' channels as today the majority of consumers and businesses respond and transact via multiple channels. Finally, it is not just about building profitable lifetime customer relationships but starting or acquiring new customers.

From mass marketing to digital marketing

For many years, until the 1990s, marketers loosely defined marketing as 'identifying and satisfying customer needs at a profit'. Up to the 1950s and 1960s, mass marketing and mass communication dominated marketing practice. The technologies that drive marketing are information and communication. Twentieth century mass marketing was propelled by high-speed rotary printing, high-quality colour reproduction, film, radio and finally television broadcasting. These were the technologies of mass communication. In the 1970s and 1980s 'target' marketing grew rapidly as brands proliferated and extended to reach specific large market segments.

Marketing depends on information about markets and in those times decision making was aided by sample survey-based research. This provided media readership research, TV audience research, consumer panels, retail audits and ad hoc surveys. Media audience research answered the question, 'Who are we reaching with our advertising?' Consumer panels and retail audits answered the question, 'Is it working to create sales?'

At this stage in marketing's evolution many major companies were distant from the customer (apart from those companies who practised direct marketing). The company still controlled the key navigation tools; it decided the product, price, promotion and place (distribution channels). The company told its customers and prospects about its products and services when it wanted to, through which media channels it chose and dictated where and when the customers could obtain their products.

The champions of this form of marketing were Unilever and Proctor & Gamble. They researched their new products, test marketed and launched with brand advertising primarily through television. This was pre-BSkyB and the 300-plus channels available today, TV offered companies an unparalleled reach to market as well as low CPT (cost per thousand). Yet still consumers were anonymous buyers.

As Alan Mitchell, the well-known columnist and author commented, the pillars of marketing in the 1970s and 1980s were branding, advertising, and research marketing. These he suggested were surrogates:

- brands were a surrogate for a relationship between the company and the product;
- advertising was a surrogate for the dialogue which a relationship brings;
- marketing research was a surrogate for the learning that takes place with a dialogue.

Direct marketing grew rapidly in the 1980s and 1990s as it provided the missing dialogue between customers and company – it encouraged customers to respond and these responses were recorded and measured. Coupled with the cost of computer storage declining exponentially, it led to the creation of large customer databases containing full transactional, geographical and lifestyle information about their customers. This was particularly true in the service sector: financial services, travel and leisure, utilities and telecoms.

The information and technology revolution

The immense increase in affordable computer power now allows today's direct marketer to hold as much relevant information on *every* customer as the twentieth-century mass marketer held on the *entire* market.

This represents nothing less than a revolutionary change to the marketing opportunity. Furthermore, the revolution is not over: computer power keeps on getting cheaper and marketing continues to become more sophisticated. Yet the communications technology revolution created by digital media may be of even greater significance.

Communications technology and digital marketing

Digital media represent the convergence of information and communications technologies. Through digital media, information is transferred from one computer to another. The information can be in the form of sounds or moving pictures. One of the computers can be a TV receiver, a phone, a smart card or, soon, devices in the home, like the refrigerator and alarm system.

Now the marketer and customer each have a computer. And their computers can exchange information. The so-called dialogue of direct marketing can be turned into something approaching a real conversation in which information is exchanged and acted upon in real time, hence leading to the expression 'real-time marketing'.

It is useful to give a definition of digital marketing.

Digital marketing is:

APPLYING...digital technologies which form online channels to market (Web, email, databases plus mobiles and digital TV)

TO...support marketing activities aimed at achieving profitable acquisition and retention of customers (with a multi-channel buying process and customer life cycle

THROUGH DEVELOPING...a planned approach to improve customer knowledge (of their profiles, behaviour, value and loyalty drivers), then delivering integrated targeted communications and online services that match their individual needs.

The first part of the definition illustrates the range of access platforms and communication tools that form the online channels which marketers use to build and develop relationships with customers. The access platforms or hardware include PCs, PDAs, mobile phones and interactive digital TV and these deliver content and enable interaction through different online communication tools such as websites, portals, search engines, affiliate and viral marketing, blogs, email and text messaging. Some also include traditional voice telephone as part of digital marketing.

The second part of the definition shows that it should not be the technology that drives digital marketing, but the business returns from gaining new customers and maintaining relationships with existing customers. It also emphasises how digital marketing does not occur in isolation, but is most effective when it is integrated with other communication channels such as phone, direct mail or face-to-face. Online channels should also be used to support the whole buying process from pre-sale to post-sale and further development of customer relationships.

The final part of the definition summarises approaches to customer-centric marketing. It shows how it should be based on knowledge of customer needs developed by researching their characteristics, behaviour, what they value, what keeps them loyal and then delivering tailored web and email communications.

In many ways the above is the same as the definition of direct marketing except it is limited to digital media. This is why many direct marketers see digital marketing as just adding a new front end by offering new media channels to market, whereas the back end – logistics, fulfilment and customer service – remains as before. If you think about the old-fashioned mail-order catalogue, Sears Roebuck or Montgomery Ward, the modern-day equivalents are companies such as Amazon and Direct Line. Digital marketing is still direct to the customer but utilises the new media channels.

Digital media have, however, permitted two further things of the utmost importance to marketing: they have revolutionised the cost structure of the functions they perform, and they have altered the balance of power between supplier and customer in ways that are only gradually playing themselves out.

Customers now can control the 'navigation' functions mentioned before. They can build proprietary databases of their preferred suppliers, investigate products and services on the Internet at a time of their choosing, and in return expect an unprecedented level of customer service with goods delivered in first-class condition within 24 to 48 hours.

Direct marketing has become mainstream marketing

The Internet revolution is the first real progression in marketing since it originated in the mid-nineteenth century. It has changed the balance of power between companies and customers and created many new marketplaces such as online auctions including the global phenomenon of eBay. Currently online advertising spend annually is set to overtake television advertising, reaching more than 20 per cent of all advertising spend. Google.com is the most successful search engine in the world; the biggest issue many major brands are tackling today is how they get their brand up to the top of the Google.com search ranking. Meanwhile, mobile marketing is just set to explode. British Airways believes the future lies in ba.com and is directing its budgets to online. The concept of real-time one-to-one marketing has finally arrived.

Direct marketing has been at the forefront of this change. It has absorbed the technological advances faster than any other discipline. It has created the 'dialogue' with customers. It has always been based on measurable and accountable advertising. Today, as the disciplines of direct advertising, branding and sales promotion begin to blur, it is direct marketing which has led this change and is now considered as mainstream marketing. Direct marketing can build brands (Direct Line, MORE TH>N, Amazon and easyJet); it can target sales promotion, but at the same time collect the data and use it for future business planning, while combined with market research it can provide powerful customer insights. It continues to exemplify the rigour of personal, measurable and accountable marketing. And to the effective twenty-first century marketer, it should be second nature to think first and foremost: direct, data and digital.

DIRECT MARKETING: THREE APPLICATIONS

There are many kinds of direct marketing applications. The majority fit into one of three broad categories: single channel, multi-channel and support.

1. **Single channel**

   Applications refer to situations where direct marketing is employed in organisations that have no other means of transacting business. In most cases this will mean email, telephone orders or online.

   Single channel applications include home shopping: for example, the traditional mail order companies such as GUS and Grattan, together with newer entries like Scotts of Stow, Boden and Amazon.

   But it also includes new single channel exponents such as First Direct (the HSBC direct bank) and Direct Line (RBS). Next Directory is a borderline case, being separately promoted from the stores while sharing the branding, the inventory and much of the logistical support.

   Many charities are also borderline cases because direct fundraising is kept separate from volunteer activities except to the extent that postal donors may be approached to become proactive helpers.

2. **Multi-channel**

   Refers to organisations that have other ways of transacting business but through the use of their customer database are in a position either to make direct offers to their customers or to support their other activities with direct marketing techniques. These are frequently organisations whose databases were initially built as a by-product of another activity, such as accounting control, e.g. banks and insurance companies such as Barclays and Lloyds TSB.

3. **Support**

   Applications are those where direct marketing techniques may be used but direct marketing is not used as a sales channel. Organisations using direct marketing in a support role will generally maintain customer databases but these will not include full or summarised transactional history. Organisations which cannot readily identify all their customers individually may use direct marketing activity in support of other marketing activity. It would include companies who produce consumables such as pet foods, washing products or newspapers.

These users, however much they might like to use direct marketing, will often be organisations for whom it is simply impracticable to compile or maintain records of all their customers*.

*We use 'customers' to describe consumers, not just direct customers.

Figure 1.1: Direct marketing applications

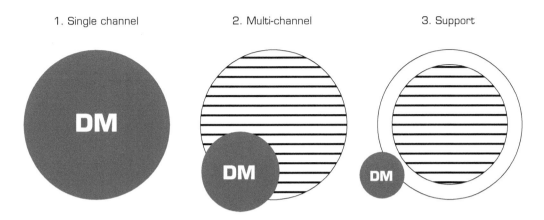

FIRMS THAT DEAL DIRECT

In 1994, the year Michael Dell launched his first website, the Dell Direct call centre was already receiving nearly 50,000 calls from customers daily. Even then, Dell was the world's largest *direct* marketer of computers.

Like First Direct and easyJet, Dell is a direct marketing company (although Dell today has a multi-distribution strategy distributing its products through PC World and Currys), dealing with its customers through its websites *and* call centres. Home-shopping companies, like La Redoute, provide another example.

The logic for dealing direct is based on efficiency – stripping out overheads or unproductive running costs. Such costs can include bricks-and-mortar outlets, sales forces, dealer margins, large stockholdings and so on. The direct model works for both business-to-consumer (B2C) and business-to-business (B2B) applications. In fact, Dell's customers range from large corporations, such as Barclays Bank, to individuals ordering from home. A particular advantage of the direct model is that it can reduce the cost of international expansion.

Table 1.1: The direct model

THE DIRECT MODEL		
Features	Benefits	Examples
Online, fax, telephone	Lower overheads	First Direct
and mail transactions	Cuts out middlemen	easyJet
Catalogues and	Faster stock turn	Dell
websites	Facilitates exporting	La Redoute

A point to note is that it is not only producers of goods or services that conform to the direct model. First Direct, easyJet and Dell are all producers. But La Redoute is a pure retailer, not making any of the clothes or other items that it sells. The insurance company, Direct Line, is a producer. But direct insurance brokers, sourcing policies from a large number of insurers, are not producers.

Furthermore, Dell may sell software and peripherals that it does not produce. In fact Dell's chief production job is to assemble components made elsewhere. Thus the direct model can work for retailers providing that it increases retailing efficiency or makes buying easier or more attractive.

Interest in the direct model has been given a huge boost by the Internet, fostering the development of new types of direct business including:

Virtual exchanges – for example, Covisint, the world's largest B2B automotive marketplace; online auctions and reverse auctions, such as eBay and priceline.com; and infomediaries, search services and buying clubs.

These entirely new types of organisation are not controlled by sellers. They are either neutral or working for buyers.

The Internet has the potential to increase the efficiency of the direct model exponentially through a reduction in transaction costs and materials sourcing costs, superior supply chain management and a greatly enhanced ability to tailor the product to the buyer's specification. In principle it is immaterial whether access is achieved through a PC, iTV or a mobile phone. In practice the 'front-end' can affect the quantity and quality of the information that can be exchanged.

To the customer, the direct model is not always the answer. Many people prefer to go to the shops or send for a sales representative. Others will use the Internet as an information source, but complete their transaction through a traditional channel. In fact our channel preferences are likely to depend on what we are buying.

MULTI-CHANNEL MARKETING

Marketing today is more challenging than it ever was before. On one side there is immense competition for the attention of today's over-messaged, out-of-time and in-control buyers. On the other side new channels for connecting buyers and sellers are appearing all the time. Marketers now have to master this multi-channel revolution and the opportunity to connect with always-on consumers, anywhere, anytime.

Mobile devices increasingly are linked to the Web, TV and the Internet are converging while online and offline are seen as seamless channels. Marketers today are interacting with their customers via 10 to 15 different channels. The problem is it is one thing to interact through multiple channels in parallel, it is another to maximise response and conversion rates across channels.

The channels in question include the traditional brand channels as shown in Table 1.2. What these traditional channels have in common is they are **'non-addressable'**, i.e. message is delivered to whoever is seeing and listening to the channel. Individuals, in this case, are not identifiable – as Alan Mitchell referred to earlier 'they are anonymous'. Audiences here are defined by survey-based research and media readership research.

Table 1.2: Overview of brand advertising and direct response channels

Brand advertising channels Not addressable	Direct response channels Addressable
TV/radio/print	Store (purchases)
Out-of-home	Call centre
Marketing events	Direct mail
Product placement	Sales and service teams
In-store displays	Mobile devices
	Email
	Web display ads
	Search engines
	Website

The **addressable** channels allow marketers to talk to individual prospects, hence they act in the conversational 'direct' sense – tailoring the message, prompting a response and measuring the response.

As online and offline converge, more and more channels are becoming addressable particularly with digital media (i.e. display ads can now be targeted at individuals).

Consumers are multi-channel buyers

Typical buyers do not think in terms of channels, only the most convenient way of achieving their goal. They often exhibit cross-channel behavioural patterns, choosing paths across channels during the lifecycle of the purchase. Figure 1.2 shows the multiple pathways a prospect can take. The start of the journey may be initiated by a store visit leading to a website and then a call centre to order.

Figure 1.2: Sample wiggly line paths of buyers through the buying cycle

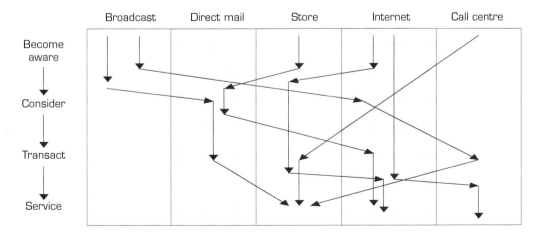

Source: Unica Corporation

While it may appear there is no pattern, the behaviour of groups of buyers may be aggregated. In this case it becomes clear certain channels are more typically frequented during certain stages of the customer life cycle. Table 1.3 shows which multi-channels are most used at different stages of the buying cycle.

Table 1.3: Channels most typically used in each stage of the buying cycle

		Awareness	Perception	Consideration	Trial	Initial Purchase	Retention	Cross-sell, Up-sell
Offline	TV/radio/print	●	●	◉	○	○	○	○
	Out-of home	●	◉	◉	○	○	○	○
	Events	◉	●	●	●	○	○	○
	Product placement		●	●	○	○	○	○
Online	Web ads	●	●	●	○	○	○	○
	Blogs	◉	●	●	○	○	◉	○
	Search	◉	◉	●	○	○	○	○
	Website	○	◉	◉	●	●	●	●
	Email	○	○	○	◉	◉	●	●
	Mobile	?	?	?	?	?	?	?
Offline	Direct mail	○	○	○	◉	◉	●	●
	Call centre	○	○	○	◉	◉	●	●
	Store/sales	◉	◉	◉	◉	●	●	●
	Service team	○	○	○	○	○	●	●

Source: Unica Corporation

● A full ball indicates the channel is typically used at this buying stage
◉ A half ball indicates the channel has limitations
○ An empty ball suggest the channel is ill-suited for a particular stage in the buying cycle
? As mobile is new there are no results for this channel as yet

What multi-channel behaviour suggests is that multi-channel metrics are a critical factor in making marketing accountability a reality. Few companies to date have yet mastered multi-channel metrics.

Who uses multi-channels?

GUS is a multi-channel retailer selling through websites and its retail stores, including Argos. Tesco is a multi-channel retailer, although its website sales are dwarfed by its store-based sales. Producers, too, may use multiple sales channels. GM (Vauxhall) and Ford sell (a few) cars directly to private motorists on the Web. IBM sells direct and through dealers. British Airways sells direct and through agents. Magazine publishers, such as *The Economist* and *Reader's Digest*, sell both through newsagents and through direct subscription. Charities raise funds through direct mail, through charity shops, through events and through street collections. Today, many charities are looking to online techniques such as viral marketing.

Some companies have spawned direct brands. Prudential insurance launched egg as a direct brand. First Direct is a subsidiary of HSBC. Direct Line is owned by the Royal Bank of Scotland.

Home-shopping catalogues have diversified both to website trading and to high street retailing – Lakeland and Past Times are examples. *Next* is an example of a high street retailer spawning a home-shopping business.

For most of these companies, the logic of stripping out costs by conforming exclusively to a direct model does not work. They do better by offering customers a wider choice of ways to deal with them. In a few cases differential pricing may be used – magazine subscription is a prime example – but in most cases the pricing is the same and the inventory is much the same.

Next believes that its catalogue and website assist shop sales and vice versa. By offering customers the widest possible choice of ways to browse and buy they maximise the return on their marketing investment.

Direct marketing is more than selling direct

All of the companies we have named use direct or digital marketing or both; not just when they are selling through their mailings, catalogues and websites. Direct marketing has come to mean more than just selling direct.

> Any company that uses direct response advertising, online or offline, and maintains a customer database, is using direct marketing.

Tesco would remain a major direct marketer if it scrapped its website tomorrow. Tesco maintains a huge customer database (Clubcard) and tailors offers to its customers, through personalised direct mail, based on their past purchasing behaviour (Table 1.4).

Magnetic strip cards like Clubcard enable retailers to link customer identities with purchases and use the data to offer the customer rewards offers, events and services which, to all intents and purposes, are tailored to the customer's needs and preferences. Although more than 14 million Clubcard statements are mailed quarterly, there are nearly 10 million variations to these mailings reflecting customers' different shopping patterns.

Even though the vast majority of Clubcard members visit Tesco to do their shopping, this is still termed direct marketing because the programme is based on the collection of shop visit and purchase data and careful analysis of individual customer preferences. The activity may also be termed relationship marketing or even loyalty marketing. Of these terms, direct marketing is the most meaningful, being capable of precise definition.

Direct and digital marketing

Let us look again, a little more closely, at McCorkell's definition of direct marketing:

'Direct marketing is the process in which individual customers' responses and transactions are recorded...'

Table 1.4: Tesco Clubcard

TESCO CLUBCARD

History, operation and scale

Tested October 1993, launched nationally February 1995

Card applications in-store, communications in-store and direct mail

More than 200 million product purchases a day by more than 14 million customers

Customer information and applications

Customer data:

Visit patterns	Spend levels
Departmental usage	Types of purchases
Coupon users/non-users	Profile/geographic data

Broad customer typologies:

Loyalists	Infrequent customers
Regulars	New customers

Applications include:

Recruitment	Lapsed and win back
Clubcard Plus (savings card)	Helpline
Local marketing	

McCorkell's definition does not specify the media through which customers' responses and transactions are invited or received. In fact a customer might spot a bargain on a website, make further enquiries by telephone and complete the transaction at a dealership. If the item purchased were a second-hand car, such a scenario would be very likely.

In this definition, *customers' responses are recorded*. If the car dealership did not bother to do this, then the process would not qualify as direct marketing. On the other hand, the form of response is not specified – for example, the data could include clickstream data as readily as phone calls or posted coupons.

'...and the data used to inform the targeting, execution and control of actions...'

Note that the definition does not specify any interval between recording the data and using it. It may often apply to data stored on a customer database and used months later (as in the Tesco Clubcard example) but it can equally apply to data used in real time during a telephone call or website visit.

In fact the use of profile, preference and purchase data in real time was pioneered in call centre software before the Web was used for marketing. An early example was (still is) car insurance quotations. The quote given to the caller is driven by the answers to scripted questions. A later example is add-on offers triggered by home-shopping orders (e.g. matching accessories). In this case, no questions are asked to prompt the offer, it is driven by the content of the customer's order.

Again, the nature of the actions is not specified – they could include:

- restricting an emailed invitation to the best customers;
- targeting new customers who match the profile of the best established customers;
- personalising a website to make relevant offers to previous visitors.

The purpose of the actions is clearly specified:

'*...that are designed to start, develop and prolong profitable customer relationships.*'

This part of the definition excludes no business with expectations of success. However, the idea that customer data collection and analysis is the key to success was peculiar to direct marketing, although management consultancies and customer relationship management (CRM) software vendors now also claim ownership of it.

DIRECT MARKETING AND PARETO'S PRINCIPLE

If Thomas Jefferson (...all men are created equal) was the hero of mass marketing, Vilfredo Pareto is the hero of direct marketing. Pareto's Principle (of the distribution of incomes) was that 80 per cent would end up in 20 per cent of pockets however society attempted to regulate matters. To Pareto, whether all men are created equal or not, they certainly don't end up that way.

So it is with customers. Every direct marketer knows that some customers are much more valuable than others. Every astute direct marketer knows who the valuable ones are. The really smart direct marketer has a system for forecasting who the valuable ones are going to be.

Why is this so important? Let's consider the example:

Customers who cost money

Typically, 75 per cent of new customers gained by a home-shopping business will have lapsed without providing enough business to recover the cost of recruiting them. All of the profit will be contributed by the remaining 25 per cent.

If the company learns which are the best sources of good customers, it can work to reduce the 75 per cent of loss-making intake. If it fails to learn, the 75 per cent will become 80 or 85 per cent, ensuring that the company loses money.

Again, typically, a bank will lose money on at least 80 per cent of its private customer base at any one time. By devoting special attention to the remaining 20 per cent, it can expect to satisfy more of them and so keep their custom. If it fails to differentiate between its good (and potentially good) customers and its loss-making customers, it is the good customers who are most likely to defect.

Figure 1.3 shows a real-life example of segmentation of charity donors based on their response to the last appeal made to them:

Figure 1.3: Segmentation of charity donors

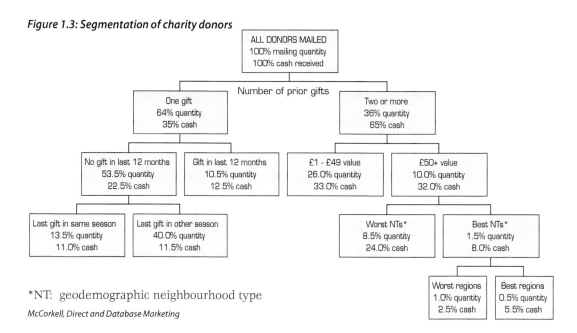

*NT: geodemographic neighbourhood type

McCorkell, Direct and Database Marketing

Figure 1.3 displays the result of applying a statistical model called CHAID (chi-squared automatic interaction detector). This is also sometimes called tree segmentation. Here we are using CHAID to analyse the results of our last mailed appeal. We want CHAID to tell us how to recognise the differences between our most generous donors and our less generous donors. In particular, we would like to know who – if anyone – not to mail next time around.

CHAID splits the mailing base (all donors) into two, by picking out the most important of all the discriminatory variables that distinguish the best donors from the others. This variable turns out to be the number of previous gifts. The 36 per cent who have sent us two or more previous donations contributed 65 per cent of the money. This result is shown near the top of Figure 1.3.

Looking further down, we can see that CHAID keeps on dividing each segment into two, like an amoeba in a Petri dish; each time it takes the most significant of the remaining discriminatory variables. What CHAID is answering each time is:

> Of all the differences between the more generous and less generous donors in this segment, which is the most important single difference?

Looking at the left-hand side of the model, we see that the least generous 40 per cent of donors contributed only 11.5 per cent of the cash received. The model demonstrates that 88.5 per cent of the cash could have been raised from 60 per cent of the donors by not mailing single gift donors who had been inactive for over 12 months and who last gave at a different time of the year.

If we assume it cost £1 in mailing expense to raise £4 in cash, the overall result from 100,000 donors would be £400,000 raised at a cost of £100,000. However, the least responsive 40,000 would have cost £40,000 to mail and brought in only £46,000 cash. We might decide to send an appeal to these donors only once a year, at Christmas time, when they are most likely to respond.

Meanwhile, the other 60,000 donors sent back £354,000 – almost £6 for every £1 of expense.

> Restricting our appeal to these donors only would improve our income to expense ratio by almost 50 per cent.

The direct marketer looks for solutions by listening to what the data says. As always in direct marketing, actions speak loudest. What people do matters more than their demographic, socio-economic or lifestyle profile.

B2B = Pareto x Pareto

However strongly Pareto's Principle applies to B2C marketing, the B2B scene is Pareto squared, one company having 10,000 times the purchasing power of another. So companies differentiate between larger (corporate) customers and smaller customers. Frequently, call centres or contact centres deal with smaller business customers while field sales teams deal with larger customers.

PRINCIPLES OF DIRECT AND DIGITAL MARKETING: TICC

Direct marketing and its information systems focus on what the customer or prospect does. To put it another way, data about past behaviour is used to predict future behaviour. This data is processed on an individual basis and can be analysed and acted upon on an individual basis, even if the number of customers reaches millions. This does not render marketing research obsolete but if we can rely only on marketing research information we are forced to make assumptions about customer behaviour which may be generally right but will often be wrong in an individual case.

Successful direct marketing practice depends on four elements. These are: targeting, interaction, control and continuity.

Targeting, Interaction, Control and Continuity (TICC)

You will see from Figure 1.4 that the four elements of successful direct marketing can be looked at either as one triangle or alternatively as four triangles inside another one. *Interaction* is in the centre. Interaction includes the stimuli we marketers create in the hope of producing a response from the people in our target market; their response is also included in the interaction triangle. In all cases we will attempt to attribute a response to the correct stimulus. Thus the results of our activities form the core of our information system and enable us to become progressively more efficient at *targeting*, *control* and *continuity*. That is because we are learning by experience.

Figure 1.4   Targeting, Interaction, Control and Continuity (TICC)

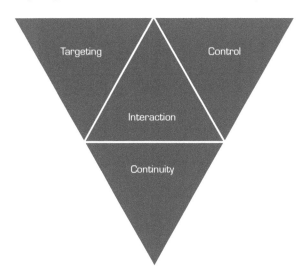

Interaction takes centre stage in direct marketing's information system.

Targeting refers to our decisions on who will receive our message and includes our media selection: TV, banner ads, print advertising, direct mail, telemarketing, email and so on. We may be targeting our established customers, identified prospects or a much larger audience of 'suspects'. In all of these cases our targeting decisions will generally outweigh in importance decisions about what to offer and how to frame our message. By examining the results of our previous attempts to target correctly, we can keep on refining our future targeting. All targeting is dependent on accurate data – whether it be external data such as circulation or audience figures, or internal data about an individual's characteristics and buying habits.

Control is the management of our marketing. It includes setting objectives, planning at the strategic and operational levels, budgeting and assessment of results. The process is cyclical, future planning being informed by past results.

Interaction is at the heart of direct marketing. The completeness and accuracy of our data within the interaction triangle will be crucial to the exercise of control. Interaction quantifies the effects of our marketing.

Customer interactions may not just be orders. They may be returns (of unwanted goods), queries, complaints, requests, suggestions, questionnaire responses and so on.

Continuity is about retaining customers, cross-selling other products to them and uptrading them. In the vast majority of business enterprises, the bulk of profit arises from dealings with established customers.

Our painstaking care in recording interactions enables us to communicate with customers, recognising their interest and showing appreciation of their custom. The special challenge of e-commerce and of contact centre management is to respond to customers in real time.

All four of the TICC elements are critical. Direct marketing is not direct marketing unless they are all in place. Sometimes it is not possible to data capture the identity of every customer and sometimes it is necessary to record the transactions of a sample of customers only. These conditions apply in FMCG (fast moving consumer goods) markets. Nevertheless, if the four TICC elements are in place, it is possible to employ direct marketing methods in these markets.

TEN WAYS IN WHICH DIGITAL MARKETING IS DIFFERENT

1. **The challenge of 24/7**

   A trading website is always open. There is no downtime to restock, correct programming errors or repair broken links to other business systems.

2. **Marketing in real time**

   A website deals with customers in real time, raising expectations of instant query resolution, immediate response to requests and, even faster delivery. Furthermore customer interaction data is being gathered continuously.

3. **Personalisation**

   Personalisation of a website is very different from personalised print. It must be based on a variety of data sources (e.g. clickstream, personal data and previous purchases) and used within a single site visit if appropriate.

4. **Data volumes and integration**

   A website can collect much higher volumes of data of different types than can be collected from other reception points. (This poses a systems integration problem and a potentially crippling data volume problem, sometimes referred to as data overload.)

5. **Many-to-many communications**

   Customers do not phone call centres just for a chat. But the Internet is different. It is open, democratic and even revolutionary. The plus side may be viral marketing. The downside could be flaming (abusive replies).

6. **Comparison shopping**

   Never was comparison shopping so easy. A company's pricing policy may need to be changed for digital marketing.

7. **Global reach**

   The reach of the website is wide but logistical or legal constraints may apply. It may be necessary to restrict orders geographically.

8. **Keeping in touch**

   Unlike direct mail, email can be time sensitive, especially when sent to a business address. But because emailing is so cheap, it is tempting to overuse it. It is easy to measure the response but not so easy to measure customers lost through irrelevant emailing.

9. **Low transaction costs**

   The cost of handling online orders and information requests, as well as of email solicitation, is much lower. This may permit lower ticket or lower margin transactions. However, credit card payment queries will be high and delivery costs will remain the same, wherever physical products that are not electronically transmissible are involved.

10. **A website is more like a shop than a catalogue**

   Unlike a catalogue, a website cannot be sent to a list of prospective customers. Like a shop, it must wait for them to call in. Unlike a high street shop, it is not visible to passers-by. It needs promotion.

Can you think of any other ways in which a website is more like a shop than a catalogue? Here are two ideas:

1. Out-of-stock items (stock-outs) cannot be deleted from a printed catalogue. They continue to occupy selling space and disappoint customers who try to order them. On the other hand, stock-outs can be deleted from websites almost as readily as the goods disappear from stores.
2. The direct marketer can measure the sales performance of each page and position in the catalogue. But the lessons cannot be applied until the next printing. Furthermore, the cataloguer cannot follow the customer's route through the catalogue, making it harder to explain the sales performance of individual items.

The website designer can use clickstream data to track customers' journeys through the site and can relate these patterns to sales. Then the site layout can be altered to optimise performance. The store can make similar adjustments although the data will rarely be so accurate or so complete.

LANDS' END – THE CYBER MODEL

A home-shopping company for nearly 30 years and the world's most experienced Internet clothing retailer, Lands' End has found another way to make its website more like a shop. You can have your own personal cyber model try on the garments that interest you to ensure they will fit.

   Lands' End will mail you its catalogue even if you buy from their website. Some people prefer to browse in a printed catalogue and shop online; others enjoy the interactive website but order by phone. See point 10 under 'Ten ways in which digital marketing is different'.

A last word about digital jargon

Viral marketing is the turbocharged Internet version of the direct marketers' referral programme or MGM (member-get-member) scheme. As customers congregate in newsgroups or chat by email and social networks, recommendations can spread like a forest fire.

   Personalisation has a similar meaning in both direct and digital marketing but the possibilities are more exciting in a dynamic environment than in print.

   Cookies are the small text files stored on your computer to enable the website to recognise it when you call again and record your clickstream. This enables personalisation. However, unless you register separately, the website will think that all users of your computer are the same person.

   Permission marketing is a significant concept that underpins online customer relationship marketing, known as CRM. Permission marketing is a term coined by Seth Godin to apply to email marketing. It is best summarised in his book (Godin, *Permission Marketing*, 1999).

Customers agree (opt in) to be involved in an organisation's marketing activities, usually as a result of an incentive. It is now a legal requirement enforced by the UK Privacy and Electronic Communications Regulations 2003 that there must be a proactive agreement to receive electronic communications. This core principle of permission marketing is now a legal requirement throughout the EU. Unfortunately it has done little to reduce the flood of unwanted emails (spam) which largely originate from outside the EU.

DATA: THE DIRECT AND DIGITAL MARKETER'S INFORMATION SYSTEM

It is essential that the direct and digital marketing information system includes customer history data. The minimum history required is a history of the customer's transactions. Often this will be summarised, showing us little more than the value of each transaction, the product or the merchandise category and when it occurred.

Without this minimum amount of data, we cannot practise efficient direct marketing because:

'Direct marketing is the process in which...individual customers' responses and transactions are recorded...and the data used to inform the targeting, execution and control of actions...that are designed to start, develop and prolong profitable customer relationships.'

Graeme McCorkell, Direct and Database Marketing

Figure 1.5 makes the point graphically:

Figure 1.5: Direct marketing is the process in which...

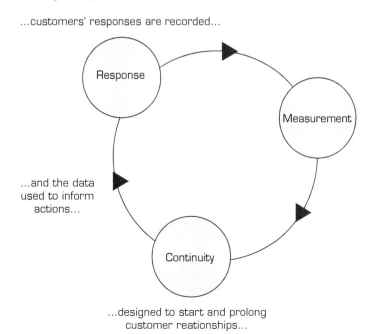

The components of response, measurement and continuity are common to all direct marketing activity:

- *Response*. A response is needed to acquire a customer and to begin compiling data relating to that customer. It is very unusual to hear of a direct marketing initiative that does not have response as a key stage in the communication programme.
- *Measurement* has always been central to direct marketing. Before cheap computing power became available, it was already possible to record and measure the immediate results of marketing expenditures. Reply coupons and telephone numbers included codes to identify the source of responses. Cost-per-response (CPR) and cost-per-sale (CPS) were and still are useful measures. Now measurement is extended to individual customers' activity. Because each customer is identified, their buying behaviour can be tracked over time. This enables the eventual return on marketing investments to be measured and forecasting to be improved.
- *Continuity* is the aim of every competent direct marketer who seeks to maximise the gearing on the customer acquisition investment by doing more business with the customer for a longer period.

The customer marketing database

An electronic library is needed to receive fresh data, keep it and make it accessible, so as to maintain the continuous learning loop that characterises direct marketing.

This is the customer marketing database system. It brings together information from a variety of sources and links the information to customers.

Figure 1.6: The customer marketing database

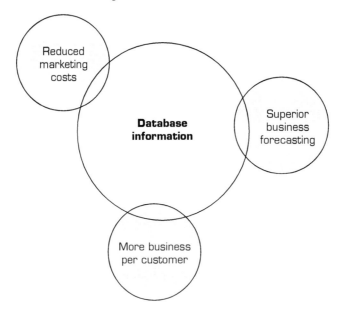

The database enables marketing costs to be reduced. This is achieved through using information derived from:

- the cost, number and value of new customers obtained by source;
- the results of contacts with established customers.

For example, it may cost twice as much to acquire customers from advertising in *The Economist* as in *The Times*. But the database may reveal that *The Economist* readers buy more and stay longer, increasing their lifetime value and making them more profitable.

More business per customer is achieved through using customer purchase histories, leading to:

- better identification and segmentation of customers;
- greater personalisation and more relevant offers.

For example, customers giving high value orders and paying promptly may receive special treatment. Offers may reflect customers' specific interests.

Superior business forecasting is achieved by analysing campaign and customer history data, using past performance as a guide to future performance. Because the errors in past activities need not be repeated, efficiency should be subject to continuous improvement.

The database answers six questions

At its simplest, the database is the heart of an information system that answers the six simple questions shown in Figure 1.7 every time interaction occurs.

Who?

- Name and contact data
- Status (e.g. customer or prospect)
- Associations (i.e. same household or company as another customer)
- Credit status (if relevant)

What?

- Order or enquiry
- Items ordered
- Product category
- In stock/out of stock

Where?

- Sales channel
- Branch or media code

The system should allocate a unique reference number (URN) or alphanumeric code to each customer. This enables customer queries to be answered all the more quickly, the URN guiding service and sales staff to the customer record or transaction details.

The system will recognise whether an order is a repeat order from an established customer or a first order from a new customer.

How much?
- The price of each item
- Gross order value
- Fewer out-of-stocks
- Fewer returns

When?
- When last instruction/order received
- When last instruction/order fulfilled

Why?
- Response/non-response to last promotion
- Identifying code of promotion causing response

Figure 1.7: The customer marketing database answers six questions

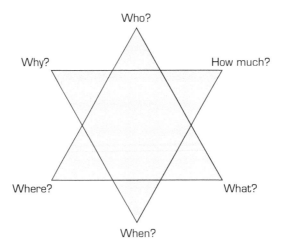

Not every system will contain transactional data because it won't always be available. For example, Lever Brothers would not have full transaction data for every Persil buyer, but would have promotional responses recorded on their database.

Business-to-business customer marketing data is often more extensive and complex. A company may have a number of identities (branches, departments and divisions) and a good many individual buyers or decision-makers. A business customer may also use multi-channels to secure supplies of different items. Purchases are increasingly likely to be automated, using electronic data exchange (EDI), Internet exchanges or an extranet.

REAL-TIME DATA

Websites and contact centres can, with the right software, respond to purchase data in real time. When a customer puts a Manchester United Annual in the shopping basket this may trigger the offer of Ryan Giggs' autobiography.

Opportunistic marketing of this sort will be used in combination with offers or other special treatments that are driven by previously captured data.

Advantages of the database

A database exploiting transactional information tells the marketer everything about customers' purchases updated with each new response (and non-response).

For example, the transactional database:
- includes *all* customers, not just a sample or cross section;
- gives customer value data, e.g. Recency, Frequency, Monetary Value (RFM) of purchases culminating in the lifetime value (LTV) of each customer;
- tells us about new customers: what they responded to and, perhaps, which creative treatment appealed to them;
- tells us about lost, lapsed and inactive customers;
- tells us about who buys which products and responds to which types of incentive or message;
- gives continuous information which is automatically updated with each new transaction;
- reports upon, and analyses, marketing campaigns and tactics;
- facilitates controlled tests of alternatives, e.g. product and price comparisons;
- provides back data (historical data) which helps the process of predicting the future behaviour of each and every customer.

Correctly used, a transactional customer database gives a running commentary on the marketer's ability to serve the needs of customers, highlighting opportunities to increase efficiency.

PARETO AND THE DATABASE – AMERICAN CAR RENTAL MARKET

- 20 per cent of American adults rent a car at least once a year.
- Only 5 per cent rent a car more than once.
- 0.2 per cent rent a car ten or more times.
- This 0.2 per cent represents one in a hundred customers.
- One in 100 customers provide car rental companies with one quarter (25 per cent) of their business.

Facts from *The One-to-One Future*, Don Peppers & Martha Rogers. London: Piatkus Books, 1996.

At one time car rental advertising was almost untargeted. But the direct marketer differentiates between customers and non-customers, then between casual customers and regular customers and finally between regular customers and frequent customers. The example of the American car rental market shows why.

The top 25 per cent of customers are those who rent a car more than once. But within this exclusive group, one in 25 of them rents a car ten times or more in a year. This group, amounting to one in a hundred customers (0.2 per cent of adults) is worth 25 times as much as the average customer. These extremely valuable customers provide car rental companies with a quarter of their business.

It would be cheaper to telephone these customers personally to thank them than it would to reach them all once with a TV commercial.

Recognising the value of these 'super customers', car rental firms offered loyal users free rentals at weekends. But frequent business travellers want time with their families. When this idea failed, National Car Rental came up with a better idea. Targeting the tired, stressed and status-conscious business traveller, their answer was the Emerald Club, having its own aisle in National's car lot at the airport. Members could pick any car in the Emerald Aisle and drive off, pausing only to have their card 'swiped' at the checkout.

National's database enabled them to:

- recognise how much more valuable their best customers were than others;
- discover how much business was at risk if these customers were lost (it would take 33 average new customers to replace one lost top customer);
- recognise the circumstances of these customers, i.e. frequent business travellers;
- send Emerald cards to the right customers.

Notice that the database is used to provide both management information and the means of communicating to customers.

The customer marketing database serves two functions:
1. It provides management information.
2. It facilitates one-to-one customer communications outbound and inbound.

The customer marketing database not only facilitates outbound communications but enables customers to be recognised when they telephone or visit the website. The contact centre agent (operator) can call up the customer's transaction record on screen so that the customer does not have to repeat information that the company should already know.

Data, CRM and eCRM

In recent years, many large companies have been dealing with the problem of integrating data from a multiplicity of management information systems. The ideal solution of bringing together all relevant customer information into one customer marketing database system was not available to these companies. The systems they used in different parts of the business were incompatible.

Looking at the captions in Figure 1.8: accounts, sales, marketing, buying, distribution, customer service, stock control and credit control, we can see these might all provide information for the marketing database.

Because some of these functions were seen as completely separate in many large businesses, and may have become computerised at different times, their systems are unlikely to be fully compatible. They will certainly not be compatible with e-commerce systems. Old systems are referred to as *legacy* systems.

However, if essential details, such as file formats, are harmonised, it is possible to store data that would otherwise simply be archived, in a data warehouse. Now, the data can be processed in such a way that it can be analysed by a competent person, using a PC.

The process of retrieving and analysing data from a data warehouse is called *data mining*. Data mining is often used in businesses with masses of transactional data, such as banks and airlines.

The idea of the data warehouse is to bring systems together to form an enterprise-wide management information system. In theory at least, this permits a customer relationship management (CRM) system to be employed. The idea behind CRM is that the whole of a customer's dealings with the company can be put together. Such systems are devised by outside software vendors and may need extensive adaptation.

Figure 1.8: The data warehouse

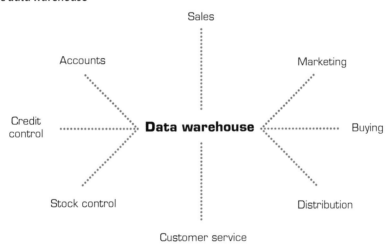

THE WHOLE CUSTOMER

As well as having a current account and a savings account, a bank customer may deal with the home loan division, the life and general insurance divisions, the credit card division and the personal investment management division. Since the average customer holds only 1.2 accounts, such a customer would be very valuable to the bank. Yet, before the creation of an enterprise-wide CRM system, the bank would not have recognised all of these different relationships as being with the same customer.

In practice, company divisions or departments (including marketing) may find their needs better served by *data marts*. These are fed by the data warehouse but contain only information that is relevant to the departmental interest and are designed to make the data easier to interrogate and analyse.

Integrating eCRM

When the company's front office is a website, the volume of data being collected, processed and managed is very large. Some data, e.g. DNS (domain name system) and clickstream data, is peculiar to digital marketing. The latter, particularly, can overwhelm a system unless it is *summarised*. It is not necessary to keep this information for individual customers as long as customer preferences, either declared or implicit through transactional behaviour, are recorded.

> **When human interaction is by email or chat, there is a full, self-generated digital record of the contact – unlike a phone call or field sales visit. This record may be used to auto-generate e-marketing contacts.**

Summary data

The transactional database needs historical data. Otherwise there can be no record of a customer's business relationship with the company. Usually, the data used to portray a customer history (or the results of a promotion) is summarised, so that it doesn't occupy too much space (memory) in the system.

While this is very sensible because it saves costs, the problem is that essential detail is sometimes lost. Generally speaking, the *number*, *value* and *dates* of a customer's transactions will be retained but the *merchandise categories* and, certainly, the actual *products purchased* will often be lost for all except the most recent transaction. Furthermore, companies are usually bad at keeping customer service records. A marketing analyst can waste hours or days looking at customer purchase profiles, seeking an explanation for why some customers are disloyal. The true explanation may lie elsewhere. Perhaps the disloyal customers ordered goods that were out of stock or had to return defective items.

Meanwhile, the sharp reduction in data storage and retrieval costs has encouraged firms to keep more raw data for analysis instead of summarising it and archiving old data. This is a major benefit of data warehousing.

CRM and database marketing

Although enterprise-wide CRM systems may have grown out of database marketing (some would say call centre operations), they have become distanced from the marketing function.

- CRM systems are essentially operational whereas marketing database systems can exploit data that is downloaded from operational systems without disturbing them. Marketing database needs may be supplied by a data mart within a CRM system.
- The CRM system is generally seen as the software that automates the front office. The front office includes the call or contact centre, the website and any other point of interaction between the company and its customers. Front office functions include service as well as sales.

▪ The impetus for the adoption of CRM has not necessarily been increased customer knowledge, but cost-cutting. Cost-cutting is achieved by increasing productivity of customer-facing staff and by diverting transactions down completely automated routes.

▪ The CRM system may work in tandem with an ERP (Enterprise Resource Planning) system that handles the back office functions. The emphasis is on operational efficiency.

CRM and relationship marketing

The very name 'customer relationship management' implies that customers are a resource that can be managed, like the supply chain and sales staff. Although CRM feeds off customer data, it is essentially neutral. It may be customer-focused in a marketing sense or it may be enterprise-focused, being employed to seek ways to save on customer service. It all depends who is extracting actionable data and for what purpose. However, the fact that a common information system is being used throughout the organisation is clearly advantageous.

THE CUSTOMER AS RELATIONSHIP MANAGER

Two features that are apparent in all forms of interactive marketing are transparency and customer empowerment. The US software producer, MicroMarketing, has devised software that enables customers to pull information out of data warehouses in order to complete transactions by web or phone. This looks like the way of the future.

CRM should not be confused with *Relationship Marketing*, which is the title of an influential book first published in 1991. Its author was Regis McKenna, a marketing consultant known widely for his work with Apple Computers.

McKenna believes that marketing is everything and doing marketing is everyone's job. The key elements of McKenna's notion are:

▪ Select a specific market segment and dominate through a superior understanding of customers' product and service needs. Integrate customers into the design process

▪ Use monitoring, analysis and feedback to maintain 'dynamic positioning' that is always appropriate to the marketing environment

▪ Develop partnerships with suppliers, vendors and users to help maintain a competitive edge

Note that this concept of relationship marketing is also quite distinct from direct marketing, although direct marketers may be ideally placed to exploit it, especially in an e-commerce environment. One example of a direct and digital marketer apparently following McKenna's strategy to the letter is Dell.

RELATIONSHIP MARKETING IN ACTION

▪ Dell sets out to develop and dominate the direct distribution segment of the PC market, a segment which (by value) consists primarily of business buyers.

▪ Dell customers 'build' their own computers on ordering from the Dell website. In practice, Dell believes they 'uptrade themselves' – specifying a higher performance machine than they could be 'sold' by a salesperson. By inviting customers' comments and suggestions and responding accordingly, Dell is also able to keep innovating in a relevant way. For example, DellHost allows customers to rent space for their website from Dell, removing the necessity to buy, monitor and maintain servers. In this way Dell generates revenue by solving a known problem, not merely by selling hardware.

Through opening up its order book on the extranet, Dell is able to make suppliers responsible for maintaining just-in-time parts deliveries. Suppliers can also meet on the extranet and collaborate to solve mutual problems. Superior supply chain management has given Dell a competitive edge.

LIMITATIONS OF THE CUSTOMER INFORMATION SYSTEM

The database is inward looking to the extent that it refers only to those customers that a business already has on its books.

Although it is possible to import external data to profile customers and compare them with the market at large, this is not a substitute for marketing research.

The database, however good, remains introspective.

It does not admit or report upon external influences. Disturbance to plans and forecasts may result from environmental influences, e.g. the economic situation, environmental concerns or other newsworthy preoccupations which affect purchase behaviour.

Worse, it does not report on customers' use of competitors or on the success or otherwise of competitive initiatives. Share of customer (or share of wallet) is a key success measure in direct marketing.

WHO IS LOYAL; WHO IS NOT

The database can often reveal whether a customer's purchase pattern indicates loyal or disloyal purchase behaviour. However, it cannot report directly on customers' use of competitive offerings. This can only be done on a sample basis, using marketing research. N.B: The sample for this research can be taken from the database.

Unless marketers are in a monopolistic situation and have absolutely no competitors (and who is ever in that position?) they need to be fully alert to competitive influences. Competition and disruption may come not only from direct competitors, but also from indirect competitors.

Quantitative market research is required by all marketers, direct or otherwise. Qualitative research is also needed because the database can only reveal what customers are buying or not buying. It cannot say why, or suggest alternative new product avenues with much confidence. Data analysis relies on back data (customer history) to predict future behaviour. While this is generally the best guide, it is certainly not infallible. Circumstances and attitudes may change, causing sudden shifts in demand.

SUMMARY

The world, people and communications are changing.

The marketing landscape is vastly different to a decade ago. Google dominates online, while Facebook, Twitter and LinkedIn continue their global social media growth. Consumers are much more savvy and shop seamlessly through multiple channels online and offline. Marketers need to re-evaluate their established fundamentals.

Today the rise of 'customer-centric' marketing (where the customer not the product or campaign is the focus) places a premium on marketers having a deep understanding of their customers.

Marketing was always about a buyer and seller, a prospect and an offer, a need and a solution. In simpler times a shop owner, say back in Victorian times, would know every customer by sight and may have a record of their orders. RFM (recency, frequency and monetary value) is not a new concept. In Victorian times shopkeepers would write to their customers, but only the ones who spent the most, bought frequently and bought recently. Marketing was even then very much a one-to-one proposition.

Over time mass markets emerged and marketing evolved into a large, complex business process, pumping value through the twenty-first century global information-based economy.

Now a vision is emerging of a new type of marketing, one which is capable of engaging millions of prospects and customers – one-to-one. This vision is made possible by the fusion of disciplines of direct and digital marketing. For the first time marketers can engage millions of prospects and customers in personal, real-time dialogue which is fully accountable and measurable.

One to-one marketing further holds the key to two of today's most critical marketing needs: controlling costs and assigning accountability from a predictable, measurable return on all marketing spend.

Brand marketing conveys what manufacturers want people to know about the product and services. Direct marketers use the behavioural and transactional data marketers know about their customers and prospects; their interests and preferences and willingness to engage in a continuing relationship. With the advent of multiple digital communication channels in every aspect of life over the past two decades the boundary between brand and direct has long-since blurred.

Customer-centricity requires the marketer to understand relationships that span online and offline channels. However, weaving together disparate customer insights and marketing metrics has rarely been achieved to date.

Today, marketing spending is clearly shifting into the direct and digital, and within the direct marketing process, the migration from traditional addressable channels, such as mail, to new digital channels, such as mobile, is clearly accelerating.

An integrated, one-to-one approach to marketing in online and offline channels uses many of the same fundamental principles as direct marketing: testing response variables, analysing marketing data, and adjusting to improve effectiveness, especially in ongoing relationships. Experienced marketing executives know that measuring the impact of traditional brand mass marketing requires months, if not years.

Combining today's instant digital communications with marketing techniques developed and perfected in the original 'addressable' channels – mail and telephone – can provide marketers with benchmarks in minutes instead of weeks. Advances in data processing, analytics, list compiling, digital asset management, and other new technologies, have turbocharged the direct and digital marketing process with powerful new tools for guiding and executing marketing campaigns and strategies to achieve the highest returns.

Each step in the evolution of direct marketing – from mailbox to telephone, to personal computers to mobile devices, and now to digital boxes and readers – has broadened both the scope and economic impact of direct marketing. At the same time, its fundamentals, including the mathematics of testing and measurement, remain constant. Proven direct marketing tools – addressability, personalisation, and direct response – add value in every channel, from email and postcards to catalogues and websites, from text messages to online video, social networks, mobile, and addressable digital services, and beyond.

From online to offline, the new discipline of direct and digital marketing is all about one-to-one.

REVIEW QUESTIONS

1. Define direct marketing and how it is different to general marketing.
2. How is digital marketing different to direct marketing?
3. What are the three main applications of direct marketing?
4. What features and benefits does a business advise by going 'direct'?
5. Name five companies from different industries who use multi-channel marketing.
6. What does TICC stand for?
7. Why is the Pareto Principle fundamental for direct marketing?
8. List five ways digital marketing is different?
9. What are the six questions a marketing database answers?
10. What is a data warehouse?

CHAPTER 2
THE ONLINE REVOLUTION

IN THIS CHAPTER

We will introduce the concepts and key drivers of Web-based digital marketing.

Over the past ten years the Internet has come to be an integral part of the marketing strategies of all successful companies. Although Internet and digital factors will be interwoven throughout each chapter, at this point we introduce the basics of the Web.

After reading this chapter you should be able to:
- Briefly outline the history of the Internet and its commercial applications
- Understand the role of the Internet in direct and digital marketing strategy
- Be able to identify the online audience and understand their behaviour
- Understand a range of online applications
- Understand where to go for further information and advice

Specific topics include:
- How the Internet has changed all forms of marketing
- The rapid growth of e-commerce
- Metcalfe's Law and Direct and Digital Marketing
- The Internet as a marketing and selling tool
- The Internet as a means to improve business processes
- Brands and the Internet
- How to develop and manage an Internet strategy
- The website – the ultimate relationship builder
- How the Internet has put consumers in control
- The social networking phenomenon – social media, blogs and discussion groups
- Intranets and extranets
- The barriers to the use of the Internet
- Measurement and evaluation of online initiatives.
- Design and usability issues – with links and references for further study
- Summary

INTRODUCTION

A recent report from the Chief Marketing Officer (CMO) council in the US reported in the *Financial Times* signalled the fact Chief Marketing Officers in the US were having to 're-engineer' their marketing staff. Their marketing staff had been trained in an analogue world and were not ready to embrace the digital age. Of the 600 CMOs surveyed, 46 per cent identified that the digital demand generation and online relationship building were among the top priorities for their organisations, with 38 per cent saying they were exploring new online media and channels to market.

The good news for direct marketers is that the CMOs tell us that this is approach will be based around the use of data to drive strategy. Of those surveyed, 62 per cent said that the use of customer data to drive segmentation and targeting was a priority. The corollary of all this was that 59 per cent identified training and development of staff in digital marketing as a major need. Maybe they should take an IDM course!

Table 2.1: Marketing projects to be undertaken base – 600 US CMOs

PROJECT CATEGORY	Per cent of respondents stating
Digital marketing makeover — platforms, programs, people)	46
Sales and marketing organisational alignment	40
Customer data integration and analytics	32
Marketing performance measurement	31
Lead qualification and harvesting system	28
Reorganisation of marketing group	28

Source: www.cmocouncil.org 2010

The marketing revolution

The IDM identifies ten ways the Internet has changed marketing. It certainly has: when we think about any market sector from publishing to banking from grocery retailing to travel, business managers have had to cope with an unprecedented period of change. Metcalfe's Law states that the value of a network is proportional to the square of the number of users connected to the system. Whilst there is some debate about the detail of Metcalfe's argument it is clear that as access to, and usage of, the Internet expands, so the online network becomes more valuable for all applications. We have long ago passed the tipping point and the pace of change has been phenomenal since the early days of the Web. It is hard to believe that Facebook is only six years old, Twitter has just turned four and Google is about to become a teenager.

A short history of the Internet to 2000

- **1969** ARPANet commissioned by US Department of Defence to protect military communications in the event of nuclear war.
- **1971** Email programme is invented, allowing network messaging.

- **1973** First international connections to the ARPANet: UK and Norway.
- **1981** TCI/IP is introduced, a common protocol for the ARPANet.
- **1991** Tim Berners-Lee develops World Wide Web at CERN. The NSF lifts ban on commercial traffic from the NSFNET network.
- **1995** Pizza Hut accepts first pizza order over the Internet.
- **1996** Commercial Internet users now outnumber public sector users. Jeff Bezos forms Amazon.com. Research project at Stanford University begins, leading to Google founded in 1998. 150 countries connected. Ten million hosts. $1bn changes hands.
- **1998** Dixons launches Freeserve, offering free Internet access and attracting 1.3m subscribers. Google founded.
- **1999** UK online subscribers top 12m, spending £2bn.
- **2000** Nearly 20 million websites online.

Since the dot.com bust just after 2000 the Internet has come of age.

The major changes to the Internet

The Internet is available 24/7, this can be valuable to global companies who can take advantage of time zone differences but it also means that there is no downtime to restock. It also raises the question – 'If we are managing customers 24/7 do we support them offline 24 hours a day?'

The Internet is global and whilst we can put language and geographic boundaries on our website many of the Web's success stories have been around the global development of previously local brands this raises issues for companies in language and legal issues and means that logistics and currency issues come to the fore. The freight companies and banks have reacted quickly to these opportunities but there are still increased costs of selling and service delivery issues that can create additional administrative burdens

As business has changed so have customer expectations. We no longer want to wait for delivery we want what we want *now*. It is the king baby syndrome, if we don't get served properly then we throw out our toys and go somewhere where they will serve us better. So online delivery promises have to be fulfilled. It is clear that sometimes they are not. The number of incomplete shopping baskets is testament to this. Research at Cranfield University identified that it took on average five days to respond to a request for information and of 100 sites contacted for information only 50 per cent responded. Poor navigation, overlong checkout procedures and unnecessary form filling remain major frustrations for online consumers. A very useful book on this and other aspects of Web design is *Don't Make Me Think! A Common Sense Approach to Web Usability* (New Riders, 2005) by Steve Krug.

Online marketing has enabled greater personalisation of content and this has been one of the great benefits of a direct approach. The right message to the right person, in the right way at the right time has long been the holy grail of marketing. We can combine a series of data sources including volunteered data and clickstream information to drive advertising and products to a far more precisely defined audience than before. We still have some way to go on this and scepticism and mistrust of behavioural targeting, overuse of display advertising and poorly targeted email run the risk of killing the goose that laid the golden egg

The rise of many-to-many communications has been a major factor. We will look in more detail at social media later on but it is clear that the Internet allows for relationship marketing to take place in a faster and more relevant way. Twitter, blogs and discussion boards allow customers to engage in something that has always been done, talking about the products they love – and hate – on a much wider even global basis. The website I Hate Ryan Air (www.ihateryanair.org) is an example of the lengths that some consumers will go to have their say on companies they feel strongly about. Typically we tell more people about bad experiences than good ones. Pre-2000 research revealed that we tell four people about good experiences and 17 about poor experiences. Today the figures can be millions. Look at the range of comments on review sites; typically they are dominated by customers who believe they have been treated poorly. The Web forces companies to consider customer service and the damage poor reputation management can cause. To see this in action search YouTube for United Breaks Guitars – in total well over 15 million people have viewed this protest campaign.

The open democratic Web is a boon to great companies but constant vigilance on discussion boards and blogs is required. You can look at www.boardtracker.com and www.technorati.com for further advice as well as Google alerts.

The fact that the Web enables cheap contacts to be made is a clear benefit to companies and potentially delivers value back to customers. For example, the use of SMS to remind customers about appointments or deals can be really useful. However, spam is a major issue. Many years ago Robert Liedermann one of the pioneers in telemarketing recommended that the phone should only be used as part of a relationship strategy. The same might be recommended for email and SMS marketing. According to www.pingdom.com, 81 per cent of emails in 2009 were classified as spam – a 24 per cent increase on the previous year. As Seth Godin states, permission is important and increasingly so.

Comparison shopping websites abound, with meerkats and comedians dominating UK insurance advertising media. Consumers are also using the Web to make their own price comparisons. It is easier to visit five websites than to trawl five out-of-town shopping centres. However, consumers are still looking for the reassurance of offline brands and use retail stores to look at the functionality, design and quality of products. Around a third of customers look at products in store before buying online and about a quarter look online before buying in store.

The temptation to drive customers into online purchase is attractive due to typically lower transaction costs. However, the long-term development of the relationship and ongoing value may be better served by a combination of bricks and clicks. In the banking sector the relative costs of dealing with the estimated 30 per cent of customers in the UK who bank online is significantly lower; new business and complex transactions are still done face to face.

The banks may be joining forces with coffee outlets but will still maintain some degree of high street presence. How long it will be before we see a banking supermarket with multiple brands located in one venue remains to be seen.

Table 2.2: Transaction costs in the banking sector

BANKING TRANSACTION	COST
Phone operator	40p
Interactive Voice Recognition (IVR)	15p
PC	12p
Internet	7p

Source: IDM Course Material/Datamonitor

The area that has perhaps had most impact is the area of data and data integration. We will look at this in the next section but the amount of data generated online is significant. For many businesses the ability to capture data is different from the ability to act on the data successfully. In a wider context we can see that Tesco handles terabytes of data a year and successfully translates this into business strategy. Tesco aligns data within a broad approach to operational strategy to produce results that have been breathtaking over the last 15 years. Tesco's competitors have failed to keep pace. It is important to understand what is important to measure as opposed to what is nice to know and how far this data can be acted upon within the resource base of the business. Companies need to discover how to integrate existing systems and functions with Web data to produce effective strategies for the future.

Finally the basic questions are: what is the Web for? Why is it being used? Why would customers come to your site and why should they come back?

Is your website a:
- shop
- brochure
- credentials pitch
- shop window
- meeting place
- centre for learning
- playground
- doorway
- channel for communicating
- part of your overall strategy

Or is it:
- a barrier
- out of date
- not controlled
- inconsistent

- hard to reach
- hard to navigate

In this sense we return to marketing basics – we must understand our market and define clearly the value we offer relative to the competition. We must get the basics right, i.e. what ultimate benefit do we offer to which market, compared to which competitors? Then craft the online experience through navigation and design. Next we develop an online strategy that is integrated with other routes to market using appropriate scalable technology. And lastly we start to drive traffic to the site though optimisation and online and offline marketing campaigns.

Website design lies beyond the scope of this book but it is important to realise that it is a vital part of online marketing. If the site is not well designed in terms of functionality and navigation, then people will not stay on the site. If the site is not focused on delivering benefits, they will not stay, if the site is not maintained and is out of date, your customer will leave.

Equally important is that if this characterises a website it will be classified as low quality by the search engines and this will affect your search rankings (more about this later).

Website usability is a fascinating area and if you have an Intranet (a website belonging to an organisation which can be accessed only by members, typically its employees); an Extranet (a private site that may link your company with preferred suppliers) or a simple customer-facing website, it is worth looking at Jakob Neilsen's site at www.useit.com.

Brands and the Internet

Interbrand one of the world's most influential branding agencies defines a brand as:

'A mixture of tangible and intangible attributes symbolised in a trademark, which, if properly managed, creates influence and generates value.'

The Internet introduced consumers to a number of new brands. Some burnt brightly and faded quickly – who remembers www.boo.com? Others made a great impact initially and have settled down into a less favourable but still viable position – www.lastminute.com is an example of this. Others have changed the way the world works and have become global leaders in their sectors. Google and Amazon are obvious examples.

If we look at the leading global brands we can see that pure Web-based businesses are relatively thin on the ground. According to Interbrand data, Google and Amazon are not in the top five by brand value. What we see are two very traditional companies; GE operating in the industrial sector and Coca-Cola in the consumer sector. The remaining three, interestingly, are companies who sell systems and hardware to use and access the new technologies. Rather like the US gold rush it is not the prospectors that get rich, it is the companies that sell shovels to the prospectors that make money.

Table 2.3: Brand values 2009 $million

Rank	Brand	Sector	2009 Brand Value ($m)	Change in Brand Value
1	Coca-Cola	Beverages	68,734	+3%
2	IBM	Computer Software	60,211	+2%
3	Microsoft	Computer Services	56,647	-4%
4	GE	Diversified	47,777	-10%
5	Nokia	Mobile technology	34,864	-3%

Source: Interbrand 2010

If however we look at the growth rate in brand values Google is top of the list and Amazon is second.

Online brands therefore have to cope with the same challenges that offline brands have had to cope with for many years. However, in the online environment the process of brand management with its multiple touchpoints and communications channels, including peer to peer, is much harder to manage.

Successful branding depends on the company being organised in such a way that customers receive a consistent and rewarding experience when and wherever they come across the brand. It's important that all members of the organisation understand what the brand stands for. It means tracking and measuring core brand metrics both with customers and also with key internal and external stakeholders. A brand can be seen as a promise; indeed in the early days of branding brands were described as trust marks. If we make a promise to a customer or prospect we must keep it. This means products that perform, a website that works and is easy to navigate, and clear and consistent communication to all our audiences. A very good book on branding is *From Brand Vision to Brand Evaluation: The strategic process of growing and strengthening brands* (Butterworth-Heinemann, 2010) by Leslie de Chernatony, now in its third edition.

The need to develop and sustain brand equity is central to almost every business's marketing effort. There are several areas that need to be considered and these are:

- The dimensions or perceived quality and value – how satisfied are brand users?
- Brand image and position – does the brand feel right and is this image consistently communicated?
- How trusted is the brand – does the brand meet expectations?
- How committed are the brand users to the brand – do they make repeat purchases, do they recommend, are they loyal?

These areas are vital to get right in terms of planning execution and evaluation. In many ways it is easier to manage this in an online environment because of the facility to measure, but the technology must facilitate the development of brand equity. The Internet must not act as a barrier to the development of assets that will, if managed effectively, last longer than the careers of the marketers who manage them. Coca-Cola was introduced to the UK in 1900.

The online market

If the basic principles of revenue generation and marketing remain constant, certainly the growth in online activity over the last ten years has been a true revolution. Fortunes have been made, lost and made again as new applications and approaches have turned the early days of dot.com boom and bust into an integral part of every company's overall business.

There is a vast array of data that tracks the growth of e-commerce and online activity worldwide. Some of this is very contradictory and confusing in the detail of sectors tracked, methodology etc. In the UK we are lucky. We have a very reliable source of information on online activity through the Office for National Statistics at www.statistics.gov.uk. The information they publish is both reliable and free of charge and is often used by companies who repackage the data and sell it on.

Access to this data can be found at www.statistics.gov.uk/cci/nugget.asp?id = 8, although it can all be accessed through the main site.

The latest available data from the Office for National Statistics tells us that in 2008 Internet sales represented 9.8 per cent of the value of all sales of UK non-financial sector businesses. This was up from 7.7 per cent in 2007. The 2009 data was released in November 2010 (after this book went to press). The report excludes the financial services sector due to the difficulty in defining online sales in the financial sector but if we consider how many consumer products are traded and bought online then we can see the huge importance of the online market to the global economy.

In 2008 total sales value across all distribution excluding the financial services sector in the UK was £2,274bn and the value of internet sales rose to £222.9bn, an increase of 36.6 per cent from the 2007 figure of £163.2bn.

Sales consisted of £104.7bn website sales and £118.2bn EDI (electronic data interchange) sales over the Internet.

The proportion of businesses using the Internet to sell rose from 14.4 per cent in 2007 to 15.2 per cent in 2008. The proportion using a website for their Internet sales was 12.6 per cent in 2008 compared to just under 4 per cent in 2004.

At the same time advertising revenues have continued to grow in the online space in 2009. Ofcom data drawing on a study from the IABUK and PWC put the total value of online advertising at £3,541.1 million.

Table 2.4: Internet advertising expenditure, by category 2005–2009

(£m)	2005	2006	2007	2008	2009	4 yr CAGR	Growth
Paid-for search	768.3	1165.6	1619.1	1986.9	2148	29%	8%
Display	335.9	453.7	592.0	637.4	709.3	21%	-5%
Other classified	262.2	379.0	585.3	715.2	677.0	27%	11%
Solus email	0	17.5	16.2	10.2	6.8	n/a	-33%
Total display	335.9	471.2	608.2	647.6	716.1	21%	11%
Total classified	1030.5	1544.6	2204.4	2702.1	2825	29%	5%
Total	1366.4	2015.8	2812.6	3349.7	3541.1	27%	6%

Source: Ofcom/IABUK/PwC

Note: CAGR = compound annual growth rate.

Solus email is an opt-in form of advertising where the body of the email is determined by the advertiser,
and is sent on their behalf by an email list manager/owner.

In the first half of 2009 this accounted for 23.5 per cent of total advertising spend in the UK, although this depends on the definition of advertising. The figure for expenditure on all forms of direct marketing was around £18 billion in 2009. If we use this measure, then online accounts for around 19 to 20 per cent of all activity.

Figure 2.1: Online share of UK advertising expenditure 2003-H12009

Source: IABUK/PWC

In the first half of 2009 headlines were made when it was reported that online advertising expenditure had overtaken television advertising for the first time (see Figure 2.2). This is slightly misleading as the figure for online included all online activity including paid for search. Since this announcement it has also been reported that television advertising revenues have increased, as has television viewing, which is now nearly 4 hours per day in the UK.

Figure 2.2: Adverstising expenditure by medium H1 2009 £million

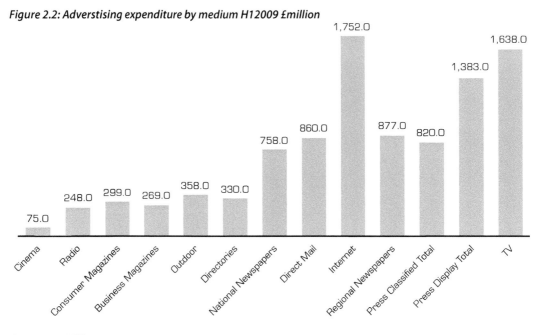

Source: IABUK/PWC

Despite the somewhat confusing picture it is clear that online marketing is significant and growing and whilst as direct marketers we must manage the customer experience across all touch points, the sexy part of the business at the moment is online.

However, it is necessary to generate a degree of balance: have the basic principles of marketing changed? We would argue that these remain more important than ever.

In a highly confused and fragmented media world the need to keep close to customers is greater than ever. In some ways online delivers the data we need to achieve this and this is why it has grown so fast. We can use a variety of techniques to meet our customers' needs faster and more efficiently. However, in other areas we see a great deal of dissatisfaction with online service, a lack of trust in online brands and accusations of sharp practice.

At its best the integration of online and offline can deliver more effectively and more efficiently the promise of marketing, the mutually satisfactory exchange of value.

So while this book is called 'Direct and Digital Marketing in Practice', it could be argued that what we are talking about is just marketing, pure and simple. Direct and digital techniques should be fully integrated within all organisations' marketing plans. We are at a point in history that means value can be created by the words digital and online, but in a few years these terms will be unnecessary, it is just the way we do our work as marketing professionals. That said we do need to understand these new techniques and how they have changed business.

The online audience
The great advantage of digital and online marketing is the amount of data that is available to us. The great disadvantage of digital and online marketing is the amount of data that is available to us.

As we have said, there is so much information that it is sometimes hard to find the resources to deal with it effectively and the same is true for audience data.

Worldwide the online audience grew by nearly 400 per cent between 2000 and 2009. The highest growth rate was in Africa but Africa still has the lowest penetration of Internet usage at just under 9 per cent. Internet usage is highest in North America at just over 72 per cent, Oceania and Australia is second at 61 per cent and Europe comes in third at 53 per cent penetration.

Table 2.5: World Internet usage and population statistics

World Regions	Population (2009 Est.)	Internet Users 31/12/2000	Internet Users Latest Data	Penetration (% Pop.)	Growth 2000-09(%)	Users % of Table
Africa	991,002,342	4,514,400	86,217,900	8.7	1,809.8	4.8
Asia	3,808,070,503	114,304,000	764,435,900	20.1	568.8	42.4
Europe	803,850,858	105,096,093	425,773,571	53.0	305.1	23.6
Middle East	202,687,005	3,284,800	58,309,546	28.8	1,675.1	3.2
North America	340,831,831	108,096,800	259,561,000	76.2	140.1	14.4
Latin America/ Caribbean	586,662,468	18,068,919	186,922,050	31.9	934.5	10.4
Oceania/Australia	34,700,201	7,620,480	21,110,490	60.8	177.0	1.2
WORLD TOTAL	6,767,805,208	360,985,492	1,802,330,457	26.6	399.3	100.0

Source: www.internetworldstats.com. Reproduced with permission

NOTES: (1) Internet Usage and World Population Statistics are for December 31, 2009. (2) Click on each world region name for detailed regional usage information. (3) Demographic (Population) numbers are based on data from the US Census Bureau . (4) Internet usage information comes from data published by Nielsen Online, by the International Telecommunications Union, by GfK, local Regulators and other reliable sources. (5) For definitions, disclaimer, and navigation help, please refer to the Site Surfing Guide. (6) Information in this site may be cited, giving the due credit to www.internetworldstats.com.

In the UK the latest data available show the extent to which the business and social life of the UK has changed due to the rapid uptake of the Internet. In 2010 around 18 million of 26 million households in the UK representing approximately 71 per cent of total households had Internet access.

This represented an increase of just under 2 million households over 2008 and four million households since 2006. Whilst this level of penetration is high it does mean that 29 per cent of British households do not have direct access to the Web and the range of services available. This may be an issue for some organisations in the not for profit sector and those that target lower income households or those that choose not to be part of the Internet revolution. The government publishes data on digital exclusion and a recent report can be accessed via www.communities.gov.uk/publications/communities/understandingdigitalexclusion.

Of those households with Internet access, around 90 per cent had a broadband connection in 2009, an increase from 69 per cent in 2006.

Table 2.6: UK Internet and Web-based content market – key statistics

	2005	2006	2007	2008	2009	2010Q1
PC/laptop take-up (%)	68	67	71	72	74	76
Internet take-up (%)	60	60	64	67	70	73
Total broadband take-up (%)	31	41	52	58	68	71
Fixed broadband take-up (%)	n/a	n/a	n/a	n/a	65	65
Mobile broadband take-up (%)	n/a	n/a	n/a	n/a	12	15
Social networking site take-up (%)	n/a	n/a	n/a	20	30	40
Use of mobile phone for web/data access (%)	n/a	n/a	n/a	20	20	23
Internet advertising expenditure (£bn)	1.4	2	2.8	3.4	3.5	n/a
Mobile advertising revenue (£m)	0.02	0.12	0.38	1.04	1.03	n/a

Source: Ofcom research / IABUK/PwC / Screen Digest

In regional terms, as might have been expected the area with the highest level of access was London, with 80 per cent. The region with the lowest access level was Scotland, with 62 per cent.

Sixty-four per cent of all adults who were recent Internet users (having accessed the Internet in the three months prior to interview) had ever purchased goods or services over the Internet in 2009. Of these, 83 per cent (26 million) had purchased within the last three months.

In terms of age Internet users tend to be younger although the skew towards younger audiences is beginning to even out; 25 per cent of UK citizens online are over 50 and 30 per cent of total time spent on the Internet is by the over-50s.

Table 2.7: UK home Internet access, by age

(%)	UK	15–24	25–34	35–54	55–64	65–74	75+
2009	70	78	80	85	63	44	20
2010	73	80	83	85	69	51	23

QE2: Do you or does anyone in your household have access to the Internet/World Wide Web at home?

Source: Ofcom technology tracker, Q1 2010

Base: all adults 15+ (n = 9013 UK, 1351 15-24, 1378 25-34, 3038 35-54, 1334 55-64, 1109 65-74, 803 75+, 2029 AB, 2631 C1, 1735 C2, 2569 DE, 4298 male, 4715 female).

There has been growth in Internet access by all age groups. Although the youngest age group (those aged 16–24) had the highest level of access, at 96 per cent, the largest increase in the proportion of those accessing the Internet was in the oldest age group (65 +). Access by those aged 65 plus increased proportionally by 15 per cent, compared with an increase of 3 per cent for the 16–24 age groups.

Table 2.8: UK home Internet access by social class and gender

(%)	AB	C1	C2	DE	Male	Female
2009	85	79	68	49	71	69
2010	88	80	71	54	75	72

QE2: Do you or does anyone in your household have access to the Internet/World Wide Web at home?

Source: Ofcom technology tracker, Q1 2010

Base: all adults 15+ (n = 9013 UK, 1351 15-24, 1378 25-34, 3038 35-54, 1334 55-64, 1109 65-74, 803 75+, 2029 AB, 2631 C1, 1735 C2, 2569 DE, 4298 male, 4715 female).

Usage

The range of reasons for using the Web is diverse and the tables and the following charts outline the core applications.

Table 2.9: Reasons for using the Internet, by age 2010

	All Adults	16–24	25–34	35–44	45–54	55–64	65 +
To keep up to date with news	39%	40%	48%	35%	41%	35%	34%
To find out or learn things	76%	72%	69%	79%	85%	76%	71%
To keep up to date with sports	21%	26%	27%	18%	21%	18%	13%
To relax	41%	51%	46%	42%	41%	25%	26%
For fun	50%	70%	59%	47%	46%	30%	20%
To pass the time	36%	54%	42%	33%	28%	21%	22%
For contact with other people	60%	70%	62%	60%	53%	56%	57%

IN42 - Which, if any, of these are reasons why you use the Internet? (prompted responses, multi-coded)

Source: Ofcom research, fieldwork carried out by Saville Rossiter-Base in April to May and September to October 2009

Table 2.10: Reasons for using the Internet, by gender and SEG 2010

	Male	Female	AB	C1	C2	DE
To keep up to date with news	47%	32%	50%	40%	37%	25%
To find out or learn things	78%	74%	76%	80%	81%	64%
To keep up to date with sports	36%	9%	25%	21%	24%	16%
To relax	41%	41%	38%	43%	47%	38%
For fun	50%	49%	42%	52%	55%	53%
To pass the time	39%	33%	33%	37%	38%	37%
For contact with other people	60%	59%	65%	60%	56%	57%

IN42 - Which, if any, of these are reasons why you use the Internet? (prompted responses, multi-coded).

Source: Ofcom research, fieldwork carried out by Saville Rossiter-Base in April to May and September to October 2009

The category of learning is mentioned extensively in all user categories and some of this clearly relates to research into purchases as 70 per cent claim to use the Internet to make purchases, whilst 58 per cent claim to use the Web for banking services.

Figure 2.3: Claimed use of the Internet for various activities

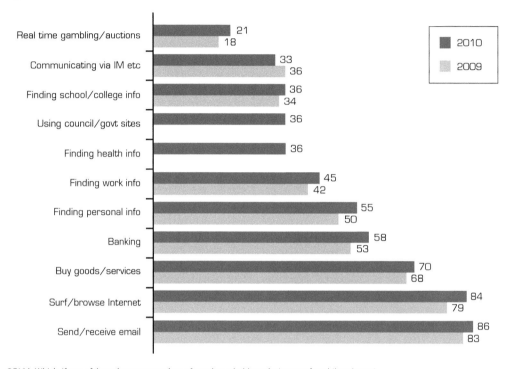

QE10A: Which, if any, of these do you or members of your household use the internet for while at home?

Base: All with internet access (n=6163).

Source: Ofcom technology tracker, Q1 2010

Ofcom reports that the results of the credit crunch have been that consumers are using the Web to try to shop and save money. Their research shows that significant numbers of people are now more likely to take advantage of some of the money-saving opportunities online than they were in 2008–9.

Of those with broadband access, 53 per cent reported that they were more likely to try to save money by purchasing goods and services online than they were 12 months ago, 61 per cent said they were now more likely to use price comparison websites (such as uSwitch, pricerunner and moneysupermarket.com) than they were 12 months ago, while 47 per cent of broadband users said they were more likely to use online vouchers and voucher codes.

Online gaming is the most popular form of online media consumption, with 39 per cent of Internet users carrying out this activity in Q1 2010 – up from 38 per cent in Q1 2009. The next most popular category is music and film downloads with 38 per cent claiming to download music and films online compared with 39 per cent in Q1 2009. Among 15 to 24-year-olds, the figures for these activities are 55 per cent for playing games and 51 per cent for downloading content.

The Internet usage category that declined was uploading and adding content. Given the massive growth of user generated content since Web 2.0 this is interesting. The exceptions to this were photo sharing and social networking, which remain popular – 49 per cent claimed to have uploaded photos while those with a social network profile had doubled from 2007 to 2010 with 44 per cent now claiming to have created a profile on a social networking site. Blog contributions were another growth area. Those claiming to add comments to blogs grew from 19 per cent to 27 per cent between 2007 and 2009.

Mobile content

Mobile access to Internet content has also increased significantly, and the range of applications has increased. This growth has largely been down to the rise of Apple's iPhone, although many rivals are now offering highly sophisticated competitive products. Regarding mobile applications, social media accounts for the majority of time spent online, with 45 per cent of total mobile time spent accessing Facebook accounts.

Table 2.11: Use of mobile data services 2007–Q1 2010

(%)	Internet access	Emailing	Instant messaging	Downloading programs
2007 Q2	13	8	11	
2010 Q1	18	10	11	8

QD9A: Which, if any, of the following activities, other than making and receiving voice calls, do you use your mobile for?

Base: All mobile users aged 15+ (n=7826).

Source: Ofcom technology tracker, Q1 2010

As expected search, telecoms sites, entertainment and news sites are the most popular. However, commerce, finance and travel sites are not far behind. In May 2010 the typical user spent nearly 24 hours online. In same time the average UK citizen watched the equivalent of five days of television, or more than 120 hours. (See Table 2.12 on page 46)

Clearly there is a growing, increasingly sophisticated, valuable online market that is accessing the Web from a variety of platforms, including mobile.

The next question is how can we create a business from these customers?

Designing an online strategy and implementation

Despite the claims for the Internet, when we look at the development of strategy for the Web we see that very often the same models and frameworks apply. There are a few tweaks to the traditional models but essentially the structure is the same. We look at developing a direct and digital strategy in Chapter 6 but here we will briefly touch on the core frameworks that support digital strategy development and this section might usefully be read in conjunction with Chapter 6.

Table 2.12: Most popular site categories, by active reach

	Active reach (%)	Time/Month per person (hh:mm:ss)
Total	98.15	23:23:09
Search & Communities	95.43	06:38:37
Telecoms Internet	88.73	03:26:58
Entertainment	87.09	04:43:46
News & Info	78.18	01:14:35
PCs & Electronics	76.29	01:14:41
Multi-category commerce	74.14	02:14:37
Finance	67.78	00:56:33
Travel	66.76	00:56:42
Home & Fashion	63.35	00:48:20
Family & Lifestyles	58.6	01:00:35
Govt & Non-Profit	50.71	00:28:00
Corporate Info	50.25	00:20:57
Education & Careers	41.78	00:44:36
Automotive	35.38	00:27:25
Special Occasions	25.61	00:13:12

Source: Ofcom/UKOM/Nielsen home and work panel, applications included, month of May 2010

The major issue is that there are very few brands that are pure play online brands, i.e. those that use only digital media, channels and distribution to reach their customer and prospect base. The majority struggle to integrate online and offline activity and it is interesting to note that the two major growth areas in marketing included digital online marketing and experiential marketing. Experiential marketing attempts to make the intangible experience and communities that exist online, tangible and meaningful to consumers in the real rather than the virtual world.

So, what is strategy? Marketing strategy can be defined as optimising the fit between an organisation and the customer groups it seeks to serve in order to create value for all parties involved over the longer term.

Its core characteristic is that it concerns interaction between the products and services that we offer to the customers/clients that we target. In general, strategy has the following characteristics:

- indentifies and allocates resources
- identifies the way the organisation will meet its goals
- broad in scope
- descriptive
- general
- offers a set of guiding principles

Strategy is inextricably linked to delivery and execution through tactics which typically are focused on:

- the detailed implementation of strategic choices
- operational execution
- specific activities are scheduled, timetabled, budgeted for and measured
- narrow task driven activity with a degree of flexibility built in

A digital strategy therefore simply means that the relationships and the characteristics of strategy are delivered through digital channels, media and methods. Put simply, what are our online business objectives, which customers will we serve and how, what will the costs of this activity be, and how much will it return over time?

The next task is to integrate digital strategy with offline strategy to produce an optimal outcome for customers and the organisation across all channels to market.

It has to be clear that a digital strategy cannot be developed in isolation. As we will see later we need to understand the customer experience and successfully integrate online and offline approaches as appropriate.

This is not to underplay the role of digital marketing and there are many techniques and methods that must be mastered in order to become a competent direct and digital marketer, however many of these apply to the tactical level.

Dave Chaffey, in his book *Internet Marketing: Strategy Implementation and Practice* (Prentice Hall, 2009) presents a useful framework for the discussion of strategic development of digital approaches to customers. (See Figure 2.4 on page 48.)

The strategic planning process for direct and digital is covered in more detail in Chapter 6.

However, the online strategy planning process in brief covers the following areas:

- Our current market position or situation analysis
- Internal resources, external factors including Pestel and competition
- Business and marketing objectives acquisition versus retention and related costs
- Strategy – how we deliver the objectives
  - Segmentation, targeting and positioning, which markets, with which brands
  - Data and information strategy, the integration of web analytics database and marketing research
  - Broader mix issue including product decisions, pricing approaches, channel choice, systems and processes, customer service and HR
- Tactics – the detailed plan
  - Detailed communications and contact strategy across communications channels, including search, email, social media and online display
- Measurement and review against marketing objectives and at campaign level
  - Web metrics and analytics
  - Campaign reporting
  - Market research on brand, customer perceptions and attitudes

Figure 2.4: Digital channel strategy

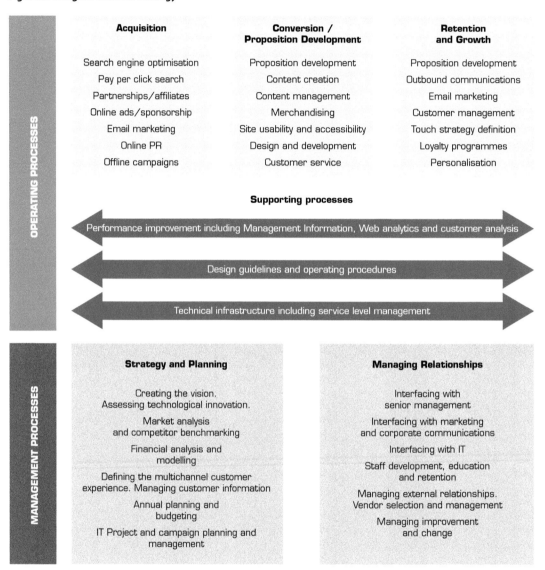

Source: Dave Chaffey. Internet Marketing: Strategy Implementation and Practice, 4th edition (Prentice Hall, 2009)

So while there is a significant intersection between the overall strategic plan and the digital plan, there are some significant differences, which we will focus on in the rest of this chapter.

Search engine marketing (SEM)

Search is a very important part of the marketer's armoury. SEM is a combination of two activities; one is the work done to optimise a website for what is called natural search, the other is the output from pay-per-click (PPC) campaigns. These two activities are linked in that they aim to drive traffic to a website, but they are separate in key areas.

Search has several overriding benefits. Firstly it is highly targeted. When we enter a search term we are actively looking for products and services, in effect we are calling the company's messages to us. Paid search is highly controllable and very cost-effective. Investment in search can help drive branding strategies. Top listings are far more noticed than banners, and conversion rates typically are higher than other online media.

The search marketplace

According to Ofcom, paid-for search now accounts for 61 per cent of total Internet advertising expenditure and its proportion of online advertising spend has increased as the popularity of display formats have declined. Search sites are the most popular in the UK with Google dominant as can be seen from the table below. Of the total search engine traffic, Google accounts for around 80 per cent of all searches and the top four search engines account for nearly 97 per cent of all traffic.

Table 2.13: Top ten sites by unique audience, split by age

Rank	2–17	18–24	25–34	35–49	50–64	65 +
1	Google	Google	Google	Google	Google	Google
2	Google search	Google search	Google search	Google search	Google search	Google search
3	MSN/ WindowsLive Bing	MSN WindowsLive Bing	MSN WindowsLive Bing	MSN WindowsLive Bing	MSN WindowsLive Bing	MSN WindowsLive Bing
4	Facebook	Facebook	Facebook	Facebook	Yahoo!	BBC
5	YouTube	WindowsLive Hotmail	Yahoo!	BBC	Facebook	Yahoo!
6	BBC	YouTube	BBC	Yahoo!	BBC	Google Maps
7	Windows Live Messenger	Windows Live Messenger	Google Maps	Google Maps	Google Maps	Microsoft
8	Yahoo!	Yahoo!	YouTube	eBay	Microsoft	Amazon
9	YouTube homepage	BBC	eBay	Microsoft	eBay	Facebook
10	Google Image search	eBay	Windows Live Hotmail	YouTube	Amazon	Wikipedia

Source: Ofcom/ UKOM/Nielsen home and work panel, applications included, month of May 2010

Note: 'Unique audience' = the total number of unique persons that have visited a website or used an application at least once in the specified reporting period. Persons visiting the same website or using the same application more than once in the reporting period are only counted once.

Figure 2.5: Unique audience of search engine sites 2008–2010

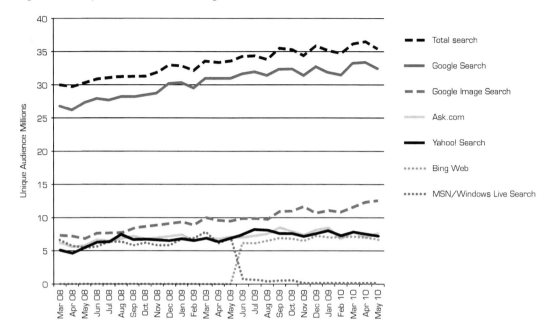

Natural search

Natural search is the activity that drives our 'organic' listings. This is the area on the left of the Google search return screen below the pink shaded premium search listings and separate from the return on PPC campaigns which are on the right-hand side of the screen.

Figure 2.6: Structure of the Google search return page

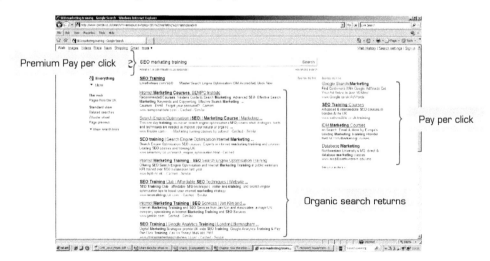

The heat map below shows why it is useful to be top of PPC and organic search as our eyes fall naturally on the top left of any page. The crosses mark where the eye lands and the whiter the image the longer the eye is fixed on that area of the screen.

Figure 2.7: Google screen heat map

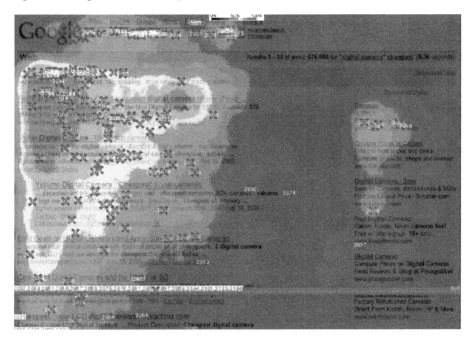

Natural or organic search listings are free and the Holy Grail for search engine marketers is to understand how to raise the position in natural search rankings.

The work here is ongoing as the market is constantly evolving there are several things to consider.

Analyse keywords

Search engines are reconciling the interests of three parties, advertisers, users and the search engine itself. Relevance becomes a very important driver of ranking. Put very simply, the fit between the search term and your website may deliver a better position. These keywords are important. When writing copy for a website it is important to realise that you are writing for two audiences – the readers and the search robots or spiders which trawl your site indexing content.

Google has a very useful tool to explore keywords. The tool can be found at www.adwords.google.com.

Another useful tool is to check the key word density of your site and your competitors' sites. There are many such tools and one can be found at www.abakus-internet-marketing.de/tools/topword.html.

The temptation is to pack the site with keywords, but the recommendation is to use keywords carefully at a maximum of around 10 per cent of content.

Do not simply choose keywords that generate the most impressions as all competitors will be doing the same. There may be several hundreds of keyword combinations.

You must consider your objectives, if you are competing against aggressive, significant and numerous competitors it will be tough. In this case you can look for alternative or niche words that will compete effectively. Often it is better to achieve high-quality traffic rather than large numbers.

It is important to be honest and up front. Google knows all the tricks and you can be removed from Google's listings very easily.

Index content

For your site to be indexed it must be submitted to all major search engines. For Google the Web link is www.google.com/addurl. Submitting for indexing does not necessarily guarantee that your site will be indexed but you can check what pages are indexed by entering the search operator site: yourdomainname into your search engine.

There is a range of such operators and they include:

- site: indexed pages in your site site:www.yourdomain
- link: pages that link to your site's front page link: www.yourdomain
- cache: the current cache of your site cache: www.yourdomain
- info: information we have about your site info: www.yourdomain
- related: pages that are similar to your site related: www.yourdomain

Optimisation of page and website content

The next stage is to optimise content and navigation. Google looks at quality and measures of reputation. So a good, well-designed landing page is vital, and good links through your site and correct use of web standards is important.

Web standards are controlled by W3C, which develops technical specifications and guidelines through the creation of technical and editorial quality standards. Their mark-up validation service is available at: www.validator.w3.org/.

This is an area that can become very technical and the relationship you have with your web designer will be crucial. However, there are a few key areas to be aware of.

Keywords can be included in body copy but can also be included in:

- Page titles which appear at the top of the Web page:
  — Keyword rich and descriptive
  — Most important words at the beginning
  — No longer than 80 characters
- Meta descriptions part of the source code
  — Attractive and should present a call-to-action
  — Communicate the content on the page
  — No longer than 250 characters
- Meta keywords
  — Should include synonyms, pluralisation, misspellings
  — 7–9 keywords per page

If you right click on a Web page and click view source code you can see a range of opportunities for keyword insertion.

There are a vast number of sources on practical Web design. A starting point is Google: www.google.com/websiteoptimizer.

Develop link partnerships

Google increasingly defines itself as a reputation engine and it tries to return search results of the highest quality to its users. Part of this measure relates to links.

Page rank is one way that Google measures the quality of websites and it appears to be more effective to link to companies with a higher page rank score

Page rank is logarithmic like the Richter scale for earthquakes. Five is twice four, which is twice three. A good website will have a page rank of five or higher. The BBC has a page rank of nine out of ten.

It appears that more links with a higher page rank into another page increase the page rank score. Outbound links appear less valuable. Internal links are also useful.

Figure 2.8: Google page rank

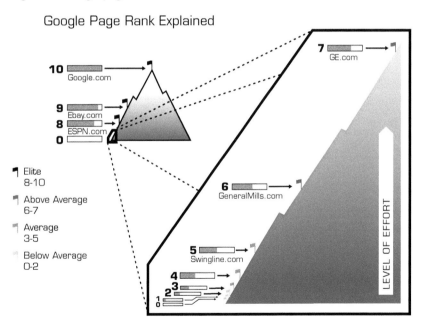

Pay per click

Pay per click returns the right-hand results in the Google search screen.

Because this is a paid-for service there is a vast amount of help available from all the search engine operators. If you follow the links for business and advertisers from the Google home page, then you can be taken through the approach stage by stage. For further information see: www.adwords.google.com/support.

The way PPC works is that you enter an auction for keywords. You bid on keywords or phrases and your bid in part determines your ranking position.

However, Google also takes into account three other areas, combining the bid with a measure of quality.

Quality is determined by:
- historic click-through rates (CTRs), users are returning evidence to Google on the quality of ads, i.e. those with higher CTR are given a higher quality score;
- relevance, language and context of a query related to keywords;
- landing page quality. Does the landing page provide relevant and original content quick load times and transparency about the nature of the business?

So these principles can drive strategy. We need to ensure:
- We have selected the most appropriate keyword and phrases.
  - we need to select a level of bid.
  - we need to write advertising copy for our entry; in Google this is limited to 25 characters for the title, 70 characters for the ad text, and 35 characters for a display url including spaces. On Google, this is displayed on four lines: a title, two lines of ad text (each with 35 characters), and a url line.
  - we need to link to relevant high-quality landing pages.
  - we need to set up measurement and review systems to track the success or otherwise of our campaigns.

Search is an ongoing process and is vital to get right. Unlike a high street, people will rarely stumble upon our website. We need to take every opportunity to get people there.

Behavioural targeting

This is a relatively new and somewhat contentious area for online marketing. It can be applied within the company and Google, through its AdSense product, is providing access to a new revenue stream by serving ads to customers based on a range of factors including online behaviour. See www.google.com/adsense.

The aim is to serve relevant content to the right person at the right time and this basic approach to segmentation simply reflects what has been done offline for many years. However, the difference in the online version is that it is far more sophisticated, wider ranging and can be automated. Also today, consumers are far more sensitive about the way companies gather and use their 'personal' information. There are various ways to capture an anonymous customer's behaviour. Cookies with permission can identify a range of very useful information.

These include:

- site type visited most frequently or recently
- messages seen
- frequency of exposure
- click history or ad interaction
- search terms clicked
- onsite behaviour
- areas visited
- processes started
- sign-ups
- geography
- access platform (mobile, Wi-Fi or broadband)
- frequency of access
- time of day/day of week
- exposure count

This information can be used to serve highly targeted executions using multiple variables.

Social media, blogs, discussion boards

Social media is defined by the IDM as 'the creation of useful, valuable and relevant content and applications by brands, or by consumers with specific reference to brands, that can be shared online, facilitated by Web 2.0 technologies.' Web 2.0 refers to technologies that allow users to create or amend content online.

Social media has been the phenomenon of the first decade of the twenty-first century. The flag bearer of the social media revolution has been Facebook established in 2004 and in the UK in April 2010 nearly 25 million unique visitors went to the Facebook site. Facebook is an example of a social networking site. Other social media include:

- Blogs: an abbreviation of 'weblog', a blog is a personal online diary, journal or news source. The author is referred to as a 'blogger' and the act described as 'blogging'. This includes 'micro blogging' services such as Twitter.
- Discussion boards: Also known as newsgroups, forums, discussion groups and Internet discussion boards or IDBs. Discussion boards allow users to read all the messages left by other users on a particular topic and post new or follow-up messages. The fact that (unlike chat rooms) discussion boards don't happen in 'real time' can also be a significant advantage because people can participate without having to be online at the same time.
- Wikis: The word 'wiki' is derived from the Hawaiian word for 'fast', an online editable document created by many Web users. It is an open, public collaboration, authored and edited by users without the need for registration or subscription. A famous example is the encyclopaedia Wikipedia.org. One thing for users of Wikipedia to be aware of is that many of the definitions quoted are incorrect, or only partially correct, as they are posted by individuals without any formal monitoring. The idea is that incorrect statements will be corrected by better informed people, but this does not always happen.
- Podcasts: Podcasting is coined from Apple's iPod range. The term is now generally used to describe audio file downloads (usually in the form of .mp3 and related file types) for subsequent listening; otherwise known more prosaically as audio-casting.
- Social bookmarking: Social bookmarking is a method that allows the online community to share content via a system of tags. The material itself is not shared as the tags simply reference material. Additional content may be added to tags to place greater context

around sources. Tags are shared within specific networks and these can be viewed by other members of that network. Examples include www.delicious.com and www.reddit.com.

The above definitions are sourced from the IDM's very useful glossary of direct and digital terminology. This can be found at www.theidm.com/resources/jargon-buster.

Social networking

These sites allow users to create personal profiles, upload content such as photographs and video, send messages and interact with each other.

There have been a huge number of changes in this marketplace with new entrants and enhanced functionality. There has also been a shakeout in the number of players with the demise of Bebo. com and various mergers and acquisitions and joint ventures, for example Twitter's venture with Bing and Google allowing search of Twitter updates through these search engines.

According to Ofcom, social networking in the consumer world is a younger person's preserve. Over 60 per cent of 15 to 34-year-olds access social networking sites and 89 per cent of these do so at least once a week. This compares with 20 per cent of 55 to 64-year-olds only 50 per cent of who use social service at least once a week. The services are used more by the higher social grades and more women than men are likely to use the sites. Forty-two per cent of women and 39 per cent of men access social networking sites. However, the same data indicates that 45 per cent of those with Internet access have never accessed social networking sites.

Table 2.14: Proportion of adults who access social networking sites on the Internet at home, by age

%	UK	15–24	25–34	35–54	55–64	65–74	75 +
Q1 2008	20	38	31	21	9	3	1
Q3 2008	26	50	40	25	14	2	(-)
Q1 2009	30	50	46	35	13	3	1
Q1 2010	40	61	61	48	20	7	3

QE12: Which, if any, of these do you or members of your household use the Internet for while at home?

Source: Ofcom technology tracker, Q1 2010

Base: All adults aged 15+ (n = 5812 Q1 2008, 1581 Q3 2008, 6090 Q1 2009, 9013 Q1 2010).

Note: Q1 2008 data in this chart are not directly comparable to data published in the 2009 Communications Market Report due to updated data provided to Ofcom.

In the consumer market Facebook leads the way, and in 2010 the site's user base grew by 31 per cent. At the same time in the business to business market LinkedIn's user base grew by 96 per cent. The story is not all rosy. MySpace and Bebo both declined in the same period by 37 per cent and 60 per cent respectively and Friends Reunited usage fell by 39 per cent. Friends Reunited was sold in 2010 for £25 million. It was acquired in 2005 for £175 million. AOL sold Bebo also in 2010 for a reported £10 million, a huge loss on the $850 million it paid for it two years previously.

Figure 2.9: Unique audience of selected social networking sites 2008–2010

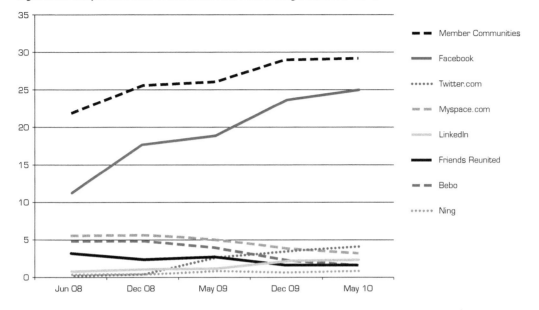

NOTE

The picture, then, is one of turbulence and change and the emergence of a consolidated approach based around a few core services who dominate the sector. Whilst large audiences are not a prerequisite for successful online marketing where we may be targeting highly defined target audiences, stability is helpful for marketers.

Social media sites in April 2010 accounted for around 23 per cent of UK users' total Internet time, up from 9 per cent in 2007.

Table 2.15: Time per user per month spent on selected social networking sites 2008–2010

(hh:mm:ss)	Jun-08	Sep-08	Dec-08	Mar-09	Jun-09	Sep-09	Dec-09	Mar-10	May-10
Facebook	03:36:22	04:23:34	06:08:19	06:02:11	05:41:20	06:06:03	06:56:02	07:02:36	06:31:49
Member Communities	02:42:06	03:34:58	05:15:11	05:04:02	05:14:08	05:39:31	06:08:06	06:24:03	06:14:18
Bebo	01:26:52	01:23:38	01:59:03	01:10:30	01:59:54	01:15:55	01:08:44	01:17:49	00:56:35
Twitter.com	00:02:21	00:04:15	00:07:25	00:34:25	00:25:34	00:24:08	00:45:29	00:29:50	00:35:25
LinkedIn	00:04:46	00:16:55	00:11:44	00:22:55	00:12:07	00:18:21	00:12:34	00:18:40	00:20:39
Friends Reunited	00:13:49	00:12:34	00:11:37	00:19:11	00:14:22	00:13:21	00:11:13	00:19:12	00:13:42
Ning	00:13:31	00:10:52	00:13:32	00:08:45	00:09:41	00:08:58	00:05:22	00:09:54	00:12:06
Myspace.com	00:54:37	00:48:17	00:51:27	00:39:00	00:26:49	00:19:13	00:13:52	00:11:39	00:09:37

Source: Ofcom/UKOM/Nielsen

Note: Home and work panel, applications included.

The table below shows the range of activity carried on online.

Table 2.16: UK Internet sectors' share of total Internet time

	Apr-07	Apr-10	Relative change
Social Networks/Blogs	8.80%	22.70%	159%
E-mail	6.50%	7.20%	11%
Games	5.90%	6.90%	15%
Instant Messaging	14.20%	4.90%	-66%
Classifieds/Auctions	5.00%	4.70%	-6%
Portals	3.70%	4.00%	10%
Search	4.10%	4.00%	-3%
Software Info/Products	5.30%	3.40%	-36%
News	1.50%	2.80%	84%
Adult	2.80%	2.70%	-3%
Other	42.20%	36.80%	-13%

Source: Ofcom/UKOM/Nielsen

Note: Home and work panel, applications included. Email excludes work-related email.

Increasingly, social media sites are accessed via mobile devices – 20 per cent of the social networking of 16 to 24-year-olds is done via their mobile whereas only 4 per cent of over-45s do the same. Again this has implications for the way that marketers configure their strategies.

Integrating social media into strategy

Despite the rapid pace of change we can go back to basics when developing a social media strategy; as with everything in marketing, strategy starts with customers. The following approach can be applied.

- Review business and marketing objectives
- What contribution will social media make to these objectives?
  - New business
  - Retained business
  - Service development
  - Member get member or referral
  - Generate site traffic
  - Enhance reputation through review or other content generation
  - Engage with the brand
- Define the target audience
- Which social media are they using, when, why and how?
- Benchmark and analyse your competitors' use of social media – what is your point of differentiation and core value proposition?
- Develop campaigns and ensure integration with other communications activity including

offline and online channels. Communicate this to all involved and interested partners within and outside the organisation.

Allocate responsibilities for

- Content development – for example, who is responsible for keeping blogs up to date?
- A simple classification of social content covers:
  - Entertainment creates an interactive potentially viral experience
  - Information – shares exclusive knowledge
  - Conversation – creates a personal and credible dialogue
- Search optimisation
- Handling customer response – who will monitor and report response data?
- How will the organisation respond to positive and negative input?
- Measurement and evaluation – what tools will be used and how frequently will we report?

Measurement of social media

There is a variety of ways that we can track social media, these include:

- We can use social bookmarking services and monitor the number of tags on our content.
- Technorati (www.technorati.com) provides real-time search for UGC including blogs using tags or keywords. Provides a system of alerts on relevant content.
- Google alerts (www.google.com/alerts) provide email alerts of the latest Google results based on your choice of topic – for example your brand name.
- There is a range of services that provide detailed reputation and tracking services online. Some of these are listed below.
- Onalytica (www.onalytica.com).
- Market Sentinel (www.marketsentinel.com).
- Nielsen Buzz Metrics (www.en-us.nielsen.com/content/.../nielsen_buzzmetrics.html).
- Radian6 (www.radian6.com).
- Trackur (www.trackur.com).
- Brandwatch (www.brandwatch.com).

Online advertising

The detailed execution of online advertising campaigns is covered in Chapter 10. At this stage we will simply explore the nature of the medium.

Forms of online advertising

The main forms of online advertising are:

- display: using banners or rich media utilising special technology such as video or expansion;
- contextual advertising relates the advertising to the content displayed on the screen;
- in-stream advertising relates to advertising served within audio or video streaming;
- mobile advertising relates to advertising on mobile devices including sms;
- email advertising is advertising within an email context;

Search is often included under advertising but has been dealt with elsewhere in this chapter.

The developments in the market are towards more technically sophisticated rich media formats. For examples of these go to www.flashtalking.com.

In the UK, the market for display advertising has grown significantly over the last five years although growth has recently slowed as more budget has been pushed into search. In 2009 the marketing was worth £716.1 million, up from £335.9 million in 2005.

Banner ads have a fairly poor reputation, largely due to the early use of indiscriminately targeted pop-ups. However, banners can still deliver results if the price is right. That said, response rates and other key measures have been stable at best.

Latest figures from DoubleClick™ show CTRs for the EMEA region average 0.09 per cent, and this is down from around 0.2 per cent four years ago. Interaction rates (an interaction is some form of engagement with the ad served, e.g. when you run your mouse over the advertisement) are 2.41 per cent and these too show a significant decline over time.

Table 2.17: Overall EMEA campaign performance norms for 2009 across DoubleClick™ Image, Flash, and rich media campaigns

Country	Click-through Rate (CTR) %	Interaction Rate %	Average Interaction Time (secs)
EMEA Region*	0.09	2.41	9.31
France	0.12	3.90	7.14
Germany	0.11	2.90	8.60
Italy	0.10	3.52	7.46
Netherlands	0.14	4.49	7.46
United Kingdom	0.07	2.29	9.62

Source:www.doubleclick.com

Advertising formats in the UK are overseen by the Internet Advertising Bureau (IAB). They can be found at www.iabuk.org. The standard formats are:
- Banners 728 x 90 pixels
- Small banners 468 x 60 pixels
- Small skyscrapers 120 x 600 pixels
- Skyscrapers 160 x 600 pixels
- Half page 300 x 600 pixels
- Mid page unit (MPU) 300 x 250 pixels

Other standards relate to rich media.

Internet advertising standards

Table 2.18 on page 62 relates to online advertising including traditional banner and skyscraper adverts, but also incorporates new rich media products such as video within banners and expandable banners. IAB recommends that media owners, agencies and advertisers follow these recommendations to make the media creation and buying process easier. This aims to help drive down growth of the formats and reduce confusion.

The move to larger formats and more sophisticated rich media formats relates to the improved performance of these formats.

DoubleClick™'s figures for 2009 show that 90 per cent of advertisments are rich media or flash based.

Figure 2.10: Advertising impression by creative type 2009

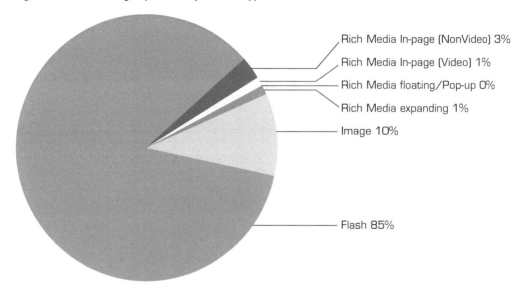

Source: DoubleClick Benchmarks, EMEA DFA campaigns, January to December 2009

Advertising online can both build brands and build response and sales in a traditional brand response strategy. Ads can be targeted in a very sophisticated way using geographic, demographic, or behavioural targeting tools.

Advertising space can be bought in a variety of ways:
- Run of category is the purchase of a given number of impressions from an ad network on a defined set of websites that have some similarity in their content or in the demographics of their customers.
- Run of network involves purchasing advertising space on a network. The advertiser purchases by number of ads but cannot specify where they will appear on the network. It is a cheaper but less targeted system.
- Run of site is the most common way of buying space which involves the purchase of a given number of impressions on a website without any constraints on which pages the advertisement appears.

Table 2.18: IAB advertising standards

	Format Category	Format (WxH) (pixels)	Max File Size* (flash)	Audio Initiation	Max Animation Length	Controls (to skip ad)	Labelling and other items
In-page	In-page units (universal sizes in bold)	Banner: **728x90**; 468x60 Skyscraper: **160x600**; 120x600 Square: **250x250**; 200x200 Rectangle (h): **336x280**; 300x250; 180x150 Rectangle (v): 240x400 Button: 180x150;125x125	30KB	User initiated (on click)	15 secs	Not applicable	Label = 'Advertisement' Font = 16pt
Over the Page	Expandable units	User-initiated expandable ads, initial size based on the above in-page units with expanded area decided by publisher	30KB	User initiated (on click / mouseover)	15 secs	Control = "Close X" Font = 16pt Location = on edge of original (non-expanded) unit Feature = enable mouse-off retraction	Label = 'Advertisement' Font = 16pt
	Floating units (overlays)	Floating ads Landing spot for floating ads	30KB	User initiated	15 secs	Control = "Close X" Font = 16pt	Label = "Advertisement" Font = 16pt
	Between-the-page (transition ads)	Decided by publisher	30KB	User initiated	15 and 30 secs	Control = "Skip advertisement" Font = 16pt Location = above the fold in lower right corner	Label = "Advertisement" or "Brought to you by" Font = 16pt Location = above the fold (top of ad)
	Pop-up units					Cannot be recommended	

Adapted from IAB US.
*Note: not all publishers carry all formats. * Initial file downloads only.*
Source www.iabuk.org

When buying online space we normally issue a request for information or proposal (RFP) and once we have decided to go ahead an insertion order (IO) is issued – this is the equivalent of a purchase order.

The insertion order will include the following details:
- Client and campaign name
- Campaign start and end dates
- Deal type (CpM/CpC/CpA – See below or whether the campaign is based on tenancy, sponsorship or partnership)
- Placement (network/site/channel)
- Volume of booked inventory by placement/format
- Rates by placement/format
- Total budget (gross cost, agency commission, net cost, net cost inc. VAT)
- Any other information
- Targeting options – i.e. demographic/behavioural
- Frequency capping – i.e. cap to three per user session
- Phasing of activity – i.e. equal delivery or weighted
- Space for booking reference number

Online advertising measurement and review

This is dealt with in detail in Chapter 10, but there are some key terms to consider here.
- An impression is a single exposure to a single user of an advertisement
- CTR – click-through rate
- IR – interaction rate, single mouseovers
- VCR – video completion rates
- CPT or CPM – cost per cost per thousand impressions
- CPC – cost per click
- CPA – cost per acquisition

There are a range of other approaches to online advertising and these include:
- sponsored content
- co-branding and affiliate networks
- advertorial
- email placement to opted-in lists
- in-game advertising, advertising placed with computer games

Mobile Internet

Include the use of mobile broadband through the use of dongles and the use of mobile phones and other devices to access Internet services.

Mobile broadband using dongles accounted for 15 per cent of total connections to the Internet in 2010, up from 12 per cent in 2009.

The use of mobile phones to access the Internet has also increased significantly and in 2010 reached 26 per cent.

Table 2.19: Use of mobile phones for Web/data access

(%)	Total	15–24	25–34	35–54	55–64	65 +
2009	22	39	35	21	6	4
2010	26	46	38	25	9	2

QD9A: Which if any, of the following activities, other than making and receiving voice calls, do you use your mobile for?

Source: Ofcom technology tracker, Q1 2010

Base: all adults 15+ (n = 9013 UK, 1351 15-24, 1378 25-34, 3038 35-54, 1334 55-64, 1912 65+).

Note: Web/data access includes accessing the Internet, downloading and streaming content, connecting using WiFi and using VoIP.

Mobile marketing techniques have developed to take advantage of the growth of the use of the devices. The iPhone apps are perhaps the most vibrant sector at present. There have been more than three billion downloads of iPhone apps from the iPhone store. In the UK 8 per cent of iPhone users downloaded apps on their mobile in 2010.

Other mobile marketing techniques include:
- mobile promotions including text to win competitions;
- the use of mobile barcodes, shotcodes, QR codes to link devices to content or to use as vouchers. qr codes are photographed by phones and using appropriate software can link the phone to a website. See Figure 2.11 for an example of QR code;
- microblogging the best known example being twitter/ugc;
- managing of customer relationships using permission-based sms or email;
- mobile advertising;
- sponsored content;
- bluetooth enabled outdoor site;
- the use of mobiles for marketing research;
- location-based marketing using gps enabled devices.

Figure 2.11: Example of a QR code

Mobile advertising revenues reached £1.03 million in 2009 and this area has demonstrated rapid growth.

Figure 2.12: Mobile advertising revenues 2005-2009

	2005	**2006**	**2007**	**2008**	**2009**
Mobile TV (£m)	0.02	0.11	0.34	0.92	0.78
Mobile VoD (£m)	0	0	0.03	0.1	0.18
Mobile games (£m)	0	0	0.01	0.02	0.07
Total (£m)	0.02	0.12	0.38	1.04	1.03
Mobile as % of total Internet advertising	0	0.01	0.01	0.03	0.03

Source: Screen Digest / Ofcom / IABUK

Mobile marketing's future seems bright as the smart phones and new fast data networks extend functionality. MMS and SMS marketing campaigns are producing results

Mobile advertising requests served in the UK by Admob, part of Google, doubled to 585 million in 2010 and this is a useful indicator of the scale of activity. Admob can be found at www.admob.com.

Email

Email is a major Web application although its commercial use has to some extent been compromised by spam email. However, 86 per cent of Internet users use the Web for email and the time spent on email sites accounts for 7 per cent of total time spent online. The use of mobile email is also increasing with 10 per cent saying they used their mobile to access email

The value of solus email (i.e. email to opted-in cold lists) declined to £6.8 million in 2010 from a peak of £17.5 million in 2007. However, the use of email as a retention device has increased significantly with around 50 per cent of companies saying they will increase their email spend in the retention area.

Email is a huge area and we cover some of the details in Chapter 10. However, the IDM publishes a very useful guide to email marketing and here are their top tips to create a successful email campaign.

IDM EMAIL 20 TOP TIPS

1. Start with a simple campaign – just because you can't do everything it doesn't mean you can't do anything.
2. Sign up for emails everywhere (B-B and B-C) – make a note of the things that other people are doing well as it's the fastest way to learn.
3. Build your privacy policy to cover the minimum legal requirements and then a little more to reassure prospects.

4. Refine your data capture strategy – start with only an email address and invite people to update their profile over time.
5. Build a simple un-subscribe process – let people go with grace and dignity, and it will provide reassurance to waverers.
6. Use software and training to minimise the amount of invalid addresses that get on to your file.
7. Create a policy to manage deliverability into your top 20 ISPs.
8. Understand the implications of blacklisting.
9. Have consistent 'From' fields to define the relationship with the recipient.
10. Test 'Subject' lines to find the ones that generate the highest open rates.
11. Keep 'Subject' lines as short as possible.
12. Recognise how the 'Preview Pane' can help open rate.
13. Use personalised content to make your campaigns more relevant.
14. Use people's click-through activity to segment and target for follow-up campaigns.
15. Monitor activity beyond the email – how many people do what you want them to do?
16. Read your 'Reply to' messages… they may contain good news as well as bad.
17. Test email support for direct mail campaigns – even a small uplift in direct mail response will cost-justify.
18. Track conversion rates from website – this is probably the only metric that really counts.
19. Personalise the Web landing pages to create a seamless journey.
20. Test something on every email and test everything on some emails – it's the only way to improve, and remember the leverage points.

Source: The IDM Guide to Emarketing, published by The Institute of Direct Marketing

Measurement and tracking

One of the great strengths of the Internet is the ability to track and measure. In this sense it is simply an extension of the basic qualities that allowed direct marketing to stand out so successfully. Of course, the corollary of this is that there is so much data it is sometimes overwhelming. The typical analytics package offers around 200 separate analysis variables. Fine if that is what is needed.

The most important thing is to establish key metrics early on and benchmark against these using reliable sources. This must be done within campaigns, between campaigns both on and offline, against the competition and over time. The aim is to learn and improve effectiveness and efficiency within and across channels.

There are dozens of snake oil sellers out there it is a question of establishing the reputation, reliability and methodology of the companies that are aiming to serve you.

The starting point for web traffic on your website is Google analytics. This is a free service offered by Google that allows you to track traffic into around and out of your site. It is simple pretty powerful and easy to use: www.google.com/analytics.

There is a range of other providers, which are listed in the appendices. They include Comscore, Hitwise, Neilsen Netratings and Alexa.

Analysis packages should be able to offer:

- funnel analysis, where people enter and leave the website identifying pinch points i.e. those pages that tend to lose browsers;
- navigation and process data;
- registration analysis;
- page analysis;
- campaign analysis across all key measures, CTC, Conversion, CPR, CPA;
- search and keyword analysis.

To this can also be added core brand measures, lifetime value and finally return on investment more about this later in the book under measurement.

Email too is a rich medium for data and again a decent email marketing company such as Emailvision, should be able to advice on key metrics and provide a package that delivers what is required.

Typical email measurement and analysis:

- Delivery statistics
  - Messages Send
  - Hard Bounces
  - Soft Bounces
  - Messages Delivered
- Key Performance Metrics
  - Open Rate
  - Click-through Rate
  - Multiple Click-through
  - First-time Click-through
  - Date and Time of each activity
- Post-email activity
  - Actions Completed post-email
  - Conversions
  - Average Order Value
  - Total Value of activity
  - Feedback
  - 'Reply To' Activity
  - Unsubscribes
  - Profile Updates

It is often the overall picture that is harder to extract. Perhaps the final word on measurement is simply use your research, data, judgement and experience to determine the key performance indicators and rigorously track these. Remember the brand and link all activity back to overall business and marketing objectives. Look at the contribution to the bigger picture: Are your customers happy? Do they come back? Are they referring above industry standard level?

Remember that off-the-peg analysis is available to all your competitors. Think about what is unique and special about your business. Don't forget the core principles of strategy, customer insight and testing.

Finally, Forrester suggests the following approach to online measurement. One thing that could be added is return on investment. Don't forget why we are in business.

Table 2.21: Online measurement and analysis

Involvement	Interaction	Intimacy	Influence
What to Track			
• Site visits	• Contributed comments to blogs	• Sentiment tracking on third-party sites (blogs, reviews, forums, etc.)	• Net Promoter (NP) score
• Time spent	• Quantity/ frequency of written reviews, blog comments, forum discussions, and UGC	• Sentiment tracking of internal customer contributions	• Product/service satisfaction ratings
• Pages viewed			• Brand affinity
• Search keywords			• Content forwarded to friends
• Navigation paths		• Opinions expressed in customer calls	• Posts on high-profile blogs
• Site logins			
How to Track			
• Web analytics	• E-commerce platforms	• Brand monitoring	• Brand monitoring
	• Social media platforms	• Customer service calls	• Customer service calls
		• Surveys	• Surveys

Source: www.Forrester.com

SUMMARY

In this chapter we looked at the history of the Internet and its commercial applications. We looked at the core changes that have come about as a result of the rapid take up of Web technologies in all areas of business and society. We explored a framework for establishing digital strategy, outlining the fact that it must never be considered in isolation. We looked in detail and the online audience and considered how this is evolving rapidly over time. We looked at a range of tools to help us identify customers and their behaviour, linking this into the next section of the book on data and research.

We looked in detail at a range of Web marketing applications including social media, mobile marketing and email. Some of these areas will be dealt with in more detail later in the book.

Finally we looked at the role of measurement and review and looked at key areas for measuring and tracking Internet performance.

REVIEW QUESTIONS

1. List five ways that the Internet has changed marketing.
2. What is Metcalfe's law?
3. What is the starting point for the development of digital strategy?
4. Give three examples of social media.
5. What is Web 2.0?
6. What was the value of Internet advertising in 2009?
7. What is a QR code?
8. List three ways mobile devices can be used for marketing.
9. List five key website metrics.
10. List three companies that provide online analytics and measurement services.

CHAPTER 3
COLLECTING CUSTOMER INFORMATION

IN THIS CHAPTER

We discuss the types of information you should gather about your customers and prospects; the sources and methods of obtaining such data.

After completing this chapter you will be able to:

- Identify the role of information in developing effective direct and digital marketing strategies
- Understand the role of the marketing research and how it links to the database
- Understand and apply qualitative and quantitative market research methods
- Identify sources of further information

Specific topics include:

- What information do we already have?
- How and where can we get the missing information?

INTRODUCTION

Here we look at the importance of collecting and applying information. As we discussed in Chapter One, direct marketing relies for its success on the collection and application of information. Without detailed information we are not able to focus on the right customer groups or segments, and without this focus we cannot take advantage of the power of direct communications. The great advantage of direct and digital marketing is that it generates better information about our customers and prospects and this should help develop more effective and efficient marketing strategies.

This chapter will discuss:

- the types of information you should gather about your customers and prospects;
- the sources and methods of obtaining such data.

You may be wondering how, with costs already so high and margins under threat, you can afford to develop a more sophisticated marketing system. Can you afford to increase the frequency of customer communications?

The first point is that you cannot afford not to, because if you do not do all you can to lock in your customers a competitor may lure them away.

The second is that you do not need to communicate with all customers in the same way or with the same frequency.

The third is that by focusing on specific segments, with highly relevant offers, you will increase your return on investment, despite perhaps spending more on the overall programme.

EXAMPLE

A UK bank used to send around 70 promotional mailings a year to its customers. Return on investment (ROI) was adequate but not exciting. One year they decided to send more than 350 mailings, each to a carefully selected segment of the customer base. This programme increased the cost per customer contact but generated more than 200 per cent increase in ROI.

Segmentation is the key

One of the main benefits of gathering customer information is that it enables you to segment customers into groups of a similar kind. Your database analyses will help you select those segments that are more likely to buy or buy additional products. It will also highlight those less likely to buy, and enable you to quantify the potential from each segment.

You can then focus your main additional marketing efforts on those who will provide the greatest return on the investment.

What information do you need?

Let's consider what customer information might be useful to you. After that we can talk about how you can get hold of it. Chapter 7 will look at some ways you may be able to use the data you have gathered.

There are generic categories of customer information that apply across sectors. The examples of data field that may be kept are not exhaustive but might help you understand the sort of data marketers are using. Of course all this is subject to data protection legislation and relevant codes of conduct. These will be discussed in more detail later in the book.

- Identification data
  - Name and contact data, including address, email, mobile phone, account number, region, territory, salesperson.
- Demographic data
  - Customers: age, marital status, gender, family/status. Business customers: company type, size, employees, turnover, size of business, head office, budget, financial year end.
- Financial data
  - Credit history, income, products bought, order size, service history, response, method of acquisition etc.
- Lifestyle data
  - Attitudes, media usage, brands bought, interests, hobbies etc.

- Behavioural data
  - Purchase patterns, referral rate, loyalty status, date of last purchase, frequency and value of purchases.
- Other
  - Length of time at current address, customer service history, complaints, VIP, MPS/TPS (see Glossary), Do Not Promote, shareholder, etc.

TYPES OF DATA/INFORMATION

1. Consumer data

Name and address The obvious starting place. It is vital to have accurate and complete details.

Transactional information What products they have bought from you; what they enquired about; what you offered them in the past.

How long have they been a customer? The longer you have had them the more chance you have of retaining their business.

Property type For example, geodemographic systems ACORN, Mosaic, etc. There are a number of these systems and you'll find further details in the next chapter. Property type can be a very useful indicator for lots of products. Its main limitation is that it deals with properties rather than people and it relies on the premise that people who live in the same type of house will have the same needs, wants and buying characteristics as their neighbours.

While this may be broadly true you only have to compare yourself with your next door neighbour to see that it is a huge generalisation.

Property type indicators would be quite accurate in identifying high and low value areas – they are less good at identifying the characteristics of individual occupants.

There are other property descriptors that may also be helpful: do they have a garage, is the property detached, semi-detached or terraced? Is there a garden, and so on.

Household composition Number of adults, number of children, their relationships to each other. It is often important to know the ages of the various occupants.

2. Lifestyle data

Although geodemographic systems such as ACORN and Mosaic can be very useful in broad targeting and evaluation of customer types, they have in the past been limited by the fact that they do not deal with individuals. The geodemographic systems are increasingly competing on the lifestyle arena and the boundaries are blurring between the different systems.

Generally psychographic or 'lifestyle' data on the other hand focuses on individuals but its limitation is that not all UK households are represented on the various lifestyle databases.

Collectively, the various lifestyle companies now have detailed volunteered questionnaire information on around 41 million UK adults. There are many duplicates across the various lifestyle databases but Axciom, the largest UK practitioner now claims to have detailed information on more than 80 per cent of UK households.

This information covers details of products preferred across a wide range of consumer areas from holidays to toothpaste, cars to insurance. These databases also contain information on age, income, occupation, brand and media consumption and interests and attitudes. The data is refreshed at a rate of 2.5 million records per year. The products are increasingly branded and the PersonicX profiling system combines data held within the following product areas:

- Behaviour Bank
- InfoBase Lifestyle Universe
- The Lifestyle Selector
- Consofile
- Email Selector
- Interactive Individuals

The lifestyle companies have worked in partnership with other organisations to produce some very sophisticated profiling techniques (profiling is explained in Chapter 4).

Further information can be found at www.axciom.co.uk.

3. Business-to-business information

The above classifications relate to consumers of course, but similar information is available for business-to-business marketing using classifications such as:

Business type (perhaps by industry code, known as standard industrial classification). It is often productive to segment businesses into industry types.

Company size Employees and/or turnover etc. This could clearly be a highly relevant factor for certain products and services. A car fleet supplier would obviously want to segment a prospect file based on the number of employees, or ideally on the number of employees with company cars.

Age In this case the age of the business. How relevant do you think age is? One major marketer, in a search for new business prospects, studied its most recent new customers analysing the significance of 30 different business factors. These included turnover, assets, number of employees, industry type and so on. **The most significant factor in identifying propensity to purchase was 'number of years since founded'.** The company was able to identify a clear **relationship** indicating that when a business reached a certain age it was much more likely to be interested in their products.

A business database can be enriched with a wide variety of additional information such as sales per employee, growth rate etc.

How to get hold of the information

So how can we collect the necessary information? There are three main sources:

1. **Internal** By talking to and asking your existing customers and prospects via the sales force, via the contact centre, in retail outlets or by email, telephone or post. Any interaction is an opportunity to capture information. The problem we have is whether this information can be maintained, and kept up to date. Under the 1998 Data Protection Act we have a legal duty to keep data accurate and up to date. If you have a customer database your information gathering will start here.

2. **External** From sources such as the Edited Electoral Roll, lifestyle databases, credit reference houses and business information brokers such as Dun and Bradstreet and Experian, rented databases (lists), response to advertisements and other marketing communications etc. Data is also available from a huge range of industry studies and omnibus surveys.

3. **Through original marketing research** Using a range of techniques that we will discuss later in this chapter.

Collecting information from existing customers

1. **Train your people to gather information at every opportunity**

   Every employee must understand the power of good up-to-date information, and each must be encouraged (preferably), coerced, or if necessary forced to gather data at every opportunity.

   When a customer telephones the organisation, almost regardless of the reason for the call, you should try to complete the missing fields in your database. Most customers, when approached politely, are prepared to give basic information about their circumstances, their properties, the number of cars they own and similar details. Equally, every opportunity for customers to update their data should be taken. This might be if they are completing an online registration form, ordering a product or recommending a friend.

   This is so important that many successful companies incentivise their employees to ensure that this happens.

2. **Specific questionnaires**

   Have you ever asked your customers, formally, what they think about your service? How many do you think would respond to a questionnaire? 5 per cent, 10 per cent, 25 per cent or more?

   Would you be surprised to know that many companies receive more than 50 per cent response to a customer questionnaire? Of course to achieve such high levels of response your survey must be 'customer-focused'; asking questions which are seen to be relevant and giving good reasons why you would like to have the information.

   Many companies use additional 'incentives' to encourage people to respond and there is no doubt that these can work, though you may not wish to pay for hundreds of free gifts, nor to provide a prize for a free draw. Equally there are a range of legal issues about the use of prize draws in marketing research and remember data must be used for the purposes specified at the time of capturing that data.

The good news is that you do not necessarily need to do these things to generate a good response.

In face-to-face and telephone research the interviewer relies on their training, skill and charm to persuade the respondent to participate. The intended respondent does not know what questions are in store and a mini-relationship is developed during the interview. In this way a skilled questioner using a well-designed questionnaire can elicit a remarkable amount of sensitive information, even information about personal hygiene and sexual matters.

The marketing research industry has professionalised significantly and interviewers can be accredited under the interviewer quality control scheme (IQCS), run by the Market Research Society

(MRS) www.iqcs.org and www.mrs.org.uk. The IQCS guarantees minimum levels of training and supervision of interviewers and aims to help raise professional standards in the industry.

It is not possible to develop the relationship so cautiously when the interviewee is completing the questionnaire themselves however.

With self-completion questionnaires either in print or online, recipients tend to read the whole thing before deciding whether to fill it in. So how can you persuade more people to fill in your questionnaire?

Make it interesting

One of the most effective techniques is to find a way of making the questionnaire more interesting and relevant to the recipient. If you can identify some specific interest of an individual you may be able to use this.

For example:

Supposing you were an oil company planning to send a questionnaire to a file of company car drivers to discover their opinions of the standards of service at your petrol stations. You could build in a question or two that would be of specific interest to them such as:

> From time to time the oil industry has an opportunity to give motor manufacturers its views on the additional safety and security features which have been developed for cars recently. To make sure we take account of your own views would you mind giving us a few moments to complete the following section:

Please tick the box that most closely reflects your view.

All new cars should now be fitted with:

	Agree Strongly	Agree	Neither agree nor disagree	Disagree	Disagree strongly
Air bags for all passengers	☐	☐	☐	☐	☐
Anti-collision systems (ACS) and so on.	☐	☐	☐	☐	☐

Such questions may have little bearing on the main information you are seeking, but they can increase response to a survey by 20 to 25 per cent.

This may sound surprising but it is simply the application of one of the basic rules of communication – make it interesting and relevant and more people will read and react to it.

At each stage of the process, the researcher should stop and ask 'Is the question really necessary?'

Each question should be carefully evaluated on its own, in relation to other questions on the questionnaire and the overall objectives of the study.

If the question does not contribute to the overall purpose of the research, it should not be included in the questionnaire.

Here are a few more hints about questionnaire design:

Make it easy Do not ask people to spend a long time writing out answers. You should give as many pre-populated options as you can, asking respondents to simply tick the box that is closest to their view, like the example above.

It is also a good idea to add open questions for that small percentage who feel so strongly about something that they wish to write some additional comments. Such comments can be quantified for analysis through editing and but can be noted and reported for further action where necessary. With appropriate permissions this is also an excellent source of testimonials.

Make it relevant Use special interest questions like the example above.

Promise a benefit A copy of the outline findings, perhaps (this is only really relevant to businesses). Often you can promise a general benefit such as 'Your answers will enable us to provide you with a better service, more closely aligned with your needs.'

Don't make it too glossy It should look like a research document not a promotional leaflet.

Give clear instructions where necessary Don't leave anything to chance. Give worked examples for more complex questions.

Break it up Use prominent section headings where necessary.

Don't cram it in Large type and plenty of space will make it look easier to fill in and you will receive more responses.

Leave room for discretion If you are asking for things including age, some people will not want to tell you. Rather than deterring them from returning the questionnaire, reassure them that you would still like to hear from them, even if there are certain questions they cannot or do not wish to answer. Unless this data is required to screen out respondents at the beginning of a questionnaire it is better to ask the sensitive questions towards the end.

Test You should run a small pilot of maybe 15 to check that the questionnaire works, that it is clearly understood and if it is delivered online the technology functions correctly

Check for meaning Ensure meaning is understood. For example, whether dinner is a meal consumed in the evening or midday. In international markets you might find clarification of meaning is more important. Translation of questionnaires can cause major problems. The secret is to translate and then back translate into the original language. A question that was asked to young people 'What was the prime motivator behind your impulse purchase of confectionery countlines?' is clearly inappropriate for the audience. Using appropriate language is important and the questionnaire must be written in a way that can be understood, using appropriate terms.

Use clear and simple language Use words of one or two syllables. Use simple English:
    Instead of 'observe', use 'look'
    Instead of 'construct', use 'build'
    Instead of 'regarding', use 'about'
    Instead of 'at this moment in time', use 'now'.

Remember, very often the questionnaire will be read out loud. It is good practice to speak the question.

Avoid ambiguity 'Do you buy a newspaper regularly?'
    What does regularly mean? Every day? Once a month? Once a year?

Avoid two questions in one 'What do you think of our prices and product quality?'
    This is impossible to be answered accurately.

Avoid leading or loaded questions 'Should the council spend money regenerating the poor environment in Brookmill ward?' It is hard for anyone to disagree with this question. 'Most people think that our membership of the European Union is a good thing. Do you?' is a leading question. The aim has to be to reduce the potential to lead respondents.

Avoid assumptions 'When driving, do you listen to your MP3 player?'
    This makes a number of assumptions about the respondent: That he drives, that his car has an MP3 player, even that he is not hearing impaired.

Avoid generalisation 'How much do you usually spend on beer in a week?'
    There are much better observational or panel methodologies to ensure accuracy here. If the respondent is spending more than a few pounds, the chances are that he will not remember in any case.

Avoid negative questions 'You don't think that drink driving should be more strictly regulated, do you?' is confusing and leads to problems.

Avoid hypothetical questions 'If West Ham were relegated, would you still buy a season ticket?'
    Speculation and guesswork is an outcome of this type of question.

THE ROLE OF THE DATABASE

The database is an invaluable source of information on your customers. Try profiling your own customers. Direct marketing succeeds because it helps to eliminate wastage by focusing on the individuals or segments with the most potential. Profiling and data analysis is one of the ways in which this wastage can be identified. We will look at this in more detail later on but database marketing can deliver the benefits outlined below.

What can we do with the database?

- Target marketing

  Marketing a particular product to a specific customer or group.

- Cross-selling

  Marketing new or additional products at a particular time of contact.

- Sales analysis and forecasting

  Monitor and predict sales.

- Market basket analysis

  Understanding how products 'pull' or trigger others.

- Promotions analysis

  Evaluating the effects of marketing campaigns on response and sales.

- Customer retention and churn analysis

  Understanding customers who have left for competitors.

- Profitability analysis

  Understanding which customers are most profitable and when.

- Customer value measurement

  Designing and analysing the results of marketing research.

- Product packaging

  Understanding physical and logical packaging (bundling).

- Contact centres

  Directing calls and preparing contact centre representatives for calls.

- Sales contract analysis

  Understanding the sales funnel and contract renewal processes.

Gathering information through external research

Traditionally direct marketers have ignored marketing research, believing that the database and testing programmes provided all the information necessary. This view has changed over the past 10 or 15 years but there are still many diehards who cling to the view that research is money wasted. Remember the database only tells us about the customers whose data we capture, it does not cover the market as a whole, data tells us *what* they buy not *why* they buy, testing tells which creative option pulls the best response, it does not tell us which options to test.

Here are just some of the ways a direct and digital marketer could use research:

- **To learn about customers** – needs, wants, buying patterns off and online, who else they buy from, and why.

- **To group customer by typology** – e.g. organised/disorganised; sophisticated tastes/simple tastes; older and affluent/younger aspiring and so on.
- **To measure attitudes towards our company and our products** – research can help us measure those things beyond raw response data, e.g. did our mailing make people think differently about us? Did our email campaign improve our brand reputation?
- **To find out what positioning we have achieved in the marketplace** – we may well aspire to be thought of as the 'Rolls-Royce of customer service' but if our customers and prospects think of us as an Austin Allegro we need to know. Only research will tell us this.
- **To identify prospects** – people or companies having the same needs or inclinations as our best customers.
- **To understand better the buying processes and decision-making** – especially in business-to-business marketing or high involvement purchases where the decision-making process is complex and involves multiple channels.
- **In planning** – campaigns, business development, new products, pricing, and so on.
- **To identify trends in the marketplace** – good planners need to stay ahead or at least abreast of what is happening out there.
- **To monitor competitors and their marketing activities**
- **To refine communications** – ensuring that people understand and relate to what we say.
- **To measure the effectiveness of non-response activities** – it is easy to count responses and even to measure the quality of those responses. But some communications are designed to change attitudes rather than attract replies. The only way of measuring their effectiveness is research.

Types of marketing research

There are broadly two kinds of marketing research: **desk research** and **primary or original research**.

Desk research or **secondary research** is that which is already available, you simply have to locate it and read it. Some is available free of charge, other studies can be subscribed to. Most of this is available online and is easily accessible. Indeed the major problem is rationalising the vast amount of data that are available and ensuring that they are pertinent, accurate, reliable and up to date.

Industry statistics

These are not always of much practical use to an individual business but they can help to explain trends. Among the reports produced are:

- **Trade associations** – often produce periodic high-level market analyses. These are often based on reports from members and can be very useful in tracking market trends and establishing value and volume sales. Brewers of Europe, for example, produces great data on its members' activity and issues affecting the industry in the European Union (EU) and beyond. Trade associations exist for almost every industrial sector. A directory of trade associations is published by CBD Research Ltd and this identifies trade associations with contact details and details of activities. These can be found at www.cbdresearch.com.

- **Stockbroker and financial analysts' reports** can also be very useful.
- **Independent companies** produce annual analyses of government-produced returns for various industry sectors. You will see these quoted in the Trade Press relating to your own industry, and you will often be able to buy all or part of one of these reports.
- **Government data** These include Companies House data, which provides companies' annual reports and accounts. These often contain commentary/statistics on the broader industry involved. Take a look at the government statistical service at www.statistics.gov.
- In addition various government bodies produce wonderfully complete data on a variety of sectors. For example, Ofcom on the telecommunications sector.

Syndicated research services

Many companies exist to provide services to industry in the area of secondary research.

Companies including Mintel, Euromonitor, and Frost and Sullivan provide what are known as syndicated or multi-client studies on a huge range of markets. These are published market research studies that are available to anybody who wishes to buy them.

Prices range from a few hundred to many thousands of pounds depending on the complexity of the report and number of markets covered.

Typically, reports will cover:

- market size, structure and trends;
- import, export and production data;
- key players' competitive profiles including financial data;
- market share data;
- advertising and marketing communications spend.

Details can be found at the following websites:

- www.mintel.com
- www.euromonitor.com
- www.frost.com

Online aggregators

The development of the Internet and its diverse capabilities has lead to the emergence of a new breed of information providers who aggregate or bring together information from diverse sources and allow access on a subscription basis or for a one-off payment. Examples include general services such as Hoovers, Profound and Lexis Nexis, and specialist services including the World Advertising Research Centre (WARC) or MAD which covers the UK marketing press. These may contain translations from a range of international publications.

Details can be found at the following websites:

- www.mad.co.uk
- www.profound.com
- www.hoovers.com
- www.lexisnexis.com
- www.warc.com

Information on online markets

There is a great deal of information on the Internet on online markets. Not all of it is reliable. The government, as indicated above, is often the most reliable source and there are more reputable suppliers in the market. The best sources for online research are often based in the US, but there are a range of other useful suppliers.

Look at some or all of the following websites. They have been shown to be useful sources of research or data on the online sector.

- www.clickz.com/stats
- www.alexa.com
- www.comscore.com
- www.intersperience.com
- www.forrester.com
- www.oracle.com
- www.ncr.com
- www.gartner.com
- www.broadvision.com
- www.accenture.com
- www.pwc.com
- www.bcg.com
- www.idc.com
- www.bitpipe.com
- www.ovum.com
- www.hitwise.com

Public domain data

In addition to individual company and industry sector reports there is much general information available from the government and most of this is free or reasonably priced. The office of National Statistics (www.statistics.gov.uk) publishes a catalogue of all its publications these include:

- Family Expenditure Survey
- General Household Survey
- The National Food Survey

Eurostat, the statistical service of the European Union, also publishes a vast array of data for member countries.

Much of this is now accessible online.

Other government reports provide information regarding populations and household compositions by area and major conurbation.

Register of electors

At present the edited electoral roll is still available for marketing purposes but this is likely to change. The edited register leaves out the names and addresses of people who have asked for their names to be excluded on the edited version. It may be bought by any organisation or individual who asks for a copy and they may use it for any purpose.

Approximately 26 million people are recorded on the 2010 Electoral Roll.

There are a significant number of companies who make this data available in a variety of formats for quite a modest cost. A search online will reveal most of them

Companies House Records

When looking for information about businesses Companies House is a good source. Their records contain simple raw data that is not always very user-friendly. However, it is easily accessible and cheap. The Companies House website also has a range of links to international disclosure of company data. Companies House is found online at www.companieshouse.gov.uk.

Other organisations provide information on companies. Services such as Dun and Bradstreet and Kompass are excellent commercial sources of company information.

Rented lists

There are approximately 6,000 consumer and business lists available to rent in the UK. All can be selected in many ways so it is possible to select highly qualified names and addresses.

Original (or primary) research you can do yourself

Original research has two broad classifications: quantitative and qualitative.

- **Quantitative research** asks and hopes to answer questions involving how much, how many etc.
- **Qualitative research** asks the question 'why' in exploring the deeper reasons behind behaviour, for example, the customer's purchase of a particular brand. This research is unstructured, largely exploratory and based on smaller examples than quantitative research. Ultimately it leads to depth of understanding and insight.

With the database we should have a lot of data on what customers do. What they buy and when and what promotional messages they respond to. What the database will not tell us is why they behave in this way. The use of qualitative research in direct marketing can add a great deal to understanding of customers.

The weakness of the database of course is that we know this information about our existing customers only. The use of marketing research can help put the database in context.

Not all businesses can afford to commission large industry-wide surveys, but the customer and prospect questionnaires discussed earlier are examples of original research you can do yourself.

You can also use your own resources to:

Build your own lists Again, not all businesses want huge lists, and if your requirements are quite specific, you may want to consider building or locating your own lists. There are various possibilities:

Direct response advertising You can often generate quite large numbers of enquiries in this way. Chapters 13 to 16 include many ways of ensuring good response from advertising.

Loose inserts Despite what critics say, inserts will generally produce more replies than display advertisements. Look at how many major direct response advertisers use them because they measure results very carefully and only repeat what works well for them. A word of warning: although they produce higher responses some advertisers find that the quality of respondents is a little lower. So, although you may produce lots more replies, the proportion who convert to purchase may be lower, but you will often end up with more customers so this is not necessarily a serious problem.

Localised insert campaigns Even small advertisers can use inserts. Many local newspapers and freesheets accept inserts and, they are usually very cost-effective. Some national newspapers now offer the facility to insert leaflets down to the level of a local wholesaler, making national newspaper insert campaigns available to local advertisers.

Door-to-door distribution of leaflets A realistic way of gathering prospect details. You cannot select specific households but you can choose streets or areas containing the sort of properties you would like to reach.

Telephone directories More useful for business addresses than personal ones. Note: some publishers now print copyright warnings in their directories, stating that the names and addresses may not be used for marketing purposes. They may well own the copyright and have a legal right to prevent such usage but why would people would buy a directory if it were not with the intention of contacting the people and businesses listed?

You should err on the side of caution. **Take the advice of your solicitor before copying any directory listings into your computer.**

Members of clubs/associations You could try to organise a PI deal with them (PI deal is an American term standing for 'per inquiry'). You arrange to pay them a small amount, say £1 for every reply you get from your mailing. Some national publishers and TV stations accept these deals so there is no reason why clubs and associations would not. Naturally they would expect to have sight of your mailing material and a right to refuse permission if it does not meet with their approval.

Previous customers Unless you had a disagreement with them, they may have left you because they were offered a better deal. If their new supplier is not able to match the introductory deal, or their service is not as good as yours, these people may be prepared to come back to you.

Existing customers Many businesses have great success with what are called MGM (member get member) offers. There are various other names for these schemes such as referral offers, friend get a friend, recommend a friend. The basic principle is that people's friends have similar lifestyles and therefore similar needs for products and services.

This certainly holds true in the e-commerce/mail order industry. I used to find this a very good source of new prospects. Furthermore, the new names tended to convert better and pay better than the average new prospect. Some business-to-business marketers also find this technique works well.

Using the Internet for information gathering

Many of the techniques described above can be managed or at least started online through the use of the Internet.

Most secondary sources of data from government statistics to the services of Axciom and Dun and Bradstreet are available online and can be accessed remotely. Certainly almost all list brokers can be contacted via their websites and most allow the online construction of list selections.

Market research is increasingly carried on via the Web and email-based surveys with a link to a survey website are effective in generating response. Packages such as SNAP www.snapsurveys.com can help design, implement analyse and produce reports in a variety of formats including online.

Online businesses have a real advantage in collecting customer information as the use of cookies (a device which allows a site provider to recognise the browser's machine) allows them to track buyer progress through a website. We cover a range of online applications later. However, the trackability of Web-based campaigns is a major advantage. We can identify the route a prospect takes through our site, where they have come from and when and where they leave for. Packages such as Google Analytics are free to users and provide very powerful Web metrics.

They can also use online surveys to measure many things, including customer satisfaction with the site. These range from sophisticated bespoke surveys, to simple opinion gathering, Dell for example has a pop up rating scale, allowing customers to rate the page.

Qualitative research can also be carried out online and in-depth interviews and focus groups can be conducted using a variety of Web-based technologies. The use of accompanied surfs can reveal a great deal about the navigability of a website and these may involve the use of eye tracking cameras to help with Web design and site construction.

Bunnyfoot has some interesting examples of how this technology can work www.bunnyfoot.com.

The use of email surveys to gain information is important but it is useful to get professional help with, for example, questionnaire design and not to overuse the medium as response rates are falling as consumers become more concerned with the effect and cost of dealing with spam (unsolicited e-mail communication).

Social networking sites, newsgroups, blogs and discussion forums

Newsgroups exist for almost every topic under the sun, including marketing research. Newsgroups can be useful sources of information and also for establishing opinions on products and services. Some companies monitor newsgroups for research purposes and some seed newsgroups with product information and recommendations. This is a dubious practice if it is not done transparently and if uncovered can lead to the user being barred from the service.

Most search engines allow groups to be searched for. Try www.groups.google.com.

Blogs can be very useful sources of information and there are significant resources available on research and marketing. Search via blogsearch.google.com to find relevant content. The site www.technorati.com will allow you to monitor blogs and www.boardtracker.com does the same for discussion boards.

Social networking sites are useful to get a deeper understanding of how your target market is talking about your products and services. Facebook and other social media sites are already using volunteered profile data to target members with advertising messages.

Data fusion

Latest trends in the management of research and data have involved data fusion techniques. For example, data from our own customer database may be enhanced with attributed, anonymous data from research based on known characteristics for example postcode or media viewing behaviour. This can then be linked to geo-demographic data such as ACORN and Mosaic via the postcode and once the geodemographic code is known this can link to lifestyle and behavioural data via Axciom's Personicx system and BMRB's TGI data.

The result is a statistically valid model of consumer behaviour and this can have value in determining marketing approaches. It is always vital to get expert advice on this as the sample size for analysis can become very small.

The Internet is not a panacea for information gathering but it does allow access to a vast range of published data and to certain groups of customers particularly in business-to-business markets. A key point in consumer markets is that the penetration of Internet in home is still only around 70 per cent of households and this is skewed towards the middle class affluent market.

It may be increasingly appropriate to use if this is your target market, but it is not suitable for all products and services.

Finally, some words of warning about gathering information via research.

Data protection

The Data Protection Act 1998 is rigorous in the way that data is held and used. It puts into law the idea of informed consent and transparency.

It means that there are restrictions in the way that research data can be held and used.

If you are in any doubt consult the Information Commissioners Office or get legal advice. The Information Commissioners' office is at www.ico.gov.uk.

The MRS code of conduct specifically states that data captured via research must be anonymous and used only for the purposes specified at point of capture. You must be careful when capturing personal data and if in doubt seek advice from the industry associations or professional research or database companies.

Statistical reliability

If you are using research simply to add information to your database most of the above techniques can be safely used.

However, if you want to use it to give you a clear picture of the state of a marketplace with a view to making accurate forecasts of likely take-up for a new product or offer for example, you must enlist specialist help and be fully aware of the need to assess sample sizes and statistical validity.

Your own in-house research or planning department might be able to help. If not, a useful starting point is the Market Research Society, which publishes a list of member organisations free of charge. All MRS members must abide by a rigorous code of conduct.

If you are looking at international markets then ESOMAR www.esomar.org does the same thing.

Marketing research is a minefield for the uninitiated, and even sometimes for those who should know better. Beware of industry publications telling you things like:

- **'Average response to direct mailings in the UK in 1988 was 6 per cent'** Well, yes, based on the samples polled in the study but these can be highly misleading. One such 'finding' that caused me no end of trouble with my own clients was that average response to consumer mailings was 8 per cent. Not having such a high average with my own mailings, I investigated this study and discovered that the 'average' was made up of:
  - two insurance company mailings producing around 1 per cent
  - one publisher's mailing that achieved 5 per cent
  - two financial services mailings generating 3.5 per cent
  - one mailing for a major soft drinks brand offering free drinks vouchers to teenagers that generated 52 per cent response.
- **The company had simply accumulated all these results and reached the impressive average of 8 per cent** So, beware of such statistics unless the report gives details of how the figure was arrived at. The Direct Mail Information Service (DMIS) publishes figures annually and, to emphasise the above point, they not only publish details of the number of mailings incorporated into the study, they show averages both in total and separately with the especially large responses removed. This gives a much clearer picture, though you should still be very wary of assuming that your own mailings would generate similar responses.

The lesson when conducting or even interpreting research is to seek professional advice at an early stage. Alternatively buy a good specialist book – you'll find a couple of recommendations in the Appendix.

SUMMARY

In this chapter we looked at the role of information in the creation of direct marketing strategies and how it should be gathered, analysed and acted upon.

We saw that, in order to construct workable segments, we need to gather information in several key areas.

We need to have access to two broad types of data:

- Consumer data – who are our customers and where do they live?
- Lifestyle data – how do they live?

In business-to-business marketing similar data is required. We need to know where they are and other characteristics such as the size and type of company in order to be able to market effectively to them.

We saw that some data is available in-house and other information can be obtained externally either through a range of secondary sources or through the use of marketing research.

We saw that information is a key asset to the business and that staff should recognise its value and seek to gather and to record information at every opportunity

The day-to-day operation of the business gives a great many opportunities to gather data but we also looked at the use of questionnaires and explored the characteristics of good questionnaire design. These included:

- simplicity
- relevancy
- reward for completion
- clear instructions
- easy to read and complete
- brevity

We also saw the need to manage questions of a sensitive nature.

We went on to explore the multiple uses to which this data is put. These included the following points. We can:

- Learn about customer needs and buying behaviour
- Create market segments
- Measure attitudes to our products and services
- Establish our brand position
- Identify future customers
- Start to understand the buying decision process
- Identify trends in the marketplace
- Monitor competitor activity
- Refine our communications
- Measure the effectiveness of other non-response activity
- Produce the direct marketing strategic plan

We then explored the different type of marketing research looking at secondary or desk research and primary research or original research.

We looked at the different sources of secondary information including government data and commercially available lists.

We saw that original research can be described as qualitative or quantitative and saw the benefits of the two approaches.

We went on to look at the applications of original research particularly in list building.

We explored briefly the role of the Internet in information gathering at all stages.

Finally we saw the necessity of complying with the 1998 Data Protection Act and of using professional researchers for certain research tasks.

REVIEW QUESTIONS

1. What is the value of customer data?
2. What is the benefit of segmentation?
3. What are the two broad types of data we need in consumer markets?

4. What information do we need to acquire in business-to-business markets?
5. Where is information available?
6. What are the two broad types of marketing research?
7. What are the two broad types of original research?
8. List five characteristics of a good questionnaire.
9. List five uses of market research.
10. What are the five types of secondary data available to direct marketers?
11. How can we build our own mailing lists?
12. What are cookies?
13. What organisation manages the market research profession in the UK?

EXERCISES

Select a company of your choice. Use the Internet find out as much as you can about this company and its markets. What are the strengths and weaknesses of the Internet as a research tool?

Go to the Dun and Bradstreet website at www.dnb.com. What are the benefits of the online service the company provides?

CHAPTER 4

USING YOUR INFORMATION

IN THIS CHAPTER

In this chapter we shall look at some of the ways the information you have gathered can be used to increase your business.

Specific topics include:

- Two main reasons for using customer information
- Segmentation: what it is and how it works
- Segmentation enables selectivity
- Bases for customer segmentation: internal data and external data
- Demographic and psychographic information
- Profiling and how it works
- How to select appropriate segments
- Example of targeting through profiling
- The Ladder of Loyalty

INTRODUCTION

There are two main reasons for gathering data:

1. To enable customer and prospect segmentation;
2. To permit companies to more closely tailor products, offers and messages to the recipients.

What is segmentation?

Segmentation is the subdivision of large customer and prospect files into smaller groups (segments). For example:

An office products company may segment into:

- companies with and without an IT department;
- size bands
    1. having up to 50 employees
    2. having 51–100 employees and so on;
- independent v. part of a larger group (possible variations in purchasing procedures);
- industry sectors – perhaps by SIC code;
- transactional history – types of product bought
    1. timing
    2. frequency
    3. enquirers only

4. no history (e.g. added to list by sales force);
■ source of first enquiry, and so on.

Such segmentation would enable the company to decide who to contact and what level of information to send about a new product (e.g. technical or non-technical material).

A business with no affiliates will present a different opportunity to one which is part of a large multinational group with a head office elsewhere in the UK or abroad, and perhaps a centralised purchasing or accounting function in a remote location.

Let's look at some consumer segmentation possibilities

Customers and prospects might break down into segments such as:

1. **Location** – distance or drive time to a retail site
2. **Owner/occupiers of large detached houses** – no children
3. **Ditto** – with children, further segmented by ages
4. **People who rent similar properties**
5. **People with smaller homes** – similar breakdowns
6. **Garden/no garden**
7. **House or flat**
8. **Households with two or more cars**
9. **Ownership of various luxury goods**
10. **Purchasing patterns** – by products/value/frequency and so on
11. **Type of occupation**
12. **Professionals such as doctors, dentists etc.**
13. **Self-employed people**
14. **Gender, age and so on.**

Even this quite short list shows the number of possibilities. Once you have your marketplace segmented like this you can see how your marketing might vary. You would quite possibly want to offer different products to prospects in the various segments.

Segmentation enables selectivity

Even though direct communication may not be competitive with mass media in terms of cost per thousand, its greater selectivity makes it the most cost-efficient choice in many cases.

You cannot achieve this selectivity without detailed information. The ideal starting position is to know who will be interested and when they are likely to be in a buying situation. Targeting is thus not only about people but also about their situations.

If you were able to subdivide the people in each of your segments according to their own personal timing preferences you would be even better equipped to send powerful, relevant communications that generated maximum response.

How can you decide whom to select from a list or audience? There are several ways:

1. **Database analysis**

   Obviously, if you have detailed individual information on each prospect this is best of all. Your database will enable you to:

   - identify the overall pool of prospects for this particular product;
   - select those who should be in the market this week/month;
   - take account of additional data about their buying methods, drawn from records of previous transactions or questionnaire responses;
   - devise attractive offers to fit their circumstances – you would not (or should not) send the same offer to a company with the potential to buy a 50-portion pack as you would to a company which uses 5,000 a day;
   - draw up profiles of your best customers and use these to identify good segments of other lists or target audiences. Profiling is explained in more detail below.

2. **Testing**

   Testing involves mailing external lists or running advertisements or inserts and analysing the replies. See Chapter 14 for more information on testing. Respondents can be 'profiled' enabling you to target more of the same. Where time and budget permit this is much more reliable than making assumptions about who will be interested.

EXAMPLE

A company selling fleet management services approached a direct marketing specialist for advice. They had tried direct mail for prospecting but found that it produced almost no response. The specialist asked, 'Who are you sending your mailings to?' and they replied 'The fleet manager, of course.'

The consultant pointed out tactfully that, although it may seem logical, fleet managers are entirely the wrong audience, as they are the ones who will lose their jobs if the company adopts the service. A simple analysis of their advertisement responses produced the answer. The people who are interested in outsourcing fleet management services are financial directors. Once the company started targeting financial directors, direct mail, previously not viable, became their most cost-efficient medium for new business prospecting.

---

3. **Research**

   A questionnaire or telephone asking, 'Who in your company will be interested?' can be highly beneficial.

   NOTE When you use this approach with businesses, make sure you ask someone who really knows. Some have started by simply asking the telephonist or receptionist but this will not always work. Whereas receptionists will know the answer to: 'What is the name of your Marketing Director?' they cannot be expected to answer the question: 'Who in your company is responsible for deciding on the purchase of security software?' As discussed elsewhere, many purchase decisions in a business are made by a committee (called a decision-making unit or DMU). When it comes to identifying the members of a DMU for a major purchase, the best person to ask is usually the managing director's secretary or the senior secretary at that location.

4. **Intuition or judgement**

Unless this is based on some evaluation of real events it remains guesswork. As we saw from the fleet management example above, assumptions can be dangerous.

5. **The use of profiling**

Profiling is the act of identifying a characteristic (in the fleet management example above, the relevant characteristic was job title, i.e. financial director) which appears to be common or more prevalent than the average amongst customers. This factor can then be used to select a sub-group of prospects or customers who are more likely to be interested in a specific product, offer or message.

Profiling factors

Business profiling can relate to company size, annual turnover, geographic location, financial year-end, title or job function of contact, number of locations, size of company car fleet, even the number of meals they serve in their staff restaurant. There are many possibilities depending on the types of products or services you sell.

Similarly, consumer profiling can relate to household composition (children/no children), property type (large/small, garden/no garden, ACORN or Mosaic type), geographical location, etc.

NOTE Not all profiling has to be related to such inanimate matters. Attitudinal factors can be very important too. Households could be typified by their attitudes towards home computing for instance; businesses could be subdivided by their public attitudes towards the environment etc.

If you are able to isolate such factors they can be very helpful in targeting the right segments, reducing wastage and thus your costs.

Sometimes the targeting factor is very simple, as in the following example:

HELPING HANDS

Dave and Maureen Lindsay run Helping Hands, a property management, repair and refurbishment business in Normandy.

Dave produces very low cost mailings that work well because they are targeted at exactly the right people.

The target market is English people who own holiday properties in Normandy. Their customers have a number of problems:

1. They are rarely in France and need someone to keep an eye on their property and garden.
2. They do not speak very good French and so have difficulty in organising basic repairs and maintenance.

3. They are worried about the standards of work if they are not around to supervise.

Dave and Maureen assembled a list using two main sources:
1. **A rented list:** Brittany Ferries runs 'The French Property Owners Club', people who, because they own a property in France, travel more frequently and thus qualify for discounts on car ferries.
2. **Recommendations (MGMs):** Dave gets a high percentage of his work from friends of customers.

Here's another example:

A company running high-quality, high-priced seminars was worried about declining delegate numbers and asked for advice on how to improve response to its campaigns.

The company had 18 seminars scheduled for the following six months and was planning to promote these through six campaigns (each detailing three seminars) to his entire list of 22,000 names. He had not carried out any detailed analysis of this list nor of his attendees.

It was arranged for his list of previous attendees to be profiled by a specialist company and discovered a 'nugget of gold':
- 75 per cent of all previous attendees came from companies with more than 200 employees – such companies represented 14 per cent of his list;
- the next 15 per cent came from companies having 100 to 200 employees, a further 8 per cent of the list.

This was all the information the company needed, and they changed the emphasis of the mailing programme as follows:
- every one of the top 22 per cent of delegates was telephoned and the call was followed by selective contacts covering the seminars in which they were interested. Each mailing was followed up by a further telephone call. This increased the marketing costs to this group by around 400 per cent;
- the balance received a single mailing with the full 18-seminar programme inviting phone enquiries for more information about any seminars in which they were interested. The marketing cost for this group (78 per cent of the list) was reduced by 80 per cent.

The net result was a 20 per cent increase in bookings and a 15 per cent reduction in marketing costs.

All because of the identification of a single key profiling factor – company size.

Now, if you start thinking about your own business, can you identify some factors that will help you select those prospects likely to be better customers for you?

What if you have no customer data?

Even if you have no data on your existing customers you may be able to use outside resources to help you identify characteristics which signify a higher propensity to buy.

Types and sources of external data

If you need help in profiling your customers, and indeed in finding more of the same type, there are various sources of help.

This is an area that is developing almost daily – it is problematic to write about because by definition anything I say can be superseded before this book gets into print.

I have therefore decided to deal with general principles only, and give you the addresses of the main data suppliers – you can then call for their latest brochures and ensure that you are up to date.

There are two broad types of external prospect data:

- **demographic data** – basic information about a property and its occupants;
- **psychographic or lifestyle data** – mainly about attitudes, likes and needs, and purchasing behaviour of individuals for example, from Personicx (Axicom)
- **demographic data examples** – ACORN, Mosaic, Cameo and so on.

Main uses are:

- **refining lists** – for example a list could be compared to the electoral roll to check that a name is still current at that address;
- **selecting the most likely segments from external lists** – this could be done by comparing property types;
- **gaining a better understanding of a marketplace** – knowing the household composition and property type of your best customers gives you a clearer view of your prospects.

We will discuss how demographic systems work a little later in this chapter.

Psychographic examples are:

The National Shoppers Survey, BehaviourBank, Personicx The Lifestyle Selector, Consofile, InfoBase Lifestyle Universe, Email Selector, Interactive Individuals Lifestyle Focus, Canvasse and there are many others. Main uses of these types of data are:

- **Data enhancement** You can send your own list to a lifestyle bureau and they will add information to those records that they can match with records on their own databases. In practice this is not always a very high percentage.
- **Profiling** A more interesting possibility is to have your own best customers profiled by the lifestyle company. They will then offer you additional names and addresses of people on their databases who match your customer profile and you could send these people a mailing to identify those interested in your products. Again, a good offer would help to maximise your response.

▪ Many companies who have used this 'matching' process to find new prospects from the lifestyle database have had great success. However, many of these lists are being heavily used and response rates may be starting to fall.

One of the weaknesses of lifestyle data is that it is self-selecting – only a certain proportion of people are willing to spend time filling in a highly detailed questionnaire about their living and shopping habits. This is more often seen as a weakness by classic market researchers than it is by direct marketers – it is not improbable that someone who is prepared to fill in the questionnaire is more likely than average to respond to an offer in a mailing or direct response advertisement.

Axciom now claims to have completed lifestyle questionnaires on 38 million UK adults or nearly 100 per cent of the adult population

In other words, if you have Mr James Brown on your customer file but Mrs Margaret Brown filled in the lifestyle questionnaire, although there will be a match at the address level there will be no match at the individual level.

Axciom says that it needs a minimum of 300 matches for it to develop a usable profile of your customers – if the individual match rate is less than 50 per cent you will need to supply more than twice this number to achieve a basic profile.

This basic process would be enough to identify new prospects with approximately similar profiles, but a larger number would be safer. Other companies advise clients to provide enough names, to achieve at least 1,000 matches.

In other words, the more customers you already have, the easier it is to harness the power of a lifestyle database.

How the demographic systems work

Demographic systems such as ACORN and Mosaic and so on are all based on the same starting information – the National Census that takes place every ten years. Census information is gathered in blocks of households called Enumeration Districts (ED). An ED contains approximately 150 households and the data about it relates to the block not to any individual property. Every household in an ED can be identified by postcode although the process is not exact, especially in densely populated areas.

There are 150,000 EDs in the UK so to be of use to the marketer they need to be grouped into larger units. These are given names typifying the occupants, so using ACORN as an example, we find five categories covering broad lifestages:

▪ **A – wealthy achievers**
▪ **B – urban prosperity**
▪ **C – comfortably off**
▪ **D – moderate means**
▪ **E – hard pressed**

Each of these breaks down into two or more sub-groups so we see hard pressed broken down into four groups and 13 types:

Struggling families

44 - Low-income larger families, semis

45 - Older people, low income, small semis

46 - Low income, routine jobs, unemployment

47 - Low-rise terraced estates of poorly-off workers

48 - Low incomes, high unemployment, single parents

49 - Large families, many children, poorly educated

Burdened singles

50 - Council flats, single elderly people

51 - Council terraces, unemployment, many singles

52 - Council flats, single parents, unemployment

High rise hardship

53 - Old people in high rise flats

54 - Singles and single parents, high rise estates

Inner-city adversity

55 - Multi-ethnic purpose-built estates

56 - Multi-ethnic, crowded flats

In total ACORN delivers:

▪ 5 Categories

▪ 17 Groups

▪ 56 Types

It must be stressed here that, although in addition to the basic census data, personal data is used to identify the predominant characteristics of an ACORN ED it is still only the general characteristics of the area we are observing. Thus if we mailed every house in ED type 5.13: 'Well-off professionals, larger houses and converted flats', while we would expect to reach a good percentage of homes occupied by professionals, a large number of them would not fit the pattern. We may find perhaps that professionals occupied 60 per cent of the households – i.e. 40 per cent do not fit the pattern.

Geodemographic systems are therefore more useful to describe the general characteristics of an area than to target an individual household for a mailing. This is not to say they are without value – let's take an example.

If we are wishing to target well-off families with teenage children we could mail ACORN type 3.9 and reach a good proportion of our target. If nationally only 20 per cent of homes contain teenagers then compared to an untargeted mailing we should expect to do three times as well using ACORN.

This would still not be as good as knowing the composition of each address and selecting only those that we know contain teenagers.

Mosaic's system works in a similar way.

Mosaic divides households in the country into 11 groups and 61 types. The Mosaic classification is also based in large part on census data and also includes other data sources.

According to Mosaic, 54 per cent of the data used to build Mosaic is sourced from the 2001 Census. The remaining 46 per cent is derived from their Consumer Segmentation Database, which provides coverage of all of the United Kingdom's 46 million adult residents and 23 million households.

It includes:
- the edited electoral roll
- Experian Lifestyle Survey information, and consumer credit activity
- the Post Office address file
- Shareholders register
- house price and Council Tax information
- ONS (Office for National Statistics) local area statistics

Source: http://strategies.experian.co.uk/

The Mosaic system's 11 groups are as follows:
- symbols of success
- happy families
- suburban comfort
- ties of community
- urban intelligence
- welfare borderline
- municipal
- blue collar enterprise
- twilight subsistence
- grey perspectives
- rural isolation

Mosaic offers a significant range of other services including Commercial Mosaic for B2B profiling and consumer products covering Scotland, Northern Ireland and London, as well as sector activities covering, financial services, grocery, automotive and public sector markets.

Another way of using these types of services is to send your customer list to marketing solutions and information systems providers such as CACI (run by ACORN) or Experian (owners of Mosaic) to have it ACORN or Mosaic coded. This will identify the predominant property types of the people who are buying your products. You can then target households in similar properties for a mailing or perhaps a leaflet distribution.

Although ACORN and Mosaic do not offer the precision of lifestyle data, there is an advantage for small marketers in that every household in the UK can be matched. So unlike the case with the lifestyle companies, a sample sent for ACORN or Mosaic coding will achieve a virtual 100 per cent match. So a smaller sample will yield a result.

As we said earlier, the basic difference between the two methods is that the geodemographic systems such as ACORN and Mosaic simply match property types and they do not deal with actual people. The Lifestyle or Psychographic systems deal with actual people and the resulting matches are therefore more accurate.

Business-to-business profiling services

Business marketers will find that companies such as Experian, Dun and Bradstreet, Information Arts and Blue Sheep offer profiling and other services in the B2B market. See www.bluesheep.com and www.information-arts.com.

A WORKED EXAMPLE

Let us assume you want to find new customers for your home security devices – alarms, security lighting and so on. You decide to test lifestyle lists and also try ACORN or Mosaic. Here's a procedure you could use:

1. **Using the lifestyle database**
   - Identify your best customers. You would need to have at least 600 names but as mentioned earlier a greater number would give more statistical validity.
   - Contact one or more of the lifestyle companies and ask them for a quote to evaluate your data and identify how many names they have that match your best customer profile.
   - After analysing your data they will be able to tell you how many similar names they can provide you with.
   - This same customer sample could also be sent to the owners of ACORN or Mosaic. Though, as explained earlier, you would not need so many names in this case.
   - You can then plan to produce and send a test mailing in two or more simultaneous batches:
     — the lists provided by the lifestyle company
     — those provided by CACI (ACORN) and/or Experian (Mosaic)

The response devices of each should be coded separately so that you can tell which half of the test produces the best response. If you enclose a response form you can simply print a code on it, such as 1 = batch 1; 2 = batch 2.

For telephone responses you will need to be a bit more imaginative. Unique telephone numbers would be ideal. Failing that, you could still print your codes in the response area but you will have to ask callers to quote the code when they ring. Some will not remember it and may not have kept that piece handy.

It is very important to do this coding exercise as you need to know which is your best source for 'roll-out' - i.e. sending a larger mailing to the remainder of the more productive list.

> For email and digital campaigns this process should be built into campaign planning tracking software.
>
> As mentioned earlier, if you really have no information to help you target prospects, you will probably need to use direct response advertising to generate enquiries. Once you have some enquiries you can analyse these and this will improve your targeting in the future.

Are segmentation, profiling and targeting relevant to all businesses?

Some marketers think that these techniques are only relevant to large businesses with huge marketing budgets but this is not so. In fact the opposite is nearer the mark. When funds are limited it is even more important to target carefully and gain the maximum value for every pound you spend.

Remember too, that profiling and targeting are not just for prospecting. You can increase the profitability of your existing customer activities by careful segmentation – targeting those most likely to be interested in a particular offer, or at a particular time.

Another aspect of profiling and targeting

Let's look at the **ladder of loyalty**, a useful device to help you highlight the differences between various types of people and help you produce appropriate communications for each. Such communications will be better received because they recognise the status of each person and deliver relevant messages.

You can categorise your own customers and prospects according to their positions on the ladder.

There are various versions of this but they are essentially the same.

Advocate
Customer
Considering
Prospects
Suspects

Salespeople can use the ladder to help them allocate their time, devise appropriate contact strategies for individual prospects according to their potential, and to help them decide what and how much to tell people about their products.

The ladder can be just as useful in helping you decide what and how much to tell the people to whom you are communicating.

What do the descriptions mean?

On the bottom rung are **Suspects**, people who should be in the market but about whom you have no information (other than perhaps their names and addresses). This segment will include many people who are totally unaware of your services. Referring to the car insurance companies (see page 87) whose general list of motorists produced 1 per cent response is a list of suspects.

Prospects are those about whom you know enough to be able to say they are likely to be in the marketplace now. From the same car insurance example, knowing the renewal dates enabled the company to change the category from Suspect to Prospect. This distinction is hugely important – remember this segment produced more than five times as much response as the Suspects, i.e. those without renewal dates.

Prospects include those who know about your services but who have not yet got round to doing anything about it. Perhaps they don't realise quite how well you can satisfy their needs?

Next we have those who are **Considering** giving you some business. These could also be called 'non-converted enquirers'. They are very probably considering other suppliers at the same time. It is essential that you send them all the information they require and perhaps even follow up your information pack with a helpful phone call or reminder.

Customers have bought at least one product from you. Assuming they are satisfied that you have delivered what you promised these people are potential advocates. You may find it advantageous to encourage this process by sending an 'MGM' offer. MGM stands for Member get Member or Recommend a Friend, also called Referral Promotions. Here you would ask customers to send you the names of people who might also be interested in your products. These offers can be incentivised and this often produces more recommendations but see the cautionary tale below.

Advocates are regular customers who are so pleased with your service that they tell their friends and colleagues. Advocates should be nurtured carefully because they are worth far more to you than the profit from their own orders. They will usually not need incentives to recommend you to others, although a suitably restrained incentive offer **may** prompt them into action. This should be approached with extreme care however, as the following example shows:

Some years ago the marketing director of a very upmarket furnishings company that had numerous shops and a thriving mail order business, tested an incentivised MGM offer.

The customer list contained many titled people and in fact the company had the Royal Warrant for supplying members of the Royal family.

They tested an incentivised MGM offer and, although this attracted lots of positive response, they also received a lot of complaints. Typical of these was the lady who said:

'If I want to share my suppliers with my friends I will do so without the need for bribery. Please remove my name from your list.'

What exactly do we mean by 'Prospects'?

The term 'Suspect' is a fairly clear description, meaning someone about whom we know very little, or perhaps someone who knows little about us.

The term 'Prospect' on the other hand can have several meanings. In fact, any person on any rung of the ladder could be described as a prospect for something. Those on the bottom rung are prospects for an initial order; Advocates are prospects for repeat purchase or sales of additional products.

So, with the exception of this section, the term prospect is used throughout this book to mean someone who has the potential to buy from your next promotion.

How does the ladder of loyalty help?

There are two main uses:

- **To help us decide what to say** – i.e. to develop relevant copy and offers, and
- **To help decide how and where to say it** – to enable us to select an appropriate medium for the communication

Deciding what to say – clearly if you are communicating with suspects it will be necessary to tell that person about the value of this particular type of product or service because they are probably aware that it exists but it had not assumed any sort of priority for them.

Where to say it – furthermore, unless you know enough about them to target a relevant segment (who happen to be in the market at present, say), it may not be cost-effective to send a direct communication to them all. You may opt to start with a broadscale media approach using Television, Press or even Posters with a very simple offer to tempt those interested to declare their interest.

This is why many direct insurance companies such as Direct Line start with broadscale advertising. It would not be cost-efficient to contact every householder every month when they only buy the product once a year. A broad approach, using something like 'Save money on your insurance, ring 0800 000 000 for details' will generally prove more cost-effective in such cases.

Once people have responded to such an offer they identify their interest and become prospects. In asking for further information online or via the contact centre they will have given their renewal date and perhaps the name of their existing insurer. The advertiser can now send them a highly targeted relevant offer that has a much better chance of being accepted.

The existing **'Prospects'** group is already segmented by such key factors and these will only be communicated with at appropriate times.

Those **Considering** your product are probably beyond the need for basic product information because they already have this. They may still react well to additional detail relevant to their specific situation, and a rationale for preferring yours to a competitive product.

Customers may not need fully detailed product information, although this will not always be the case. Research in many fields shows that customers do not get the best out of products they buy because they are not totally aware of all that the product can do. This is especially true in the case of PC software, for example.

At the top of the ladder are the **'Advocates'**, customers who are so impressed by your products and service that they tell their friends and colleagues about it. You do not need to explain to these customers why they should buy your products – they would be insulted if you did.

Communications to Advocates should be to say 'thank you for your business' and to give information about new developments or make special offers to encourage continued business and recommendations.

Two key considerations

From the above descriptions two things emerge:

1. People will need different levels and amounts of information according to their place on the ladder.
2. The same person could be on different rungs according to the specific product you are promoting.

Even this is an over-simplification. An Advocate who has regularly bought Product A from you, may not be aware of Product B and could thus be classified as unaware. However, there is a strong relationship already established and hopefully some information on your database, which will help you to sell Product B to this person. In this sense they should be classified much higher than the average 'Suspect'.

The important thing is that you should use these descriptions to help you identify the right people, the right messages, and the right timing for a specific product or offer.

NOTE Do not forget however, the huge value of the relationship you have with existing customers.

NOTE Common sense is a useful ally when deciding how tightly to target the best prospects – a 100 per cent response to a campaign may be highly interesting but if you have mailed only 40 people you will not build your business very quickly.

So, while it is important to try to improve cost-efficiency you must also keep an eye on the overall number of sales needed to cover costs and make a contribution to your profits.

SUMMARY

In this chapter we looked at how the information we gather deliberately or simply as a result of our business activities is used to enhance customer focus and satisfaction.

We saw that the two main reasons for gathering data are to segment the market to allow better tailoring of the product messages and offers to customers.

We looked at a range of segmentation possibilities in a range of markets including consumer and business-to-business and then explored the four ways of creating market segments

These included:

- database analysis
- testing

- marketing research
- intuition.

Of these we saw that the most risky was the last, where possible, one or more of the other three methods should support the use of intuition.

One way of managing the process of segmentation is to buy in services. We learned that there are a number of services supporting the direct marketer in this task. External services are classified into two areas:

- Demographic – the main uses of these data are to refine lists, to help selections form external lists and to gain a better understanding of customers and markets.
  Examples include ACORN or Mosaic.
- Psychographic or lifestyle – the main uses are data enhancement and profiling.
  Examples include behaviour bank and the lifestyle selector.

We then looked in detail at how the demographic systems work and looked at some of the output from the ACORN system.

The advantages of demographic systems were discussed and include the fact that there is virtually a 100 per cent match with these systems as all homes are coded.

He disadvantage was the relative lack of precision in the demographic systems. ACORN and Mosaic deal with property types not people.

We saw that Experian and Dun and Bradstreet offer similar profiling services for business-to-business markets.

We then went through a worked example of how to apply these systems in practice.

We went on to look at the ladder of loyalty and explored how it helps in the process of segmenting customers into relevant groups.

We saw that the ladder of loyalty describes the relative position of customers in terms of their relationship to the company. They may be:

- Advocates
- Customers
- Considering purchase or non-converted enquirers
- Prospects
- Suspects

Each of these categories was defined and an indication of the different direct marketing approaches to each was given. We saw that the ladder of loyalty helps us to decide what to say to customers and how and where to say it.

Segmentation finally was shown to allow us to identify the right people the right messages and the right time for a product or offer.

REVIEW QUESTIONS

1. Why should we gather data about customers?
2. Define segmentation.
3. List five consumer segmentation variables.
4. What are the four ways of creating marketing segments?
5. What are the two types of external data available for profiling?
6. What are the three main uses of demographic data?
7. What are the two main uses of lifestyle data?
8. What is an Enumeration District (ED)?
9. Who provides profiling services to business-to-business markets?
10. List five rungs of the ladder of loyalty.
11. What is an advocate and what are the implications of this description for direct marketing?
12. How should direct marketers use the concept of the ladder of loyalty?
13. What is the main purpose of segmentation?

EXERCISE

Choose one of the following markets:

- travel
- desktop PCs
- beauty products
- financial services

Describe the market segments that are available to the company.

What are the main segmentation variables used in dividing the market?

What impact do these variables have on:

- products offered;
- offers made;
- media choices online and offline;
- messages.

CHAPTER 5
THE MARKETING DATABASE

IN THIS CHAPTER

In this chapter we take will consider the entire process of constructing or specifying a marketing database.

We also explain in detail the various legal, ethical and industry standards covering the collection, storage and use of individual data.

We provide links such as www.outlaw.com to enable readers to keep up to date with these constantly changing regulations, and the way they are interpreted by the authorities.

Specific topics in this chapter include:
- What is a marketing database?
- What is the marketing database used for?
- Pareto's Principle or the 80:20 rule
- Targeting and segmentation: How?
- The role of customer data in developing relationships
- How can you capture the data?
- How can data be kept up to date?
- The importance of de-duplication
- How can the data be used?
- How does the database achieve all these things?
- Hardware and software
- Legal and regulatory issues

After completing this chapter you should be able to:
- Define a marketing database;
- Understand the process of building a database and the various applications it can support;
- Understand how the database is maintained;
- Identify hardware and software requirements;
- Identify key legal and code of conduct issues in holding customer data.

What is a marketing database?

Whether you refer to data warehousing, data marts, customer relationship marketing systems or simply a marketing database, the use of customer data has never been so widespread.

It drives successful programmes such as Tesco Clubcard, it is a significant by-product of Web-based marketing and used carefully it is improving the effectiveness and efficiency of marketing a wide range of organisations in every sector.

It is also causing a high degree of controversy following regular reports in the press of data being lost, stolen and used for various purposes that occasionally compromise the trust between organisations and the customers they serve.

In this book we will refer to the marketing database and it is clear that whatever you call it, most marketers today consider it to be an essential part of their armoury, and would consider those not having a database to be behind the times.

This opinion is put forward by most marketing people regardless of rank, job function or technical knowledge. But what exactly is a marketing database and is this view justified?

Since this book was first written (*Direct Marketing in Practice*. Oxford: Butterworth-Heinemann, 2002) there have been significant changes in the way that organisations handle data. The process of pulling diverse systems together and upgrading legacy (or out-of-date systems) has made the IT industry and consultants operating around the sector vast amounts of money.

In the 1980s before the use of customer data for marketing purposes became prevalent and when marketing database theory was in its infancy, systems were designed primarily to handle customer transactions and billings rather than marketing requirements.

Bank systems, for example, were centred around customer accounts. Data was designed to facilitate the efficient operation of functional areas of the business, for example finance or logistics. Today data systems deliver this traditional functionality but also focus on driving and developing customer relationships in ways that would never have been imagined even ten years ago.

Figure 5.1: Legacy systems and customer data

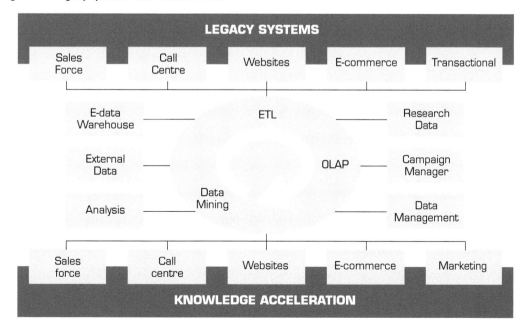

Source: IDM Diploma in Direct and Interactive Marketing Course Material 2010

The figure above shows where data often sits within an organisation. We can see at the top of the figure a variety of different sources. Often these will contain different data formats and rules and procedures. These data are enhanced through a variety of other sources including:

- research data, suitably disguised and aggregated;
- campaign data including response, contact centre data, Web metrics and a range of data from ecommerce activity;
- external overlays, e.g. Axciom, Mosaic or Blue Sheep products.

Data are Extracted, Transformed and Loaded (ETL), analysed through a variety of systems including Online Analytical Processing tools (OLAP) and mined for insight.

This is helped by campaign management software and subject to various rules relating to data management.

And this is a simple data model.

Work done by Oracle for General Motors on their data systems worldwide was rumoured to have come in at over US$1billion and to have generated similar annual cost savings.

Put very simply, the purpose of a marketing database is to enable marketers to use the company's data for marketing purposes.

This may seem blindingly obvious but the application of technology and the management of data within organisations is one of the most intractable problems for companies with constant concern about the flexibility and scalability of data solutions and an inability to manage the vast quantities of data that are being produced from multiple customer interactions.

Consider for a moment the sheer volume of data produced from the Tesco Clubcard scheme. The triumph of Clubcard is the ability of Dunn Humby, Tesco's data analysis company, to make sense of terabytes of data and to produce effective marketing outputs from this analysis. Have a look at the Dunn Humby website (www.dunnhumby.com), where you will find some interesting ideas and case studies to explore.

Through its agency EHS Brann, Tesco issues quarterly statements to more than 12 million customers, it captures an estimated 80 per cent of purchases and uses this to drive more than nine million message variations.

Tesco is now using data collaboratively with suppliers to help drive effective marketing relationships based on effective insight derived from customer data.

In order for a database to be useful to marketers it must be capable of being viewed from a customer basis rather than a functional or organisational basis.

If Mrs Jones, a bank customer, has a current account, a mortgage and a gold card we are able to plan our marketing in the light of her total business with us rather than having a variety of accounts each of which is viewed as a separate entity. Apart from enabling more cost-efficient and effective marketing programmes it also prevents us irritating our better customers, i.e. those with more than one strand of business with us, by failing to understand the extent and nature of their business with us.

The marketing database often stands separate from a company's central system. A bank's marketing database would take data from the various customer accounts records and merge them into a separate data area. This avoids the marketing functions impinging on the day-to-day activities of running the bank and assembles the data in a way that facilitates the marketer's requirements.

There are other possible sources of data. In some cases data is automatically gathered on a customer by customer basis as part of another business function. For example:

- part of a customer care system – people may ring a helpline number if they experience problems with a product or service;
- online request for help;
- a salesforce management system – where salespeople visit prospects and these are converted to customers;
- part of a facilities management system – where direct debits and standing orders are processed for, say, a charity.

The reality, then, is that a marketing database comes in all shapes and sizes. As long as you have a means of assembling data for marketing purposes you can claim to have a marketing database. What really counts is how the data is used. Used in the correct way, data is an extremely powerful tool, as we will show in the rest of this chapter.

What is the marketing database used for?

Consider the example of a company with a customer care system originally designed to:

- answer the queries of customers requiring help in operating the machines, and;
- provide information for customers wishing to buy more concentrates.

This is an excellent example of a system designed to serve essential business functions that has evolved into a marketing database.

In fact its use as a marketing tool is beginning to outstrip its original purpose. It is a good example of how customer problems can be turned to a company's advantage.

The marketing database is used to further relationships with customers. The initial contact may be negative – the customer may have a problem. The system enables this to be dealt with smoothly and ensures that remedial action takes place; a spare part is despatched, a money-off voucher is given in compensation, and so on.

Once we have logged the customer details on the marketing database we can use this information to build the relationship. We may offer further benefits such as money-off vouchers for new products, advice of forthcoming promotions, or entry into prize draws.

Our data can also be used to produce reports for other departments in the company; quality control can see where problems are arising; marketing can look at, say, age and consumption habits of specific segments of the customer base. One of the most important functions of the marketing database is to provide easily understood and actionable reports for a range of audiences within the company.

By combining data from promotions with sales records a company can develop a powerful weapon to help with both strategic and tactical marketing.

For example, when planning a local promotion the company was able to use the data to:

- identify customers in the vicinity through postcode selections, and;
- refine the list by selecting people with certain buying patterns, perhaps selecting those living within five miles of the store who last bought a drinks maker more than two years ago.

Pareto's Principle or the 80:20 rule

This well-known principle states that 80 per cent of a company's business comes from just 20 per cent of its customers. This is broadly true of almost all businesses. For example Dell aims to sell computers and then a range of accessories to extend the functionality of the machine and eventually replacement machines, thus perpetuating the sales cycle.

In practice computer buyers do not all exhibit the same behaviour – some will buy Dell once then switch; others may keep machines for a long time and never buy add-ons; a third category are regular purchasers.

Each of these segments requires a different approach.

Some will receive frequent communications and promotions; others may not prove worth any investment at all. The marketing database enables us to manage this segmentation efficiently.

The basic principles of customer segmentation are vital to successful marketing and the customer database allows us to manage this process very effectively.

In summary, the marketing database enables us to:

- develop customer relationships on a selective, cost-efficient basis;
- provide regular high quality relevant reports to our colleagues;
- select sub-sets of customers based on individual data;
- target those most likely to be appropriate for a particular communication or offer;
- manage different segments of customers according to their potential;
- apply our learning to develop new markets and opportunities.

Targeting and segmentation: Why?

Consider British Airways Holidays (BAH). This is a subsidiary of British Airways that offers top class holiday packages to the discerning traveller. These packages are designed to appeal to the more affluent customer who is more concerned with quality than price.

The BAH marketing database is made up of data from a variety of sources including information on previous bookings. Let's consider how this might be used.

When selecting an audience for a Caribbean holiday promotion we will consider customers' previous buying patterns. Would we offer this holiday to someone who went there last year?

Yes, of course this would be a good selection.

What about those who went last month? Probably not a good selection unless their buying pattern shows us that they take several holidays a year.

Buying patterns are powerful predictors. If you took a holiday in June last year, the chances are you will consider June again this year. If you have visited Paris, Rome and Amsterdam in recent years, an offer on a holiday to Prague may well appeal.

As we can see, concurrency of data and timing of offer are key factors. With an efficient marketing database BAH can make the right offer to the right customers at the right time. Clearly such precision leads to greater relevance and thus more cost-efficient marketing programmes.

By planning well-targeted campaigns like these, you can forecast how much you are going to spend and what the likely response to your promotion will be. This enables fairly accurate forecasting of sales and return on investment.

In addition to their customer database BAH have a database of people who are likely to be good prospects.

This was made possible by profiling their existing customers. A major advantage of building a good marketing database is the ability to identify prospects. We will see later on in this chapter how you can select good prospects by matching them to a profile of your current best customers.

Have a look at www.britishairways.com/travel/home.

Look at the information that is captured and think about how, with relevant permissions, BA could use the data to target customers.

In summary, segmenting and targeting specific customers means we can:

- ensure that our communications are relevant and therefore more likely to succeed;
- develop and offer more appropriate products and services;
- improve the effectiveness of all customer contacts;
- identify better prospects;
- increase the accuracy of our forecasts;
- increase the productivity of our marketing expenditure.

Targeting and segmentation: how?

Now, having looked at some of the benefits of targeting and segmentation, let's see how it can be achieved.

There are a number of statistical techniques in common use. We will not study them in detail here but rather discuss them from a marketing perspective.

Regression analysis is a technique that scores individuals according to their characteristics. Study of previous behaviour enables us to allocate plus or minus scores in relation to this particular event. Let's say that our analysis of previous customers shows us that people who take expensive holidays tend to:

- have taken one before;
- live in larger houses or at least in certain postcodes;
- be over 40 years of age;
- have children at private schools;
- have a household income of more than £40,000 p.a.

Now let's consider a study into the likelihood of a prospect responding to the offer of a Caribbean holiday. We may find this can be forecast as follows:

- add 50 if they have booked a luxury holiday before;
- add a further 50 if this was in the Caribbean;
- subtract 35 if they are aged under 40;
- add 40 if they earn more than £50,000 p.a.

We will apply this scoring method to every relevant characteristic of every prospect on file and we can then confidently predict that those with the highest scores are the ones most likely to respond to our offer.

Such analyses are carefully developed and tested, based on historical data, and then monitored during use to ensure their continuing accuracy.

Regression analysis is a good tactical tool, delivering a highly targeted set of prospects for a given offer.

On a more strategic level we may consider the use of tools like CHAID (see Glossary) and cluster analysis. These aim to allocate semi-permanent codes to customers and these are then broken down into segments having similar needs and behaviour.

So instead of reviewing the entire file for prospects for our holiday offer, we may have previously segmented the base into groups, some of whom are more likely to be interested in such offers.

We may, for instance, derive a type A1; high income, loyal customers. This works in a similar way to the popular demographic coding systems such as ACORN and Mosaic, but in this case it is applied to your own customer data rather than to a type of property.

In order to understand the workings of CHAID let's consider an example of a bank wishing to sell ISAs. At present 8 per cent of customers have an ISA and they wish to increase this to 10 per cent. The CHAID model is fed 30,000 customer records containing data on:

- number of ISAs
- household income
- size of mortgage
- years as a customer

The CHAID software considers all of the given variables and determines which is the most important in this case.

Firstly, it finds the most significant factor to cause a response/no response and splits the file down accordingly.

The process then re-iterates the first stage using the remaining variables

The process continues until the system establishes no more statistically significant splits.

Let's say it establishes that the most significant factor is 'years as a customer'. It further subdivides this factor into say: less than one year with the bank; one to five years as a customer; more than five years. It may then identify something like the following:

- less than one year as a customer – only 3 per cent have an ISA
- one to five years – 8 per cent have an ISA
- more than five years – 12 per cent have an ISA

The CHAID model then moves on to the next stage which is to take each of these three segments and considers the next most significant variable in each instance.

It may ascertain that in the most loyal customer segment (more than five years with the bank) the next best discriminator is mortgage size. People in this segment with mortgages of more than

£100,000 may have a 14 per cent take up of ISAs.

By breaking down each segment into its significant variables a number of potentially good sub-segments may emerge.

We may find that although 'semi-loyal' customers (with the bank one to five years) are not of interest as a whole group (only 8 per cent have an ISA), those in this group who have mortgages of more than £150,000, and household incomes of £65,000 or more are much better prospects. The model may show that 15 per cent of those in this sub-set have an ISA.

CHAID segments are easy to understand and apply – we know exactly what characteristics we are seeking – we then select our target audience according to these factors.

Furthermore, we can brief our creative people on these characteristics so that they can write relevant copy. We can also feed back the information to the computer programmers so they can apply the segmentation to their files.

When using CHAID it is important to set out a detailed plan of what is mailed to whom and when. Otherwise one group of prospects may well come up again and again and receive too many mailings whilst another may not be mailed enough.

Figure 5.2: CHAID analysis tree for a charity

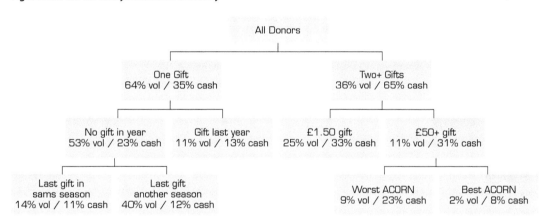

The figure above is an example of a CHAID analysis of a charity donor mailing file, showing which groups were the most generous – or not.

In the example above the number of previous gifts is best variable: 36 per cent who sent two or more donations account for 65 per cent of the money.

It also demonstrates that one group, second from the left on the last row, accounted for 40 per cent of the volume mailed but only gave 12 per cent of the cash. By omitting this group, profitability would have been improved dramatically.

The analysis shows that the number of previous gifts would have been the best variable: 36 per cent who sent two or more donations account for 65 per cent of the money.

10.5% Yields   12.5% cash
26.0% Yields   33% cash
10.0% Yields   32% cash
13.5% Yields   11% cash

60% Volume 88.5% cash

The model also shows that 88.5 per cent of the cash could have been raised from just 60 per cent of the targeted list.

Cluster analysis is a similarly powerful strategic tool. In this case the model does not deal with specific variables but general characteristics. In the same way that ACORN and Mosaic typify property, cluster analysis breaks down customers into types. So we may see more general descriptions such as:

▪ Loyal customers with a large spread of products;
▪ Struggling 'nest builders'.

Such classifications would be used strategically across the entire product range rather than to select propensity to buy a particular product like an ISA. This method has many of the advantages of CHAID but it is not so easy to understand.

Neural networks are the latest technique to appear in this sector. They apply artificial intelligence within a statistical model. We tell the model who is an ISA customer and feed in all of the other data about those people. In effect the model asks questions of the sample in order to determine who is likely to be a good ISA prospect.

With most of these techniques we base our predictions on the behaviour of those who responded to previous offers.

The main disadvantage of neural networks is that it works by splitting the response or behavioural sample into three discrete samples. In marketing we are often dealing with quite low response rates and splitting these responses into three means that there is sometimes a real paucity of data.

We will not try to explain how this technique works but simply say that given enough data it seems to be comparable with the other techniques. As our understanding and usage of artificial intelligence develops it may become the best of these tools in the future.

Doing it yourself

It is possible to use the above techniques on your own computer using a number of statistical analysis packages. The most common are SPSS now part of IBM and SAS. These are off-the-shelf packages that are relatively user-friendly and cost-effective. It is important to understand that the main skill in data analysis is not in running the software, but in understanding the data.

You can find details on SPSS and SAS at their websites: www.spss.com and www.sas.com.

For example, data from a recent petrol station promotion seemed to indicate that there were lots of youngsters driving around in expensive cars. In fact they were mainly teenage respondents to a CD promotion who filled out questionnaires with a mixture of personal preferences (musical tastes), and household data (family car). The lesson here is to know your data and understand its implications before submitting it to the model.

To use these statistical analysis packages you will need at least a basic knowledge of statistics. Most marketers will not need to use all the features but they will include advanced statistics, modules, coefficients and so on. If you are not familiar with such techniques you should start by having someone trained in statistics by your side when running these models.

Using the data

Any model derived should be actionable. It is no use finding that sales of your drinks increase during hot weather if you are not able to make use of that fact. You cannot affect the weather but such knowledge may enable you to use the weather forecasts to prepare for more rapid production and distribution when demand is likely to rise. Findings must make sense – remember your conclusions will have to be explained to colleagues, creative agencies, bureaux and so on.

Summarising this section we have:

- Regression analysis – a statistical modelling technique used mainly for tactical mailings;
- CHAID – an analysis tool that creates your own customer typology;
- Clustering – similar to CHAID but a general-purpose tool. It is the technique used by the developers of ACORN and Mosaic;
- Neural networks – the newest technology, not yet fully proven in marketing;
- All can be derived from standard statistical packages such as SPSS and SAS;
- The real skill is not in pressing the right buttons but in understanding the data, interpreting the reports and applying the results;
- Results should be easily understood by third parties;
- You need to be comfortable with the results – you have to present them and sometimes defend them.

Development of customer relationships – why?

Have you heard the story of the author who submitted a manuscript to his editor? The editor thought it would make a great book, but decided that David was not a good name for its hero. He felt that Arthur would be more appropriate. The author complained that this would entail lots of extra work but the editor assured him that with word processing it was very easy to make a simple global change.

The author agreed to the change and the book was published. Too late, a reader pointed out that in one chapter the hero took his lady away for a romantic weekend and they gazed upon Michelangelo's statue of Arthur!

The point about this story is that technology can make some operations easy – sometimes too easy. As a marketer you have to remember that your database is filled with people not just data.

The *Daily Telegraph* is an innovative newspaper and one of the first to sell subscriptions to consumers. It did this via an Advanced Payment Programme (APP) where customers can pay in advance for several months' copies and receive a discount on the normal cover price.

If you as a customer were thinking of buying something, would you be influenced by the fact that you had bought a product from the company before and you were happy with it? Of course you would. Therefore a company that has access to its customers can continue to sell to them and boost their loyalty. For the *Daily Telegraph* this future sale may be a renewal of the subscription or any other product that it offers in association with other suppliers.

Contented customers are more likely to recommend your product to their friends and colleagues. In fact, customers who have experienced problems that have subsequently been remedied are even more likely to recommend you. This shows the importance of continuing a dialogue with your customers and the marketing database offers you an excellent way of managing this process.

If you have taken out a subscription deal with the *Daily Telegraph*, you will have to decide at the end of your subscription period whether you wish to continue with the arrangement. The *Daily Telegraph* knows from its database records when this decision will have to be made and will contact you beforehand.

The paper will remind you what a great newspaper you read and restate the benefits of taking out a further subscription. The marketing database enables the company to time these communications so they are highly relevant to individual recipients.

The *Daily Telegraph* will not stop at sending you a simple reminder. They will also carry out anti-attrition studies. This is an important area – having gone to the considerable time and expense of recruiting a customer, one does not want to lose them through lack of understanding their needs. Even worse – recent studies show that dissatisfied customers tell between four and 17 people to avoid the offending product.

With this in mind the *Daily Telegraph* will ask lapsed customers why they failed to renew and will plot and analyse the reasons carefully. There may be some reasons linked to age, the length of subscription, address or household composition (number of adults, number and ages of children etc.). Whatever the factors involved, by knowing which customers are most likely to defect, the company can make a special effort to persuade them of the benefits of renewal.

Like many sectors, the newspaper industry is highly competitive. There have been price wars where rival newspapers have slashed their cover prices to increase sales. There have been expensive promotions, prize draws, wall charts, bingo games and memberships schemes. Whenever a new initiative is planned competitors will do their utmost to pre-empt it or at least spoil it.

Direct communication offers a way of talking directly with customers without telling all your competitors what you are planning. In real life, of course, your sharper competitors will be on your contact lists and will get to know what you are planning. Even so, direct communications can be used to make offers to the customer base; conduct market research or maybe just to say 'thank you for your custom'.

Direct communications online or offline are clearly a private media, enabling a continuing dialogue with customers. A newspaper is itself a private medium of sorts, communicating to its readers every day, but the difference is that the communication is one way. It also sends the same message to the entire audience whereas with direct communication we can vary the message for each segment or type of customer. The database is the tool that makes this possible.

In summary:

- All customers are different – they need differing messages;
- It is easier to sell to existing customers than cold prospects;
- The marketing database makes it easier to target and time communications correctly;
- Anti-attrition techniques can help you predict which customers are most likely to leave, and when;
- Direct communications are more discreet.

Development of customer relationships – how?

First a few questions:

- What data do you need?
- Where can you find it?
- How can you capture it?
- How can you keep it up to date?

What data do you need?

Most businesses have more than enough data, the problem is not generally one of availability but of centralisation and management. One of the key questions will be what should be kept.

> If an item of data is to be used for communications there is a legal obligation to be keep it up to date – any data is better than none but out-of-date information can be misleading, even harmful. Writing to the old address when customers have moved house may be difficult to avoid but the impression left by your mailing will be very bad.

This is not to say that old data should be destroyed; it may still be very valuable for analysis, profiling etc. However, it makes sense to remove old records to an archive for occasional use, rather than have them taking up space and using data processing time on the main database.

A good start may be to:

- **Capture data essential for current requirements**
  — names, addresses, products purchased etc.
- **Collect key profile data**
  — family size, number of cars, property type etc.
- **Collect data which will aid future activity such as cross-selling, repeat purchase stimulation etc.**
  — which offer they responded to; timing, ages of children etc.
- **Collect data relating to the marketplace**
  — peaks and troughs of demand, what other suppliers they buy from. As we saw in Chapter 1, this can be very productive.

First define the uses

A good rule is to define a use for each piece of data before you include it. If you can't think of a reason to keep it you probably don't need it. If you are really not sure then you can hold a separate file or table of such data which does not clog up the main database, bearing in mind that if you don't maintain it, it will eventually become out of date.

Where does the data come from?

Unless you are starting up a brand new company there will be lots of data already available. For example:

- **Administration data**
  You will have details of existing and lapsed products, queries and special requests, invoices, reminders, demands and payments.

- **Marketing data**
  Names of enquirers from previous communications, advertising responses, etc.
  Details of email campaigns, door drops, consumer mailings and advertisements run, promotions organised etc.

On its own, departmental data is only of use for its original purpose. When different pieces of data are combined and coordinated their true value can be much greater.

EXAMPLE

Let's imagine that you are an insurance company and want to select those clients who have some spare disposable income to offer a premium-priced but valuable additional service. Perhaps a new type of high-quality burglar alarm, linked directly to a local security firm 'flying squad'. The information you hold is either:

Segment 1: The amount of their buildings cover, or

Segment 2: The amount of motor cover and type of car

From these bits of data you know:
1. The value of their house, or
2. The type and value of their car

Neither of these pieces of data, nor even the two in combination will tell you much about their disposable income. But supposing in the case of Segment 1, you also know the size of their mortgage, and for those in Segment 2 you know their mortgage and their building value you have suddenly got a lot of marketing information.

E.g. Looking at Segment 1 only

Type	A	B	C	D
Buildings cover	£55,000	£100,000	£350,000	£350,000
Mortgage	£55,000	£50,000	£300,000	£60,000

Just relating these two pieces of data gives us a much clearer picture of the available funds in these households. Types B and D are likely to be better prospects for a premium-priced service.

In Segment 2 we have an additional piece of data – the type and value of their car(s). This adds a further dimension to our assessment – if their car is a Ford Mondeo they are perhaps not especially likely to be interested in the new service; ownership of a Jaguar indicates they are likely to be better prospects.

The continuing need for data

Although there may already be quite a lot of data in and around your business, additional data will probably be necessary and there is a continuing need to build and maintain your database.

Here's a reminder of some other sources of data:

- **Customer and prospect questionnaires** These can attract quite large responses – 50 per cent or more from established clients and 20 per cent or more from prospects.
- **Communications to outside lists** There is a wide range of lists available for rent – any respondents can be added to the database, subject to the requirements of the 1998 Data Protection Act.
- **Lifestyle database companies** Provide a similar service for consumer records – these organisations have several million names and addresses on their databases.
- **Responses from advertising, inserts and other promotions.** Again, subject to the requirements of the Data Protection Act these can be added to your database.

And for information about businesses…

- **Companies House** A good source of raw data about companies extracted from their annual returns. You can also buy the same information but with additional 'narrative', trend analysis, etc. from…
- **Information brokers** such as Dun and Bradstreet, and Experian. These companies can provide not only names and addresses but also additional data about size, performance etc. They will also verify your own records and add any additional data they hold.

How can you capture the data?

However much data you already have it will not all be in a computer, or at least the computer on which you wish to run your marketing database. Some data capture is inevitable therefore. If you have the capacity to undertake data input in-house this is the cheapest way.

It is important to avoid duplication of records so it is advisable to build some form of de-duplication process into the data-entry routine.

There are a number of software tools available such as 'Experian QAS' to help you check the accuracy of each address on entry. Most of these will save a high percentage of the initial keystrokes.

As an alternative to in-house data capture there are many bureaux offering this service and you will find these via a simple online search.

How can data be kept up to date?

Data decays very rapidly – more than 10 per cent of consumers move house every year; and up to 30 per cent of business people move (desks at least) every year. It is vital that data is maintained correctly and some of the ways you can do this are:

- **Regular communication inviting response** – such as questionnaires or offers of information.
- **Periodic comparisons with outside databases** – e.g. the edited Electoral Register, lifestyle database companies, and for businesses with companies like Dunn and Bradstreet and Experian.

Every time a contact is made with a customer or prospect, by any medium (email, mail, phone or in person), you should attempt to verify your data.

The importance of de-duplication

When you are adding names to your database, or perhaps planning to mail one or more outside lists together with your own, it is necessary to identify 'duplicates', i.e. people whose names appear more than once.

Lists from various sources and your own names and addresses can be run through a 'merge/purge' to highlight possible duplicates, which are then scrutinised and eliminated where necessary.

You should also include addresses you do not wish to mail (e.g. people who owe you money, who have asked not to be mailed, or those whom you simply do not want to do business with).

Where to get your lists de-duplicated

When adding new data you can usually program your database to identify any duplicates. For a wider exercise such as the one above you should consider using a bureau.

There are numerous bureaux that can take your own and a selection of external lists and carry out the de-duplication process for you. Most bureaux have the latest hardware, highly sophisticated software and lots of experience. This is very valuable and, despite the charges, outsourcing your de-duplication will frequently be highly cost-effective.

The benefits of de-duplication are not purely financial either – a merge/purge run can save much customer irritation and also tell you something about the potential value of an external list.

For example a prospective external list has greater potential;

- If it has no, or very few **internal** duplicates, i.e. addresses appearing twice on the same list. This problem is rare with rented lists, and if a list is very 'clean' it is likely to be well managed and therefore more likely to be up to date.
- The higher the duplication with:
  - — your own best customer list;
  - — the other candidate lists.

Names which are on all or several lists, are often the best names of all and some mailers actually single these out for special treatment e.g. better offers etc.

The addresses on different lists may well not be in the same format and some additional data processing may be necessary. However, most bureaux cope very efficiently with this problem and a merge/purge run will usually be cost-effective.

NOTE: de-duplication is important even if you are only planning to contact your own customers and prospects.

Duplication can be very common, even within internal lists unless you have been very careful in checking each new name as it is added.

Some companies keep records by account numbers or product type rather than customer names and addresses and this can lead to a high level of wastage and customer dissatisfaction.

EXAMPLE

A colleague lived in Normandy and worked in England and used the car ferry up to 20 times a year, ten or so with Brittany Ferries and the rest with P&O.

Occasionally he received a contact from P&O but Brittany Ferries really do it in style.

They clearly do not believe in de-duplication because whenever they sent out a communication he received 12 or more identical copies.

When he contacted them to suggest some more careful database management, the marketing director dismissed helpful suggestions, pointing out that as 90 per cent of all their customers travel only once a year, there was no need for such irrelevancies!

Apart from the frightening lack of concern for a good customer, this case illustrates the vital importance of de-duplication and good database management. Unless you check names as you add them to your database, or at the very least before you mail them, your best customers will receive the most copies of the same mailing.

How can the data be used?

Now that you have collected all this customer information, what can you do with it? The following section shows how and where the database can help you manage your business.

Planning The database helps you to define objectives, select customer segments, develop relevant offers and messages, and match costs to potential returns.

Contact strategy The process of deciding which medium or combination of media will be most appropriate for each task and each category of customer. Your database will also help you to identify individuals for the sending of timely communications. There are many possible reasons for contacting customers apart from soliciting orders.

Data processing The production of data and even labels for addressing a mailing; lists for follow-up activities; 'mail-merging' of letter copy and addresses; counts and reports to aid planning.

Response handling One of the key functions of your database is to record response to promotional mailings. This is easier if you use Unique Reference Numbers on your response forms.

Lead processing Helping you keep to track of enquiries (leads) received, following these through the sales follow up process and, where necessary, issuing reminders for future action.

Campaign management and reporting In addition to producing the necessary customer paperwork, your system should also produce periodic reports to help you manage promotional campaigns.

Customer satisfaction surveys Information from questionnaires can be added to customer records helping to make the planning and selection processes more effective in future.

Analysis In addition to producing pre-determined reports, a good database system enables you to do ad hoc 'what if' analysis.

Data maintenance Data, especially name and address details decay rapidly. Frequent contact can overcome this providing you update records quickly and efficiently.

How does the database achieve all these things?

As we can see in the figure overleaf the marketing database is simply a series of tables. A table can be:
- a list of names and addresses;
- a list of transactions;
- a list of suppliers/delivery methods and so on;
- a list of promotion codes;
- a list of customers who have been mailed, and their responses;
- or any logical collection of data.

Figure 5.3: Relational database schema

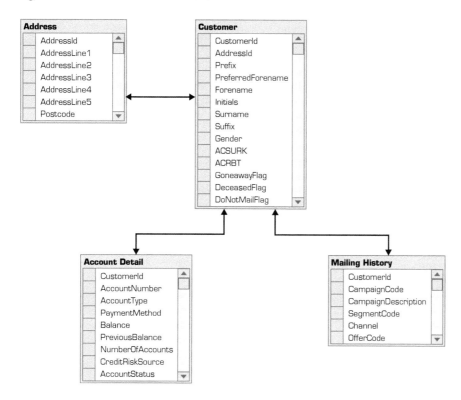

The ways in which this data is assembled and manipulated are highly complex and we do not need to go into details here. However, as a marketer you do need to be able to follow the logic of a database.

For instance, it would not be logical to store details of every transaction against every customer, in the same table. Some customers may have dozens of transactions, others only one. To avoid large areas of wasted space, transactions are stored in a separate table, with a link between the customer's name and address and the transaction.

Having assembled the data, records have to be selected for a particular mailing campaign. This is done by a process of raising queries. For instance, if we wished to mail customers who had spent more than £500 in the past six months we would:

- tell the computer to identify all transactions of £500 or more between the dates of XX and YY;
- link these transactions to the name and address table;
- get a count of how many names and addresses had been identified;
- if and when required, extract the related names and addresses for use in the promotion.

Using queries in this way enables us to model campaigns and identify whether our selection parameters have been appropriate. If the count shows we have only 50 customers who fit the category (spent £500 within last six months) we may wish to broaden the parameters.

We could extend the period to 12 months and/or reduce the qualifying total to £250. This would produce a larger number of prospects.

The exact process used depends on the software being used. Software is generally more user friendly and allows the marketer direct access to the data. This makes modelling campaigns easy and fast.

These people use the data to answer customer questions, but also to do data analyses using user-friendly Windows-based software (SAS, SPSS).

The IT people do not have to bother with marketing requests – a great relief for them! Marketing people do not have to think through the answers before they ask the questions!

Developing the database

Nowadays it is possible for almost all organisations to set up and manage an effective customer database. These can be run on computers using a range of software and systems from the simplest like Microsoft Access to Web-enabled bespoke systems costing millions from companies like Oracle and IBM.

The power and capacity of computers are expanding rapidly and today it is very doubtful that you will be managing a consumer database that will expand at a rate faster than the expansion of technology. The problem for many companies is handling the problems involved in extending the scope and functionality of older database systems.

The process of developing a marketing database is fairly standard whatever the size of the business. However, it can be complex and demanding.

A staged planning approach is outlined below.

- Business review
- Data audit
- Data strategy, specification and verification
- Data verification, capture, maintenance and enhancement
- Hardware/software
- Management issues – should the database be run in-house/out-of-house?
- Applications
- Review

Let's look at each of these stages in turn.

Business review

It is important that the overall mission and objectives are reviewed in order to inform the process of establishing the database.

It could be that a database is not required to fulfil the mission of the business or that the cost of a particular database design or hardware is too great.

All business decisions should begin with an understanding of the strategic direction of the business. The database decision is no exception. We must ask:

- How will data help the business achieve its business and marketing objectives?
- Where will the business be in ten years' time?

- What media, information and technology changes will need to be built into the system?
- What segments will the data support now and in the future?
- What business processes will the database support?
- How will the database be accessed?
- Is the database open to customers through the Internet?

Data audit

Carrying out an in-depth data audit is the next stage of the process. We need to establish the following:

- What information requirements does the organisation have now and in the future?
- Where is this information held currently?
- What unnecessary information is currently held?
- How is this information currently used?
- How will it be used in future?
- Which departments and individuals need access to this information?
- If information is not available, where does it come from?
- Who will enter the data and ensure that is accurate and complete?
- What applications will this information support?
- How does the proposed system integrate with existing information management systems?

Data strategy, specification and verification

The review of strategy and the data audit should result in a long-term strategy for data within the organisation. This should be capable of evolution and development over time as the markets served by the organisation and the organisation itself changes.

The strategy should specify the information that is required by the organisation outlining where the information is available and what additional data is to be acquired and managed.

It should determine the following:

- Who and what departments are able to use and update data held on the database?
- How will the data be kept up to date and who is responsible for this?
- What data verification rules will be put in place to ensure quality and completeness?
- What analysis systems will the database support?

Where will this data come from? Think about the ways that your company or a company of your choice may capture data on its customers. Write down as many data sources as you can.

Remember, data needs to be kept up to date. This is a legal obligation under the 1998 Data Protection Act but is also vital for good practice in database marketing. Information has a life. It is estimated that professional marketers change their job every 18 months to three years. The lapse rates for trade press titles such as Marketing and Marketing Week are around 25–30 per cent. In the consumer market, data expires almost as quickly.

- **People move house**

  About 10 per cent of households move house each year. The Royal Mail keeps a list of movers called the National Change of Address File (NCOA). The Postal Address File (PAF) will also help. This is a list of all 26.5 million addresses in the UK and is regularly updated.
- **They die**

  It is dreadful to send mailings to dead people; it is ethically unacceptable and causes distress for families that have recently suffered bereavement. There are a number of services that help the marketer avoid this, for example The Bereavement Register and Mortascreen. These services allow companies to remove the deceased from their lists. The Deceased Register is a service based on cards completed at the Register Office and is supported by the Information Commissioner and Local Government. For further details, go to the DMA website or the Royal Mail website.
- **They are enticed away by the competition**

  By better, more relevant or cheaper offers.
- **They leave due to poor marketing**
- **They move out of the market; Club 18-30 has a clear target market!**
- **Their lifestyle changes, they marry or have children, or simply stop drinking or smoking or go on a diet**
- **Their financial circumstances change, they trade up or trade down**

Kimberly Clark: Nappy talk

Kimberly Clark markets the Huggies brand of nappies. Kimberly Clark has around two and a half years to sell the estimated 4,500 nappies that the average child uses in this time. They try to ensure that every nappy used is a Huggies nappy. This involves a range of broad-scale communications and a series of data-driven targeted direct marketing communications.

The Huggies Mother and Baby Club recruits members through the Bounty list, a list of expecting mothers that is compiled through responses to take ones and other media distributed to pregnant women. The women sign up for a range of free samples including Huggies nappies that are delivered after the delivery of the child.

A series of targeted communications is also delivered to the family covering the period from the date of birth to potty training. Among these is a series of publications that provide information on care and other elements of child rearing. These include free samples and coupons.

The publications are seen as valuable in themselves. They cover the following:

- Step 1   Pregnancy
- Step 2   Birth and early days
- Step 3   Reaching out to the world
- Step 4   Sitting up
- Step 5   Crawling everywhere
- Step 6   First steps
- Step 7   Toddler days

The publications deepen and strengthen the relationship between customers and the brand at a crucial time of life and the trust developed during this time sustains other brands in the Kimberly Clark family.

Data verification, capture, maintenance and enhancement

Data verification is important. A regular review of the data is important. Data fields should be reviewed to check that they are up to date and that they hold the data they are supposed to hold. We need to check if the data is usable and if not determine what we have to do to make use of the data? As we said earlier we also need to check that we do not hold duplicate data.

De-duplication is an important part of the process of verifying data. Duplication of records may occur for a number of reasons, including keystroke error or other data entry problems, or simply the fact that volunteered information is not provided in a consistent way.

We may have two addresses with slightly different names, for example:

Lewis K	128 Greene St	SL6 8TY	12/8/62
Lewes Keith	128 Greene Ave	SL6 8PY	12/8/62.

These may be different people or the same person.

De-duplication ensures that we do not send multiple mailings or make repeat contacts in other ways.

There are a number of software solutions that allow for de-duplication of records. These packages can be set to different degrees of sensitivity and may be based on the number of matched characters and/or numbers or a string of digits or may allocate a weighting depending on the character of the data that is being assessed.

Reference tables may be used to help the verification of data. There are reference or look-up tables for titles, job description, brands, models of car and so on. These are crucial for the maintenance of data quality as they help reduce errors.

Formatting will be used to ensure that data is entered consistently, that it fits the fields and is presented in consistent style.

International databases have a range of issues around salutations, titles, address and postcode formats.

Verification and validation

It is important that data is entered correctly and is accurate; the process of verification and validation may mean that data is keyed in twice to ensure accuracy and where possible is verified against external data sources for example postal address data may be validated against the postal address file (PAF) run by the Royal Mail.

We may check that all product and communications codes are accurate by running entered data against a list of all codes.

We may check to validate the range of data within a field, for example income data may typically fall within a range of possible figures and a key stroke error may make the difference between thousands and millions.

Finally it is always recommended to carry out a visual check of a variety of data records.

Behind all data there will be an audit trail identifying when the data was captured, when it was last updated etc.

Hardware and software

There is a range of vendors in the market. There are dozens of questions that need to be asked. The key questions are:

- What type of system should we use mainframe, PC, or Cloud Systems?
- How much will the build cost and how long will it take?
- How much will maintenance cost?
- How easy is it to integrate with existing systems?
- How easy will it be to grow the system and how flexible is it?
- Do we have in-house expertise?
- What external support offered and how accessible is it?
- Analysis systems support
- Data capture, maintenance and enhancement
- Management issues – should the database be run in-house/out-of-house?

Database bureaux can host the database for your organisation and this has several advantages and disadvantages.

In-house operation has the following benefits:

- strategic orientation of the business should be assured;
- integration and access is manageable;
- greater control and ownership;
- cost may be lower.

However, there are some disadvantages:

- cost of hardware and consultancy may be significant;
- speed of development can be slow;
- service standards may be lower than those from an out-of-house provider;
- skills in IT and strategy may be weak;
- specialist processing skills may not be readily available.

  Database bureaux provide the following benefits:
- skills and systems are developed and tested;
- there are no fixed costs. You pay for what you get;
- it is fast to market;
- resources can be allocated to ensure prompt delivery and penalty clauses can be built in;
- performance measures can be built into the contract.

Often there is migration from the bureau into the organisation. This means that learning can take place at lower risk.

The usual approach is as follows:

- set-up at the bureau;

- sort out data issues;
- set up updates and enhancements;
- develop internally;
- run the two in parallel;
- import.

Building your database on a PC

As we have seen, the first point is to get your data into the PC domain. Next you may need to engage experts (internal, external or perhaps both) to design the database you require. These experts should help you define the design you need, file layouts and data selection requirements and the reports you will need on a regular basis.

For database interrogation it is a good idea to base your system on an off-the-shelf package like Access. You will identify certain standard operations that you will need on a regular basis. These include such things as:

- **Load a certain set of data from a specific source on a given day of the week** (this could be the number of responses received by the mail room last week or an automated update of email responses);
- **Produce a set of reports on the status of various aspects of the business at the end of each month** (number of new customers who have ordered; total value of new orders and so on).

These regular reports can be designed as 'push button' options whereby the operator has only to select a given 'hot key' to run these analyses. Such an approach minimises error, makes operations more efficient and allows operators to concentrate on more important tasks, such as actually checking the contents of the reports.

Such reports can be written into your database by your developer.

When choosing a software supplier choose an established company (as you would when choosing any other supplier). Ask to talk to their clients and take up references. Any reputable supplier will be happy to volunteer these details.

The initial software is only part of the story. You will need to strike up a partnership with this company, as there will be changes or upgrades required as new versions are developed. Suppliers should tell you about their testing and bug logging procedures.

A good supplier will keep you informed at every stage of development. If you are simply presented with a completed system you have had no chance to monitor or even steer the development. It can be very difficult to understand the workings of a system when you have not been party to its planning and evolution.

A final point is to ensure that your supplier caters for installation, training and on-going support. You are bound to have problems, bugs, questions and comments and you need a supplier that will cater for this.

Systems available range from bespoke fully integrated systems for multinationals to simple systems designed for SMEs. Costs and sophistication vary accordingly.

Look at the following sites for further information

Visit the following websites, browse the sites to identify the range and nature of the claims for CRM and supporting systems:

- www.ibm.com
- www.ncr.com
- www.oracle.com
- www.alterian.com
- www.salesforce.com

Another useful site is:

- www.comparecrm.com

The role of the database and customer relationship management

Customer relationship management (CRM) has been one of the business buzzwords of the last five years. It reflects the fact that marketing orientation must run through the entire enterprise. As organisations have come to recognise this, it has become clear that marketing is too important just to be the responsibility of the marketing 'department'; all parts of the business throughout the value chain, from suppliers to accounts and HR to our marketing intermediaries, have a role in promoting the organisation and its products and services.

CRM attempts to reflect the reality of the customer experience. It is an old marketing chestnut, but it is nonetheless true that customers do not recognise the output of organisations as 'sales promotion' or 'advertising' or 'sales force' activity. All they see is an organisation dealing with them as customers, potential customers (prospects) or lapsed customers, better or worse than another company.

Touching BMW

Research done for BMW by its award-winning below-the-line agency Archibald Ingall Stretton identified over 240 different ways in which a customer or prospect could come into contact with the BMW brand. Some of these are managed through communications planning, some can be controlled, perhaps through PR, some cannot be managed, for example word of mouth and day-to-day contact of customers with BMW drivers. The key output of this research was to provide BMW with a network analysis and allow them the opportunity to explore further the intensity and relevancy of these 'touchpoints' for customers.

CRM attempts to integrate an approach to customers that uses the information about them gleaned from multiple contact points to develop appropriate strategies to manage the customer experience to deliver a consistent customer experience that maximises mutual value from the relationship.

Gamble, Stone and Woodcock (2001) define CRM as 'an enterprise wide commitment to identify your named individual customers and create a relationship between your company and these customers so long as that relationship is mutually beneficial'.

It is important to realise that for many organisations 'CRM' is inevitably attached to 'systems'. However, as you can see from the above definition it is not necessary for CRM to be IT based and indeed the design of CRM programmes, as with all strategic decisions in business, should involve the matching of resources to opportunities. That is, the system design should be appropriate to the resource base of the organization and its planned future growth.

It is the IT systems that tend to cause most dissatisfaction. A survey by Gartner recently found that more than 55 per cent of managers were dissatisfied with the results of the implementation of CRM systems in their business.

The idea should be that CRM aligns the business more effectively with customers' needs and wants and promotes solutions to customers more effectively and as a result more efficiently. Too often we seem to focus on efficiency without recognising the impact that this has on effectiveness. If we raise expectations then we must deliver against these expectations.

In its optimum form, CRM integrates information sources, learns from this information and delivers a consistent targeted offer through multiple contact points.

Customer information sits at the heart of this and will include data from the following:
- websites
- dealers
- sales force
- accounts
- operation
- fulfilment and response handling
- call centres
- partners
- transaction data

As well as the marketing database.

A checklist for database systems and software would cover some or all of the following characteristics:
- cheap and off the shelf;
- widely used;
- are easy to use and train for;
- can be obtained through a large number of suppliers and developers;
- offer a wide range of options and applications including for example email and campaign management systems;
- are easier to link with other packages;
- designed for non-technical people to use;
- at the forefront of technology and flexible;
- well documented and well supported;
- enabled to supplement the standard off-the-shelf features with bespoke software additions.

External data sources

It is worth considering what external data might be available to help you enhance your database. External data helps to improve your understanding of your customers, gives you alternative ways of selecting records, and provides a useful source of new prospects. External data can be related to demographics and lifestyle information. We have looked at this in some detail in previous chapters but a brief summary is presented here to conclude this section.

Demographics

Demographics companies supply a system of categorising the country into a number of different demographic types. Each postcode in the country is assigned one of these types. This means that each customer on your database can be matched to a demographic type. When this is done across all of your customer records a demographic profile emerges.

As discussed earlier, popular demographic classification systems are ACORN and Mosaic. These are based on public domain data including the census, the edited electoral roll and County Court Judgement (CCJ) data. Key statistics such as car ownership (from the census), length of tenure (electoral roll), and any CCJs are put through cluster analysis to determine the classification system.

If you have a licence agreement with the demographics company, the codes can be used as a basis of selection. For instance, you could select all members of a Mosaic type who have spent more than £500 with you.

It can be very useful to have such additional data, although external data will never be as powerful as your own customer data. When a demographic code is allocated to a customer record, it does not refer to that customer as an individual, it refers to the neighbourhood in which that customer lives. Where demographics scores over your own customer data is that it covers the entire country.

Thus, if you know the profile of your current customers, you can apply this to find prospects who are likely to have similar needs and behaviour. You can profile your customer base and then:

- order similar names from cold (rented) lists;
- select media and advertising likely to be read or subscribed to by the sort of people who buy your products;
- identify areas of the country where your prospects are likely to live.

This final point introduces a whole study in itself. Many retailers use demographics to measure market potential. Thus if you know the sort of people who buy your products you can evaluate areas on the ground to judge the likely demand for your products. This is one of the ways supermarket companies determine whether a site is worth developing.

Lifestyle data

Lifestyle companies collect information on customers' lifestyles. The data is assembled from various sources; guarantee cards filled in, in return for an extended warranty; questionnaires inserted in magazines or mailed to previous respondents; competition entry forms and so on.

Marketers can buy lists on the basis of lifestyle data – for example you may wish to rent the names of 50,000 people in Northern England who earn more than £25,000 per year.

Lifestyle questionnaires have now been filled in by most adults and the data relates to individual not simply to neighbourhoods. Thus, though the number of addresses will be smaller, you are selecting on the basis of actual individual data so the 'fit' should be closer to your ideal requirements.

Another point to note is that the people who filled in the questionnaires are responsive and thus untypical of the country as a whole. However, as you will often be using such data as the basis for selecting names for a marketing offer this bias can sometimes be a benefit rather than a penalty.

Another way of using the lifestyle databases is to send your customer file to them for profiling. The lifestyle company matches your file against their data bank and allocates additional data such as income, car ownership and other factors you request. Typically only 25 per cent of your file will be matched but it is a much cheaper way of buying information than traditional market research.

After this exercise you will have a good idea of income, car ownership, age, hobbies, readership habits and so on. If you set up a licence agreement with the company you can use these data for selection purposes. The lifestyle company can also supply you with names and addresses of prospects whose profile matches that of your customers. Such agreements have to be carefully negotiated with the data owners.

As a general rule, the hierarchy of data is:

- **your own customer data** – most powerful as it relates to your customers and their existing relationship with you;
- **lifestyle data** – as it relates to individuals by name and address;
- **demographic data** – dealing as it does with the characteristics of neighbourhoods rather than households.

The opposite side to this coin is of course that customer data is only available for your own customer base; lifestyle data to those people who have filled out a questionnaire and demographic data is universal.

Summarising this section:

- Demographics companies allocate codes based on public domain data;
- Codes are allocated to postcodes and thus represent the characteristics of neighbourhoods rather than households;
- Data is thus not as powerful as lifestyle or individual data;
- All postcodes have been allocated a demographic code;
- It is used to profile existing customers on the assumption that prospects will be of the same profile;
- Useful for site location studies, general targeting, prospecting and measurement of market potential;
- Lifestyle companies collect data about individuals via questionnaires;
- If you send a file for profiling 35 per cent would be a good match rate (as opposed to almost 100 per cent with demographic coding);
- Lifestyle data is more powerful as it relates to individuals rather than areas;
- A company's own data is the most powerful of all (though clearly only refers to one's own customer base and thus has little roll-out potential).

Data warehousing and data mining

The amount of data collected by organisations today has been causing some difficulty. Tesco's Clubcard scheme, which has been very successful, generates huge amounts of customer data. Dunn Humby manages this process very well, and Tesco is beginning to work very tight segmentation models from this data. But it has taken some time to develop.

Data warehousing aggregates data form multiple locations and allows for quick interrogation on any variable. It should be available through the organisation and is often accessed through a very user-friendly Web interface with the database via the companies' intranet. The danger is that the information collected is not relevant and the ease with which enquiries can be made create information overload. We are all aware of the amount of information we now have access to and the old maxim 'information is power' remains true, but information without intelligence is nothing!

The increased sophistication of software and hardware has allowed the process of data mining to emerge. This is the idea of searching databases for unseen connections between apparently unrelated data sets, this is facilitated through the use of neural nets. It can be objective driven or simply be a random process of exploring statistically valid and commercially relevant connections.

SUMMARY

We started this chapter by looking at the move towards customer relationship management and the central role of the database to this idea. Despite the developments in IT, the database remains a problem area for many businesses.

We saw that as for almost everything in direct marketing the starting point for the design of the database is the customer.

We saw that the information fuelling the database is often drawn for other areas of the business, including accounts, customer care, sales management, or facilities management systems.

We looked in detail at the various uses of the database. These were:
- developing selective cost-efficient relationships;
- providing reports on marketing activity;
- segmenting our customers into more manageable groups;
- targeting groups with particular messages;
- managing these groups for maximum profit.

Segmentation and targeting were seen as central applications of the database and the ability to cost-effectively target communications and products to improve our long-term marketing position was central to this.

We looked in details at the techniques used to segment the customer base these included:
- regression analysis;
- CHAID;
- cluster analysis;
- neural networks.

We saw that it is possible to carry out sophisticated analysis of the database using tools such as SPSS and SAS. However, at least a basic knowledge is require of statistics in order to understand and to communicate the results

We looked at the *Daily Telegraph*'s customer relationship programme and using this we explored the value of developing customer relationships:

- customers are different;
- they respond better to targeted messages;
- we can acquire customers and retain customers more effectively;
- the database helps manage this process discretely and efficiently.

We looked at the process involved in developing customer relationships.

First, what data is needed?

- data for current activity, including contact data;
- profiling data including family size and lifestyle;
- data aiding future activity, including response history and timings;
- data relating to the market, including competition and supply patterns.

Second, where does the data come from? We explored the range of internal and external sources available.

Third, how can it be captured? We saw that data capture can be handled in-house or through an external bureau. We looked at the software available to help the process.

Fourth, how is it kept up to date? We looked at the need for regular communication and cross checks with external databases. To manage this process the need for de-duplication was stressed and the ways of managing this process were discussed in detail.

The use of the database was explored in detail. Uses included:

- planning;
- contact strategy;
- data processing;
- response handling;
- lead processing;
- campaign management and reporting;
- satisfaction surveys;
- analysis;
- data maintenance.

We saw how the database works to help us manage these activities and looked at the technical specification required to support the database.

We explored the advantages of desk top systems, which included:

- cost;
- flexibility;

- data portability;
- they are generally at the forefront of technology;
- they are becoming really fast;
- ease of use and accessibility.

In Chapter 6 we will see that Moore's Law, and the pace of change in computing power, means that system capability is improving constantly.

We went on to look at the range of software supporting marketing activity and saw that the recording, storing, transferring and analysis of data is being made easier by the month.

Recent development in system design allows the cheap construction of marketing databases that can be widely used and understood by non-technical staff.

We went on to explore the integration of external source with our internal data looking at demographic and lifestyle lists.

Finally we looked at data warehousing and data mining and the use of online analysis and processing.

REVIEW QUESTIONS

1. What are the benefits of using a marketing database, what are the difficulties?
2. Where do we obtain data to populate the database?
3. List five common uses of a marketing database.
4. What is the Pareto Principle, and what is its relevance in direct marketing?
5. Why do we segment the customer base?
6. List four techniques that help us segment the marketing base.
7. What is CHAID analysis?
8. What are the benefits of retaining customers?
9. What are the four types of data required to maintain customer relationships?
10. List five sources of external data.
11. What is de-duplication?
12. What are the characteristics of a marketing database that allow various applications to be supported?
13. What are the advantages of microcomputers in managing the customer database?
14. What external data sources are available to help enhance internally generated data?
15. What is data mining?

EXERCISE

You are a local restaurant manager who has recently been on an IDM training course on direct and database marketing. You have decided to set up your own marketing database for your business using Microsoft Access.

What information would you keep on the database?
How would you acquire and maintain the data?
What marketing applications would the database support?

CHAPTER 6
DEVELOPING THE STRATEGIC PLAN

IN THIS CHAPTER

We will discuss the foundation of all successful marketing campaigns – the strategic planning process.

After completing this chapter you should be able to:
- Understand the role of strategic planning in successful direct and digital marketing
- Be able to understand and apply a structure for strategic planning
- Be able to use basic analysis tools such as PESTEL analysis and SWOT analysis
- Set solid and quantified marketing objectives for new business and retained business
- Develop strategic options and decide on the best approach to achieve objectives
- Understand the role of review, measurement and contingency planning
- Link strategic planning to campaign planning in order to maximise contribution

Specific topics include:
- The structure of the strategic marketing plan
- The use of SWOT, PESTEL, competitor reviews and similar analysis tools
- Objectives, strategies and tactics – understanding the terminology
- Planning and the brand
- Planning for the customer journey
- The role of research
- ROI, LTV and other evaluation methods
- Links and references to sources of market and marketing information
- Summary

INTRODUCTION

So far we have looked at the nature of direct marketing and the new digital marketing landscape. We understand that customers' lives are far more complex than they have ever been. As marketers we have a range of ways of communicating our message and promoting our products and these include online and offline media. Almost anything can carry a marketing message. A herd of cows with branded blankets over them were used to promote *The Sun* newspaper to potential readers travelling to London from Southend. People have had temporary tattoos placed on their foreheads and asked to sit on the London Underground in order to promote brands.

More about media choices and planning later.

However, it is clear that the decisions marketers have to make are more complex and more challenging than ever before. This is why the substantial chapters of the book begin with the role of data, research and insight, and information. Peter Chisnall, in his book on marketing research, calls information the raw material of management. If we are better able to understand our customers, how they live their lives, where they go for information, and how they make decisions, we should be in a better position to create and deliver value to them. This means they will be more inclined to buy from us, stay with us, recommend our products and services to their friends and family and in doing so deliver value back into the company.

You may be thinking that this is simple common sense and in a way you are right. It is clear that revenue and profits come from customers and if we deliver what they want we should be successful and remain so.

Business is not always as simple. There are many examples of businesses which have lost sight of this basic principle. Marks and Spencer struggled to come to terms with changes in British tastes in fashion for several years. Woolworths failed to come to terms with changes in the way that we shop for music and film amongst other things. Kodak and 'Encyclopaedia Britannica' are examples of companies whose business model has had to change dramatically over the last few years.

Think about the telecommunications market. Senior marketing executives at BT will have seen their business change from a state-run monopoly to a private business operating in a highly competitive global marketplace. They may have joined their business when mobile phones were the size of bricks and the Internet was just beginning to emerge as a serious commercial consideration. Voice Over Internet Protocol (VOIP) and Skype would have not been thought about and SMS was simply a tool for BT engineers to communicate about technical issues.

FedEx is one of the world's largest airlines judging by the number of planes it operates. The promise it makes is amazing if we really consider it carefully. To deliver a package in New York within 24 hours of collecting it from a London address is a phenomenal feat of logistics management. It would not be surprising if occasionally the focus of the business were on its operational activity rather than purely focusing on its customers.

- Rosbeth Moss Kantor describes managing business as 'dancing on the moving carpet'.
- Change is endemic and change within businesses is not easy to bring about.
- Keeping close to customers whilst managing the business is not always easy.

Planning is the process that helps us reconcile the needs of the firm to make money (typically) in a turbulent, changing and competitive world from customers who needs change over time.

It delivers the promise of marketing and it may be helpful to consider a basic definition. There are several but we prefer the definition of the American Marketing Association

> Marketing is the activity, set of institutions, and processes for creating, communicating, delivering, and exchanging offerings that have value for customers, clients, partners, and society at large. American Marketing Association (AMA), 2007

Note that the definition includes the fact that marketing produces exchanges that satisfy both parties – customers, and the goals of clients and partners. Satisfaction may mean profit from the organisation's point of view, although if we are working in fundraising or any other not for profit sector, it may have a different meaning.

Planning has to reconcile several different dimensions:

- the nature of the organisation, its resources and goals;
- the changing business environment in which it operates;
- the competition;
- the customers it serves.

Now and into the future, this is not a simple task.

The planning process

Consider this quote from General Eisenhower when engaged in the planning for the Normandy invasion at the end of the Second World War:

'The plan is nothing, planning is everything.'

This is a bit of a business chestnut now and has been used by many CEOs when talking about their business planning process. What it reflects is that very often the output of the planning process varies as it is delivered due to some unforeseen event, for example a new competitor or a new piece of regulation. However, this does not undermine the value of planning and an effective plan will try to forecast and account for the range of potential changes in the market and put in place contingency plans in case these changes occur.

If we consider the problems created in the 2009–10 credit crunch we can see the results of some companies' failure to plan adequately for the downside risk of some of their activities.

What the planning process tries to do is to bridge the gap between the organisation, its customers and places this in the context in which commercial activity takes place.

This is actually one of the downsides of a direct approach to marketing. The fact that direct marketing is so rich with transactional data encourages some companies to focus quite narrowly on response. A 2 per cent response to an email campaign may seem like good news but if our competitors are achieving 5 per cent we are going backwards.

A small UK-based breakfast cereal company ran a test on a mailing to a selected group of customers and potential customers. The mailing focused on sustainability and healthy eating.

It showed the field that the grains were grown in, the farmer who harvested the grains and offered discounts on the final product. The response to the mailing was excellent so much so that if the campaign had been rolled out it would have increased the company's share of the Ready to

Eat breakfast cereals market by 2 per cent value. The company decided not to roll out.

Why do you think this was?

First, the company competed in a sector that was under pressure. Fewer people than ever are having a 'proper' breakfast. More people eat breakfast on the move or skip breakfast. This means that volume sales are very steady and value is created by higher unit prices for added value products. The small UK company competes in the market against Nestlé, Weetabix, General Mills, Kellogg's and Quaker which are some of the world's largest food companies. Rightly it was decided that the risk of retaliation from these companies was too great. The risk included the end of the company's independence. The approach to response data was correct and enabled a correct judgement to be made. The strength of direct marketing is its use of data; a weakness that it sometimes focuses too narrowly.

Strategic planning reconciles the strengths of direct marketing's bottom up approach to planning with the need to understand the bigger, top down picture.

So, what does the process look like?

First of all we need to understand that the marketing plan is only one part of the bigger approach to planning that is carried out on a corporate level, and that may need to reconcile the requirements of several business units and functions with the business. These may include finance operations and HR.

Figure 6.1: Marketing planning and the corporate context

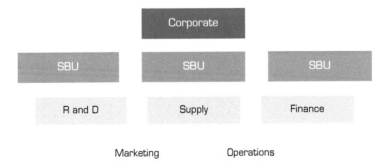

The planning process at whatever level it is set follows a similar pattern. Often this is described as a journey:

- Where are we now?
- Where do we want to be?
- How can we get there?
- How can we best get there?
- How will we know when we have arrived?
- What resources do we have to carry out our plans?

Marketing planning concerns the products and services of the organisation and the customers and clients of the organisation and considers how best to bring the two together.

Marketing planning concerns the impact of the other functional areas on customer acquisition and relationships and occurs over a shorter timescale, typically one to three years as opposed to three to ten years for corporate planning.

This does not happen in isolation. You have to work within a rapidly changing business environment, with customers who are sometimes hard to understand and hard to reach in the face of competitors who are trying to do exactly the same.

The final structure of the plan is more complex than the journey model and a full structure is presented below as a proforma.

Figure 6.2: The marketing plan structure

Procedural and reporting elements
1.   Identification Information
2.   Executive Summary
3.   Terms of Reference
4.   Procedure
Where are we now?
5.   Marketing Audit and Issue Analysis
Where do we want to be?
6.   Objectives
How can we get there?
7.   Strategy
How can we best get there?
8.   Operating Plan
9.   Contingency Plan
How will we know when we have arrived?
10.   Budget
11.   Appendices

We will go through each of the elements in turn but before we do so, let's clear up an area that can cause confusion: the difference between objectives, strategies and tactics.

Objectives

Marketing objectives answer the question:

'Where are we going?'

A company may have different objectives for each of its divisions, product groups, and so on.

The nature of objectives in business is determined by the area of the business to which they relate.

Corporate objectives tend to relate directly to return on shareholders' investment, which may impact on marketing as, for example, we may be charged with keeping customers for longer or acquiring customers at a lower cost or developing new product lines. However, corporate objectives will also relate to operations and HR as these higher level objectives may be achieved in a variety of ways, and impact upon all the functional areas of the business.

Marketing planning can be compared with a section of the orchestra. Unless it is combined successfully with the other areas of the business we will produce discord; each section and each player has to perform effectively to deliver the overall effect. Each section has its own area of expertise and skills.

Marketing skills relate to our knowledge of customers and the products and services we market and the range of tools we have to deliver this. This means that overall marketing objectives should relate to the customer groups that the organisation is serving and the products and services we are providing to them. Simply put, marketing objectives relate to customers and products. However, objectives based simply on products are out of step with the way markets are changing. It is essential that we think in terms of setting objectives and developing strategies for different customer groups.

One way to think about the way that objective setting works in marketing and how it contrasts with strategy is to consider the fact that objectives usually can be written as TO, and strategy is usually written as BY.

Objective

TO acquire 1,500 new customers at a cost of £100 each with an average order value of £250 by the end of the financial year.

Strategy

BY developing a direct response campaign using a range of online display advertising and print in selected media.

Tactics

Among others:

- To place banner ads on mums.net and babycentre.com
- To buy space in *Mother and Baby* magazine

Marketing objectives should always be stated in numeric terms, e.g. percentage share of customer sought or, more usually in direct marketing, desired percentage increase in profit or revenue.

A long-term marketing objective might be, for example, 'To increase our share of the overall market by 20 per cent and our profit margin by 5 per cent.'

However, this in itself is not enough. To qualify for the description a marketing objective must also be timed, otherwise how can you possibly measure your progress towards it? So the objectives above should be developed into something like:

'To increase our share of the overall market by 20 per cent by the end of financial year 2010–11, and our profit margin by 5 per cent in the same time period.'

Now you have an objective that can be measured. These long-term objectives can now be broken down into annual (or even quarterly) goals so you can evaluate your progress in more manageable units and take corrective action if you are not meeting your targets.

Strategies

Strategies answer the question 'How will we get there?' They are broad guidelines but should be described numerically where possible.

A strategy might be 'I am going to introduce a younger feel to all our promotional activity and increase our media coverage of the under-25 market by 30 per cent.' Again this must be accompanied by a time frame.

Strategic marketing plans (SMPs) are the all-important middle ground between long-term objectives and short-term tactics.

Tactics

Tactics (or action plans) answer the question 'What exactly are we going to do?'

An example might be 'We'll sponsor an up-and-coming rock band and feature them heavily in our next promotion to measure the effect on sales.' Your organisation might have a number of objectives, and for each objective there may be a choice of competing strategies. Each strategy, in turn, may employ a number of tactics simultaneously. All this may sound like nit-picking, but in practice a great deal of money and energy is wasted by confusing these terms. Too often you will see management examples where objectives are set without realising that strategies and tactics are needed to bring them about. You will also see companies obsessed with tactics with no strategy or objectives in place to steer the tacticians.

Procedural and presentation issues

The marketing plan is not a document to be put away and ignored. It is a plan for action and specifies responsibilities, timetables and budgets. Therefore it needs to be presented in a way that is clear and accessible. The communication of the plan may be through a variety of means including formal presentations, meetings and discussions. The end point of this process is that all parties to the plan know their role within it and are aware of the goals, dependencies and key milestones that will need to be met.

At the heart of the process lies the written plan. The plan is an action-oriented document and it must be designed to be read, understood and acted upon. The plan should be as concise as possible. It should contain only key information; supporting detail and background analysis can be put into appendices. The basic presentation should be professional and easy to read. All tables and charts should be given a title and sourced. The font size should be adequate (at least 12pt is recommended) and it should be double spaced. There should be a clear contents page and lists of figures and tables. Tables of data should be clearly labelled, with units, for example volume or value, specified. If consumer research is presented then the base sample size should always be included. Each section should begin on a new page and be clearly numbered with sub sections also numbered.

A word on style

Style and tone should be business-like, with crisp, direct prose. It should be factual wherever possible, avoiding florid language (metaphors, similes etc).

Presentation and layout should be attractive and easy to read. Use headings, sub-heads, numbering systems and paragraph indents. Statistical data should be clearly presented and concise.

Strategic plan presentation checklist:

- Confine raw data to appendices
- Put data of more than half a page in an appendix
- Tables should summarise data wherever possible
- Data should be rounded up or down to significant whole numbers
- Data with trends should be in graph form – and shouldn't be buried in prose
- Tables should have headings and sources
- Pie-charts, bar charts and other such visuals should be used whenever possible
- If data require explanation, put the explanation next to the table, preferably on the same page
- Try to avoid referring frequently to data in appendices – if they are that important, put them in summary table form in the text

The report should contain a master timetable. Presented as a Gantt chart or PERT chart (see Chapter 8 on campaign planning). Individual or department schedules should also be shown with key dependencies outlined.

Include an executive summary before the contents page. The executive summary is a very important part of the document as it is the section most likely to be read by all staff, including senior directors.

Identification

The first sections are procedural. Identification information simply lays out the details of the plan and includes the following information:

- To
- From
- Date
- Title
- Reference

Contents page

All pages and sections should be numbered and tables, figures and appendices should be separately listed.

Executive summary

An important part of the report writing process that is key to making a good first impression and should summarise your plan simply. The summary should cover all relevant section of the plan including finances and where possible should cover no more than one page. It may run to more but should never exceed two to three pages.

It should cover at least the core

- Objectives
- Findings
- Recommendations
- Top line budget

Terms of reference – these again are procedural elements and they contain a brief description of events which gave rise to the report (e.g. 'This report was requested following our meeting on August 19th when we discussed…')

Procedure or methodology – this contains a brief description of the methods you used, the major data sources you used etc.

Section one of the marketing plan

The marketing audit or situation analysis

This is likely to be one of the most important parts of the plan.

Kotler describes the audit as:

'… *a comprehensive, systematic, independent and periodic examination of a company's - or business unit's - marketing environment, objectives, strategies and activities with a view to determining problem areas and opportunities and recommending a plan of action to improve the company's marketing performance.'*

It is important to realise that the quality of your work here will determine the quality of your plan and you need to establish current resources and position in the market, with your customers, and relative to your competitors in a dynamic environment.

It is not the raw data that is most important but the analysis of this data and what we do with it.

Remember you need to reconcile internal resources with external opportunity within the broader business environment.

So what do we need to know?

- Internal and external factors

We always start with external factors. These are the factors that typically lie outside our control but which influence our ability to do business. This includes a broad environmental analysis or PESTEL analysis, a market analysis and a competitor analysis. It is also known as a macro analysis.

PESTEL analyses

The acronym PESTEL stands for:

P = political factors

E = economic factors

S = social factors

T = technological factors

E = environmental factors

L = legal factors

Other writers include other elements, including:

- ethical factors
- industrial factors
- international factors

Still others will include competitor analysis as part of this activity.

So you may read about

- Pest
- Slept
- Steeple
- Plestie
- Plestie + C

It really doesn't matter what device you use to construct the analysis, the key thing is to understand those forces that lie outside the direct control of the organisation that may prevent you from doing business.

Many companies try to control these uncontrollable factors and the objectives of the lobbying industry and the corporate PR function are to exert influence where possible.

What most companies do is to build these factors into their plans, aiming to develop scenarios and contingencies to reduce their negative impact and to optimise any positive outcome.

The PESTEL analysis is an important part of the Situation Analysis and it is concerned with establishing the current situation in order to help understand what might happen in the future. There will always be uncertainty and risk. Planning seeks to reduce the levels of risk to which the organisation is subjected. And we may get it wrong; the external environment is dynamic.

These are some quotes from old PESTEL analyses:

- It is unlikely that inflation will ever fall below 5 per cent
- Import penetration will never be above 15 per cent
- Price of oil will never exceed $2 per barrel
- Markets will grow at 10 per cent per annum
- Consumer movement is irrelevant
- Style matters more than quality
- 640k of memory should be enough for anyone

■ There will be a world market for five computers

Sources of information for the PESTEL analysis

Obtaining relevant information and then presenting it succinctly is the difficult part of the PESTEL analysis.

There is a vast range of data sources, and the emergence of the Internet as a key information consolidator and provider has increased the availability of information. It has increased access to previously remote information, for example data held overseas, and it has increased the ability to distribute this information.

Data on markets and organisations can be obtained from many different sources. Able researchers will be flexible and innovative in their approach to information searches, and the most unlikely sources can reveal important information.

For example, the publications of the HR department in a certain company revealed staffing levels at particular factories in India, which had been classified as confidential by the corporate affairs and marketing departments.

A full list of sources is available in the appendices. However, a summary of types of sources is included below. Over time you will develop you own specific list of trusted information brokers. This will be a valuable asset as you develop your career.

List of sources

The best sources of help in this area are the lists and directories of specialist publishers such as:
■ Euromonitor and Croners: Euromonitor publishes a range of information directories. Croners Executive Companion and Croners Office Companion include a list of business information services;
■ IMRI publishes a list of market research reports and agencies worldwide.

Specialist research agencies

There are many specialist research agencies that can help and organisations such as the Henley Centre Headlight Vision, the Future Foundation or the OECD provide solid research-based analysis than can add real value to the planning process.

Governments

Governments publish vast quantities of data about the economy and society. Much of this data forms the basis of commercial services, provided at some cost by research firms. It is the raw material of good PESTEL analyses. These publications are not expensive and it is always worth checking to see what is available.

There is also a statistical service for the European Union and this provides comparative data across all member countries.

Other national governments have their own statistical services and these can normally be accessed online.

Trade organisations

These are a broad range of information providers that include:

- trade associations
- the trade press
- professional institutes
- chambers of commerce
- regulatory bodies and pressure groups.

Trade associations

These exist for almost every industrial sector. Some publish amazing details on their members' activities. Associations such as ESOMAR publish annual reviews of the market research industry for its members.

Trade press

Trade press is invaluable as a source of up-to-date information on markets and companies. Almost every trade is represented, and titles such as *Pig Farmer Weekly, Tunnels and Tunnelling, Wood Based Panelling International, The Grocer, Advertising Age* and *Off Licence News* give an indication of the range of sources that are available.

The journalists quickly become experts in their field and are worth contacting.

Professional institutes

These institutes generally represent individuals within the profession and some provide excellent data on their industries.

Chambers of commerce

These can be very helpful for organisations, particularly in overseas markets, where commitment to the Chambers' mission is sometimes greater than in the United Kingdom.

Regulatory bodies and pressure groups

The activities of organisations like the Financial Services Authority, the Advertising Standards Authority and Ofcom generate information on the sectors they cover.

Pressure groups like Greenpeace or Action on Smoking and Health (Ash) can provide data on the industries they monitor and causes they represent. For instance, www.ash.org.uk has a statistical report on smoking and smoking behaviour.

Trade unions and other member organisations can provide useful data. For example, the Salmon and Trout Association covers the market for fly fishing through its activities aimed at preserving habitat and stocks.

Financial data

The activities of investment houses and stockbrokers produce regular reports on the activities of their target companies. The briefings that inform these reports often contain useful market and strategic data that can be extremely revealing.

The press

The *Financial Times* and *Wall Street Journal* are required reading for marketing professionals and their services include online archives. Other national and local press can be accessed for relevant data.

SPECIALIST SERVICES

Information about companies

The best source of information in the United Kingdom is Companies House; all companies over a certain size are obliged by law to lodge financial and other information at Companies House. The Companies House website also has a range of links to international disclosure of company data.

Other organisations provide information on companies. Services such as Dun and Bradstreet and Kompass are excellent commercial sources of company information.

Information on markets

There are hundreds of companies providing secondary or published data on markets.

Some of the more important providers include

Nielsen

Nielsen provides data on media and advertising spend and a range of data to industry. See www.acnielsen.co.uk.

BMRB

BMRB is a leading UK research agency that provides the Target Group Index (TGI) which is a valuable resource to marketers and allows customer data to be enhanced in a number of ways. It also provides a useful insight into diverse markets.

The Target Group Index (TGI) is a continuous survey where data collection runs throughout the year so that seasonality does not skew results. TGI yields information on the usage of more than 4,000 brands in 500 product areas for those aged 15 + .

It is updated four times a year on a rolling quarterly basis.

The survey is based on a sample size of circa 25,000 interviews per annum. Results are weighted to match known demographic profiles and re-weighted to the National Readership Survey.

A self-completion questionnaire is placed with selected respondents at the end of BMRB's Access Omnibus survey.

TGI data are used to assist the understanding of target markets to aid marketing and advertising decisions. The data helps the users of TGI to optimise their marketing and advertising receipts/expenditures. See www.bmrb-tgi.co.uk.

Many companies exist to provide services to industry in the area of secondary research.

Syndicated research services

Companies like Mintel, Euromonitor, and Frost and Sullivan provide what are known as syndicated or multi-client studies on a huge range of markets. These are published market research studies that are available to anybody who wishes to buy them.

Prices range from a few hundred to many thousands of pounds depending on the complexity of the report and number of markets covered.

Typically, reports will cover
- Market size, structure and trends
- Import, export and production data
- Key players' competitive profiles including financial data
- Market share data
- Advertising and marketing communications spend.

Online aggregators

The development of the Internet and its diverse capabilities has lead to the emergence of a new breed of information providers who aggregate or bring together information from diverse sources and allow access on a subscription basis or for a one-off payment.

Examples include general services like Hoovers, Profound and Lexis Nexis, and specialist services like the World Advertising Research Centre (WARC) or MAD, which covers the UK marketing press.

These may contain translations from a range of international publications.

Information on online markets

There is a great deal of information on the Internet on online markets. Not all of it is reliable. The government, as indicated above, is often the most reliable source and there are more reputable suppliers in the market. The best sources for online research are often based in the United States, but there are a number of other useful suppliers.

Other techniques include
- **Environmental scanning**
  This technique refers to the semi formal process of gathering data about the market from diverse secondary sources. These may include the general and trade press.
- **Delphi studies**
  The name is taken from the ancient Greek oracle at Delphi. In this technique we take notice of the view of industry experts to construct a forecast of the future of the market and the environment impacting on it.
- **Brainstorming**
  Is a similar technique but involves a panel of interested parties who simply express any views as to the likelihood of occurrence and the impact of any event in the market. The most extreme views can be expressed in a neutral and non-judgemental atmosphere. These are then evaluated and further analysed to create a focused approach to the problem.
- **Scenario planning**
  This was made famous at Shell. We create a range of different scenarios, which may emerge as the result of events in the environment, and we plan against these potential scenarios

▪ **Cross impact analysis**

This technique attempts to extrapolate the impact of variables on one another for example the recent foot and mouth outbreak in the UK has impact across a range of industries, not just farming, but all those support industries that supply the agricultural sector.

Whatever techniques are used there is a common sequence of activity in carrying out the external analysis.

▪ Monitor

Trends in the task environment, external consultants may be used.

▪ Identify

Trends with significance for the firm, senior executives will establish criteria for relevance.

▪ Evaluate

Significance of trends in the current product markets.

▪ Forecast

Direction of trends identified.

▪ Evaluate

Against long-term strategic development of the firm.

When carrying out a situation analysis we must ensure the trends we are evaluating are reviewed regularly and that clear criteria are set to enable analysis of the impact of changes. We then need to generate a standard report and allocate responsibilities for dealing with the impact.

With a little work and a lot of thought it is possible for any company to put together a sophisticated analysis of the business environment. In presenting the data it is important to spell out the implications for the organisation. Some good analyses simply ask the question 'Which means?' after the particular factor under consideration. Others go into much more detail indicating the likely impact of the factor the competitor reaction, the research required to monitor the area and then ranking the factors in order of the severity of their impact. We will look at this under risk assessment matrices.

How you present the data is up to you but the key point to avoid is a bland list of macro economic forecasts barely related to the company. Equally you should avoid over presenting the data. Remember the plan is to be acted upon and must be read and understood.

Below are some examples of PESTEL factors.

The socio-demographic environment

▪ Baby boomers grow old – what is the impact of the ageing population?
▪ Cocooning – we are scared to leave our homes due to fear of crime, road rage, trolley rage, traffic congestion
▪ Single parents – what is a family?
▪ Single occupancy – in the region of 1.5million new homes are required
▪ The grey panthers – the hormone- and financially-enriched fiftysomethings
▪ The growth in tertiary education
▪ Euro youth

- Ethnicity – the rise of a black and Asian middle class
- The pink pound – the gay market
- The end of the nuclear family
- Women working outside the home
- Population demographics
- Gender, age, ethnicity, race, religion, working age population
- Income distribution
- Social mobility and stratification
- Lifestyle changes
- Attitudes to work and leisure
- Consumerism
- Levels of education and training
- Social change and changing social attitudes

The economic environment

- GNP vs income distribution – the new rich
- The new poor
- Time poor/wage rich
- The Euro zone
- Interest rate convergence
- Consumer spending v. saving
- Employment – full time, part time, contract work
- Tax and spend – what about our disposable income?
- Recession?
- Dot com, dot gone

Political legal environment

- EU broadening and deepening
- EU legislation, data protection
- Minimum wage – how much?
- End of public sector boom
- Environmental protection – recycle, tax incentives
- Interest groups – data privacy
- European and global issues
- Competition law
- Employment law
- Health and safety
- Product safety
- Environmental protection laws
- Business ownership laws
- Company law

- Disclosure laws
- Planning and property law

The technological environment

- Digital convergence
- Social media
- iTV
- Analogue turn off
- Networks
- Moore's Law – costs declining
- Database integration
- Life cycle contraction
- Replication
- Government spending on research
- Government and industry focus on technological effort
- New discoveries/developments
- Speed of technology transfer
- Rates of obsolescence
- Levels of research and development
- Subsidies for research and development

Environment

- Legislation
- Ethical platforms
- Green issues
- Resource management
- Waste disposal
- Energy consumption
- Impact of fossil fuels
- Raw material resource depletion
- Air and soil contamination
- Protection of the environment
- Conservation
- Recycling
- Alternative forms of energy

Key aspects of PESTEL analysis

- It is not just a bland list
- It is about understanding drivers of change
- This will mean different factors have a different influence
- Combined outputs maybe important

Risk evaluation matrices

A risk evaluation matrix can help classify some of the variable in a PESTEL analysis.

As you can see in the table below the factors can be classified and assessed under the headings and this can encourage real insight and analysis.

Figure 6.3: Risk evaluation matrix

Issue PESTEL factor	Likelihood of occurrence Score/10	Impact Score/10	Threat or Salience Score Column 2x3

External analysis: market review

The next area to consider is the market itself. Whilst as direct marketers we understand that we are concerned with individual relationships and the value we can create from them we also need to place these relationships in a broader context to evaluate the potential in the market as a whole and the dynamics of that market.

A market review will consider the following elements where possible.

Market size

- Volume and value with trend data, growth rates, relevant market share data
- Distribution channels
- New product development and innovation rates
- Market structure in terms of product segmentation, for example the beer market might be broken down into lagers, ales, stouts, on trade v. off trade and so on
- Customer analysis. This will include analysis of our customer base and the market as a whole. It will draw on database and research analysis
- Customer insight, generic research and analysis of the customers in the market now and into the future this should cover the market as a whole and include current customers competitors' customers and prospects and suspects

Stakeholder analysis

Stakeholder analysis covers a review of those groups or stakeholders that are affected by or who influence our activity.

A UK telecommunications company weighs up every decision against a trade-off of the value created for different stakeholders.

Stakeholder analysis is an exercise in networking; it should include research into social, category and brand influencers – people (companies and individuals) who have a strong influencing power with customers and consumers.

The three factors to look at when determining stakeholders are:

1. How much stake they have in the organisation
2. How much influence – internal or external
3. How much 'attention grabbing' capacity – often used in conjunction with the media

Stakeholders may include:

- Staff
- Current customers
- Shareholders
- Local communities around the organisation
- Suppliers
- Alliances and partners
- Trade bodies
- Social, category and brand influencers
- Relevant media
- Directors
- Debtors and creditors
- Local and central government
- Consumer lobbies
- Unions
- Outside directors
- Licensing bodies
- Regulatory agencies
- Trade associations
- Environmental groups

Suppliers

Details about key suppliers should be included in the analysis where relevant.

Intermediaries

Analysis of key channel intermediaries may also be included.

A competitor review

This may involve Porter's Five Force's analysis (see following point) but should consider direct and indirect competition and assess where they are strong and weak relative to the organisation.

Porter's Five Forces Analysis

Porter's model describes the five forces that he believes influence any particular industry.

Using the five forces allows us to analyse the environment within which our organisation operates and suggest actions which can create advantage.

Figure 6.2: Porter's Five Forces Analysis

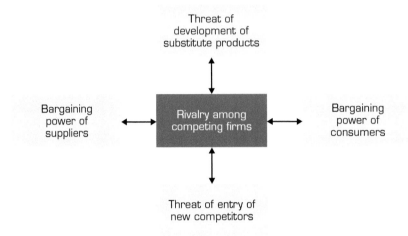

Source: Porter M. Competitive Strategy: Techniques for Analyzing Industries and Competitors, 1998, Free Press

Let's explore each of the elements in turn.

The threat of entry or barriers to entry

Successful industries with high levels of profit will always attract competitors. Rivalry will exist if barriers to entry are low however, certain industries have a high number of entry barriers.

These may include:

- high capital requirements are needed to enter the market;
- limited access to distribution channels;
- aggressive competition;
- legislation or government action to restrict entry to the market.

Bargaining power of consumers

Where buyer power is high then competing firms will have less flexibility in the way they market their products and services. This can create rivalry.

Buyer power is likely to be high when:

- there are a few major buyers;
- there are many small operators in the supplying industry;
- products are highly standardised;
- switching costs are low.

Bargaining power of suppliers

Where there are few alternative sources of supply, for example suppliers of raw materials, components, human resources and other expertise, supplier power is high and suppliers may charge high prices for supplying these scarce resources.

Supplier power is high when:
- there are few concentrated suppliers;
- the cost of switching are high;
- the supplier brand is powerful, e.g. Intel;
- suppliers' customers are fragmented and they have lower bargaining power.

Threat of developing substitute products
Threat of substitutes can arise when:
- customer needs can be fulfilled with other products;
- quality of the current product is low or high, leaving a gap in the market for alternatives;
- there's a generic substitution, for example a Harley Davidson rather than a second honeymoon;
- customers choose not to buy or to do without.

Rivalry among competing firms
This area draws conclusions from the output from the other four areas and classifies an industry in terms of the intensity of the competition.
Competitive rivalry is high when:
- there are low barriers to entry;
- there is a threat of substitutes;
- there are a large number of competitors with little differentiation;
- a company is failing;
- market growth is slow;
- there are high fixed costs in an industry and firms must produce and sell to cover these costs;
- there are high exit barriers and a company must remain in the industry and compete effectively.

Other areas to consider in the competitor review are:

The nature of competition
- Competition now.
- Five years from now.
- Sources of internal and external information about competitors.

Competitor's current strategy
How is a competitor currently competing across the major areas, for example online or offline communications, brand and reputation etc?

Capabilities
Strengths, weaknesses and level of awareness.

Competitor's future goals

What drives the competitor?

Other considerations here include:

- What is the competitor's likely response to our initiatives?
- Are they satisfied with their current position?
- How aggressive are their plans for expansion?
- What are their likely moves or strategy shifts?
- Where are they most vulnerable?
- What will provoke retaliation?
- Investment goals of competition
- Level of commitment in market sectors
- Strengths and limitations
- Changes to competitors' future strategies and their potential impact

Environmental (PESTEL) changes and their impact on competitors should also be considered.

This may deal with issues such as:

- Acquisition
- Deregulation
- Import penetration
- Distribution channels
- Technology developments
- Raw materials supply
- Legislation

To summarise, the external or macro audit includes:

- A PESTEL analysis with associated risk matrices
- Competitor review, maybe using Porter's Five Forces
- Market review
- Stakeholder analysis

We have also looked at the range of sources that are available to help us with the task.

Situation analysis – internal or micro analysis

We always start the audit with the external review as ultimately determines the limits of the organisation's activity. However, we also need to assess our own position within the market. This is the internal or micro part of the situation analysis.

Internal analysis should cover the following:

Financial analysis

A review of key financial measures including a review of the financial performance of brand and product portfolio.

Customer analysis

This will include, where possible, the value of the customer base now and into the future using lifetime value analyses. You can read more about this in Chapter 8.

It should include analysis at segment level and should include measures of acquisition and churn rates as well as relevant measures of customer satisfaction, brand perception, and where possible these should be benchmarked against the competition.

Internal resources

An analysis of the internal resources of the business should be made. This does not relate to the tangible resources of the business but intangible elements as well.

This may be developed under the 8Ms framework:

- Manpower
- Machines
- Marketing
- Management
- Money
- Materials
- Methods
- Management information

So we are beginning to reach the end of this phase of the plan. There are various ways in which the analysis can be brought together.

We might use various tools for portfolio analysis.

- BCG Matrix
- Directional Policy Matrices

The BCG matrix looks at the product portfolio in terms of the growth of the overall market and the relative market share of the products.

It categorises products in terms of the role they play in generating cash and the investment needed to maintain the products.

Accordingly the four quadrants of the matrix define four types of business:

Stars: High market growth and high market share

Generally, this unit should be retained by the business. Although it requires reinvestment to maintain its market share, the continued increase in the size of the market implies good future prospects.

Question marks: High market growth but low market share

Sometimes also called a 'problem child', the question posed here is whether the company should continue to invest and develop the unit so that its market share increases and therefore becomes a star.

Cash cows: Low market growth but high market share

Even if a market is mature, a company with a high market share can still provide good returns. A cash cow will need less investment than either stars or question marks.

Dogs: Low market growth and low market share

Where a company's market share is much less than its competitors and where the market is growing only slightly or is static, there seems very limited benefit to continue to invest in such a business. The matrix strongly implies that dogs should be divested.

Figure 6.5: The Boston Consulting Group Matrix

		Relative market share	
		High	**Low**
Market growth	**High**	Stars	Question Marks
	Low	Cash Cows	Dogs

Directional policy matrices generally look at industry attractiveness and company strengths.

Factors that may be counted as company strengths include:

Company strengths:
- Costs relative to the competition
- Financial resources
- The strength of the brand portfolio
- The nature and value of the customer base
- The sophistication of IT and systems infrastructure
- The relationship with distribution channels
- Management experience and skills
- The profit margins enjoyed on activity
- Fit with Critical Success Factors (CSFs)
- Relative market share
- Reputation/image
- The ability to manage and bargain with key suppliers
- Ability to match competitors' product quality or service standards

Factors that may indicate an attractive industry include:

Industry attractiveness:
- Market size
- The growth rate of the market

- Low customer churn rates
- High profit margins
- Intensity of competition
- Seasonality
- Cyclicality
- Resource requirements
- Social impact
- The vulnerability to regulation or legislation

These are generally plotted on a nine cell matrix.

Figure 6.6: Directional policy matrices

		Industry Attractiveness		
		High	Medium	Low
Business Strengths	**High**			
	Medium			
	Low			

The output from the matrix then suggests various strategic options and these are outlined in the table below.

Table 6.1: Directional Policy Matrices Strategic Options

Invest	Grow	Harvest	Divest
High Market Attractiveness High Business Strengths	High Market Attractiveness Low Business Strengths	Low Market Attractiveness High Business Strengths	Low Market Attractiveness Low Business Strengths
The ideal segment.	*The market potential is attractive but needs substantial investment to become successful.*	*Organisation has strengths in a market that has lost its attractiveness. Still allows short- and medium-term profits.*	*Not an attractive segment and strengths are below average. Only useful to supports a more profitable part of the business.*

Direct marketers can use this approach. One way it could be done is to look at customer segment attractiveness rather than market attractiveness. Instead of a macro approach to the definition of markets we could consider the value of customers and place this in the context of the market as a whole.

It is really important to realise that unless we link the two elements together we run a high risk of failing to understand and deal effectively with the bigger picture. We may have very profitable high value customers but if these exist within a market that is declining or under threat from competition or advances in technology then they will not sustain future profits.

Whether we choose to use the tools outlined above is a matter of their usefulness to the planning process. They can be difficult to use. The dimensions in the BCG matrix for example are difficult to populate in some sectors. The idea is to use tools that help you accomplish the task and use them in a thoughtful and appropriate fashion rather than blindly following the advice laid down in business books!

SWOT

One area that should be included is a SWOT analysis.

S   Strengths
W   Weaknesses
O   Opportunities
T   Threats

The SWOT analysis presents a summary of all the other analyses.

Strengths are company factors that give you competitive advantage.
Weaknesses are company factors that may work against you.

Strengths and weaknesses relate more to internal factors than to external but clearly there may be some overlap.

Opportunities are external factors that are likely to be in your favour.
Threats are external factors that may work to your disadvantage.

Tackle the OT list first, not the SW list.

By tackling the OT list first, you can rank the relative importance of your strengths and weaknesses in the light of the opportunities and threats that face you. Then you can establish priorities for improvement.

The OTs can be taken straight from the PESTEL analysis or the associated risk assessment.

The SWOT is really important as it tends to drive strategic decisions. The SWOT should:

- be realistic, **outcomes** of strengths are not strengths for example – 'we are a successful business' does not describe a strength;
- be detailed enough to be understood;

▪ be evidence based and specific to the organisation;
▪ represent an accurate picture of the organisation and its environment;
▪ be based on measurement where possible;
▪ prioritise;
▪ suggest actions.

One effective way of doing this is to simply add an extra column to the SWOT labelled 'implications' or 'which means…' This forces you to spell out, for each factor, the implications for the organisation and in this way you enhance the analytical output from the SWOT. You can see this in the example below. This employs a prioritisation scoring system and attempts to spell out the full implications of the factors listed. The factors are also classified.

Figure 6.7: An example of SWOT analysis

	Strengths	Implications	Score	Weaknesses	Implications	Score
Customers	Regions	North and North West are currently strongest areas for CRI. South West is also relatively strong.	1	Lack of data on architects	Only a small amount of data is available in order to understand which practices to target – do not know value by region.	3
	Contractor Insight	Manipulate to target architects by increasing advocacy levels	3	Decision makers	Unaware of DMU on database?	3
				Currently weak in regions we wish to target e.g. London	This may mean targeting higher risk segments (but with high potential)	2
Resources				Sales force not skilled/ motivated to target architects	Implications on future resources if not addressed – could impact number of leads CRI is able to manage	2
Market Share	Penetration of architect market – currently 8%	This can be considered as a positive based on no pro-active marketing activity	1			

Key issues and critical success factors

Key issues

Key issues follows the SWOT analysis and is a summary of the SWOT to some extent. It lays down four to six key areas that must be addressed in order for the business to move forward. They act as the bridge between analysis and strategy and should be as simple as possible. Occasionally these can be expressed as critical success factors (CSFs). CSFs tend to be more customer focused and are derived from customer and competitor research.

A list of CSFs may look like the points listed below. The same approach we took to risk assessment can be used here to rank the CSFs.

- Improve quality of service
- Internal staff performance; training, motivation and retention
- Need to develop service offering
- Improve database management skills
- Website redesign
- Enter B2B market

Objectives

There is an old management maxim that says if it can't be measured then it can't be managed. This is not always the case. Given the defining characteristics of direct marketing the process of objective setting is important and should be SMART:

- Specific
- Measured
- Achievable
- Realistic
- Timed

Marketing objectives are concerned with customers, markets and, maybe, products and services. It is only by selling someone 'value' that the corporate objectives will be achieved. (NB In a product strategy the thinking would be selling something to someone.)

So, objectives will be concerned with:

- acquiring new customers in current markets;
- acquiring new customers in new markets;
- winning back past customers;
- developing current customers in current markets;
- developing current customers by entry into new markets;
- retaining customers;
- efficient resource allocation in serving customers.

In setting the objectives, financial target, customer value, customer experience, market opportunity and internal capability gaps all need to be taken into account.

EXAMPLE

If the corporate plan wants to increase revenue by 10 per cent and trends only indicate a 5 per cent increase then the marketing objectives need to fill the gap by acquiring more customers or developing current ones. If customer profitability is desired above that of current levels, then objectives may be set to acquire more profitable customers; increase the profitability of current customers; or retain more profitable customers while letting less profitable ones go.

Gap analysis can help us understand the extent of marketing activity, required to meet our objectives.

Figure 6.8: Gap analysis

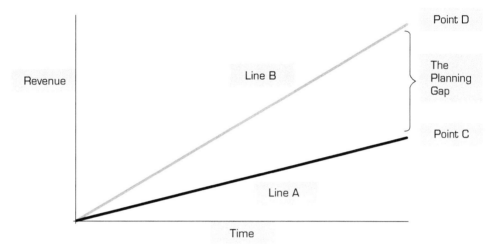

Line A shows the growth that will take place in the industry.
Line B shows the growth we are required to achieve.
The gap between points C and D is the total increase in revenue required for the planning period.

The planning gap is where our marketing objectives are set and we can see that this gives us work to do in familiar territory.

Revenue can be obtained in a variety of ways:

- Keep customers longer
- See higher value products to existing customers
- Cross-sell to existing customers
- Get existing customers to recommend new customers
- Win back lapsed customers
- Acquire new customers

The detailed use of gap analysis can take us right down to campaign level objectives. Traditionally, marketing objectives would have been about products and markets. However, in a direct context we can link the larger measure of market share to individual customer activity.

The use of gap analysis can provide a clear view of the objectives of the marketing plan and help to identify how this objective may be achieved. It allows us to drill down into the source of revenue and profit by customer and to translate very broad market definitions and market share into customer-based activity.

Ansoff presents an approach to planning and objective setting which is helpful to direct marketing in that it links what we do with who we serve. It also helps because it deals with important concepts for direct marketers.

The Ansoff Matrix considers how an organisation or company can expand by plotting four alternatives, based on the products (or services) it provides along the horizontal axis and the markets (or customers) it sells to on the vertical axis. A fifth option – consolidation – is also available.

Figure 6.9: Ansoff's Matrix

	Product	
	Present	New
Market Present	**Market Penetration**	**Product Development**
Market New	**Market Development**	**Diversification**

Source: H. Ansoff, Corporate Strategy, Penguin, 1988, Chapter 6

The idea of new and existing markets sets us off in a direction that is more familiar to us as marketers, especially if we substitute the word customers for markets. New and existing customers can be equated with acquired and retained business. It helps us to understand that customers create value for the business and those products and services are the vehicles through which value is transferred from the organisations to its customers.

From this we can see how corporate, marketing, direct marketing and campaign objectives can be link in an interlocking hierarchy:

Corporate objective
- Return on investment 15 per cent this year

Marketing objective
- Increase market share by 2.5 per cent this year

Direct marketing objectives
- Acquire 20,000 customers at average cost per order of £x in year one
- Retain 80 per cent of existing customers in year one

Communications objective
- Raise spontaneous recall of our brand by 10 per cent in our target market in year one

Campaign objectives
- Recruit 10,000 new customers using direct response television advertising in year one
- Recruit 6,000 new customers via email in year one
- Recruit 500 customers from roll out of tested list in month one

So the best objectives will be customer focused, will look at revenue and cost implications and be time limited.

Strategy

This section now translates analysis and objectives into action. It outlines in broad terms how you are going to achieve your objectives, i.e. your method (not what you are going to do). We are trying to develop a strategy that differentiates, that is competitive, that reflects the reality of the market, and sustains and develops our position within it now and into the future.

It should start with a broad statement of strategy. This may cover the markets/customer groups to be targeted, the products to be delivered and the broad approach to marketing.

Following that there should be sections that cover the following areas. This where the skills of the marketer are really brought to the fore. We aim to configure the elements that we can control to allow the organisation to meet the objectives that we have set.

Customer segments

Whilst we have analysed the customer base in the situation analysis we now look at the segments we are aiming to serve.

We can use many different criteria to split the market into more defined groups.
- Geodemographic
  - Age
  - Sex
  - Class
  - Occupation
  - Family stage
- Psychographic
  - Values
  - Attitudes

- Opinions
- Lifestyles, life stages
- Other behavioural
  - Value
  - Knowledge
  - Belief
  - Benefits sought
  - Loyalty status
  - Usage rate
  - Readiness to buy
  - Critical event
- Business-to-business
  - Size
  - Employees
  - SIC
  - DMU status
  - Order size
  - Order status

We are aiming to optimise the fit between the organisation and the customer groups we serve in order to maximise the value we provide and can receive in return.

Typically direct marketing deals with two main segments – new and retained customers and we then sub-segment within this.

We can target one or more segments depending on our resources.

Following the process of segmentation we then position our products. Are we exclusive, mass market, everyday or for special occasions? This positioning is driven by the brand and reinforces the brand promise.

There then follows the development of strategies (where relevant) for:

- Products – for example, do we need to introduce new products? What new service initiatives or warranties need to be developed?
- Pricing – are we pricing high or do we need to get product into the market quickly by setting a price for penetration of the market? What is our strategy on offers and pricing for new and retained business?
- Communications – what media and media combination will be used to reach our market? For example, what is the balance between online and offline promotions, the role of social media, advertising, PR, DM, events etc?
- Distribution – what distribution channels shall we use, do we go direct, purely online or offline or a mixture of clicks and bricks?
- Sales – how do we integrate a sales force or do we outsource the function?
- A strategy for customer care and service
- A strategy for information, database, CRM systems and market research

Operating plan

The operating plan includes the detailed tactical plans for each area of the strategy. For example the communications plan will include media schedules, campaign activity, timetables and contact programmes for each segment.

This area will include timetables in a Gantt or PERT chart and detailed responsibilities for delivering elements of the plan, showing key milestones and dependencies.

Variance or contingency planning

This area should cover the following questions:

- What will we do if we are exceeding targets?
- What will we do if we are not meeting targets?

This section should describe clearly how you propose tracking the plan and what you intend to do if things go wrong. It also needs to have a budget allocated to it.

Budget

This is often the most critical part of the plan. It should show:

- Revenues
- Costs
- Profit
- Return on investment

The area of strategy and budgeting will be covered in more detail as we move through the rest of the book.

Finally:

Appendices

These will contain raw data, tables, diagrams, charts and other evidence in support of your recommendations.

So you have now covered the overall structure of a marketing plan. It's a complex process and in many larger organisations highly technical and demanding. However, it is the means by which we link the business and its objectives with the customers we are trying to serve and places this relationship in the broader business context in relation to competitors. In this sense it delivers the only source of revenue into the business. It is central to the health of the organisation and its importance cannot be underestimated.

In Chapters 7 and 8 we will explore in more detail how the plan is delivered.

SUMMARY

In this chapter we looked at the connections between direct planning and corporate planning, and initially explored the basic process looking at the journey model and explored the difference between objectives strategies and tactics.

We moved on to look at the marketing planning process and explored the following structure:

- Executive summary
- Terms of reference
- Procedure
- Marketing audit and issue analysis
- Objectives
- Strategy
- Operating plan
- Contingency plan
- Budget
- Appendices

We explored this structure in some detail. Focusing particularly on the analysis and objective setting areas. Within the analysis section we looked in detail at two types of analysis:

- Macro or external analysis including:
  - PESTEL analysis
  - Competitor analysis
  - Customer analysis
  - Stakeholder analysis
  - Market review

- Sources of information for the external analysis:
  - Micro or internal analysis including:
  - Resources review
  - Financial analysis

We also looked at the role of portfolio analysis and directional policy matrices and risk assessment matrices.

We explored the role of SWOT.

In looking at objectives setting we looked at the role of gap analysis and use of Smart objective setting.

Finally we looked briefly at strategy setting, operational plan and budgeting, recognising that these areas will be covered in more detail in Chapters 7 and 8.

REVIEW QUESTIONS

1. What are the benefits of marketing planning?
2. What is the difference between strategy and tactics?
3. Outline the stages of the marketing planning process.
4. What is PESTEL?
5. List three sources of external information useful for the planning process.
6. What does Smart stand for?
7. What is the role of gap analysis?
8. Describe the function of directional policy analysis?
9. How useful is Ansoff to direct marketing planning?
10. What are key issues?
11. Describe the ways value can be added to a SWOT analysis.
12. Why does strategy start with market segmentation?

CHAPTER 7

MANAGING THE CUSTOMER JOURNEY FROM ACQUISITION TO RELATIONSHIP

IN THIS CHAPTER

We will introduce the basic building blocks of a successful business.

After reading this chapter you will be able to:
- Understand the link between acquisition and retention planning
- Identify methods for analysing the customer journey including touch point analysis
- Apply a structure for the development of a retention programme
- Understand the nature of customer loyalty and how it can be nurtured
- Understand the financial implications of investment in loyalty programmes
- Understand and apply a planning structure to acquire new customers for a business

Specific topics include:
- The links between acquisition and retention
- Planning a retention programme
- Developing and maintaining customer relationships
- CRM – implementation and effectiveness
- Customer satisfaction and customer delight
- The vital importance of good customer service
- Differences between B2C and B2B
- The role of data and research
- What makes customers loyal?
- What do they value in a relationship?
- The effect of reducing customer losses on new business needs
- Understanding customer life cycles
- Complainants – our best friends?
- The role of customer satisfaction surveys
- Relationship marketing
- Two types of customer communications
- Recovering the investment
- Five key stages in developing loyalty

- Two general rules for building loyalty
- Basic loyalty techniques
- Acquisition planning
- Acquiring the right customers

INTRODUCTION

This chapter discusses various ways in which you can recruit or acquire customers and develop relationships with them and so increase their loyalty. It is important to remember that loyalty is a two-way thing – you cannot treat your customers with disdain and expect unswerving loyalty in return.

If we consider the core objectives of most businesses we see that they are about creating profits or a return on investment for shareholders. The broader definition of marketing extends this into the idea of value creation. We offer something to customers, donors, clients, audiences, and they give us something back in return. In business this is typically a financial return. In charity marketing or fundraising this return may be financial or a financial equivalent, for example volunteering or other support activity. In social marketing the return may be based around a change in behaviour, for example reporting symptoms to a GP before the condition they reveal becomes serious, taking up benefits or stopping drink-driving. In political marketing the objective may be to change voting preferences. The core principle is that this return, however it is defined, comes from the audience we are targeting. Put simply, value or revenue comes from customers. For most companies, marketing is about the top line in any profit and loss account, i.e. revenue generation.

The revenue or turnover figure is simply the sum of sales to customers over a certain period of time. Some customers buy once, some are new, some are old, some are loyal, others are not. The enormous advantage of direct marketing is that it is able to understand the nature and quality of this revenue generation and look beneath the top line figures to explore, in some detail, the basic transactions that build revenue.

Other functional areas help to deliver this value. For example IT and logistics help to deliver products and create seamless Web experiences; HR seeks to employ and develop staff skills to deliver superior service; finance will help us refine our budgets and looks at managing the cost base of the business. However, in terms of contact and communication it is marketing that drives the central relationship. The sum of our activities across all functions delivers the revenue base of the business. So again, put simply, profits come from customers and the effective management of the business that serves them.

However, as direct marketers we know that not all customers are the same. The broadest level of segmentation is between customers that are new to the business and those that already buy from us. Acquired or retained business. This chapter explores this basic principle and shows how we can adapt our offer to acquire the right customers and use a variety of techniques to keep them and develop their value over time.

Recruiting new customers for any company is a very costly exercise, so once a company has acquired customers it is important to keep them. Today, when many products and services have become commodities, customer service can be the only reliable long-term differentiator. It is vital that a company plans to develop solid long-term relationships, but only with the right sort of customer. So the first stage in developing customer loyalty is to recruit the right sort of customer. This has implications for media and message planning, offer development, consideration of promotional offers and so on.

Nowadays, loyalty campaigns alone are not enough to ensure continued success. The product must be right and the price must be considered reasonable – you do not need to be the cheapest but if you are not you must work hard to make your customer feel that your service is worth the extra cost.

Acquisition or retention?

A crucial question when planning campaigns is: Should we concentrate on developing existing customers or on acquiring new ones?

The answer will clearly vary from business to business and there are two key questions to be answered:

1. How well developed are our present customers, i.e. how many of them are open to buy more or additional products?
2. How long can we afford to wait before we make a profit on a new customer? Do we have sufficient funding and sufficient confidence in our ability to retain customers to wait for a year or more to turn a new customer into profit?

The second question is the key to finding the balance between acquisition and retention strategies. If we can afford to wait for profit we can clearly allocate more margin to promotions and thus recruit more new customers by making them a better offer.

There is another consideration in finding the correct balance – the actual cost of buying new customers and the evidence of enhanced value from retained business.

Research studies from McKinsey, the management consultancy in the UK and America, have shown that the cost of obtaining a 'conquest' sale (one from a new prospect) is between three and 30 times as much as the cost of achieving a repeat or renewal. Frederick Reichheld in his book *The Loyalty Effect* showed that a 5 per cent increase in retention can lead to an 85 per cent increase in profits. Researchers at Cranfield University showed that loyal customers spend four times more in the categories to which they are loyal than switching customers.

Tesco used Lifetime value analyses to show that Clubcard customers were around £130 a year more valuable than non-Clubcard customers. Not a vast sum you may think until you consider that in 2010, Tesco has more than 18 million customers including 15 million active Clubcard members – not bad for 'electronic green shield stamps' as David Sainsbury is said to have described Clubcard on its launch. This evidence has lead to budgets being shifted from acquisition to retention strategies and investment in a vast range of 'loyalty' programmes; more about this later. However, there is a very important point to be made.

> Whatever we decide about the balance of the business, and however much time
> and money we devote to gaining new customers, we must first of all concentrate
> on maximising the business we develop from existing and former customers.

The correct sequence of allocating the promotional budget is as follows:

- **Existing customers first**

  Given the above cost factors it is essential that we concentrate first on retaining and developing existing customers before we start to allocate promotional funds to locating new prospects.

- **Existing enquirers next**

  The second best source of business will be people with whom we already have a relationship, however slight. These people have already expressed an interest and they will always yield a better return per pound than any outside list of new prospects or any new advertising campaign.

  In this category we would also include people who used to buy from us but no longer do so. Unless they stopped buying because of a major problem the chances are that, sooner or later they will look to change from their new supplier. A timely reminder may successfully resurrect a previously good relationship.

- **New business last**

  Note that we are not suggesting that getting new business is not important, simply that the best return on investment will come from promotions to existing contacts. It makes sense therefore to exhaust all possibilities of additional or renewal business from these before starting on the much riskier business of seeking entirely new customers.

  It is always worth taking any opportunity to build the prospect list by ensuring that any enquiries are recorded and not simply replied to and discarded.

The fact is that all businesses need new customers for a number of reasons:

- customers move away;
- customers are enticed away by the competition;
- customers' needs change and they move out of our market;
- customers change roles;
- customers retire;
- customers seek variety;
- we may not be able to recover all our costs from our existing customer base.

However, it will be seen from the above that new business generation should be viewed as an investment – one which will pay back in the longer term rather than in the immediate future. In deciding on the optimum point of profit we will need to consider:

- **Funding**

  Do we have the financial resources to wait for profit?

- **Competition**

  How much competition is there in this field?

How strong is it in terms of price and offer?

- **Development potential**

What additional products do we have which could be cross-sold to the same customer – in other words what is the potential for developing more business once we have sold them their first product?

- **The promise**

Will our product or service live up to the promises we made?

Will our customers feel they have been given good value for money when they come to consider repurchase? **It is always easy to increase response to a prospect offer by lowering the price or increasing the incentive, but if this raises unrealistic expectations we may find that future sales are disappointing.**

- **Level of service**

Can we afford to maintain or even increase our level of service to existing customers? What is our current retention percentage, i.e. how many customers continue to buy from us year after year?

There have been numerous recent studies into customer retention and loyalty and all have reached the same conclusion – many customers change suppliers because their existing one did not care enough about them. But how much is enough?

Customer *satisfaction* is clearly not enough these days – studies show that whilst expressing satisfaction with a supplier, a large percentage of customers would happily shop elsewhere.

An electrical company reported that whilst 80 per cent of customers stated they were quite satisfied with the present level of service, 70 per cent said they would certainly *consider using another supplier.*

In another study, a car company found that of all customers who changed to an alternative car, only 10 per cent were dissatisfied.

What are the implications of this?

Customers today are more demanding and have a greater range of options to choose from than ever before. Today therefore, customer satisfaction is the starting point not the objective.

Our objective should be customer delight. How can this be achieved?

Many studies show that it is added value that makes the difference. A study carried out by Professor Thomas O. Jones of Harvard Business School in the 1990s reinforced the idea that satisfied customers still leave. Interestingly he also showed that those who had encountered a problem with a company that had been resolved to their satisfaction, were more likely to stay and more likely to recommend that company to friends and family. This study has been confirmed in many sectors and the findings have stood the test of time.

In the UK the most satisfied customers in grocery retailing according to a *Which?* magazine survey in 2010 are Waitrose customers.

The top four stores Tesco, Asda, Sainsbury and Morrisons came in far lower than Waitrose's 79 per cent, with scores of between 49 per cent and 58 per cent. Marks and Spencer were second at

65 per cent and joint third above all the major players were Aldi and Lidl on 61 per cent.

In the automotive market the annual J.D. Power survey of customer satisfaction reveals a similar picture; first and most satisfied customers are Lexus drivers with 85 per cent satisfaction levels; close behind comes Honda on 83 per cent, ahead of BMW, Audi, Mercedes and Saab. Skoda came in sixth ahead of quality brands such as BMW, Volvo and Audi.

So, what is going on?

Waitrose offers a distinctly superior service; you may agree. Staff are well trained, knowledgeable and friendly. The stores are well stocked with high-quality products. A friend recently returned a product to Waitrose and they refunded double the money paid for the product.

Lidl is cheap, with limited staff, limited stock but it is recognised as offering real value for money and the Internet is full of positive comments on the prices they charge for certain products.

The same principles apply with Lexus and Honda. Part of the reason for this phenomenon is the link between value and the fulfilment of expectations. A Skoda or Honda driver almost certainly has lower expectations than a Mercedes driver. A Lidl customer has lower expectations than a Tesco customer. Perhaps the idea, then, is not just customer satisfaction and delight but delivering these desirable attributes by simply delivering on and keeping promises made, and where possible by exceeding customer expectations.

In the old days a grocer would offer added value in his daily contacts with customers, popping in a couple of extra carrots after weighing and pricing an order; offering a little extra which stuck in the customer's mind because it was something 'he didn't need to do'. For other companies it may be offering 24-hour support or if something has gone wrong making sure that it is put right. Indeed recovering service failure is so important that it is tempting to say put it right at almost any cost.

Such an approach builds strong customer loyalty because it says, loud and clear 'I value your business'.

You should spend some time thinking about things you could do to increase your satisfaction rating in the perception of your own customers. In other words you must offer value it whatever way you have defined it for the money customers are paying.

Developing and managing customer relationships

Today's successful companies seek a continuing relationship with their customers, not one based on occasional transactions. The costs of such an approach needs careful management but the objective must be to encourage the customer to enter into an ongoing relationship and, where possible, to extend this across several products and services.

Moving from a purely product-based approach enables you to communicate wider values to your customers; values related to the brand and the values embedded within it which include style, ethos, service standards and attitude.

Adopting such a customer-focused strategy enables you to maximise the lifetime value of each customer by anticipating needs and offering timely solutions. We will look at this in detail in Chapter 16.

This involves a shift in emphasis in measuring success. Many companies have traditionally been preoccupied with making sales to new customers. As we have seen this is not always the ideal approach when planning to build a profitable business.

Customer retention is the key

The enlightened company prefers to measure success by customer retention. Gaining a new customer is a considerable achievement but it is only half the story. The profit comes from developing a relationship that leads to repeat or regular purchases, which are achieved at a lower marketing cost than the initial transaction.

Customer retention is not the only benefit of developing customer relationships. Many customers would be prepared to buy more than one type of product from a supplier they trust and cross-selling is cheaper and therefore more profitable than conquest selling.

Existing customers can also exert a powerful influence over potential customers; they compare experiences regarding product satisfaction and customer service. Look at the customer review sites on the Internet and consider how you make decisions about purchases. Very often we ask friends and family and use review sites and magazines before purchasing,

In 2004 the Henley Centre/AOL Brand New World No. 1 evaluated people's attitudes towards and trust of various sources of information from search engines to face-to-face sales people.

Figure 7.1: Which information sources are most important?

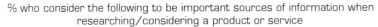

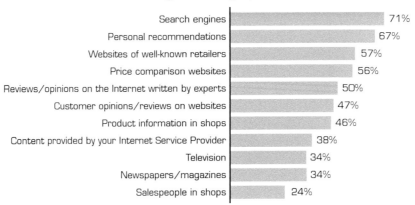

Figure 7.2: Which information sources are most honest?

% who trust the following information sources are honest and fair

Information source	%
Personal recommendations	90%
Price comparison websites	73%
Websites of well-known retailers	73%
Websites of well-known brands	68%
Search engines	67%
Customer opinions/reviews on websites	61%
Product information in shops	60%
Reviews/opinions on the Internet written by experts	60%
Content provided by your Internet Service Provider	53%
Newspapers/magazines	44%
Television	37%
Salespeople in shops	35%

Both these studies were carried out six years ago, before the advent of Web 2.0. Social networking has brought about many changes in attitudes towards media of all types. It is reasonable to assume that the bottom three in the 'Trust' table will not have improved their relative positions, although a repeat of the 2004 study would be welcome. The Henley Centre and AOL produced Brave New World No 2 in 2006 but it was confined to online media and so does not resolve the above issue.

All this is not to suggest that customer acquisition is not important; merely that customer development and retention are absolutely crucial. As mentioned earlier, the greater the long-term customer value, the more you can afford to spend to acquire the customer in the first place.

One large office equipment company places such high value on customer development that their sales and marketing managers' annual bonuses are largely based on the following two questions:

1. Of the customers you had a year ago, how many are still buying from you today?
This measures the retention or renewal rate of customers. The higher the retention rate the more valuable is the new business gained.

Customer development is not just about retention, it is also important to grow existing customers. So the second question is:

2. Compare the average value per customer now with that of the same group a year ago – how much has it grown?

Back to your database

Developing customers requires a differential approach – not all customers will require the same information, nor will they respond to the same messages. And, of course, the ideal timing will vary for each customer. We will look at this when we discuss campaign management in Chapter 8.

Developing differential customer development plans can be difficult and time consuming – unless the database can be made to do most of the work. As we have seen in Chapter 5 your database enables you to manage your customers in segments – based on customer type, amount of business, size of company, potential value or other factors, and to build a unique customer retention and development plan for each segment. It also enables you to measure the success of each plan precisely.

For each customer segment you should develop a plan containing:

- Forecasts of new product sales (cross-selling potential)
- Forecasts of upgrade sales (up-selling potential)
- Detailed action plans for exploiting these opportunities

Careful database analysis can make it easier to plan acquisition and retention by type of customer, value bands and so on.

What makes customers loyal?

Let's consider some factors about customer loyalty:

1. Although loyalty is measured by behaviour it is really about customer attitudes.

Recognising loyalty can be difficult. Continued purchase tells you that customers are not unhappy but by the time you have noticed that they have stopped buying it can often be too late to solve the problem. It is necessary to find a way of measuring customer attitudes before normal purchasing time, which of course varies from customer to customer.

Attitudes are made up of three related components:

1. What we think
2. What we feel
3. What we do

The third area is easiest to measure. We can measure behaviour, i.e. how often customers buy, how long they stay, their response history, how much they spend and their cross-sell and up-sell rate. We can also track their recommendations. This behavioural dimension is easier to measure than the other areas.

Some have tried to establish research approaches into attitudes which combine measures of relative satisfaction, commitment and trust as key drivers. The BrandZ approach from Millward Brown explores a slightly different approach using a survey instrument to establish the extent of emotional bonding. For each brand, each person interviewed is assigned to one level of a brand pyramid depending on their responses to a set of questions. The BrandDynamics Pyramid shows the number of consumers who have reached each level.

Customers are classified in the following categories:

- Bonding – Rational and emotional attachments to the brand to the exclusion of most other brands.
- Advantage – Felt to have an emotional or rational advantage over other brands in the category.

- Performance – Felt to deliver acceptable product performance and is on the consumer's shortlist.
- Relevance – Relevant to consumer's needs, in the right price range or in consideration set.
- Presence – Active familiarity based on past trial, saliency or knowledge of brand promise.

Purchasing loyalty increases at higher levels of the Pyramid – consumers at the level of bonding are likely to be active advocates of the brand. There is also an increase in share of wallet – the proportion of consumer expenditure within the category on that brand – as you ascend the Pyramid. The goal is to build as large a group as possible of truly loyal consumers, by sustaining a suitable relationship and increasing their loyalty to the brand.

The rankings are based on the responses to the following questions:

1. Which of these brands do you have higher opinion of?
2. Which of these brands have better products?
3. Which of these brands are setting trends?
4. Which of these brands are most popular?
5. Which of these brands are different from the others?
6. Which of these brands have better price?
7. Which of these brands cost more than you're prepared to pay for?

Customers that are most loyal will answer these questions about your brand positively at least four times and price will not be a consideration. Advantage customers will answer at least three statements positively and again there will be no price barrier. Take a look at the website at www.brandz.com or www.millwardbrown.com.

2. The key point is you cannot keep track of customer attitudes without regular contact and feedback

Without direct feedback you cannot hope to understand customer needs, attitudes and intentions.

3. Loyalty is not a one-way street

All of marketing consists of a two-way exchange between company and customer. Before you can expect loyalty you must offer it yourself. This means that you must be prepared to 'go the extra mile' where necessary.

4. Loyalty cannot be developed by marketing communications alone

Every aspect of your business is a factor in building loyalty, from enquiry taking to delivery and after-sales service – even a follow-up for non-payment must be made with courtesy and care.

5. It is impossible to develop customer loyalty without committed staff who share the objective of 'customer delight'.

Loyalty and commitment of staff at all levels is a base requirement for developing and maintaining customer loyalty. Promises must be fulfilled; added value must be volunteered at every opportunity. Relationship marketing strategy works internally as well as externally, all partners in creating value must be committed, resourced and incentivised to deliver that value consistently.

6. Customer loyalty is the logical outcome of caring about, and delivering solutions for customer needs.

'Loyalty' obtained with discounts and incentives is very fragile and can easily be bought by competitors.

A word of caution: you cannot go into this in the short term only. A loyalty programme is a continuing thing, a long-term commitment of time and resources. So, before you take the plunge, stand back and consider a few pertinent questions:

1. Have you quantified the benefits of investing in a loyalty programme?

You need to calculate your present and potential customer retention rates in order to forecast the likely return on your investment. If you do not have the information or the experience to do this you should consider testing your programme to a small discrete segment of customers. It is estimated that a loyalty programme can cost between 1–4 per cent of turnover and you need to be clear of the incremental value of such an investment. Payback can take several years and it must be given time to do its work.

2. Have you researched existing levels of customer satisfaction?

You may already have a very high level of satisfaction and retention. If so, do not expect to achieve huge additional gains; you are already doing a lot of things right. If on the other hand your satisfaction ratings are very low you may need more than a loyalty programme to put things right.

3. Have you defined the service requirements of your customers?

Not all will require the same levels of service. Your objective is to allocate your resources in the most cost-efficient way. For example, try to segment your customers according to the following chart:

Figure 7.3: Contact strategy differentiated on customer value

Customer value	Main method of servicing account
High	Face-to-face and telephone
Medium	Telephone account Management
Low	Email, mail + inbound phone

Segmenting customers in this way enables you to use your resources in the most cost-effective way. Companies who have adopted this approach report that many customers transferred to telephone account management actually prefer it, as they can be sure that their contact is always available when they have a query.

Telephone account management implies full service with regular communications from you to your customer. The low value customers are dealt with solely by email, or occasional direct mail (e.g. catalogues) with the telephone available to them for queries – you would not generally make calls to these customers, except for specific promotional campaigns, research purposes and trouble-shooting.

4. Do you know what will improve your customers' loyalty and how this can be delivered cost-efficiently?

You may be able to determine this from your customer satisfaction surveys. Alternatively you may need to undertake wider research. Marketing research is discussed in Chapter 3.

5. Can you offer genuine benefits to your customers?

Remember, these must be real benefits in the eyes of your customers.

What do customers value in a relationship?

In recent studies, when customers have been asked to identify the factors that make them value a supplier they generally list the following attributes:

- **Good products at fair prices** – not all customers seek the lowest prices. Many people realise that, at least to a certain extent, 'you get what you pay for'.
- **Convenience and ease of access** – they want to be able to get hold of you quickly and easily, especially when they have a problem. The old 'take two aspirins and call me in the morning' approach is a sure way to lose customers.
- **Effective and fast problem solving** – a quick, sympathetic response to their queries and complaints is highly important. Handling a customer problem may be a routine, even boring, task to you, yet the problem could be the most worrying experience of your customer's life.
- **Privileged status as a known customer** – they like to be recognised when they make contact.
- **Appropriate contact and communication** – they do not want to be bombarded with irrelevant mailings, email, SMS and phone calls.
- **Anticipation of their needs** – some call this being 'pro-active', but whatever it's called it is a key aspect of customer management.
- **Professional, friendly dialogue** – all many customers want is the opportunity to discuss things with someone knowledgeable.

Happy customers tell their friends about you, pay less attention to competitive offers, and also tend to be more receptive to offers of additional products.

Effect of reducing customer losses on new business requirements

Every business loses a percentage of its customers every year. Some of these losses are unavoidable, yet many could be avoided with better customer management. Let us suppose that you have 500 customers and your seven-year business plan requires you to grow your customer strength by 10 per cent each year.

Your targets are indicated in the table overleaf. Let us see what the difference is in your recruitment targets between a customer retention rate of 70 per cent and one of 85 per cent.

Table 7.1: Customer recruitment targets

	Now	Year 1	Year 2	Year 3	Year 4	Year 5	Year 6	Year 7	Cum. Total
Customer strength required	500	550	605	666	732	805	886	974	–
New customers needed if 70% retained	–	200	220	242	266	293	322	354	1,897
New customers needed if 85% retained	–	125	137	152	166	183	202	221	1,186
Difference	–	75	83	90	100	110	120	133	711

As this table shows, if you can improve your customer retention by 15 per cent your marketing budget needs to buy 711 fewer recruits. If an average new customer costs you £75 to recruit, this represents a reduction of £53,325 which could pay for quite a lot of customer retention marketing with some left over to boost your profits.

Looking at this from the opposite point of view, losing an additional 15 per cent of customers increases your recruitment requirement by 60 per cent – a massive additional burden on your marketing budget.

Customer life cycles

Research across many markets indicates that customers have natural life cycles, just as products and complete industries have life cycles. Also, some companies cease trading, in which case a customer 'life' may be determined by the effective life of that customer's supplier. Research also tells us that many customer relationships are cut short without achieving their natural lifespan. A crisis or competitive intervention may be sufficient to break a productive relationship.

For example, a study published a few years ago showed that the natural lifespan of a transatlantic frequent business flyer relationship is about five years, after which the individual gets promoted or changes jobs. However, the study also showed that the customer might defect prematurely when the relationship reaches 'a moment of truth' and the airline does not recognise this, or fails to respond appropriately. Such 'moments of truth' occur in all business relationships – some may be predictable and it may then be possible to anticipate and overcome them by delivering timely customer care messages.

EXAMPLE

A customer satisfaction survey carried out in the UK at the end of the 1990s identified the dangers of customer dissatisfaction over and above the business lost. The survey discovered that whereas a happy customer would tell four people about the airline, an unhappy customer would tell 17.

Today the ratio is almost certainly higher and the advent of Web 2.0 and user-generated content (UGC) means that dissatisfied customers can tell millions of people.

Dave Carroll, an American country singer was flying with his band to a gig on United Airlines. He claimed baggage handlers broke his guitar and was angry that despite a year of protests the airline would not admit responsibility. Take a look at the clip: www.youtube.com/watch?v = 5YGc4zOqozo. Dave Carroll uploaded three song videos, was featured on CNN and UK news and in less than a year in excess of ten million people saw this story. This is the new reality.

Complainants may turn out to be your best friends. Many well-known companies report that former complainants generally turn out to be very good customers. One major company set objectives for increasing the number of complaints received, on the understanding that many customers did not bother to complain they just left for the competition. It seems that a customer who complains is trying to let you know that they would value the relationship if only you would recognise their problems and try to solve them.

So it is vital to give your customers a channel to let you know when they are unhappy, at the time of dissatisfaction. Many companies run customer satisfaction surveys to a sample of their file and whilst this can be a valuable gauge of service and delivery levels it will not highlight specific cases of dissatisfaction.

If you positively encourage all customers to let you know their concerns there will be two main effects:

- **You will have a pile of complaints to deal with**, some of which can be turned into future selling opportunities.
- **You will pick up cases of dissatisfaction at an early stage** when it is still relatively easy to put them right – this will help you increase renewal rates.

There are really no infallible rules about customer retention – there are, however, some general factors, arising from research and observation of many companies, which apply to most situations:

1. Customer retention rate is the most decisive influence on marketing cost, as we have seen from the earlier example. Remember it costs most companies much more to replace a customer than to retain one.

2. Customer satisfaction can be measured through customer surveys, and many customers are quite willing, even keen, to tell you how to get it right.

3. The causes of customer losses can be established – a follow-up call to a lost customer can be an excellent investment. Not only will many of them tell you why they changed suppliers, a good telephone manner will encourage them to consider you favourably again, when their new supplier disappoints them in some way. This is a vital point: existing satisfied customers cannot tell you why others are dissatisfied

4. There is a strong correlation between absence of dialogue and customer loss rate – much of the adverse feedback concerns the fact that companies give the impression that they do not want to know about customer problems and opinions. But simply keeping in touch can make a major difference to customers' willingness to repurchase. Look at the following example from a major insurance company:

Table 7.2: Effect of marketing communication on customer retention

	Number of contacts in year	Retention Rate %
All customers	1	63
	2	74
	3	80
	4 +	82
New customers	0	43
	4 +	82

It can be difficult to measure the precise effect of a single marketing communication on customer attitudes, and it is necessary to analyse the strength of relationships continuously.

It may be possible, through customer surveys, to recognise critical points in the relationship (the 'moments of truth' mentioned earlier) which call for specific communications.

Customer satisfaction surveys

When researching customer satisfaction, an increasing number of businesses are approaching their entire customer file instead of just a sample.

There are two reasons why this is a good idea:

1. Complaints can be picked up at a very early level – as we discussed earlier it is much easier to resolve a small concern than one which has been 'festering' for a long time

2. Customers appreciate being asked – indications are that simply sending out a satisfaction survey can engender positive attitudes amongst customers

Satisfaction surveys nearly always measure the output of a process rather than question the process itself. At some point it is worth auditing processes and reviewing the entire service delivery system. Satisfaction levels should always be benchmarked over time and relative to the competition where possible.

Satisfaction surveys cannot stand apart from the service recovery process. If a problem is identified it should be acted upon. One well-known automotive company carried out regular satisfaction surveys, but if a problem was identified the respondent was simply thanked for their time. This created an even worse situation, having raised the expectation that something was going to be done and then nothing happening.

The use of two-way marketing communications plays a valuable part in building and measuring the customer's view of the relationship. But why wait until you send out a survey? Every time you contact a customer you have the opportunity to encourage dialogue.

If you want your regular communications to help you build loyalty you must make sure that they are relevant to your customers.

How can you make them relevant?

Make sure every communication:

1. Is useful and interesting to your customer. They do not want to be told how successful or clever you are. It is amazing how often this mistake is made.

2. Involves your customer. Encourage them to reply. Ask them to tell you what they think about your service. What do they need from you that you are not supplying?

3. Helps them to get better value from you. Offer useful advice on how they can get the most out of your relationship.

4. Is consistent. All communications, online and offline, telephone contacts and customer service and sales people must tell the same story.

Relationship marketing

The communications programmes described above are often called **dialogue** or **relationship marketing**. The aim of relationship marketing is not just to make customers think you are a good supplier. Your aim should be to make your customers value their relationship with you to the extent that they would not normally consider any other supplier.

The relationship marketing idea suggests that all customer touch points must be managed for customer delight. This means that relationship marketing is not just about internal excellence. A customer's view of a product is formed by a variety of influences not all directly controlled by the company. So relationship management must be extended to the network of suppliers who impact on customers.

You will not be able to lock in every customer for life, but this is not necessarily a bad thing. Building and maintaining strong relationships costs time and money and not all your customers will merit the extra investment. The key is to identify those whose loyalty will repay the additional investment and concentrate your efforts there. A further strengthening of the bond can be made by providing *added value* to your customers.

EXAMPLE

Your objective is to make them think 'they didn't need to do that'. To illustrate the advantage of added value read the following example:

A customer ordered some new business cards from Kall Kwik. When he collected the order the manager gave him a booklet entitled 'Cash Management'.

This was written specifically for small businesses by a well-known firm of accountants and funded by Kall Kwik. Although very happy with the advice of his existing accountant he was still very impressed that Kall Kwik should provide this entirely free of charge.

Such a booklet could be mailed or handed to your customers; mailed to prospects or offered as a premium in return for a sale or an enquiry.

Customer communications

There are two broad types of marketing communication:

1. Customer care, or relationship building

2. Sales orientated, designed to sell or at least to initiate a selling process, by generating leads

Sometimes it is possible to combine these so that:

- Customer care communications give customers the opportunity to send for sales information, although the sales content would be very 'soft-sell';
- Selling messages include customer care content.

Where such combinations are possible you can make your budgets work harder, but it is vital that you do not jeopardise the main purpose of each communication by trying to do too much.

Another key factor in relationship programmes is *timing*. The best customer care programmes are time sensitive. Being sensitive to customer needs and buying cycles can make your promotional mailings much more productive.

Time-sensitive communications (or series programmes) are timed to coincide with critical customer life stages or 'moments of truth'. Therefore, the messages go to different customers at different times.

For example, a 'welcome' message may go to a new customer very soon after their first purchase. Another message may be timed to arrive shortly before they could be expected to re-order. The important point is that these communications should be timed according to the customer's requirements, and not to fit in with your sales or planning cycles.

Automated marketing systems allow this to be done far more effectively than ever before. For example, if a subscription is due for renewal this will trigger an automated mailing, email, SMS or combination to try to achieve the renewal. These very precise event-triggers are easier to manage than some more general trends. In the business-to-business world financial year end is an important date as many companies are anxious to allocate contingency funds to projects. In the express packages sector companies like FedEx target the fashion industry around the time of the major Designer Collections. Mobile phone companies will identify if you have travelled abroad and send offers relating to data and voice services.

These event triggers can be identified through an analysis of transactions on the database coupled with investment in research that tries to establish the nature and length of the decision making process. For example in car marketing the most important piece of data is expected date of renewal. The communications programme is based around this volunteered data. Look at baby products companies including Kimberly Clark and Procter & Gamble, and use the Bounty list (a list which includes the details of pregnant women) to identify the expected date of delivery of the new baby. Take a look at the Bounty website for an idea of how powerful this simple piece of data can be: www.bounty.com.

You will also want to consider *how* your messages are delivered: some selling messages may be better delivered face to face, whereas customer care messages will more usually be delivered by email, mail and/or telephone.

Finally, you will want to consider *who* should receive each message. In selling to consumers this may not be so important but with business customers there may be differences between the ideal distribution of customer care and selling messages.

Although there may be one key decision maker in a business, there may well be others who can block future orders.

One of the key advantages of direct marketing communications is the ability to deliver *appropriate* messages to each member of the decision-making chain. Messages can be varied whilst maintaining a consistency of style and tone.

The precise effects of a customer relationship programme are not so easy to measure in the short term. However, retention marketing is relatively cheaper than customer acquisition. One never wants to lose a good customer but so long as you are retaining a high percentage you are probably doing well in comparison with your competitors. A few years ago PricewaterhouseCoopers published the following survey finding:

'A 2 per cent increase in customer retention is equivalent to a 10 per cent reduction in marketing costs.'

PricewaterhouseCoopers

Recovering your investment in retention marketing

Retention programmes cost money to develop and maintain. As mentioned earlier, they will not prove cost-effective for every customer. It is vital to segment your customers and to target your retention marketing at those who have the propensity to repay your investment.

The five key stages in developing retention and loyalty are:

1. **Customer classification**

   The first step is to segment your customers into categories such as:
   - business and consumer, where you serve both;
   - high and low value;
   - percentage of their annual expenditure you already receive (share of customer);
   - single and multi-product purchasing patterns;
   - payment performance;
   - lapsed customers, split into 'time since last order' bands;
   - property type, where relevant;
   - Possessions, e.g. cars and other luxury goods for consumers or type of equipment installed for businesses.

   There are no fixed rules; you must apply your own segmentation according to the specific circumstances in your own business.

2. **Segment analyses**

   Here you will be concerned with the potential value of each type of customer. You should consider:
   - profiles of those in each segment;
   - customer needs and expectations and the costs of servicing their business;

- potential lifetime value;
- expected re-purchase rates;
- acquisition costs and potential payback periods.

3. **Programme streaming**

   The idea is to vary your investment level according to the segment analyses carried out above. You should also vary your strategy, because what will be appropriate for one customer may be totally inappropriate for another.

4. **Communications planning**

   Your objective should be a continuing programme of communications running through the following stages:

   - Welcome
   - Up-sell
   - Cross-sell
   - Prevention of dormancy, and where this fails
   - Reactivation

5. **Testing and evaluating**

   If you have a large enough customer file, testing will answer many questions (see Chapter 14 for more information). However, even where testing is viable you may also find it valuable to carry out some marketing research. Marketing research is discussed in Chapter 3.

   Not all customers can be made loyal. It's a matter of basic character. Some customers tend to be loyal (subject to good service, of course); others tend to be fickle or 'promiscuous' shoppers.

   Research by one of the UK's largest direct marketing agencies indicates that although still difficult, it may be easier to attract the loyal customers of another company than to change the basic attitudes of one's own fickle customers. This does not necessarily mean that it is a waste of time to try to build customer loyalty, simply that it will take a very strong bond to totally remove the chance of a customer being attracted to another supplier.

Two general rules for building loyalty

1. **Develop dialogue**
   - Questionnaires can identify present and future needs, levels of satisfaction with products, service, delivery, etc. and generate nice warm feelings amongst your customers.
   - Regular communication programmes including welcome letters, special offers and incentives where relevant, can help you build good relationships.
   - 'Personalised' communications are appreciated, but make sure it is true personalisation and make sure the personalisation is correct.
   - Knowledge gained from such feedback can help you develop products, services, events and occasions which are valued by customers and prospects.

2. **Make your database work for you**
   - Your database enables you to send effective, timely and appropriate communications.
   - Tracking recency, volume and order detail identifies cross-selling and up-selling opportunities, and incentive allocation where appropriate.

- Fast fulfilment of requests and orders builds customer confidence and satisfaction.
- Instant access to customer information enables you to deliver real personal service.

Some basic loyalty techniques

Welcome: Numerous researches have shown that welcoming new customers has a measurable effect on the level of renewals and repurchase. One major car manufacturer noted an increase in repurchase of 23 per cent as a result of them introducing a welcome sequence.

EXAMPLE

A major UK bank tested two ways of welcoming new customers. The details were:

Control group No welcome activity
Group A Welcome letter
Group B Same letter as Group A but followed up with a telephone call.

Detailed results are confidential but the bank reported that over a three-year period, customers in Group A were better than those in the control group, but Group B customers 'significantly out-performed those in the other two groups'. These customers were measured on their payment performance and repeat purchase of loan and/or investment products.

The value of the 'Welcome' stage is clearly recognised by many charities, which find this an effective opportunity to 'upgrade' new supporters. Donations sent to the NSPCC will trigger a simple 'thank-you' communication from the Chief Executive, followed by an upgrade communication from the Appeals Manager.

The Appeals Manager says, in three simple paragraphs:
1. Thank you again.
2. Here's some more information (reassuring the donor that their money is being put to good use).
3. A hope that the donor will be persuaded to think about other ways they can help.

They enclose a form to sign donors up for regular donations but they also say they plan to telephone 'shortly' to talk about it. They pre-empt the possibility that this might be seen as unwelcome by enclosing a form that can be returned to say 'do not call'.

Dialogue: Customers want to tell you when they are happy and when they are not. Making this process simple and friendly increases the level of dialogue between you and your customers. It also increases the number of complaints – most dialogue increases renewal and repurchase.

Developing the relationship across more than one product is in itself beneficial to retention.

Another well-known bank study into customer retention showed the following odds of a customer changing banks:

Table 7.3: Product tenure and retention in the banking sector

Accounts held	Odds against changing
Current account only	Evens
Savings only	2 : 1
Savings and current	10 : 1
Savings, current and loan	18 : 1
4 accounts	100 : 1

This study demonstrates the increased grip one has on a customer by extending the business across more than one product line. This tends to hold true in most businesses and it highlights the benefits of cross-selling.

Selling additional products to a customer not only increases your revenue it also locks in your customer more strongly.

Helplines: These are generally beneficial but are especially significant in a field where customers are apt to be confused by jargon and technical detail. Sadly, many helplines are not very helpful. Firstly they tend to take a long time to answer, though whether this is due to staffing levels or the fact that most queries take a long time to answer is not clear.

Secondly they are often staffed by people who are not trained adequately or not given the authority to act in a way that solves the problem.

An example of a good helpline is that set up by Nestlé in France to advise mothers of young babies about health and nutrition. The company reported that this and other similar customer-focused initiatives has enabled them to increase their share of the very competitive baby food market from 26 to 43 per cent.

The telephone should not just be considered as an 'inbound' tool. Calls made to customers to see if they are happy are sometimes called 'cuddle calls'; a brief call asking, 'Is everything all right? Do you have any problems?' can work wonders for customer loyalty. You can also be lucky and achieve a major gain as the following example shows:

EXAMPLE

A small computer retailer in Belfast delivered a new laser printer to a customer. One week later the marketing executive telephoned the customer to ask 'Is everything okay?' The customer replied 'Well, the printer is fine but we are not sure if our carpet will ever recover.'

Apparently when loading the printer with toner there was a major spillage and their nice cream carpet ended up with a large black stain.

The marketing executive sent round a firm of cleaners who lifted, cleaned and refitted the carpet, which cost around twice as much as the profit on the laser printer and she was in trouble with her sales manager.

Not for long, however, because the customer was so impressed that he telephoned the TV station who ran a feature on the computer retailer with the message: 'If it's customer service you are looking for this is the company to buy from.' Since then business has never been so good.

Newsletters (online or offline): These can be very effective but are often misused. Customers do not want to read about your luxurious new offices, they want to know how to get more out of the product they bought from you. Make sure your 'News' is of interest to them not just to you.

EXAMPLE

The European subsidiary of a large international company opened a huge new warehouse on the continent. This cost more than $4 million and they were naturally very proud of this facility. The head-office marketing department produced a newsletter announcing the new facility under the headline 'New $4 million warehouse now open – most modern in Europe'.

Before they sent this to customers, the UK marketing department asked their consultant for advice. 'Bin it' was the response.

The reason for this advice was that the company already had a reputation for high prices (and for very high-quality products it must be said). What they did not need was something that might cause customers to think: That's why they are so expensive.

What they did need was a headline that demonstrated a benefit for the customers. After a discussion with the operations director they eventually came up with a crucial fact: the greater efficiencies of the warehouse would reduce the average delivery time of five days to three days. Now they had a headline:

'New warehouse reduces delivery times by 40%.'

Not surprisingly this had greater customer appeal.

So, although it must be prepared with care, a good newsletter can have a major impact on your customers' attitudes towards you.

Gifts/rewards: These have their place but remember that a customer who can be bought by a gift can be bought by someone else offering a better gift. Try to think of gifts as a 'thank-you' rather than a 'please'. Several studies in the past 20 years have shown that, whilst short-term customer behaviour can be changed by rewards, once the rewards stop, buying behaviour often reverts to its original pattern.

Some studies suggest that if you are able to offer a gift that is relevant to your product there is a better chance of a longer-term attitude change.

Third party offers: This is where you are able to offer something funded or part-funded by a third party. For example, you may be able to do a deal with your local theatre and offer seats at a special discount to selected customers. Such offers are a chance to give your customers a special extra value opportunity.

There are currently numerous offers of free weekend breaks at hotels. Many customers are becoming suspicious of such offers, which usually require the participant to buy meals in the hotel restaurant. The accommodation is free so the offer is genuine, but if a customer had not intended to go away for a weekend it still incurs a cost.

If your offer is a genuine no-strings attached discount, make sure you say so, loud and clear.

Time communications to suit your customers not your sales department: Remember that customers buy according to their time cycles not yours. Don't mail all your customers at the same time because it's convenient to you, remember that relevance relates to timing as well as to content.

Ad-hoc communications: This relates to the previous point. If you can send people some information that is appropriate to them they will appreciate this far more than a stock mailing.

An alternative to the 'cuddle call' mentioned earlier is the 'love letter', which is a similar approach but by mail or email. You cannot afford to overdo this – your customers will not appreciate being bombarded with such notes.

Questionnaires: As mentioned earlier, customers appreciate being asked their opinion and if complaints are identified early, products and services can be developed which are exactly what customers need.

EVPs: The Extra Value Proposition, or added value item such as the booklet on 'Cash Management' given away by Kall Kwik, can be hugely beneficial in retaining business.

Web FAQs: Frequently asked questions areas on websites can help. However, research into the effectiveness of your FAQ section must be done and the opportunity to allow customers to contribute to this through, for example, Wiki and Web 2.0 technology, should be considered. It is also important to realise that FAQs cannot answer every possible question, so there must always be a prominent 'contact us' facility on every site.

Online user groups, discussion boards and forums: The use of user-generated content can be very helpful. A major computer company guaranteed a response to user queries within 24 hours; 85 per cent of these queries were dealt with by other users. The monitoring of these sites can reveal service and product issues and help pre-empt more serious problems.

Loyalty drivers or bonds

These can be classified in three ways:

1. Financial bonds
2. Social bonds
3. Structural bonds

- **Financial bonds** are those that focus on financial incentives for example air miles. They can be distinguished from simple sales promotion due to their long-term nature.
- **Social bonds** focus on the status and nature of membership organisations – for example Diners Club offers special privileged status to its members It is a card payment service but its point of differentiation is the idea of the club, offering 'personal and exclusive' benefits to its members. In the online world, social networking sites and forums replicate this approach. They seek to create a community of interest managed and facilitated by the brand owner. They offer appropriate contact and communications based on the history of the relationship, which may be enhanced through database analysis and a professional and friendly two-way dialogue between the brand and the member. They also facilitate peer to

peer communications and appropriate third party involvement with, for example, carefully targeted offers and partnerships.

   A good example of this is A Small World, a social networking site focusing on high net worth individuals and available by invitation only: www.asmallworld.net. Social contacts between members may be offered online through user groups or offline. Harley Owners Group (HOG) is a community of Harley-Davidson enthusiasts. Have a look at the HOG website at: www.harley-davidson.com/wcm/Content/Pages/HOG/HOG.jsp. (Be warned that, according to Harley, 'prolonged exposure may lead to extended periods of uncontrolled euphoria'.)

- **Structural bonds** Create convenience for customers and easy access to products and information, for example FedEx's package tracking system. Other examples include best plan schemes from the mobile phone companies that migrate customers to the best price plan according to their usage, and the use of extranets to enable automated repurchase or restocking.

Switching costs

In many cases there are costs, in either time or money, involved in switching suppliers. This can be considered from two angles.

1. As a reason for an existing customers not to switch – although this is not an easy topic to introduce to a customer. Ideally we would focus on positive reasons to stay with us.
2. As a benefit to those considering switching to us – this is why banks now offer to manage the changeover of existing payments and standing orders for new customers.

Switching costs can include:

Habit: the costs associated with a change in behaviour, spending habits or routine

Set-up costs: these are costs associated with forming relationships

Search costs: the cost involved in searching for and evaluating an alternative providers

Learning costs: costs involved in learning how to use a new product

Sunk costs: are those invested in past experiences – these may not be relevant economically but may be psychologically relevant to the consumer

Continuity costs: relate to the risks incurred because of a possible reduction in the level of service rendered if a new company is used

Contractual costs: costs that are present because of involvement in reward schemes or due to contractual obligations requiring the customers to pay a penalty if they leave, for example fixed rate mortgages

So far, because of the reasons outlined at the start of this chapter, we have been concentrating on customer retention. However, we also need to consider acquisition.

   The financial aspects of this will be covered in Chapter 8 but acquisition planning is important and it is worth noting that customers do not think in terms of acquisition and retention. They simply see a relationship that develops with a company over time. They expect loyalty to be rewarded and major issues occur when better offers and processes are given to new customers. Managing the customer experience in such a way that this does not happen is an important part of the planning process.

Acquisition planning

The acquisition plan fits alongside the retention plan and is a part of the overall plan for marketing. The plan starts with a review of objectives and the analysis of customer groups to be targeted.

The acquisition plan

1. Review business and marketing objectives
2. Set direct marketing objectives:
    - How many customers do we need to recruit, at what average order value and cost to meet our overall targets?
    - What will be the value of these new customers over time (LTV analysis)?
    - What do we want our audience to think and feel as a result of our campaign?
3. Analyse the target market, their decision-making process and their characteristics

There are many sources of new business and the diagram below outlines them.

Figure 7.4: Sources of business

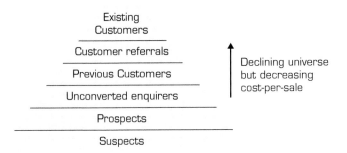

Source: IDM course material

Existing customers obviously form the basis of our retention programmes, but they also have a role to play in our recruitment programmes. They help in two ways:
1. They can refer new business through member get member schemes
2. They can be profiled to help us identify the ideal acquisition targets

We looked at profiling in Chapter 4. We want to recruit the best customers at the lowest cost and the analysis techniques we looked at in Chapter 4 can help with this. We can also draw on internal and external research data to give media buyers and our communications team the answer to the questions:

'What do our best customers look like? How do they make decisions? Where do they go for information? What messages do they respond to?"

The answers to these questions allow us to plan our communication strategy.

Communications planning

We need to align our plans with the prospect's journey, this means coordinating timing and media scheduling to determine how best to move the prospect towards a sale. We must determine what type and style of communications will best determine successful achievement of the objective set and then test these options. This is covered in detail in Chapter 8.

The plan will cover:

- a contact strategy: a one-, two- or multi-stage approach aligned with the customer decision making process;
- integration with contact centres, retail and e-commerce channels and the sales force;
- media choices and scheduling, forecast response, revenue and costs;
- creative execution and message;
- contingency plans;
- testing strategy;
- timetables and budgets.

Communications implementation

Evaluation and programme analysis: The feedback loop needs to be set up to measure the individual campaign results and the contribution to overall marketing and business objectives.

This means looking in detail at areas including:

- cost per enquiry;
- cost per lead;
- cost per sale;
- click-through rates;
- interaction rates;
- overall response rates;
- conversion ratios;
- average order values.

We also need to look at longer-term measures such as:

- renewal rates;
- subsequent order values;
- brand response, i.e. the broader appreciation of the brand and reinforcement of brand values and positioning;
- likeability and recall measures;
- satisfaction rates;
- the effect of integration between campaigns and channels;
- lifetime values;
- ROI – at the right time.

SUMMARY

In this chapter we looked at the value of customers to the company over time. We saw that loyalty is a 'two-way street'; loyalty to customers generates loyalty from customers. We saw that profit comes from customers who transact with the company over time and that levels of profitability generally increase over time. That said, all companies will need to acquire new customers. A balance between acquisition and retention is required, but the greater the customer value over time the more a company can afford to acquire them in the first place. In managing this process the database provides us with an invaluable tool, segmenting customers and helping identify plans to develop these segments.

We explored the six factors to consider when developing customer loyalty. These were:

- explore attitudes as well as behaviour;
- communicate on a regular basis;
- be loyal to your customers;
- all customer touch-points should be managed to foster loyalty;
- highly motivated staff are vital to the delivery of customer satisfaction;
- loyalty must be deeper than a response to price discounts.

We saw that there has to be a long-term approach to the development of loyalty. We need to ask the following five questions.

- What quantified benefits accrue to the organisation through the introduction of a loyalty programme?
- What are existing levels of satisfaction?
- What are the service requirements of your customers?
- How can you deliver loyalty to maximise financial return?
- What genuine benefits can you offer your customers?

We went on to explore what customers value in a relationship and saw that meeting these expectations and retaining more customers can have a significant effect on profitability.

We saw the value of encouraging complaints as a key source of feedback on your activities. Customer satisfaction surveys will not always lead to loyalty but are a good indicator of potential. We saw that the process of measuring customer satisfaction is crucial for four reasons.

1. Retention is key to profitability
2. Customers will tell you what they want
3. The cause of defection can be established
4. The absence of dialogue can cause dissatisfaction

Key to the process is to make all communications consistent, relevant and involving with the potential always to add value to the relationship.

We went onto explore the five stages of establishing a retention programme. These were:

1. classification of customers

2. segment analysis
3. programme streaming
4. communications planning
5. testing and evaluation

We saw the importance of the database triggering appropriate timely interaction with our best customers.

We explored some simple but effective devices for encouraging and developing loyalty. Finally we looked in detail at the role of acquisition planning and considered the structure of an acquisition plan looking at the following process.

- Review business and marketing objectives
- Set direct marketing objectives
- Analysis of target prospects, their decision making process and their characteristics
- Communications planning
  - A contact strategy: a one-, two- or multi-stage approach aligned with the customer decision making process
  - Integration with contact centres, retail and ecommerce channels and the sales force
  - Media choices and scheduling, forecast response, revenue and costs
  - Creative execution and message
  - Contingency plans
  - Testing strategy
- Timetables and budgets
- Communications implementation
- Evaluation and programme analysis

REVIEW QUESTIONS

Where does profit come from? Describe the contribution of retained customers to costs, revenues and profit.

1. Describe the role of the database in evolving a retention strategy.
2. List six factors that make customers loyal.
3. What are the five things a company should do before investing in a loyalty programme?
4. What do customers value in a relationship with a company?
5. Why should companies encourage complaints?
6. What are the five stages of a retention programme?
7. Why is it important to encourage dialogue with customers?
8. Discuss the importance of measuring customers' satisfaction levels.
9. What are the two types of customer communications?
10. According to PricewaterhouseCoopers, a 2 per cent increase in retention will reduce cost by how much?
11. What are the five elements of the communications planning process in delivery of a retention programme?
12. List and critically assess five loyalty building techniques.

EXERCISE

Consider the five stages of communications planning in delivery of a retention programme. Gather and analyse marketing material that you think attempts to deliver against each of the five stages. How effective do you think they are in encouraging loyalty?

Explore how the retention process might work in each of the following businesses:
- a small car dealership
- a large pharmaceutical company
- a marketing consultancy

What are the differences and similarities in establishing loyalty across these sectors?

CHAPTER 8
CAMPAIGN PLANNING

IN THIS CHAPTER

We will discuss the planning of direct marketing campaigns, looking at each stage of the process from concept to evaluation.

After reading this chapter you should be able to:

- Understand how direct marketing campaigns differ from traditional awareness campaigns
- Prioritise targeting to achieve the most cost-efficient results
- Deploy the 13-stage planning process to develop effective campaigns
- Develop critical path analysis with PERT or Gantt charts

Specific topics include:

- How direct marketers approach campaign planning
- Acquisition or retention – getting the priorities right
- The 13 stage process from setting objectives to campaign evaluation
- The importance of SMART objectives
- Managing campaigns using PERT
- A campaign planning checklist
- Case study – Launching Virgin Media

INTRODUCTION

Before we can start to plan a campaign we need to decide on our main priorities. Do we want to build the business we have with our existing customers or find new prospects and convert them into customers?

The answer will often be 'both' but we need to get the balance right and to prioritise each phase of the plan.

As we have mentioned previously what makes advertisements and mailings work is relevance.

It is not easy to send a totally relevant message to a wide audience through broadscale advertising simply because the audience is made up of individuals who each have their own interests and needs.

So what is relevant to one will not be relevant to another.

This is why, whatever the starting point, sooner or later we will find it more cost-effective to communicate selling propositions through direct communication methods such as face-to-face, Internet, mail and telephone, rather than broadscale options like television, radio, newspapers and magazines. But this relies on accurate and comprehensive data.

Even if we have the names and addresses of suspects or even prospects, direct communications will not necessarily be the most cost-efficient place to start.

> **Suspects = all those in the target market, e.g. for buildings insurance all home owners are suspects; Prospects = home owners whose insurance will shortly be due for renewal.**

With many products, especially those that are bought infrequently, it is not easy to establish the right time to communicate with suspects. For example, a company selling car insurance will only find direct mail cost-effective for targeting new customers if they know the motorist's renewal date. Without this there would be very high wastage.

Under these circumstances some form of broadscale prospecting may be more cost-efficient. When using this route it is vital to find something relevant and interesting to say which will grab the attention of the prospect and persuade them to contact us for more information.

Once we have details of their precise requirements we will often find that direct communications are much more cost-efficient.

It is worth looking at the way a direct marketer would approach a communications campaign and comparing this with the method used by traditional advertisers.

The traditional 'awareness' campaign approach consists of four basic phases:

Whereas the direct marketing approach is a continuous cycle of planning, testing, measuring and modifying as the campaign progresses.

Direct marketing cycle

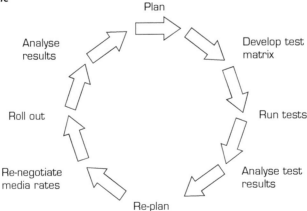

Summarising, the direct marketing approach sets out to:
- identify prospect clusters that offer the greatest potential to…
- …deliver the required number of responses…
- …at the lowest cost per response.

It is a continuing process of testing, measurement and refinement.

Acquisition or retention?

A crucial question when planning campaigns is:

Should we concentrate on developing existing customers or on locating new ones?

The answer will clearly vary from business to business and there are two key questions to be answered:

1. How well developed are our present customers, i.e. how many of them are open to buy additional products?
2. How long can we afford to wait before we make a profit on a new customer? Do we have sufficient funding and sufficient confidence in our ability to retain customers to wait for a year or more to turn a new customer into profit?

The second question is the key to finding the balance between acquisition and retention strategies. If we can afford to wait for profit we can clearly allocate more margin to promotions and thus recruit more new customers by making them a better offer.

There is another consideration in finding the correct balance – the actual cost of buying new customers. Research studies in UK and America have shown that the cost of obtaining a 'conquest' sale (one from a new prospect) is between three and 30 times as much as the cost of achieving a repeat or renewal.

This means that, whatever we decide about the balance of the business, and however much time and money we devote to gaining new customers, we must first of all concentrate on maximising the business we develop from existing and former customers.

The correct sequence of allocating the promotional budget is as follows:
- **Existing customers first**
  In view of the above cost factors it is essential that we concentrate first on retaining and developing existing customers before we start to allocate promotional funds to locating new prospects.
- **Existing enquirers next**
  The second best source of business will be people with whom we already have a relationship, however slight. These people have already expressed an interest and they will always yield a

better return per pound than any outside list of new prospects or any new advertising campaign. It is always worth building the prospect list by ensuring that any enquiries are recorded and not simply replied to and discarded.

In this category we would also include people who used to buy from us but no longer do so. Unless they stopped buying because of a major problem the chances are that, sooner or later they will look to change from their new supplier. A timely reminder may successfully resurrect a previously good relationship.

■ **New business last**

Note that we are not suggesting that getting new business is not important, simply that the best return on investment will come from promotions to existing contacts. It makes sense therefore to exhaust all possibilities of additional or renewal business from these before starting on the much riskier business of seeking entirely new customers.

It will be seen from the above that new business generation should be viewed as an investment, one which will pay back in the longer term rather than in the immediate future. In deciding on the optimum point of profit we will need to consider:

■ **Funding**

Do we have the financial resources to wait for profit?

■ **Competition**

How much competition is there in this field?

How strong is it in terms of price and offer, i.e. are we likely to be able to keep customers long enough to recover our investment?

■ **Development potential**

What additional products do we have which could be cross-sold to the same customer, i.e. what is the potential for developing more business once we have sold them their first product?

■ **The promise**

Will our product or service live up to the promises we made?

Will our customers feel they have been given good value for money when they come to consider re-purchase? **It is always easy to increase response to a prospect offer by lowering the price or increasing the incentive, but if this raises unrealistic expectations we may find that future sales are disappointing.**

■ **Level of service**

Can we afford to maintain or even increase our level of service to existing customers?

What is our current retention percentage, i.e. how many customers continue to buy from us year after year?

The campaign planning process

The process of developing a campaign is quite straightforward. The essential steps are:

1. specify the objective
2. identify the target audience and where to find them
3. define our positioning

4. forecasting and budgeting
5. select the broad communications approach
6. decide on the best timing
7. choose external specialists where necessary, and brief them
8. plan and commission media and creative
9. organise tests where necessary
10. 'sell' the campaign internally
11. prepare for the response
12. execute the campaign
13. measure everything

Now let's examine these in more detail

1. **What's the objective**, i.e. what do we want to achieve with this campaign?

   To encourage enquiries from new prospects?

   To convert previous enquirers?

   To persuade previous customers to buy again?

   To up-sell – sell more of the same products to existing customers?

   To cross-sell – sell additional products or services to existing customers?

   Clearly, each of the above objectives will require its own unique strategy. All marketing objectives should be SMART.

S Specific, i.e. precise and quantified – if it's not specific it can't be measured

M Measurable

A Aspirational – the original says 'achievable' but we prefer aspirational

R Realistic

T Timed – if it isn't timed we can't measure our progress

Specific objectives

'More sales' is not an objective, at least not a SMART one. If it's not quantified and timed it can't be measured; if it can't be measured how will we know we are getting there?

So a marketing objective for a campaign to existing customers may be something like:

'To achieve 200 orders from our existing customers within a marketing cost of £2,000 by the end of Q1.'

This would be even better if we also quantify the amount of revenue we expect these 200 orders to generate.

If the purpose of the campaign is to acquire new customers our objective could be:

'To achieve 500 enquiries from subscribers to business magazines by the end of Q2 at an average cost of £15 each; and to convert 30 per cent of these enquiries into sales by the end of Q3.'

2. **Identify the target audience and where to find them**

Who do we want to communicate with?

Do we know enough about them to send a truly relevant message?

What else do we need to know – how will we fill the gaps?

Where are they – do we know their names and addresses?

Does someone else have a list available? Can we find other businesses who are targeting the same sort of people but not selling a competitive product?

The answers to these questions will tell us how targeted the initial approach can be.

3. **Define the ideal positioning** (see Chapter 12 for more on positioning)

Is our positioning credible – do we need support – have we got testimonials approved for use?

4. **Forecasting and budgeting**

What response do we need – are we looking to break even; make an immediate profit; invest for a longer term payback?

How much can we afford?

5. **Select the broad communications approach**

Will the campaign be multimedia or standalone – can we specify at this stage?

If multi-media do we need to vary by medium? E.g. if we want to build some awareness and trust with board directors before sending a targeted offer to the IT Manager, how long in advance should we run the awareness advertising? Once this is decided we can start to think about media.

Broadscale media such as:

Business publications – for the above application

National newspapers and magazines

Broadcast – TV and radio

Outdoor advertising such as posters and bus sides

Online advertising – banners and pay per click (PPC)

Search engine optimisation (SEO)

(Media are covered in detail in Chapters 9 and 10)

Targeted communications such as:

Direct mail

Email

Door-to-door distribution

Telephone/text message

Sales force – telephone and face to face

Public and press relations (PR)

PR is not generally seen as part of a direct marketing campaign but if you can get a mention in a relevant medium and a unique phone number or the URL for a specific landing page on your website you can sometimes generate a good volume of enquiries. One mail order company received more than 1,000 enquiries from a two line mention in *Good Housekeeping* about their new catalogue.

Successful campaigns will often incorporate a combination of the above options.

6. **Decide on the best timing**

The next step is to establish the correct timing for each prospect segment. If we know the right time it is easier to make a highly specific approach, it is also more likely to be productive.

For example, all parents will know that September to December is the time toy retailers target their prospects; but for a toy manufacturer selling through retailers, the season starts in January.

In business-to-business marketing a very productive time is often around the financial year-end, when very often there is budget available for discretionary activity. So one useful piece of information about a company is the date of their year-end.

7. **Think about specialist suppliers – even for a brief campaign any of the following may be involved:**

A direct marketing agency

Online advertising or search specialists

A bulk email consolidator

External print consultants

If we use external suppliers we have to brief them. Selecting and briefing suppliers is covered in detail in Chapter 15.

8. **Plan and commission media and creative**

External specialists will often be required for these tasks. They must be briefed thoroughly and allowed enough time to do their best work. The more time a media buyer has the more chance there is to negotiate the best deals. Having decided on the right media and timing we can now start to think up offers in preparation for writing copy or briefing an outside creative team. Good creative work takes time – if we ask for the impossible we may get the work on time but it is likely to be adequate rather than brilliant.

9. **Organise tests where necessary**

As we will see in Chapter 14, testing can achieve dramatic improvements. Every campaign manager should at least consider including some tests.

10. **'Sell' the campaign internally**

We must make time to tell colleagues what will happen and when; all campaigns run more smoothly when internal departments buy into them.

11. **Prepare to handle the response**

If we are asking people to send for more information, we will need to estimate how much response to expect. We can then produce enough 'response packs' to satisfy demand. It is important to avoid keeping people waiting – this is a good rule in any circumstance, but it is vital when responding to enquiries. It is wise to assume that prospects may have sent for details of two or three alternatives; the first one to respond has a better chance of getting the business. The quickest way of course is to give prospects the option of downloading a pdf brochure from the website, which also overcomes the problems of estimating how many brochures to print.

However, unless we can be sure our target is likely to prefer an online response we must also cater for the offline respondents.

When generating leads for follow-up, speed is equally important. Leads should be passed directly to the sales or telemarketing people with any supporting information, e.g. what the respondent asked for, any special requests and so on. Salespeople may acknowledge the lead by telephone when making an appointment, but if this cannot be done quickly a written acknowledgement is advisable.

12. Execute the campaign

We must remember to include a way for prospects to respond; ideally they should be offered a choice, e.g. website URL, email address, telephone number, and even a fax number or coupon and reply paid envelope. Many people feel that fax is no longer relevant but in mid-2009 one UK office products company found that, because of the huge volume of emails now being received by business people, they were getting more responses to faxes than to emails.

13. Measure everything

Future campaigns will be easier to plan, and more likely to succeed, if they are based on previous experience. The best approach is to develop a 'guard file'. This is a 'scrapbook' containing all relevant details as in Figure 8.2 below.

Figure 8.2: Sample guard file

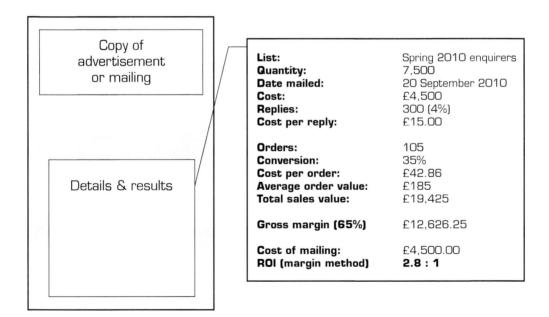

The details recorded will of course vary according to the activity, e.g. banner advertisement, email, mailing, telephone follow-up campaign, etc. The creative shown could be a scanned-in advert or mailing, a video of a commercial, and so on. We can add in any relevant costs such as sales-force time, etc.

Comprehensive guard files also carry additional information such as the weather on the day the advert appeared, and details of any competitive offers appearing on the same day (not possible with mailings and emails, of course). Such details can be very helpful when analysing results six months down the line.

The example ends with a calculation of ROI (return on investment). There are several different ways of expressing ROI and these are explained fully in Chapter 16. The one used above is the 'Margin Method', i.e. we made £2.80 margin for every £1 we spent on the promotion? This is the preferred option for direct marketers. Whatever method is decided on the important thing is always to stick to the same method so we can be sure we are comparing like with like. This is then a sound basis for comparing results and selecting the best, most cost-effective, approaches for redeployment in future campaigns.

Managing the campaign

All experienced campaign managers use some form of tool to help them keep tight control of the many elements. This used to be called Critical Path Analysis (CPA) and the two most common tools used today are Gantt Charts and PERT Charts. The simplest is the PERT chart and here's an example.

Figure 8.3: Direct market campaign PERT chart

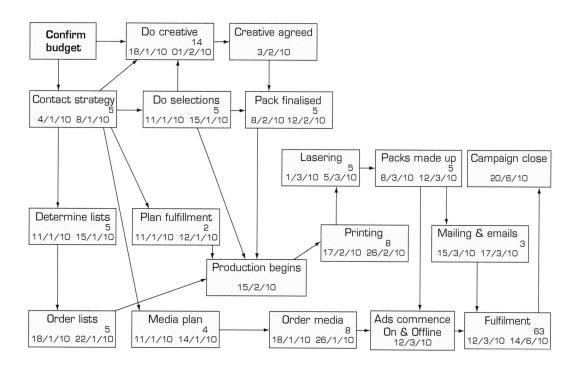

The PERT chart is simply a spreadsheet that links the various boxes so if a significant change is made to the dates in any box the chart automatically updates every subsequent box so the manager can immediately see the effect on the planned completion date. Very useful!

Campaign planning checklist

Objectives – must be SMART A precise, quantified statement

Acquisition or retention? An acquisition campaign takes a lot longer to organise

One stage or two? One stage is easier; not always possible with complex or costly products

Timescales? Have you allowed enough time to do a great job? Three months is not long enough to plan a campaign

Profiling/analysis/research Do you know your target? How much do you know? Is this enough to ensure your communications will be relevant? If not how will you fill in the gaps? Do you need primary research? That can add months to your schedule.

Communications strategy Single medium or multimedia? If the latter remember that you may have to build some awareness among your client's budget holders before sending them your targeted offers. Timing needs to be carefully planned so each element can do its job properly. For example, if you are planning to sell an enterprise-wide hardware network to a company you may need a couple of months of advertising in business magazines to 'prime' the members of the Decision Making Unit before you send your targeted communications to the IT Manager.

Think about suppliers

Do you have, or need a direct marketing agency; mailing house or telemarketing bureau; bulk email provider; online/search specialists?

Will you buy print direct?

Prepare comprehensive supplier briefings – poor briefing is one of the main causes of campaigns going 'off-track'.

Keep everyone informed – maybe set up an extranet; any changes are entered as they happen; all involved check it daily.

Remember to brief colleagues as well as suppliers – call centre, customer service, despatch.

Budgeting and finance

What is your financial objective for this campaign? Break even? Profit? Investment in future business? You must make a clear case here as this is how your budget holders will decide whether to fund your project. If it's an investment programme you may have to develop a lifetime value analysis (LTV) to justify your payback projections. LTV is explained in detail in Chapter 16.

Media evaluation and selection

Think about identifying advertising media, mailing lists/email lists, Online targeting, Selecting TV regions.

Make your media choices early to give partners the chance to negotiate the best spaces and deals. Remember that the best media can be hard to get into at short notice.

Testing

Unless you have a good strategic reason for not doing so you should always test new advertisements, mailings, emails and so on.

Communications – key tasks for you

Set up a project file so if you are taken ill, or delayed on a business trip, a colleague can pick it up and run with it immediately. This must contain: **Schedules** detailing what happens when; **Contact lists** with out of hours numbers too.

Response handling

Will you have enough phone lines and people – if you don't know that's another good reason to test first.

Creative aspects

Remember your acronyms – run through AIDCA and 5 x W – have you covered everything? Remember that creative people don't work nine to five – give them all the back-up information they need to answer questions out of hours. Make sure they have fully understood your corporate guidelines.

Programme analysis

Measure everything. Replies, conversions, revenue, follow-up activities, competitive activity, even the weather! Remember that your measurements may be scrutinised very carefully in six or 12 months' time. Make sure they are complete.

SUMMARY

- Schedule everything.
- Allow for slippage and remember Murphy's Law, 'what can go wrong, will go wrong' and remember, Murphy is an optimist!
- Break everything down into key tasks and assign completion dates to every task.
- Identify dependencies and re-plan if necessary.
- Brief everyone – internal and external.
- Keep people informed of changes – and remind them of key dates.
- Keep checking budgets and schedules.

CAMPAIGN CASE STUDY:
LAUNCHING VIRGIN MEDIA

INTRODUCTION

Virgin Mobile and NTL:Telewest merged in February 2007, creating the UK's first consolidated quadruple-play company, offering a bundled cable television, broadband Internet, and fixed and mobile phone service. There were two main reasons for the merger:

- The immediate potential of cable technology, and
- the longer-term possibilities offered by quad-play.

Virgin Media had a great opportunity in the UK, provided that it, and its lead agencies Rapier and Rainey Kelly Campbell Roalfe Y&R, could overcome several major challenges within tight timescales and financial constraints.

This study looks at how Virgin Media and Rapier overcame consumer misconceptions about cable to rapidly establish Virgin Media as a leading UK home digital brand.

BACKGROUND

Government policy is that all UK TVs will receive a digital, rather than an analogue signal by 2012. A digital signal can be transmitted via an aerial, cable or satellite. The first cable TV licence was issued in 1984, and the first satellite did not launch until 1989, but UK cable take-up remained stagnant during the 1998–2005 digital TV boom years. In 2003, Telewest's cable infrastructure covered 25 per cent of the UK and it was considering using Wi-Fi as an alternative way to expand, rather than laying more expensive fibre-optic cable.

UPGRADING TO DIGITAL TV

By 2005, a combination of a flurry of free broadband offers designed to incentivise the take-up of pay TV, and the impending digital TV switchover meant that UK digital TV penetration had reached 90 per cent. Although digital satellite TV (BSkyB) and terrestrial digital TV (Freeview) take-up was steadily increasing, the number opting for cable delivery remained static; in spite of the fact that fibre-optic cable potentially offers the best technical digital service delivery solution.

OBSESSION WITH SHORT-TERM RESULTS

By 2007, cable technology was in serious danger of missing out on the UK's digital revolution. Obsession with short-term results had driven Telewest and NTL into pursuing price-led marketing strategies, concealing the real benefits of cable from consumers. This strategy resulted in UK consumers regarding cable as a poor man's alternative to BSkyB's satellite technology.

NTL and Telewest merged in March 2006 to create Britain's second largest residential telecommunications organisation after BT, in addition to its TV and Internet provision. Prior to the merger, NTL had acquired a reputation for poor, unreliable customer service: Telewest was widely regarded as the superior brand of the two.

TARNISHED IMAGE

So, in 2007, NTL:Telewest had a somewhat tarnished image and, by association, so did cable technology. Virgin Media's principal, larger, better-established pay TV rival in the UK was BSkyB.

BSkyB, had been a dominant presence in UK TV broadcasting since its inception in 1989. In 2001, BSkyB had 5.3 million UK household subscribers, compared to cable and digital terrestrial's combined two million households (*Source*: *The Independent*, 23 July 2001). Even post-merger, NTL:Telewest was still playing catch-up with around five million UK households, compared to BSkyB's eight million.

VERTICAL INTEGRATION

BSkyB's vertical integration throughout the supply chain is a key strategic factor in its hold over the UK market. As a channel provider and distributor, Sky has exclusive prime content rights in some important areas, such as some films, and the sporting events now available only through its premium channels, Sky Sports 1, Sky MovieMax and Sky Premier.

BSkyB has a history of dealing ruthlessly with potential rivals. In 2002, it was the subject of several complaints about anticompetitive practice made to the Office of Fair Trading. Telewest, NTL and ITV Digital (insolvent by 2002) raised three separate concerns, but the OFT decided there was insufficient evidence to uphold the complaints.

In *The Guardian* in 2003, Greg Dyke, then Director-General of the BBC, commenting on the recent demise of ITV Digital, expressed his concern about the balance of power in UK broadcasting: 'A healthy broadcasting market in the UK needs a third gorilla alongside the BBC and Sky. Having seen off the threat of ITV Digital, BSkyB has the corporation in its sights.'

Within two months of its launch, Virgin Media was in dispute with BSkyB. Virgin queried the distribution price of some of BSkyB's programming and BSkyB promptly withdrew its Sky basic channels, including hit programmes like first run editions of *Lost, The Simpsons* and *24*. This meant Virgin was unable to supply its customers with the promised programmes. This cost Virgin Media customers, many defecting to BSkyB, and could easily have derailed its entire launch strategy. By November 2008, however, a mutually satisfactory deal had been struck with both companies agreeing to exchange broadcasting content without High Court involvement.

'AS BRILLIANT AS IT SHOULD BE'

It was against this unenviable back-drop that Virgin Media and Rapier's mission to create 'an entertainment and communication world that was 'simply brilliant' was mobilised – a carefully orchestrated series of integrated communications designed to awaken the public to the possibilities that Virgin Media's cable technology had to offer.

AMBITIOUS OBJECTIVES

The principal objective was an immediate 25 per cent improvement in cable performance.

Virgin also had a visionary brand objective based on Virgin's brand values: to establish Virgin Media as the consumer champion in the communications and entertainment market; and to use the arrival of the Virgin brand to prompt a mass reappraisal of cable technology.

In addition to the main objectives, supporting objectives were designed to function as communication planning principles for the campaign:

- Demonstrate how cable, unlike any other delivery technology, can resolve typical consumer gripes.
- Show that bundled services offer superior value.
- Liven things up and challenge the status quo.

DEVELOPING THE CAMPAIGN PROPOSITION

The launch delivered the uncompromising message that Virgin Media offers consumers superior value to that of existing service providers. The new brand had to create an immediate impact on consideration measures and elicit an equally swift response from consumers.

The campaign needed a strong creative idea to provide a focal point for the integrated communications strategy. The immediate potential that cable technology offers was the most compelling source of a unifying idea. The fibre-optic cable technology gave Virgin Media its unique service proposition by offering:

- Superior products. Better broadband with more advanced functionality and better on-demand offerings, just as these requirements were becoming more common among consumers.
- Superior value. Virgin Media's bundled quad-play service offered consumers a cheaper alternative to purchasing broadband, TV, landline and mobile services separately.

GENUINE DIFFERENTIATION

Cable technology gave Virgin Media the opportunity to genuinely differentiate itself from the current pay-TV and telephone market leaders, Sky and BT.

Virgin Media now turned to research to unearth the insight that would allow it to create the right communications approach to excite consumers across different product categories and demographic segments.

The results of the consumer perception research were stark. Overall, the UK consumers' experience of the home digital marketplace was commoditised and scary:

- Consumers faced a bewildering array of choices, offers and providers.
- Brands were engaging in confusion marketing – complex price offers (Talk Talk, Orange), product specifications (Sky broadband), jam tomorrow (BT Vision) and weirdness (Bulldog).
- All expected woeful customer service; sadly led by NTL customers.

These research findings enabled Virgin to identify the core insight:

'Services that are supposed to make my life easier and more fun are making it more complicated and painful.'

COMMUNICATION STRATEGY

Virgin wanted to communicate the emotional and rational impact of their brand offer:

'To show people just what a duff deal they'd been putting up with from media owners like BBC, Sky, BT, Vodafone telling them what content they could watch and when, how long they could go online and so on.'

POSITIONED AS A CONSUMER CHAMPION

Virgin positioned itself as a consumer champion, simplifying the sectors and shifting power from corporations to the consumers. Essentially Virgin Media empowered consumers by giving them control of the technology, opening up films and TV schedules to customers and removing Internet and phone usage restrictions.

The marketing challenge was that the core products and services customers received had not changed. The campaign had to redefine the existing customer experience, rebuild the value proposition and engage people in genuine dialogue.

The strategy was to make customers feel they were part of something special. The creative reflected the power shift from corporations to consumers over time and then deepened and personalised the message. The creative idea was 'Over to you', with messages focusing on the new freedom and possibilities offered by Virgin Media services. Messages used everyday language, rejecting the technical jargon that had previously typified home digital communications.

RE-ENGAGING DISAFFECTED CUSTOMERS

Importantly, Virgin Media needed to speak to its own customers. Current cable customers' experience was reflected in the worst satisfaction scores in the industry. The communications strategy aimed to re-engage disaffected consumers in the same technology that had already turned them off. The acid test would be its ability to convince the existing customer base that Virgin Media represented something new and different.

The launch initially targeted the franchise areas that Virgin Media could service using the existing cable infrastructure. Early launch communications were focused geographically, using traditional brand-building communications such as TV, radio, PR and poster sites.

BLEND OF TARGETING APPROACHES

The geographically targeted communications were followed with tightly targeted messages aimed at segments that offered the greatest potential to increase cable uptake:

1. Interest-based – targeting groups like sports fans and gamers, with relevant messages in PC magazines, portals, and sports bars.
2. Trigger-based – identifying moments of consideration and targeting audiences such as home movers, new mums.
3. Switcher activity – identifying key targets for switching, or for packaged value-based solutions. A combination of propensity and demographic modelling was used to target all direct personal communications.

CAMPAIGN EXECUTION

Customers were the first group to be told about the launch. The entire customer base of over five million households received a letter from Richard Branson outlining his vision for the new company. The letter directed customers to a specially designed microsite offering a new kind of dialogue; customers were asked for their views on the business and about Virgin Media's services in general.

The spirit of open dialogue continued throughout the year, with the introduction of Penny Movie festivals; customers voting for suitable films that could be offered for 1p via the on-demand service.

Virgin Media and Rapier delivered a series of integrated campaigns during 2007 in order to deepen UK consumers' understanding of specific products and the brand's value proposition.

Richard Branson spent the day of the launch with the famous burlesque performer, Dita Von Teese and an array of other celebrities in an eight-hour live TV broadcast, answering texts and emails; the business, news and entertainment airwaves buzzed.

Figure 8.4: Advert for Virgin Media

Teaser-style TV and radio spots, and a huge outdoor campaign built awareness and raised issues about the way consumers were being served by the existing providers. Broadcast communications were ideal to demonstrate the benefits of cable's unique product attributes. Commercials featuring iconic film stars were tailored according to broadband capacity; Uma Thurman explained the benefits of Virgin Media's products, using a calm and intimate tone, to cut through the cluttered marketplace.

Broadcast communications were supported by press advertising and posters at high-traffic sites. Direct response media were used to explain Virgin's manifesto for change, engaging consumers in a one-to-one conversation.

'THE TRUTH ABOUT BROADBAND'

This creative idea tapped into consumer confusion and leveraged Virgin's brand equity as a consumer champion. Communications appeared in geographically targeted mass media, direct response adverts in the national press and long copy executions in targeted online and offline media. Provocative adverts prompted people to check whether or not they were getting the speed they were paying for by visiting a specially created microsite.

Figure 8.5: Example of provocative advert for Virgin Media

This creative idea stretched seamlessly into acquisition communications, featuring a simple £10 offer to encourage a prompt response.

Other campaigns focused on the value delivered by Virgin Media's bundled service. Direct response TV ads featured well-known media personalities such as Ruby Wax. All campaigns were supported by direct marketing activity targeting key acquisition opportunities:

- Home movers received a mailing with the message: 'Settling in? Lucky you, you're already connected to Virgin Media.'
- Sub-segments were targeted with specific messages; for example, gamers were reached through tailored ads in the 'gamers' press.

RESULTS

The launch campaign met or exceeded all its objectives. At launch, NTL had much higher awareness than Virgin Media. Within three months of the launch spontaneous awareness of Virgin Media passed that of NTL and prompted awareness reached 80 per cent.

BRAND IMAGE QUICKLY ESTABLISHED

Virgin Media's brand image was quickly and precisely established by its launch campaign. There were reassuringly low scores on negative associations that might have been an NTL legacy, and high scores on Virgin Media's priorities: 'changing the view of the market' and 'products easy to understand'. Public perceptions of the brand improved dramatically over the course of the campaign, giving Virgin Media a leading rational and emotional image.

By the end of 2007, total consideration of Virgin Media stood at 40 per cent, 10 per cent higher than ever achieved by NTL or Telewest, and Virgin now dominated Sky in its broadband Internet space with respect to brand consideration.

IMPROVED CUSTOMER SATISFACTION

Customer satisfaction scores improved dramatically during the year, accompanied by an increase in new customers arriving as a result of existing customer recommendation.

The campaign also had a positive impact on hard measures, such as cost per acquisition and return on investment (ROI).

The overall cost per response dropped by more than 50 per cent compared to 2006. Crucially, ROI grew steadily during 2007, despite the multi-million pound relaunch cost. Virgin Media customers were not just buying, they were buying more; the average number of services taken by new customers grew from 1.8 to 2.3.

CABLE DECLINE REVERSED

The campaign caused a major reversal of years of cable decline. Within three months Virgin Media was enjoying dramatic growth. It continues to focus on specific products with an emphasis on niche targeting and customer engagement.

Consumers now have a credible alternative in a sector that was moving towards monopoly before Virgin Media stirred things up.

LESSONS LEARNED

Virgin Media, Rapier and other partner agencies achieved a complete turnaround of the brand in less than 12 months, overcoming public misconceptions of cable and confusion about home digital services. Virgin Media's positioning as a consumer champion challenger brand is in complete harmony with the Virgin Group's brand and positioning.

The marketing communications strategy was built on a solid foundation of cable technology's untapped potential, combined with genuine consumer insight. For 12 months, UK consumers were simultaneously targeted with an integrated series of carefully crafted messages about the brand and specific products and services, using mass and personalised communications.

The campaign was a complete success; cable technology is high on UK consumers' consideration lists, and Virgin Media's customers are the happiest in the sector.

Many thanks to Virgin Media and to Rapier for permitting us to include this case study.

SUMMARY

In this chapter we have explored the process involved in developing a direct marketing campaign. We identified that we must first develop a clear understanding of the priorities of the business.

We presented a 13-stage process which covered the following elements:

1. specify the objective;
2. identify the target audience and where to find them;
3. define positioning;
4. forecasting and budgeting;
5. select the broad communications approach;
6. decide on the best timing;
7. choose external specialists where necessary, and brief them;
8. plan and commission media and creative;
9. organise tests where necessary;
10. 'sell' the campaign internally;
11. prepare for the response;
12. execute the campaign;
13. measure everything.

We discussed the need to make our objectives SMART: Specific, Measurable, Aspirational, Realistic and Timed.

We looked at the need to identify and locate the target audience, including the use of bought-in lists.

Media options were discussed in relation to the characteristics of the target audience and the reach and impact of the media options.

The process of communications development looked at the production of creative, booking of media and crucially preparing to fulfil any response.

We discussed the importance of campaign measurement and evaluation and explained the benefits of the 'guard file'.

We considered the crucial question of the balance between acquisition and retention. Understanding the source of profit within the company the cost of acquiring customer was seen as a crucial factor in this.

The sequence within the allocation of the marketing budget was discussed and we looked at the most profitable source of business, i.e. our existing customers moving to existing enquirers and finally to new business as generally the most expensive source of business. We saw that in many cases customers become more profitable over time and our aim should be to optimise profitability over time. Our ability to do this was dependent on our financial resources, the state of competition, our capacity to create value from the relationship through up-selling and cross-selling, and our ability to maintain customer satisfaction through on-going customer service.

The chapter closed with a campaign planning checklist.

REVIEW QUESTIONS

1. What does the acronym SMART stand for?
2. List four possible objectives for a direct marketing campaign.
3. List two broadscale media and two targeted media.
4. What is a guard file? What are the key benefits of maintaining this?
5. Why is it important to target existing customers first?
6. Describe the sequence of allocating marketing communications budgets.
7. How does a PERT chart help the campaign planner?

EXERCISE

Identify two recent multimedia campaigns that you think worked well. Where did you first see the campaign, i.e. in what medium. How do they carry the theme through from one medium to another?

Follow through by visiting the website and checking the linkage between the ads and the landing page – do they fit?

CHAPTER 9
PLANNING OFFLINE MEDIA

IN THIS CHAPTER

We will discuss the planning and buying of offline marketing media.

After reading this chapter you will:

- Understand the special problems of measuring media effectiveness in multimedia campaigns
- Appreciate the effect that digital developments have had on traditional media
- Know where to find detailed information on audiences, costs and characteristics of all offline media

Specific topics include:

- The difference between planning direct response and awareness campaigns
- Brand versus response – the traditional conflict – and the new way
- Planning integrated campaigns
- The use of follow-up techniques
- The importance of accurate targeting
- Sources of media information
- Strengths and weaknesses of the main offline media including
  - newspapers and magazines
  - loose and bound-in inserts
  - the telephone
  - door-to-door distributions
  - third party leaflet enclosures
  - direct mail
  - DRTV
  - radio
- External data sources – rented lists, lifestyle data
- Buying and evaluating offline media

INTRODUCTION

In the past few years there has been a significant shift in budget allocations. Press, TV and radio budgets have been reduced in favour of online advertising. This is partly because audiences continue to decline whilst advertising rates have remained static and thus represent less value for money.

Another reason often quoted is that response rates to traditional media are declining but this is not quite so clear-cut. Before the advent of integrated multimedia campaigns measurement of direct response advertising was simple. Each insertion was a standalone event with precisely measurable results. We would use individually coded reply coupons, unique telephone numbers and unique website landing pages so every response could be correctly attributed to its source.

The special problems of campaign measurement in multimedia campaigns

Direct marketers today face a conundrum. Our entire marketing philosophy of direct communication with individuals, which has often meant that our cost per contact has been much higher than traditional broadscale media costings, has always been underpinned by the measurement tools peculiar to direct marketing. We have been able to prove through our precise response analysis that direct marketing can be hugely cost-efficient.

Today, however, we have two problems:

1. We have established beyond doubt that multimedia campaigns are more effective than single medium approaches – but this means that we cannot measure individual media with our previous precision. We can get close through the use of complicated regional testing, e.g. omitting one medium from the mix in one area and measuring the effect, but it is not as precise as before. And in any case we are really only measuring the response route that the customer finally chose – there is no way of measuring precisely which and how many of our communications the customer saw before responding. **And that is the simpler of the two problems.**

2. More complicated is the involvement of the Internet. Most offline ads and mailings, even if they ask respondents to respond by phone or mail, include a URL. This is not a problem in one sense as it can only increase response but it does create a problem when it comes to attributing the response to a specific stimulus. Of course we can design specific landing pages so that we can measure the final decision point but, again, we will never know what other messages they saw before deciding to contact us. A further complication is that, based on anecdotal evidence, even when seeing an ad in the press or on television, many prospects go first to a company's website because they realise that there will often be a better deal for orders placed online. And that's the offline evaluation problem. With online ads it is even more difficult. If someone sees an online banner we know for sure that they are online, so that means they have several options available at the click of a mouse, and for them it is even easier to go direct to the company site.

   Here's an example of the online problem. A recent research study by Neilson NetRatings and the agency Harvest Digital asked 'If you see an online ad for flights or holidays, which of the following actions do you usually take?' Here are the responses:

Click on the ad i.e. directly attributable response

26 per cent

Go directly to the advertiser's site using the URL
attributable if the URL led to a unique landing page

29 per cent

Go to a travel agent or other route – not attributable

8 per cent

Use a search engine – i.e. 'Google it' – not attributable

57 per cent

The above percentages total more than 100 as some respondents chose more than one option. Whatever the precise statistics are, it is clear that a high percentage of these responses cannot be correctly attributed. So, at least in this case, measurement of online advertising is inherently unreliable. It is fair to say that if we can judge an online campaign as successful from the attributable responses, the true situation can only be better, but it does not offer us our usual precision. And in any case, without further research we will never know whether travel advertising stimulates different behaviour to that for other product areas.

And we are still left with the offline/online conundrum.

Before we consider individual media it is worth looking at the way a media planner would approach a direct communications campaign and comparing this with the method used by traditional advertisers.

Brand versus response – the traditional conflict

Ten years ago a new term came into marketing – Brand Response Advertising – though despite the claims of many agencies it wasn't a new concept, simply a new name for Rapp & Collins's invention of the 1980s – double-duty or dual-purpose advertising. Rapp & Collins identified that awareness ads could generate response and direct response ads could achieve awareness provided they were written and designed to do so. Hence dual-purpose or double-duty advertising.

Although things have changed for the better since then, many companies and agencies still cling to the same old split between 'awareness' and 'direct response' with each side sure theirs is the right way. These conflicting camps are often totally opposed to each other and the debate continues.

But the new way is catching on

And it is the way all advertisers will eventually go. Already a high percentage of TV commercials carry a website URL and often a telephone response number too. And most print advertisements now include at least a Web address.

Brand response advertising works

It is proving effective for many advertisers targeting both consumers and business people. Major brand advertisers have found that well-designed attractive ads **can change attitudes and generate response** if the two sides will simply put aside their prejudices and work together. There are a number of advantages for planners:

- **Greater choice of media**

  Because of the dual-purpose objective, the campaign can be extended into media that would not quite satisfy the pure evaluation of either awareness or response planners.

- **More creative flexibility**

  During a campaign different elements will contribute more or less to either objective. However, it will always be necessary to ensure that the basic principles of communication are followed. We will return to this in Chapter 13.

- **More response methods**

  Today we can receive responses in at least five ways: website, email, phone, mail or fax. Most of these do not require a coupon so there can be less pressure on space. However, an interesting development recently is that coupon responses have been increasing – perhaps because some people are concerned about the integrity of their personal data when they send it online?

These advantages and the fact that many advertisers are experiencing great success means that brand response or 'dual-purpose' advertising is here to stay.

The start of the digital age

Today, digital technology has brought about changes in all directions:

- **New working practices**

  The virtual office is a reality – at least it is technically. There are still many people who will not willingly embrace, or perhaps do not have the self-discipline to accept, the freedom to work from home. But those who do can easily stay in touch with the office online.

- **New communications vehicles**

  Now that we can go online through our mobiles and TVs, we no longer need even a laptop to stay in touch. Video conferencing makes 'face-to-face' meetings possible from anywhere in the world. The Internet also enables closed user groups to share bulletin boards and diaries across companies and countries.

- **New channels of distribution**

  The Internet is also a major distribution channel, enabling written and audio-visual material to be shared or sold around the world.

- **Changes in social behaviour**

  Although there are now more than 400 commercial television channels in the UK (compared to one in 1980) overall viewing time has not increased. Consumers have greater choice, greater control and the opportunity for greater interactivity. Many people now spend more time online than they do watching television.

- **Web 2.0 and social networking**

  One of the biggest changes in the last few years has been the advent of Web 2.0 and the massive growth in social networking and user generated content (UGC). In just six years, Facebook has become the big one with more than 500 million members worldwide. Twitter, YouTube, My Space, Bebo and many others are also huge.

■ **New ways of getting news**

In all developed markets newspaper circulations and television audiences are in decline. Old-established papers in UK, Europe and the USA are facing closure and many television contractors are also in trouble. The newspaper decline is undoubtedly because of the ease of getting up-to-the-minute news online; television because of the increase in online activities and the switch of budgets to online. At the end of 2009, 70 per cent of all UK homes had Internet access and 90 per cent of those had broadband (63 per cent of all homes).

All of the above factors have to be considered when planning a communications campaign.

Planning direct response versus brand awareness

Let's look at the differing objectives of the two types of media planner and then see how these might be brought into alignment.

A traditional advertising planner aims to achieve maximum coverage of the marketplace in the shortest possible time. High frequency and repetition are considered desirable, maximising 'opportunities to see'. In the following chart we can see how coverage is built up week by week.

Figure 9.1: Traditional media planner

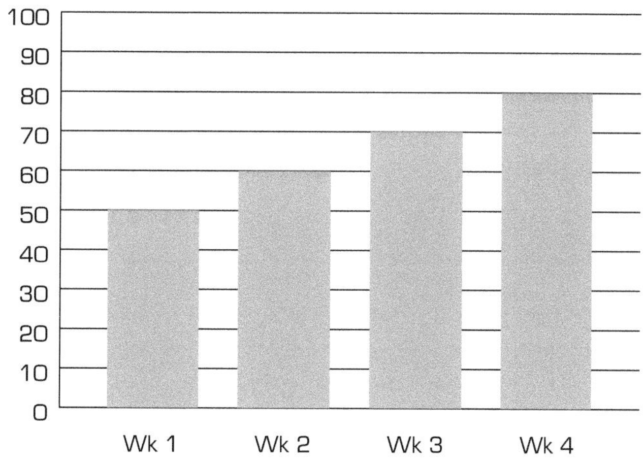

However, from a direct marketing perspective this is not the most cost-effective use of the budget. When we examine the response data from each individual insertion we find that effectiveness of each subsequent advertisement declines rapidly if the insertions run too closely together.

So the direct marketing planner's chart looks very different:

Figure 9.2: Direct marketing media planner

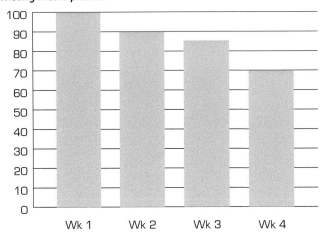

This shows clearly how response declines as the campaign progresses and the DM planner aims to minimise this decline in two ways:

1. By testing to find the ideal 'gap' between each insertion – broadly the longer the gap the less the decline. There is of course a trade-off required as no advertiser can afford to wait too long between insertions. Careful testing enables the DM planner to optimise the budget.

2. By developing two or more versions of the same offer, i.e. two different advertisement approaches. This enables frequency to be increased without the same level of decline in response. We will discuss this again when we cover testing in Chapter 14.

Integrated media planning – bringing it all together

The integrated media planner uses a mixture of media to achieve a variety of impacts that collectively add up to a successful campaign. The planner will use media for achieving positioning, understanding and to create **noise** – having this going on even in the background enables response-oriented advertisements to be more cost-effective.

Using media in this way means that occasionally we need to accept a slightly higher cost per response than we would expect from a strict DR campaign but we will have achieved a greater overall effect by adding the awareness elements to our campaign. This can have a beneficial effect on retention and repeat sales. It will also make future campaigns more cost-effective. There are two different types of media integration – strategic and tactical. Strategic integration will be covered in Chapter 11.

Tactical media integration – follow-up techniques

Many direct marketers have found that combining two or more media in close proximity can have a significant effect on response levels. The first technique was the follow-up mailing and this has been used for many years. A typical follow-up mailing is sent to arrive around 10 to 14 days after the initial contact. This works quite well and generally results in an overall response gain of around 33 per cent, i.e. a 3 per cent response might increase by a further 1 per cent. However, a warning is necessary here.

Some marketers, on experiencing a poor response to a mailing, think immediately about sending a follow-up. But this is a very bad idea. If the first mailing was unsuccessful, a follow-up of the same offer will be three times as bad. The first requirement is to try to establish why the mailing failed. There might be several reasons – including:

1. Poor targeting – in this case a follow-up to the same people will not solve the problem.
2. A poor offer – again, repeating the same offer will be no solution. Changing the offer, perhaps by adding a promotional incentive or offering a discount, may increase response.
3. A problem with delivery – you may be able to establish this with the postal organisation – did all your seed mailings arrive on time? (See Glossary.)

> The main thing to remember is that follow-ups to failed mailings are usually a waste of money.

Using the telephone for follow-up

This technique was first developed in the early 1980s when B2B marketers began testing the telephone to follow up a direct mailing.

When used in this way the telephone has to be deployed in a different way to a traditional mailed follow-up. A mailed follow-up can repeat all the information that was included in the initial mailing – a telephone call cannot. Therefore the call has to be made much earlier. Telemarketers will say that calls can be made up to five days after the mailing arrives but this is too long. Many tests have shown that the optimum day for the call is two days after the mailing touches down – i.e. starting in the middle of day three. This allows for a spread of delivery, which is quite common, especially when using Royal Mail's discount scheme, Mailsort.

Waiting longer than this means there is a good chance that the mailing will have been binned or at best filed and the call will not work.

When this technique was first used it generated large increases in response, sometimes up to 10 or 12 times as much as that from the control sample. It is not so effective today for two reasons:

1. It has been used heavily, especially in B2B, and the effect has worn off.
2. The increasing disaffection with receiving unsolicited telephone calls, witness the rapid increase of numbers registered with the Telephone Preference Service (TPS) and the corporate equivalent (CTPS).

Despite this the technique still works but to a lesser extent. Gains today are more likely to be two or three times control rather than the higher levels of the 1980s and 1990s.

Recent examples include:

- a UK charity that used the telephone to follow up a mailing asking prospects to commit to a monthly donation by direct debit – the telephone call increased acceptance by more than three times;

- a card company mailing asking retailers to take the card generated 3 per cent response. The follow-up call increased this to 7 per cent;
- publishers of business magazines also find that telephone follow-up to subscription renewal mailings is effective.

Follow-ups are not confined to the telephone of course. Any two or more media can be combined to enhance effectiveness:

- a car manufacturer found that sending a mailing (frequently referee to as 'dropping a mailing') after a substantial press advertising campaign was significantly more effective than when mailed in isolation;
- similarly, several companies have had success by linking mailings to DRTV campaigns;
- the organisers of an IT symposium found than following a direct mailing with an email one week later, doubled the number of registrations.

The planning process

We start with targeting – always the most important factor in the success or otherwise of any communications campaign. There have been many researches into the relative effectiveness of each factor in determining whether an advertisement or mailing will work well.

A study we did at Ogilvy & Mather showed the following weightings between the four basic factors:

Factor	Value
Targeting – list or medium	6
Offer or key benefit message	3
Timing – in relation to prospects needs	2
Creative treatment	1.35

A more recent study in America found the following:

Targeting	60 per cent
Offer	30 per cent
Creative	10 per cent

Methods and minor details vary from study to study but all come to the same broad conclusion – that targeting is undoubtedly the most important factor.

So, **who** are the people in our target audience?

- What are they like?
- Where do they live?
- What do they do?
- What do they think?
- What do they want, like and need?

When is the right time to approach them?

- What is the decision-making process for this audience/product?
- When are decisions made?
- When is the ideal time to influence them?
- When are they most likely to respond?

Where can they be found?

- Where do they live/work?

What media do they consume?

- What newspapers and magazines do they read?
- Are they receptive to direct mail?
- How much time do they spend online, and what sort of sites are they likely to be using?
- Do they listen to radio – at home? – in the car?
- Television? – which channels/time slots?
- Cinema – what sort of films?
- Do they use trains, buses or the underground?

How do they consume media?

- What is their location?
- What are they doing?
- Are they involved/uninvolved?
- Active/passive?
- Interested/disinterested?

How much will it cost to reach them? The objective is to reach the maximum number for the minimum cost. So, build your ideal media plan by understanding the market forces, and using flexibility and negotiation skills to achieve an acceptable compromise.

The next step is to identify the available media – there are hundreds of options:

- national commercial television contractors
- regional ITV companies
- hundreds of satellite and cable channels
- commercial radio stations
- mobile and landline phones

- poster sites
- cinema screens
- national newspapers
- regional paid-for newspapers
- regional free newspapers
- consumer magazines
- trade publications, and of course
- many thousands of websites for online advertising

Not to mention sponsorship, promotions, interactive media, product, packaging and the many 'ambient media' opportunities. You can advertise in 'ambient media' such as:

- in public toilets
- on petrol pumps
- in golf holes
- on supermarket floors
- in concert programmes
- on entertainment and travel tickets
- on escalators and so on
- WOM – word of mouth marketing. This is a fairly new 'medium' but one that is growing rapidly with specialist WOM agencies and departments springing up as we write. Marketers can now hire people to speak well of their products in bars, clubs and so on. Taxi drivers who recommend a show or a holiday destination to their passengers are often being paid to do so.

Media planning is about understanding your audience and where to find them, then using appropriate media intelligently so your message is seen as relevant and interesting. So how do you identify the right medium from the thousands of options? You start with research and profiling your existing customers if possible. This helps you identify the characteristics of good prospects and of individuals likely to be low value/high risk and so on. Profiling characteristics may include:

- geographic factors. Identifying people by region, town, TV area, vicinity to stores and so on;
- demographics. Age, class, gender, household composition, marital status and so on. With businesses you may be looking at size, industry, number of company cars, sites, coffee machines and so on;
- geodemographics. Using some of the many property classification systems such as ACORN and Mosaic (see Chapter 4 and the glossary);
- psychographics. Here we are considering attitudes and lifestyle characteristics with products such as Acxiom's PersonicX (see Chapter 4);
- behavioural. Purchasing patterns, frequency, value and so on.

The objective of profiling is to identify the best customers and then use research to locate similar people/companies with the highest propensity to become good customers.

Identifying the audience – sources of media information

Once we have defined our target there are a number of media research sources to help us locate prospects:

- TGI – Target Group Index. This is based on a sample of 24,000 UK residents aged 15+. The survey covers 200 publications across 500 product fields and 4,000 brands. It can be used simply to identify the most appropriate publications for reaching a specified audience or in a much more complex way to identify attitudes, lifestyle characteristics and publications read by, say, Marks and Spencer shoppers.
- NRS – National Readership Survey. A larger (38,000 people aged 15+) but simpler study covering 287 publications. It is used primarily to identify the characteristics of, say, *Daily Mail* readers. These can then of course be compared to your own customer profile.
- BBS – British Business Survey. Conducted by the Business Media Research Committee this bi-annual report provides readership information on more than 3,000 business people.
- BARB – Broadcasters Audience Research Board. This reports on size and viewing habits of the UK television audience. A sample of almost 5,000 households is measured continuously using a combination of automatic and manual diarising covering each individual member of each household.
- RAJAR is similar to BARB but reporting on radio audiences.
- POSTAR is similar for poster audiences.
- FAME (Film Audience Measurement & Evaluation, formerly called CAVIAR) – reports details of audiences by film and frequency of visit.

Rather than going into great detail about these studies, which change frequently, I simply recommend that you contact each organisation for their information pack – you'll find their addresses in the Appendix.

Most media are capable of carrying a direct marketing message. Their effectiveness varies according to:

- the size of audience you wish to reach;
- how much you can afford to pay for a response;
- the complexity of your message;
- how appropriate a particular medium is for your message, and so on.

A good media plan:

- is built to deliver the number of responses your business needs;
- covers branding as well as response requirements;
- makes your communications stand out through innovation;
- allows for constant testing and change where necessary.

Media selection

Now let's review the various offline media options open to us.

Press: Newspapers

We can use press advertising in a variety of ways:

1. To initiate a relationship either through inviting a request for information or sometimes through a direct sale. The former is called two-stage or two-step advertising and the objective is to generate a 'lead' or enquiry. Direct sales are referred to as one-stage, one-step or 'off-the-page'.

2. In a dual-purpose role where we can achieve awareness and generate leads at the same time. Some critics say that dual-purpose advertising does not work but my experience and Stan Rapp's experience with Rapp & Collins prove otherwise.

3. As a support medium – a well-timed press campaign can increase response to a concurrent activity such as a mailing, door drop or even a television or radio campaign. It can also make sales force activity more productive and it can be highly effective in driving traffic into a website. In business-to-business it can reach decision-makers that we may never ever know about. However well targeted a direct mailing is it may not result in an order if the budget holder has not heard of us. An awareness campaign in newspapers or business magazines, in advance of a targeted offer, can be the deciding factor in achieving an order in a business-to-business campaign.

Newspapers offer several advantages:

■ Large audiences – despite the general decline in circulations some press audiences still run into millions so press can be an effective way of reaching large numbers of people quickly.

■ High response volumes – although response percentages are low, the actual number of responses can be large. 0.02 per cent of *The Sun*'s 2.9 million circulation is still 580 replies.

■ Fast results – a daily newspaper has a very short 'life' – consequently 80 per cent or more of your responses will come in within a week. This shortens the process of testing and re-planning media.

■ Flexible rates – good negotiators will find many publications are ready to be realistic on price. We are currently in a buyer's market and this is unlikely to change in the near future if at all. The best discounts are obtained through short-term buying and especially distress buying. This is when the paper has a space it cannot sell in tomorrow's edition due to a last-minute cancellation. If you have an advertisement ready to go you may find you can get a good space for well below half price. You cannot depend on this for an entire campaign of course – many professional space buyers avidly seek such spaces so there are not many such spaces that hit the open market. However, you should brief your media buyers to watch out for these opportunities.

■ Testing opportunities – many newspapers offer A/B split run facilities enabling direct response advertisers to test alternate copy or offers. A/B splits are explained in Chapter 14.

■ Reader relationships – many regular readers tend to trust their paper and therefore the advertisements appearing therein. Some advertisers have discovered that writing advertorials for specific papers, i.e. with copy in the style of the editorial, increases response.

- Low entry cost – because of the lower production costs, it is cheaper to test press than television. It is sometimes possible to test a region of a paper before 'rolling-out' nationally, thus minimising the cost until the publication is proven to work.
- Cost-efficiency – press responses can be surprisingly cheap. Some advertisers can actually make a profit 'off-the-page' though this will not always be the most important factor. As you will see when we discuss budgeting in Chapter 16, many advertisers are prepared to invest in generating new customers and to wait a year or more to achieve profit.
- Short lead times – if you have an advertisement ready you can book a space this afternoon and see your advertisement appear nationally tomorrow morning.
- Creative versatility – the range of sizes, shapes and special positions available in most papers enables a high level of creativity to be applied.
- Regional opportunities – some national publications print separate regional editions – ideal if your business is centred in one region only.

The perceived weaknesses of press advertising are:
- Competitive clutter – unless you buy large spaces or pay a premium for a solus* position your ad is likely to be accompanied on the page by at least one other. If it is competitive, as are so many in say the financial pages of a paper, your ad will lose some of its impact.

> * **A solus space is where your ad is the only one to appear on that page; semi-solus means there will be one other advertiser on the same page.**

- Cost – even though the 'cost per thousand' is low in national newspapers, even a small space can cost hundreds of pounds.
- Short 'life' – today's paper is 'dead' tomorrow.
- High wastage – however carefully we target, there will be high wastage in newspaper advertising. This is mitigated of course by the low cost per thousand.
- Low quality of response – short copy and broad audiences tend to produce unqualified replies, so in two-stage advertising* conversion to sale can be quite low.

> * **An advertisement or mailing that asks for an order immediately is a one-stage activity; one where the prospect is encouraged to send for further information or say, an application form for a credit card, is two-stage.**

- Low readership of any individual advertisement – research shows that as little as 5 per cent of 'readers' will actually notice any individual advertisement.
- Lack of environmental selectivity – again, unless you pay a premium or negotiate hard, your advertisement will be placed 'run-of-paper'. This means it could go anywhere from city pages to sports section. The surroundings may not be appropriate for your offer, and therefore not attract the right sort of readers.

■ Direct response 'graveyards' – some publications tend to group direct response advertisements and place them all together in the back of the paper (this is particularly prevalent in newspaper magazine supplements). The publishers argue that this creates a 'department' and this can be true. However, unless actively seeking a direct response opportunity your prospect may not even enter the department and will thus not even see your offer.

What size of advertisement will be most cost-effective?

Traditional advertisers, with their requirements for 'coverage' and 'opportunities to see' prefer to take large dominant spaces and these may often be highly effective of course.

Because they can test and measure individual insertions, direct marketers know that the smaller the space the more cost-efficient it will be (assuming that the smaller space contains the same wording and offer as the larger one).

There have been a number of researches into the relationship between size and cost-effectiveness and Philip Sainsbury analysed the results of several of these studies when developing his 'Square Root Principal'.

Sainsbury noted that, although doubling the size of an advertisement might be expected to double the response, in fact it only increases response by around 41 per cent. The square root of two is 1.41 and, as multiplying size by two gives a response of 1.41 times he called this Sainsbury's Square Root Principle.

The principle works in both directions as the following table shows:

Table 9.1: Sainsbury's Square Root Principle

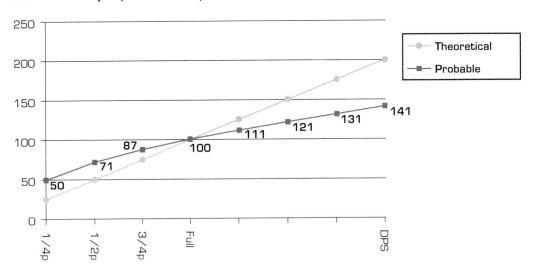

What Sainsbury showed is that, if a full page produces 100 replies, a half page will produce around 70 replies and a quarter page around 50. So, if your objective is to achieve the lowest cost per reply you should plan to use the smallest space into which you can comfortably fit your message.

There are, however, three caveats:

1. If your main aim is to impress your distributors and channel partners with the effort you are putting behind this product, small spaces will not be effective.
2. Equally, if your objective is to build awareness, large spaces will do this more quickly.
3. You can usually negotiate better discounts on large spaces – thus, if you could buy an ad twice the size for less than 1.4 times the cost it could still be cost-effective.

Magazines

There are several types of magazines in the UK:

1. Broad interest magazines targeted at females such as *Woman, Woman's Weekly* etc.
2. Men's sports magazines and 'glamour' titles such as *FHM, Zoo* and others.
3. Special interest titles such as those for golfers, photographers and boat enthusiasts.
4. 'Serious' news magazines such as *The Economist, Time* and *Spectator*.
5. Age-related titles like *The Oldie* and *Saga* magazine.
6. Satirical titles such as *Private Eye*.
7. Free supplements with weekend newspapers.

Magazines are frequently used by direct marketers for both one-stage and two-stage campaigns. They can be useful when you want to target specific groups, whether based on demographics, such as 'women aged 25 to 34' or special interests such as angling or golf.

One thing to bear in mind about both newspapers and general interest magazines is that people don't buy them to read the advertisements. Special interest magazines are different. It is not unusual for people to buy one of these specifically because they are looking for some equipment. For this reason the earlier comment about 'graveyards' does not apply in these titles.

Major strengths of magazines include:

- High reader interest – if your offer is well targeted your advertisement is likely to be better read than the same copy run in a general newspaper.
- Long life – many magazines are in circulation for months or even years. Some advertisers in special interest publications receive replies months after running their offers.
- Pass-on readership – some magazines have a very high 'secondary' readership – this can increase the exposure to your ad.

There are also some weaknesses and these include:

- Long copy dates – whereas a newspaper ad can be booked and run in a few days, colour magazines quite often require artwork several weeks before the publication is distributed. This can make testing and roll-out a lengthy process.
- Cost of testing – large ads can be expensive so testing can be costly.
- Limited testing capabilities – although some magazines offer split run facilities these can be withdrawn at short notice when the volume of advertising exceeds a certain limit. With the exception of TV programme journals, there are no regional testing opportunities.

■ Graveyards – here again publishers tend to group direct response advertisers into 'graveyards' at the back of the magazine.

Loose and bound-in inserts

Many of the above limitations can be overcome by the use of loose or bound-in inserts. These leaflets arouse criticism from many people but they are a highly effective advertising medium. Studies have shown response increases of 500 per cent and more by using a loose insert against a full-page colour advertisement in the same publication.

There are several types of inserts

■ Loose inserts (the most common) are the leaflets that fall out of your newspaper or magazine. However, after criticism from newsagents, major publishers often enclose these in plastic envelopes.

■ Bound-in inserts are usually made of card and this in itself can increase readership, as the magazine tends to fall open where the card appears – this is called a 'hot-spot'.

■ Outserts – this is the name given to a leaflet bound onto the outside of a magazine. This can be expensive to arrange but is of course very responsive as no one can look at the magazine without seeing the advertisement. These are also sometimes called 'wraparounds'.

■ Tip-on cards are typically postcard-size cards that are spot-glued on to the page on which an advertisement appears. They are fairly expensive as you have to pay for production and print of the card, a full-page advertisement in the magazine and an additional charge for gluing ('tipping-on') the card. However, like the bound-in version they produce a hot-spot and this generally increases response.

A word about design and printing: most leaflets are inserted by machine so there are some restrictions regarding size, shape and positions of folds and perforations. It is important to discuss your plans with the publication before finalising design and print.

One reason why inserts receive criticism is they are obtrusive. Yet this is the very reason they work so well. Research tells us that only around 5 per cent of newspaper readers notice any of the advertisement; 100 per cent notice a loose insert, even if most only throw it away. If the headline catches their eye with something relevant they will read it.

Research often takes the form of a 'reading and noting study'. Here are the results of two noting studies (see Glossary) comparing magazine advertisements with loose inserts:

Space Advertising

Size/Position	Noting Score (%)
DPS colour	59
Page colour	57
Page mono	42

Loose inserts

Advertiser	Size of insert	Noting %
Toy retailer's catalogue	48 pages	87
Insurance offer	4 pages	83
Mail order catalogue	4 pages	79

As we can see, the noting scores are much higher with inserts than with advertisements. The use of inserts has grown dramatically over the past 15 years and there are several reasons for this:

- High responsiveness. In the final analysis the only reason for a medium to continue to attract advertising is that it produces results. As most loose inserts carry direct response advertising they are highly measurable, though the 'leakage' to websites mentioned earlier makes precise attribution difficult. They have consistently produced more cost-effective replies than page advertising.
- More media opportunities. Very few newspapers 15 years ago would accept loose inserts. Today many newspapers, including major national titles, carry inserts. Most local paid-for and free newspapers also carry them.
- Ease of response. Prospects can tear off a reply card or post or fax back the entire piece, although often the main thrust is to generate a Web response.
- Creative flexibility. There is almost no limit on space (but see note opposite about enclosing machinery). It is quite common to see A5 catalogues of up to 64 pages used as loose inserts.
- Use of existing leaflets. If you have some spare leaflets, inserting can be a very cost-effective method of distribution. This again is subject to compatibility with the inserting process, and it may also create a problem with precise attribution.
- Test opportunities. Inserts offer much greater flexibility for test programmes.

Additional benefits

1. Part circulations can be bought. With a newspaper you have to buy the whole circulation, or an entire region and cannot test to a small percentage of readers. With a loose insert you can specify the quantity you want to test and in many cases the region too.
2. Economical testing. You can place, say, 250,000 inserts in *The Sunday Times* (less than 25 per cent of its circulation), and then supply two or more different leaflets each carrying a unique offer or copy approach. In this way you can answer many questions with quite a modest test budget.
3. The ability to vary copy by type of reader, or region. For example, you might want to run an offer to all European readers of *The Economist*. If you place an advertisement you are restricted to a single language but with loose inserts you can vary the language for each batch of magazines – ensuring that readers in each country can read the offer in their own language. The ad reps will tell you that this is unnecessary as they wouldn't buy the magazine if they couldn't speak English. True, but they still prefer to read in their own language and so are likely to pay more attention to your offer.

- Localised use of a national medium. National publications often contract out the inserting and this is sometimes done at local wholesaler level. In these circumstances a business in, say, Worcester could advertise locally using a national paper. This is not done by all publishers so you would need to check it before assuming it could be done in your region.
- Quality control. With some magazine advertisements the colour reproduction of your product may not be as good as you would like. With inserts you control the print quality.

Among the stated weaknesses of inserts are:

- Cost. Inserts are quite expensive as you have to produce the leaflet and then pay for insertion. A full distribution of inserts may cost three or four times as much as a full-page advertisement. However, response will often compensate for this, so it is not necessarily a weakness.
- Timing. Because of the leaflet production time it can take a lot longer to set up an insert campaign than an advertisement campaign.
- Quality of response. In the past some insert users reported that the quality of insert responses (measured by percentage conversion to sales) was slightly lower than advertisement responses. This is, I think, based on a period when most responses came by post. Under those circumstances the existence of a convenient tear-off reply paid card did tend to stimulate a greater number of casual replies. Nowadays, however, when more than half of the responses come by phone or Web this factor is not so relevant. Today, some advertisers report that conversion to sale from insert responses is as high or higher than from those received through the mail.

Buying and evaluating press advertising

Most publishers have a 'rate card' that sets out charges according to a variety of circumstances. The main factors affecting cost are:

- Date. If your advertisement must appear on a fixed date you will be expected to pay a premium on top of the basic charge for the size of space you require. You can avoid this extra charge by specifying 'run of week', this means that the publication can place your ad when it is most convenient to them. There is a mid-point when you may specify a three-day period – say Tuesday to Thursday when the additional charge will be less.

  There is also the seasonal factor; advertisements in early December may carry a premium simply because all traders are advertising their Christmas offers so space is literally 'at a premium'.

  If your business does not require your ads to be so precisely timed you may be able to negotiate very good discounted rates in off-peak times. When I was marketing controller for a mail order company I used to buy as much space as possible over bank holiday weekends. Major advertisers avoided these times assuming that fewer people actually read their papers over holiday periods. Response levels do tend to fall at these times but because the papers need to sell their space it becomes a buyer's market and I was able to buy at very low rates. This more than compensated for the drop in response.

- Position. Not all pages attract the same level of readership. Publications will either research their audiences or often simply go with the accepted 'wisdom' that says that the following positions attract more readers and are thus worth a higher charge:
  1. Cover positions – front cover, back cover, and to a lesser extent inside front and inside back cover. Outside covers are usually worth the premium.
  2. TV programmes page – generally accepted to attract a high readership, but only of TV viewers.
  3. Readers' letters page – this would depend on the product and the sort of people who would be interested in it. Probably worth a test.
  4. Early pages, especially right-hand pages – again, worth testing
  5. 'Solus' and 'semi-solus' positions. A solus position is where you are the only advertiser on a page. Semi-solus is where you share the page with only one other advertiser.
  6. Facing matter – if your advertisement is placed on a page that faces editorial rather than more advertising it is considered to be worth a premium. Of course this may depend on what the editorial is about, but it is generally beneficial.
  7. Within a feature – an obvious one if your product will appeal to those interested in such a feature.
  8. Front of section – a financial advertiser would pay extra to be on the first page or perhaps the contents page of a financial section of, say, *Money Mail*.
- Size – the larger the advertisement the greater the cost. Spaces of less than full or half pages are usually charged by the single column centimetre (scc).
- Colour – obviously a colour advertisement will cost more than a black and white (mono) space.
- Market demand – this can be seasonal as discussed above. But there are also times when, because of general economic booms and recessions, space is more or less freely available. Ten years ago it was very hard to buy TV or press space because of the dot.com boom. Once this bubble burst it became a buyer's market again. The current recession (2010) combined with the general decline in audiences discussed earlier is making rates very soft.

Keeping your costs down

The first thing to do, if you have a sizeable budget, is to appoint a good media buying agency. They can often save you lots of money through their experience, knowledge and sheer buying power. They will advise you but the things you can do to help them buy economically are:

- Keep your plans flexible – don't specify a fixed day if you will be happy with a two- or three-day option.
- Specify the front third of the paper, say, rather than the first right hand page.
- Don't use non-standard sizes, they are very difficult to buy at discount rates.
- Allow for short term/distress buying. All publications have problems occasionally – an advertiser may be forced to cancel at short notice and the publisher will need to sell that space in tomorrow's paper immediately. If you have an advertisement ready to run your agency may be able to buy a space at less than half of the rate card cost.

Third party distribution of leaflets

In addition to inserting leaflets in newspapers and magazines there are numerous opportunities for enclosure in mailings, invoices and parcels despatched by non-competing 'host' companies.

For example, some consumer mail order companies will enclose your leaflets in their parcels. Your product must be non-competitive with theirs, but this is often an excellent way of targeting good prospects. This is a popular medium with an annual capacity of many millions of leaflets. Among the many such opportunities are enclosures in:

- customer mailings;
- catalogues and statement mailings;
- product despatches;
- directory distributions;
- sample packs;
- shared envelopes;
- subscription magazines and newsletters.

Among the benefits of such distributions are:

- implied endorsement from the host;
- leaflets are highly targeted at mail-responsive audiences;
- low cost – a fraction of the cost of a mailing;
- it is difficult for competitors to monitor your campaign.

One reservation about this form of distribution is that you buy volume on the company's estimate of the number of packages it is expecting to send. If this volume is not achieved, you will receive fewer responses, though you will of course only pay for the volume actually despatched.

There are a number of companies that organise these leaflet distributions and you will find some addresses in the appendix.

The telephone – inbound

In the past 10 years many major UK companies, notably in the financial services and IT industries, have outsourced their call centres to Asia, primarily as a cost-cutting exercise. Some of these have been very successful but there have also been many problems. Some of the complaints are prompted by British xenophobia but many are genuine.

There have been some problems with understanding strong accents (in both directions it must be said) but one of the major factors has been the poor infrastructure supporting the overseas call centres. In some cases the operator has been totally unable to access the customer's details and this means that however efficient and polite the operator, the customer experience is unsatisfactory.

The high volume of customer complaints has prompted some companies to repatriate their call centres and some now even feature 'British call centres' as a benefit in their advertising. In 2010 there are more than 750,000 people employed in UK call centres.

However, many of these companies are still trying to cut costs which results in a different sort of dissatisfaction. If one has to spend several minutes negotiating automatic menus only to be given a pre-recorded message saying 'we are experiencing an unusually high call volume at present so please call back later', satisfaction is highly unlikely.

Before we leave the inbound functions of call centres it is worth considering the differences between outsourcing customer service call centres and those specifically dealing with technical help. In my view a customer service centre should be either an internal department or at least seamlessly linked to the centre of the business so that however complex a query is, the operator can either find the answer quickly or transfer the caller to a colleague in another department. Where someone in a remote country is trying to sort out a problem of late or damaged delivery, many problems can arise. We will return to this topic in Chapter 15.

Technical help on the other hand can be outsourced with fewer problems. Technical help centres have operated effectively in this mode and this may well be because technical knowledge can easily be trained into highly educated people of any nationality whereas customer service operations require much broader knowledge of local conditions and idioms.

Another factor here is that a technical help call is typically self-contained and does not require much involvement of other departments.

The telephone – outbound

The use of the telephone as a sales medium excites much criticism and debate. The preference services statistics bear this out:

The Mailing Preference Service (MPS) was set up in 1983 and in the past 27 years a total of 4.5 million people have registered their wish not to receive unsolicited direct mailings.

The Telephone Preference Service (TPS), which is barely 10 years old, already has more than 15 million subscribers. A further 1.9 million business numbers are registered on the Corporate Service (CTPS). The preference services are administered by the UK Direct Marketing Association and you can find out more by visiting http://corporate.mpsonline.org.uk.

Note that registering your number or address details with the preference services will not stop existing suppliers calling or writing to you. By giving them your details you are deemed to have approved their use (this is called a 'soft opt-in') and to stop these communications you will have to contact each company direct.

The telephone is ubiquitous and the mobile telephone revolution has added to the power of the telephone. More than 70 million mobile phones are owned in the UK. The current third generation (3G) mobile devices offer a truly integrated experience, enabling email and Web access almost anywhere in the world.

More than 15 per cent of UK homes now use only mobiles and do not have a landline.

The telephone is most effective as a support medium but it is also still used as a standalone direct marketing medium. Its use for cold-calling is not recommended, although some companies still use it in this way. Many people complain that despite being registered with the TPS they are still receiving cold calls, often from telephone service providers. These calls are generally made by a small number of rogue UK operators or from outside the country.

Cold-calling gives the industry a bad name but the fact that it is still used shows that it does work. My advice is not to use the phone in this way and if you do choose to go ahead, make sure you check your new prospect numbers with the TPS as the penalties for transgression can be severe.

For inbound work and outbound work to existing customers the telephone is unparalleled as a medium:

- it is immediate and interactive;
- it can personalise the brand;
- it is highly personable and targetable;
- it is extremely flexible cross-sell and up-sell opportunities can be exploited immediately;
- it is superb for customer care, complaint handling and information gathering;
- in combination with other media it can significantly boost response.

Against this the telephone is expensive, its immediacy means that even existing customers find calls intrusive. It demands skilled well-trained and motivated staff.

The mobile phenomenon

The mobile is a hybrid medium in that it combines online and offline. Therefore it could belong in this or the next chapter. As most of the current applications are really digital we will cover it mainly in Chapter 10.

The Mobile Data Association (MDA) tells us that 265 million text messages (SMS) and 1.6 million picture and video messages (MMS) were sent every day in 2009. A study by the international Mobile Marketing Association reports that 95 per cent of text messages are opened compared to only 25 per cent of emails.

But sending texts is only a small part of the potential of a modern-day mobile phone. An increasing percentage of users access the Internet for news, to locate services, book tickets and appointments and so on. The mobile network can be used in all aspects of direct marketing from acquisition to retention and customer service. We will return to this in the next chapter.

Direct mail

As we saw earlier, the most important factor in making communications campaigns successful is targeting. So in direct mail the targeting element is the list of people we want to approach. Getting this right should be easy when we are targeting existing customers. We should have enough current data to enable all mailings to existing customers to be relevant. Good quality data enables us to select only those for whom our offer will be relevant and thus reduce annoyance and also save cost.

And relevance is the make or break factor in direct mail as the following example shows:

One UK high street bank recognised the importance of relevance several years ago. Prior to that point they had always mailed 'the list', i.e. all customers who were considered creditworthy, every month. Response rates were adequate but not exciting.

They started to use their data more intelligently and began a different monthly mailing programme. Each month they would review all customer accounts and select the 50,000 or 100,000 for whom a particular product or offer would be appropriate at that time. This created much extra work, and the smaller mailing volumes meant that they lost the economies of scale they had previously enjoyed.

In the first year of running this new programme, instead of the 40+ mailings they would normally have sent they sent more than 500, all to small segments.

The results? Despite the additional costs the programme generated a return on investment (ROI) three times higher than that of the control group. The programme satisfied the three golden rules of successful marketing communications:

Send the **right message** to the **right person** at the **right time.**

Volumes of mail despatched and response rates have both declined in recent years but there are a number of reasons for this:
1. All experienced direct marketers strive hard to reduce costs and avoid wastage by using sophisticated research and segmentation tools – we do our utmost to eliminate 'junk mail'.
2. Among the heaviest users of mail are financial services companies and the current deep recession in this sector has caused them to cut back on their promotions.
3. Use of email has grown dramatically, especially in B2B, and this too has had an effect.
4. Direct response rates are also being affected by the tendency of customers to go directly to a company's website rather than respond to a mailing. This is partly a matter of convenience although customers are also becoming aware that many companies offer better deals and discounts to those ordering online.

Despite the above concerns, direct mail and the telephone (especially mobile) are still first choice offline media for contacting existing customers and prospects. There is very little wastage provided your data is well maintained. If you also have email addresses then that will be the lowest cost option, although many people, especially business people, complain that they are receiving too much email. We will discuss online communications fully in the next chapter.

Direct mail is very flexible – the message can be varied according to what we know about this customer's likes and dislikes and their purchasing history. We can vary timing too, increasing relevance even more. Direct mail messages are remembered far longer than those sent by other media. A study for an international airline found that 74 per cent of those mailed had remembered the key messages three months after the final mailing was received. In another study, more than 60 per cent of young females (16 to 24 years old) remembered the main message six months after a mailing. This was possibly enhanced by the fact that under-18s do not receive so many mailings, but it is still an impressive statistic.

Companies undertaking lifetime value analysis (LTV – see Chapter 16) frequently find that customers who started with them as a result of a direct mailing are generally more valuable than those from any other medium. This is believed to be because a mailing is likely to give a much more detailed description of the product and the company; thus the eventual purchase is a more considered action.

Although there is a lot of talk and press criticism about 'junk mail', research tells us that the majority of consumers and business people they like to receive direct mail 'providing it is relevant and interesting'.

External mailing lists

Direct mail and email are clearly among our first media choices for communicating with existing customers and prospects. But they can also be used effectively for prospecting providing we can find appropriate names and addresses. And that is where rented lists are very valuable. We will deal mainly with email in the next chapter but list location is the same for both types of mail so we will cover both here.

There are thousands of mail and email lists available for rent in the UK – split approximately 50/50 between business lists and consumer lists. It is possible to buy lists outright rather than renting though this can be expensive and is not always the best option. Unless you have a product or service that will appeal to the majority on a list you may simply buy a lot of data that will never bring you any business.

My own preferred option is to rent first and make a good offer that encourages interest from the maximum number of good prospects. Once these people have responded you can put them onto your own database and, subject to the provisions of the Data Protection Act, and for email The Electronic Commerce Regulations 2002, mail them as often as you like.

Most rented lists are available from List Brokers and there are several ways of finding brokers:

1. **Simply search online for 'rented mailing or email lists'**
2. **Read the advertisements in the marketing trade press** – you will also find lists advertised in the business to business sections of national newspapers.
3. **Call the Direct Marketing Association (DMA)** and ask for their list of members who are list brokers. Contact these brokers for details of any lists they can suggest to reach your target audience.
4. **For direct mail lists, talk to your Royal Mail customer service executive** – you will sometimes hear of new lists that are not yet on the open market.

The different types of lists

There are several types of lists on the market:

Basic lists of people by general descriptor – for example a list of financial directors, or homeowners.

Lists of people who did something – e.g. responded to a mailing for a loan; subscribed to a magazine and so on. These are sometimes called 'response lists'. If you were a publisher looking for subscribers to a new magazine about business finance, the first type of list, e.g. financial directors might be worth a test; but you would do much better with a list of FDs who already subscribe to Accountancy Age. Experienced direct marketers invariably find that behavioural data is the most powerful. Which leads us to...

Lifestyle databases – there are several companies that have built databases of prospects with extensive data about their lifestyles and buying preferences covering everything from toothpaste to holidays. You'll find a list of these suppliers in the Appendix. These companies offer a huge number of consumer names and addresses and they can be used in a variety of ways:

1. They can compare your own list with their data, profile your customers and offer to rent you additional names that match your best profiles.
2. They can add data to your own customer records, enhancing your selection capabilities.
3. They can link customer data to the target group index (TGI) so you can also get help in selecting the correct broadscale advertising media to find new prospects.

Here's an example of the value of additional data when selecting prospects:

A client launched a new mail order venture – a selection of activities, games and books aimed at teenagers. I asked a lifestyle database company for their list recommendations. Their first suggestion was to simply mail their general list of mail order buyers – this would cost £95 per thousand names. I decided to use this as a control (see Chapter 14) and against that I tested:

Mail order buyers – having one or more children, aged 10+, having bought toys, games or books to the value of £50 or more, in the previous 12 months – this list cost the basic rate of £95 per thousand plus the four extra 'selections' at £7 per thousand – so a total cost of £123 per thousand names. The results were:

Basic list – £95 per thousand – 2 per cent ordered – average value £51 = 20 orders value £1,020

With extra targeting – £123 per thousand – 3.5 per cent ordered – average value £55 = 35 orders worth £1,925

The extra £28 per thousand generated additional sales of £905 per thousand.

Business-to-business lists – lifestyle lists are obviously about consumers, but there are many business lists that include much additional data that can help you in targeting the right prospects.

List rental contracts

List rental contracts are quite specific and should be read carefully. Usually a rental covers a single use of the names and if the renter does not honour this agreement the broker will know through the use of 'seed' names – people who report to the broker when they receive a mailing. Using a rented list more than the agreed number of times is a breach of contract and brokers would be quite within their rights to sue offenders.

Tell the list broker who you are trying to reach – they should be able to offer a number of suggestions of suitable lists. Before the data is supplied the broker or list owner will want to know the content of your mailing or email.

Note: In some cases the list owner will not release the names to you at all and will expect you to use a mutually agreed mailing house or email consolidator.

De-duplication

Even when renting a single list it is worth considering a merge/purge or de-duplication run. This is helpful in a number of ways:

1. It will prevent you from sending people more than one copy, saving prospect irritation, and in the case of a posted mailing your money.
2. Analysis of the de-duplication run will tell you whether you have chosen good lists
   - the higher the duplication with your best customer list the better the rented list will perform
   - the lower the duplication within a list the better that list is managed, therefore the more up to date the data is likely to be.
3. You will avoid renting names of people already on your database.

Good de-duplication is a highly technical process and not something the average mailer should attempt. An off-the-shelf PC database package may claim to be able to de-duplicate records but not in the way a specialist company would do it.

We do not need to go into the technical details here but a specialist de-duplication service is likely to be more accurate and more cost-efficient in the long term. When a list de-duplication is planned, brokers can supply 'industry compatible' data. In other words they will all send their data in compatible formats making the job of matching the lists quicker and easier.

Don't worry about having to find a specialist for this job, most list brokers will be able to recommend a suitable supplier.

Making direct mail interesting

Direct mail offers great creative freedom and uniquely can carry a large range of enclosures to attract attention. Companies have had great success with mailings enclosing full-size house bricks, shoes, hats and footballs and many other items. In a research study business people were asked 'Which of the mailings you receive do you open first?' The most frequently chosen option was 'those that are bulky or look most interesting.'

Until the early 'noughties' many companies mailed CDs and DVDs to offer software and sound and visual demonstrations of their products. This has been superseded in developed markets by 'drive to web' where a much wider range of options is available and often at lower cost to the company. In markets where broadband usage is less developed (such as most African countries including South Africa) the CD route is still popular.

Direct mail is an excellent testing medium allowing valid comparison of lists, offers, timing, creative approaches and response devices.

The cost of mailings

Critics of direct mail often cite the high cost of mail compared to broadscale advertising. A mailing can cost £500 per thousand or more, whereas a television audience can be bought for less than £10 per thousand.

However, the much tighter targeting and greater relevance can reduce wastage to such an extent that the differential is often more than compensated for by lower cost per response. This depends on the mailings being based on sound data enabling precise targeting. Where we are prospecting with no knowledge of who in the universe will be interested right now, we will often find that broadcast or print advertising is a more cost-effective place to start.

This is why, for example, insurance companies advertise for new customers in broadscale media. They may be able to rent names of motorists or house owners but, unless they know the date of renewal of a prospect's existing insurance, expensive media will not be cost-effective given that 80 or 90 per cent of those contacted will not be open to buy at any time.

EXAMPLE

If we wanted to sell home decorating products by direct marketing, the first requirement would be to identify people who are thinking of decorating in the immediate future. We could identify some broad targeting factors such as 'People who have just moved house may want to decorate' or 'People tend to decorate in the spring', but these are almost impossible to isolate from the broad mass market. So a sensible first step may be to run a series of advertisements in homemaking magazines, national press, selected television programmes (e.g. home makeover programmes) and relevant websites, offering free advisory booklets for decorators. Those who respond are identifying themselves as good prospects. Now it would be possible to follow up with direct mail without high wastage. Costs could be contained even further by offering the booklets as pdf files for downloading from the website.

Door-to-door distribution

Door-to-door (DTD) is a huge medium in the UK. Millions of leaflets and 'unaddressed mailing packs' (Royal Mail term) are delivered to UK homes in this way. Response rates are much lower than for addressed mail but this is still a cost-effective medium. There are numerous distribution companies offering this service and costs can be as low as £20 per thousand (plus printing costs).

Royal Mail also offers this service but their rates are higher. This is not necessarily a bad thing because advertisers using Royal Mail delivery tend to get a higher response rate. This is simply because anything delivered with the daily post is likely to be given more attention than a leaflet pushed through the door at any other time.

There is much confusion in the newspapers and therefore with consumers about what constitutes junk mail. My definition is 'addressed mail that is badly targeted or irrelevant'. However, when consumers are asked about junk mail they are often referring to 'unaddressed mail', i.e. door-to-door leaflet distributions. Given the decline in newspaper advertising revenues it perhaps not surprising that journalists are biased against alternative media but a recent example demonstrates the negative slant applied to any news relating to Royal Mail.

It was announced in March 2010 that in negotiations with post delivery unions the number of unaddressed leaflets they would deliver in the future would increase. In a hysterical article on Telegraph.co.uk, headed 'Royal Mail deal sees junk limits abandoned', the author implied that from now on householders could expect to be inundated with a sea of unwanted mail. This is naïve on two counts:

1. The fact that Royal Mail will accept more of the existing volume does not mean that most marketers will suddenly rush to send more leaflets. They are likely to transfer some of their existing volume to Royal Mail simply because, as explained above, it tends to generate a higher response than that delivered by other methods.

2. The fact that the DTD medium has grown so much over the past few years indicates that it works. In other words many people do respond to it. So an increase in the proportion of leaflets being delivered with the post is probably not going to ruin people's lives.

Many major financial services companies use DTD so it is clearly working cost-effectively for them.

Television

Direct response television (DRTV) was very popular in the 1980s mainly because of the PI (per inquiry) deal. Started in the USA (hence 'inquiry') PI is where a TV or radio station is prepared to run your commercial for a nominal charge and the advertiser then pays an agreed amount for each enquiry generated. The late Al Eicoff, the Chicago-based DRTV specialist used this technique extensively, sending copies of his client's ads to all 700 TV contractors in the US and asking them simply to run them whenever they had a gap. Many of his clients did very well out of this.

In the UK it fell out of favour with the TV contractors because the major consumer goods companies complained about advertisers being offered 'free' time and used their weight to squash it. The recession in the early 1990s saw the reappearance of some of these offers, and they can still be found today but mainly on radio and in certain local newspapers. It is always worth enquiring about such deals as they reduce the risk for small or first-time advertisers. And the perfect response to a pushy space salesperson is to ask them to put their money where their mouth is and offer a PI deal.

Despite the loss of the PI deal, DRTV has been growing consistently since the mid-1990s. Most television advertisements now carry at least a website URL and often a telephone number. DRTV grew for several reasons. One is the number of channels now available to direct marketers, which in turn means greater opportunity for targeting.

Until recently, the declining audiences were not always reflected in advertising costs but the current recession together with the switching of budgets to online has caused the contractors to be much more realistic. Rates are now more negotiable. The cost is negotiated up-front, but the final cost paid is based on the actual audience reached (based on panel research data). TV time is bought by TVR or Television Rating point – put simply, one TVR is equal to 1 per cent of the audience the advertiser is aiming for. For example, if an advertiser is targeting housewives in Lancashire, and an episode of 'Coronation Street' is viewed by 25 per cent of housewives in the region it is said to deliver a TVR of 25. TVRs are measured for each minute of a programme by a panel of some 5,000 households around the UK.

However, apart from some blockbuster programmes, it is unusual these days for a programme to deliver a high number of TVRs. With several hundred satellite channels now available, TVRs are generally counted in single digits, especially on the satellite channels. Buying TV is a complicated subject and one best done by media specialists.

The development of digital interactive channels has extended the capability of building brand awareness TV into the potential to create a very rich one-to-one direct marketing experience, but this has not become such a big success as predicted. There have been some successes but generally viewers have been disinclined to leave the programme they are watching to visit a website when they can easily do so once the programme is finished.

A major reason for the increase in DRTV is the ease of using the Internet. Today with more than 75 per cent of UK homes having access, it is easy for an advertiser to feature a URL and drive interested prospects to the website.

Television has several advantages:

- it still reaches large audiences at a low cost per thousand;
- off-peak air time can be very cost effective and is used by many direct response advertisers;
- it can reach specific audiences due to the increase in the number of satellite channels, though audience numbers can be very small. However, if you have a good offer on a golf accessory you can be sure of reaching golf enthusiasts by advertising during a golf programme;
- credibility – in the eyes of the consumer television still carries weight;
- it is ideal for demonstrating products;

That said, television has several disadvantages:

- it is complex to buy and to manage;
- it generally offers low response rates;
- response handling can be a problem – most of the response will occur directly after the commercial has aired, and if that is during a peak time programme, call centres must be adequately resourced to cope with this sudden influx;

- messages are limited due to regulation and airtime costs – it is difficult to deliver a lengthy description of a product in 40 or 60 seconds.

The keys to the successful use of DRTV include:
- be clear about the objectives and the audience;
- use a good creative team; you have 60 seconds or less to get your message across;
- remember that the key objective is response so always give viewers time to note the details – the URL or telephone number should be displayed throughout the ad;
- use a simple memorable response number or URL (good examples are 0800 40 40 40 for Trust House Forte; pcworld.co.uk; text ECON129 to 60300 for instant call back and so on);
- demonstrate the benefits of the product, i.e. use the advantages of the medium.

Radio

Radio has always been an important option for direct marketers. Many local stations offer attractive cost effective targeting opportunities. There are hundreds of radio stations in the UK and the weekly reach of commercial stations is more than 28 million adults.

The Radio Advertising Bureau produces some excellent research on the effectiveness of radio as an advertising medium. Its strengths include:
- creative flexibility – words can create very persuasive images in the mind;
- intrusiveness – although a strength this can also be a weakness;
- relationships – many consumers describe the radio as 'a friend'. This makes it powerful as a standalone medium but also in support of an integrated campaign;
- cost-efficiency – radio audiences can be reached quite cheaply; cost per thousand is among the lowest of all media. However, response rates can also be low;
- local identity – many stations have a strong local identity making them ideal for local campaigns;
- production costs – it is possible to spend a lot of money on radio production, but this is mainly due to the fees of the presenters. Most radio stations can produce commercials using their own presenters and these can be a lot cheaper;
- testing – the low costs make testing inexpensive;
- targeting – audience research is extensive and it is possible to target specific audiences well.

There are some weaknesses to be aware of:
- there is no visual element, this can reduce memorability;
- frequent repetition can lead to channel switching; if the same commercial is repeated several times during the same hour of 'drive time', listeners tend to switch channels; the best campaigns rotate several different versions of a commercial to avoid this problem.

SUMMARY

In this chapter we looked at the process of communicating with our customers offline. We started by discussing the increasing problem of measurement and attribution of responses brought about by two relatively new factors:

- the increase in multimedia campaigns. These are more effective than single media communications, but mean that precise attribution of the cause of a response is much harder;
- the 'leakage' of response to the Web, as many consumers today go directly to a website when an advertisement or mailing interests them.

We saw that the traditional approach of awareness advertising is giving way to dual-purpose advertising where direct communications and awareness are integrated and work more effectively together.

The issue of follow-up was discussed and we saw that, although the effect is reducing, the telephone is still a valuable method of following up a mailing, though it is important that the call is made within three days of the mailing arriving. We saw also that email can be used as a follow-up tool, and that linking mailings to press or TV campaigns can produce significant gains in response.

We saw that sending out follow-ups to failed campaigns is a poor strategy as the reminder will produce much less response than the original already unsatisfactory effort.

Relevance of message was seen as central to the effectiveness of marketing communications and it is this that is continuing to drive the growth of direct marketing.

We examined the effects of the digital revolution on the media landscape; the declining demand for printed news media; and the fragmentation of television audiences due to the multiplicity of channels available today.

We went on to look at the importance of integration in planning media and looked in detail at the planning process. The process started with targeting.

We saw that we had to ask six key questions:

1. Who are they?
2. When is the right time to approach them?
3. Where are they?
4. What media do they use?
5. How do they use media?
6. How much will it cost to reach them?

These questions were examined in detail as we touched on the role of research in identifying audience and their patterns of media consumption. These included geodemographics, psychographics and behavioural research. We saw also that services such as TGI could help significantly in the task of media selection.

We looked at the strengths and weaknesses of the following media:

Press

Magazines

Inserts

Ambient media

Word of mouth advertising

Third party distribution (enclosures in other companies' despatches)

Door-to-door distribution

Telephone

Direct mail – including the location of suitable mailing lists

Television

Radio

REVIEW QUESTIONS

1. Explain why relevance is vital in the process of delivering marketing messages. Why is this leading to an increase in the use of direct marketing media?
2. What are the advantages of media integration?
3. What is the main difference between awareness and response advertising?
4. Explain the direct marketing planning process, how does it differ from the awareness approach?
5. What is the most important factor in the planning process?
6. What is TGI? How can it help the direct marketer?
7. List the strengths and weaknesses of at least three direct marketing media.
8. Explain Sainsbury's Square Root Principle.

EXERCISE

Your company is a provider of financial services in the United Kingdom.

You have been asked to launch a new flexible mortgage product. The target market is affluent 35 to 45-year-olds with an outstanding mortgage balance of more than £100,000. You need to acquire 25,000 customers to reach the financial targets for this product, and 10,000 of these will come from your existing customer base.

How will you communicate with your existing customers?

What media choices are open to you when you look to acquire new customers? What media would you choose to test?

CHAPTER 10
DIGITAL MEDIA PLANNING

IN THIS CHAPTER

We will consider the digital media landscape in relation to the planning of direct marketing campaigns.

After reading this chapter you will be able to:

- Differentiate between the various digital media
- Build your own online intelligence unit by setting up RSS feeds and subscribing to relevant newsletters
- Understand how online and offline media can work together

Specific topics include:

- How budgets are being switched towards online
- Consumers' preferred sources of produce information
- What sources are trusted most
- The various ways of delivering marketing messages online, including
  - search engine optimisation (SEO)
  - pay-per-click advertising
  - affiliates
  - RSS feeds
  - online advertising (banners)
  - social network advertising and blogs
  - email
  - viral marketing
  - mobile marketing

Overview of digital media

The offline media review which we have just seen in Chapter 9 was fairly easy to write, mainly because little has changed in recent years, or at least little has been added apart from some additional TV channels.

It's very different with online media. The online media landscape is growing and fragmenting at an amazing rate. We started to write this chapter in December 2009. At that time Facebook had just announced they had 350 million members worldwide. By October 2010 they had more than 500 million. Twitter, while not having so many members, is undoubtedly the fastest-growing online community today – in the year from 2008 to 2009 membership increased by well over 1,000 per cent. In March 2010, five new social networking sites were announced.

The original intention was to review each medium in detail, but given the background of such rapid change we have altered the plan. We will talk about each type of online opportunity but to get the most value from this chapter you will need to do a lot of research of your own. We will give you links to a number of newsletters and blogs that will help you keep up to date – they will also fill your inbox – hundreds or thousands of relevant newsletters are published every day so you will have to be selective. However, without a regular flow of such news you will struggle to keep abreast of the rapid changes. A way of saving you time while still receiving lots of important news is to use RSS feeds. More on that later.

Switch or integrate?

We have mentioned earlier the fact that many advertisers are switching budget from offline to online channels but the key to real effectiveness is finding a way of blending offline and online to create a truly integrated communications strategy. And we have to start by understanding customer behaviour. **And, most importantly, the fact that despite all the present day discussion about managing customer relationships, we have to understand that we do not manage the relationship, the customer does.**

Writing in the magazine *Interactive Marketing* in 2000, consultant and author Alan Mitchell said:

'In future, the first one in one-to-one marketing will increasingly be the customer or his agent, and this development will shake marketing theory and practice to its very roots…

All other developments have been mere changes in the marketing weather. We are now at the beginning of a global climatic change.'

And he was right. Since 2000 the media universe has changed dramatically. In March 2000 the dot.com boom burst, and media buyers felt that normal service had been resumed. No longer was all the prime space being commandeered by Web entrepreneurs happily prepared to pay the asking price – direct marketing space negotiators must have felt they had been let out of jail. But in place of the dot.com bubble a whole new situation was developing.

Direct marketing started as a business-to-consumer channel (B2C) and then in the 1980s the main growth was in business-to-business (B2B). Since the advent of Web 2.0 and the massive growth of the social networking channels there is a third route to market – and that is consumer-to-consumer (C2C). The first two are well understood by all intelligent marketers today but the third is raising many questions.

The social media revolution, with C2C sites such as My Space, Facebook, YouTube, Bebo, Twitter, Second Life and so on brought about a third 'channel' that advertisers are still coming to terms with. LinkedIn is similar except that its members (worldwide membership of more than 62 million) are business people. They are still using the network primarily to pass on information about their work and their business contacts but it represents a good opportunity for advertisers.

The 2004 'Brave New World' study done by the Henley Centre and AOL, asked consumers 'Which information sources are the most important when considering a product or service?' The results make sobering reading for the media planner:

Figure 10.1: Which information sources are most important?

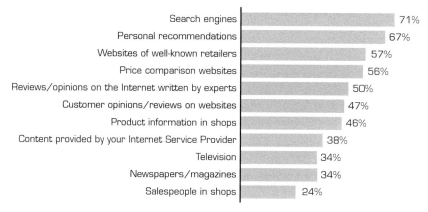

% who consider the following to be important sources of information when researching/considering a product or service

Search engines	71%
Personal recommendations	67%
Websites of well-known retailers	57%
Price comparison websites	56%
Reviews/opinions on the Internet written by experts	50%
Customer opinions/reviews on websites	47%
Product information in shops	46%
Content provided by your Internet Service Provider	38%
Television	34%
Newspapers/magazines	34%
Salespeople in shops	24%

Offline media can start the awareness process but further research is highly likely to happen online – usually through a search engine query (Google, Yahoo, MSN, Bing etc.). However, there is also an intermediate stage where consumers, and increasingly business people, ask friends and contacts through social networking sites and blogs (weblogs). They also use price comparison sites at this point. Note that personal recommendations were only a few points behind search and this study was done before Facebook went public.

Consider this; Facebook membership now exceeds 500 million; in January/February 2010, according to comScore, the four major search engines reported a decline in searches while Facebook recorded a 10 per cent increase in searches over the same period. Bing meanwhile showed a slight increase in searches and there is speculation that this may be because of its partnership with Facebook. If a Facebook search doesn't produce the answer it defaults to Bing.

A further question in the Brave New World study asked 'Which sources do you trust to be honest and fair?'

From this perspective personal recommendations are far ahead. So people trust their friends rather than advertisers – this has always been true but today it is much easier to implement. With social networking you can ask hundreds or thousands of people their opinions, instantly.

Figure 10.2: Which information sources are most honest?

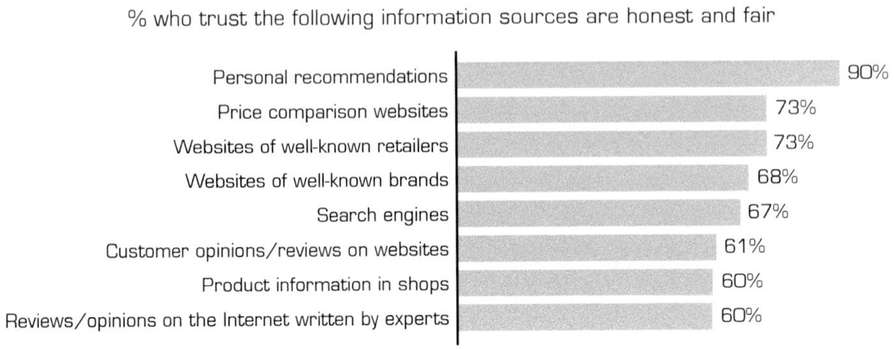

% who trust the following information sources are honest and fair

Information source	%
Personal recommendations	90%
Price comparison websites	73%
Websites of well-known retailers	73%
Websites of well-known brands	68%
Search engines	67%
Customer opinions/reviews on websites	61%
Product information in shops	60%
Reviews/opinions on the Internet written by experts	60%

Who can we reach online?

The Office for National Statistics (ONS) reports that 18.3 million households in the UK (70 per cent) had Internet access in mid-2009. And 90 per cent of those now have broadband (that's 63 per cent of all UK households).

In 2009, 37.4 million adults (76 per cent of the UK adult population) accessed the Internet in the three months prior to interview; 70 per cent of these (26 million people) had bought something online within that three-month period.

And although many feel that the online audience is mainly younger people the statistics don't bear this out.

According to Neilson NetRatings in mid-2007 the over-50s now account for 30 per cent of all UK Web usage; and the over-65s spend more time online than any other age group.

The rapidly increasing percentage having broadband access, linked to the ISP's drive to deliver faster broadband speeds, means that usage is changing. While the big three uses continue to be email, general surfing for news and information, and buying products, more and more users are downloading video, using social networking sites, gaming and using VOIP (Voice Over Internet Protocol) services such as Skype.

Let's review the digital media. We'll start with the assumption that whatever your product or service your first objective in using digital media is to get the prospect to visit your website. With that in mind we can see that there are many possible ways of reaching Internet users and drawing them in:

- search marketing (SEO and PPC)
- affiliates
- online advertising
- social network advertising, blogs
- email
- viral marketing
- mobile marketing

Search marketing

The two basic versions are natural search and pay per click.

Theoretically, natural (or organic) search is free in that you don't pay to bring the prospect to your site – they are searching for something and if your site appears to the search engine to offer the solution your listing will appear. The objective is to be on the first page – the percentage of users that go to page two is quite small. You may be lucky and get onto page one without spending anything other than your site development costs, but, as Damon Runyon (almost) said 'that's not the way to bet'.

Search engine optimisation requires a lot of experience, a lot of skill and quite a lot of luck, it must be said. So, if someone promises to get you to the top of the listings, beware. Of course an SEO specialist can help you improve your chances but there is really no one solution to achieving success here, and as soon as it appears to Google that the SEO specialists are learning the secrets, they change their algorithms. The base requirement is that your site and the text behind it must contain the keywords that searchers are using to answer their questions.

There are some online tools that can help you by showing the most popular keywords that are currently being used by searchers – Yahoo used to have a free tool called Overture but this has now disappeared. There is a link on their page to the tool offered by Wordtracker: freekeywords.wordtracker.com. This used to be a free service but I think that so many people have been using it that they have seen a money-making option and all you can get now is a seven-day free trial. That could still be very helpful. There is also another way of identifying relevant keywords although it isn't free. If you experiment with a pay-per-click service such as Google AdWords you will eventually find out which of the keywords you are using attracts the most visits. This will cost you some money but the results are rapid and you can fine-tune as much as you want. If you are interested in this simply visit www.Google.co.uk/AdWords where you will find lots of helpful advice. They will also offer you a link to another keyword tool www.wordstream.com, again you can sign up for a free trial. The illustration on the following page shows a typical search result – in this case I simply searched on Google AdWords.

One thing that all SEO specialists agree on is that the more sites your own site is affiliated to the better chance you have of being elevated towards the top of the listings.

However, this is not as simple as it sounds. The search engine will not only count the number of affiliations, it will also assess their relevance and their popularity. And the people or systems that evaluate these things are pretty smart. One SEO 'expert' was recently caught out after he had developed an affiliate-sharing scheme whereby a large group of his clients agreed to become affiliated to each other. It didn't take the search engine people long to spot this and suddenly all his clients' listings disappeared from the early pages.

It will also not help you to use popular keywords that are not relevant to what is on your site. The search engine software can also measure how long a person stays on your site having clicked through – clearly the longer they stay the more relevant is your offering to the customer. Greater relevance is the cornerstone of a search engine's promise, so that scores points.

Figure 10.3: Google AdWords Search Results

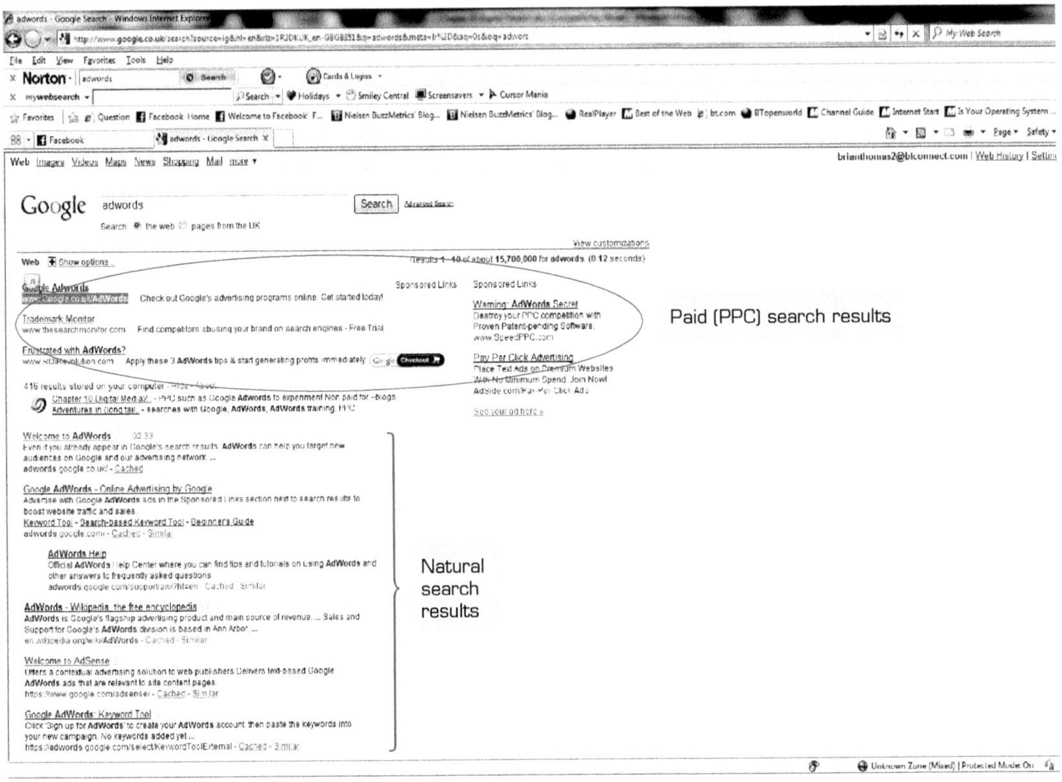

Incidentally, greater relevance can also elevate you up the sponsored (PPC) listings. What this means is that, all things being equal, the more you are prepared to pay for a keyword, the higher up the listing you will appear – except that if another PPC listing is clearly more relevant as described above, it may rise above a purely cost-based ranking.

The added value of a PPC campaign

Google say that adding PPC to your natural search activities can boost click-throughs dramatically. An example recently quoted is that if you are top of the paid search listings and 1 per cent of the people seeing your ad click through; it is likely that being top of the natural listing would generate double that traffic (i.e. 2 per cent would click through). However, if you were top of both natural and paid listings you could expect around 6 per cent to click through to your site.

Pay per click such as Google AdWords is easy to arrange and there are plenty of helpful tools and hints on the AdWords site. You only pay when someone clicks through to your site and you can try a whole range of alternative wordings then eventually arrange for Google to run the most popular one after you have evaluated their effectiveness. And once you get the hang of it and have tested a few alternatives the results can be seen very quickly.

Pay-per-click advertising is offered by all major search engines.

Affiliate marketing

The basic premise is that you pay other sites an agreed commission, usually for each new customer acquisition – cost per acquisition (CPA). You may be able to negotiate different terms such as cost per click-through, cost per registration on your site, cost per successful sign-up for your newsletter, or cost per eventual sale. You can try to negotiate your own terms and rates with individual sites, or you can use an external specialist to organise this for you. The larger and more successful sites are likely to have fixed terms of business for affiliates and these are less likely to enter into non-standard arrangements.

Remember the warnings above – linking with irrelevant sites will not only fail to benefit your business, it may damage your ranking in natural search listings.

So the principal things to remember about affiliates are:

1. The more relevant and popular sites you are linked to the more business you will achieve from your affiliate programme.
2. The less relevant and popular your affiliates are, the less business you will gain and the greater the chance that your natural search rankings will suffer.

Online advertising

Ideally a banner ad will cause the viewer to click through to the advertiser's site and the buyer will want to buy on a cost per click or cost per visit basis. Alternatively it may only be available on a CPM (cost per thousand impressions served) basis. However, the advertiser will generally want to measure it by click -throughs (CTR = click-through rate – the percentage of impressions that actually resulted in a click-through). CTR is usually quite low, less than 1 per cent is quite normal. There is also likely to be an awareness effect but this is much harder to measure.

There are numerous options in terms of shape and size. Most frequently used are the horizontal banners and vertical banners (skyscrapers) but there are various levels of interactivity. The most simple banners contain a single static image which can be clicked on to go direct to the advertiser's site, although it is more common to see an animated banner with two or more images that change giving the appearance of animation. Site owners may impose file size limits to limit page loading times.

The MPU (or mid page unit) will typically feature rich media, animations and video. These will cost more to produce and to serve as they can be very large files. However, they are likely to attract more attention and thus hopefully more clicks. Overlays are more obtrusive as they do actually overlay the Web page the user was intending to view. They can be very powerful but are less likely to work if the user is given the option of opening it or not. A variation on this is the expandable banner. This is perhaps the ideal middle way as the normal size banner will be served with a message inviting the viewer to click or roll over the banner to expand it.

There are numerous shapes and sizes of banners and different websites have their own variations. They often impose a limit on memory size simply because excessive memory can slow down page loading time.

Figure 10.4: Examples of horizontal and banner ads

Figure 10.5: Examples of mid-page unit and mini-banner ads

Making banners work

As with all forms of advertising there are no shortcuts, at least no inexpensive shortcuts. You either need to carry out extensive testing or employ external specialists who will cost money but whose experience should reduce risks and shorten testing times. There are a few obvious pointers such as:

1. Banners at the top or in the middle (MPUs) tend to get more clicks, and those on the left-hand side seem to attract more attention that those on the right.
2. Even a very simple animation will catch the eye better than a static banner.
3. The more relevant your ad is to the content of the site on which it appears the more likely it is to be of interest to the site user.
4. With this in mind, an ad featuring a specific product or promotional offer is more likely to be clicked on than one with just a basic corporate statement.

If you are fortunate enough to get the prospect to click on your banner, make sure that the landing page they arrive at 'matches' your banner. If the prospect has to spend time seeking out the details they will click away in seconds.

The purpose is generally to persuade the visitor to visit the advertiser's website. However, a visit is not the real objective – unless the visitor buys something or at least registers for further information the click-though is virtually wasted. Virtually because there is a small chance that a visit will result in the memory being stored in the prospect's mind.

This branding element is very difficult to measure, but as we saw earlier the other measures are more manageable.

There are four basic ways of buying banner ads:

1. Use an online media buying agency – this is the recommended route unless you have lots of experience.
2. Build an affiliate network – this can be effective but unless you employ external specialists it can take lots of your time.
3. Approaching relevant site owners and negotiating direct – again, this can be effective but takes lots of time and effort.
4. Swap arrangements where you arrange reciprocal advertising on each other's sites. These can be negotiated direct or through a banner exchange programme such as www.ukbanners.com which can help you get distribution quickly.

Behavioural targeting

This relatively new form of targeting is based on tracking a consumer's browsing habits and then serving online advertisements that are deemed to be relevant.

This is an emotive subject, having even stimulated debate in a parliamentary round table in March 2009. Both sides feel strongly about their stances. The privacy lobby argues that it is a clear invasion of privacy while the opposite side claims:

a. That any information used in targeting is anonymous and is thus no more of an invasion than any company using other forms of behavioural data to identify prospects for whom an offer would be relevant.

b. In surveys consumers have stated that they would prefer to receive only relevant advertisements.

The debate continues although in September 2009 the UK government decreed the practice to be legal. It can be highly effective with tests showing uplifts of 40 per cent to more than 100 per cent against run of sites (ROS) advertisements.

Google and, presumably, other search engines are using a form of behavioural targeting by refining search results they offer based on earlier searches. The UK Internet Advertising Bureau (IAB) has developed a new code of practice regarding behavioural targeting. The code requires operators to notify users when their data is being collected and give them the opportunity of opting out.

The IAB runs a website called YourOnlineChoices.co.uk to explain to consumers how behavioural advertising works. You can keep up to date with developments by visiting the IAB site or Googling 'behavioural targeting' and following one of the links.

Pop-ups – most powerful, and most unpopular

Pop-ups are advertisements that appear in their own small window. They are impossible to ignore although users can set their browsers not to allow pop-ups. In the various studies of acceptability of the various forms of online ads, pop-ups are consistently the most disliked. Nevertheless, like door-to-door selling and telephone selling, they continue to be used, so that means they must work.

A mid-way version is the interstitial – this is a pop-up but it will generally close automatically and is thus less annoying than the standard pop-up that must be closed manually.

Text-links

In some cases these have been found to be more effective than banners because they seem to be a natural part of the flow of text the visitor is reading.

Clearly there are many options for online advertising and new versions appear all the time.

Advertising on social networking sites

There are various ways of promoting your company on social networking sites.

1. Placing an advertisement – see below for the Facebook advertising page. Like Google, Yahoo and MSN they offer lots of help in devising and optimising your ad. You can choose a pay-per-click or cost per thousand (CPM) model. The ads are quite discreetly served so are not likely to annoy many members.

You can set up your own page or form a 'group' and invite Facebook members to become 'fans'. For example, the main Coca-Cola page has more than five million fans.

Figure 10.6: Advertising on Facebook

YouTube

Here's another opportunity. You can upload your own video ad on to YouTube. Or have your ad embedded into an existing video. A third possibility is to run a static or animated banner like those on any other website. Again, visit the site and follow the instructions and you will find lots of help offered.

LinkedIn

The difference with LinkedIn is that their worldwide membership of more than 62 million is almost exclusively business people. So it has attracted advertisers large and small. There are buying models for large and small advertisers.

Blogs

Not strictly an advertising medium but an opportunity nevertheless. The term 'blog' is an abbreviation for 'weblog' – a website that is used by an individual or company to offer news and comment about any number of issues. 'Blog' is also used as a verb – to blog is to add news or comment to a blog.

Some blogs are simply online diaries of individuals, but many of these collect a wide following. The number of blogs online is growing daily and is estimated in early 2010 to be around 2 billion worldwide.

Blogs often contain images, and links to other sites. Many offer a facility for comment from readers. There are many popular blogs by marketing and business consultants and also lots of corporate blogs, some more interesting than others. To succeed, a corporate blog needs to offer worthwhile news and comment.

One thing to be aware of is the existence of paid 'word of mouth' (WOM) bloggers who, in the guise of giving personal recommendations are actually hired by companies to promote their products and services.

Note that WOM is not confined to the Web. WOM 'employees' can be found in bars and clubs; taxi drivers are often paid to recommend shows, holiday destinations, restaurants and so on.

Second Life

Second Life needs a rather different approach in that they don't actively sell advertising space. However, companies can set up their own Second Life presence, maybe a shop or a music festival, where their brand is heavily displayed. They can then promote this on blogs and other social networking sites. To see some samples search on YouTube for 'Brands in Second Life'. Dell, BMW, Reebok and many other brands have been active there.

RSS feeds

You will find many regular newsletters that you will want to receive in full but there is another way. You can keep up to date with news without having to spend lots of time scouring websites. Popularly known as Really Simple Syndication the letters really stand for Rich Site Summary – a method of delivering regularly changing Web content. Many news-related sites, weblogs and other online publishers syndicate their content as an RSS Feed to whoever wants it. Simply sign up to an RSS reader such as Google Reader or Bloglines. You can then set up automatic news feeds to your reader from any website that carries an RSS Icon or button. As always, you can keep up to date with developments simply by searching 'RSS Feeds'.

Email

A recent study indicates that more than 80 per cent of all Internet traffic is now spam – unsolicited and largely unwelcome emails.

Another study done in the US by Cohesive Knowledge Solutions (CKS) reveals that business people there spend more than 40 per cent of their work time dealing with emails, and they estimate that more than a third of that time is wasted. And companies are now starting to calculate what this costs in lost productivity and profits.

We are probably not yet at that stage at which email volumes significantly disrupt workflow in the UK but the danger is clear. There is not enough space to explore email in great detail but some important considerations are:

1. 'Cold' emails can only be sent to people who have **opted in** to receiving them, so if you plan to use email as a prospecting tool, make sure that the list you are buying or renting conforms to the The Privacy and Electronic Communications Regulations 2003.
2. There is a level of consent called **soft opt-in**. This means that the person you are planning to email has either sent your company an email; subscribed to one of your services, e.g. a regular newsletter, or at least registered with your website, included their email address in that registration and clicked the 'submit' button.
3. When using such names for future email marketing programmes you should always include an unsubscribe option. You should also provide a clearly visible link to your company's privacy policy.

4. Many recipients at work or at home use a preview pane to decide whether an email is worth opening – the wording of the subject line and the sender's name are key factors in that decision

We will discuss creative aspects of email in Chapter 13.

Planning email campaigns

The overall considerations for email marketing are essentially the same as for direct mail campaigns. The database, targeting and selection issues that have been described for mailing list work should be applied to email marketing. The biggest single difference between email marketing and direct mail is cost, but it should not be thought that because the media costs of email are so tiny that any less effort is required at the planning, testing and evaluation stages than would be the case in any other medium. Indeed, given the amount of data generated in the course of an email campaign, the reverse may be true.

There are three main sources of email addresses:

1. **Your own email list**

   As a general principle, companies should try and collect the email addresses of all new customers, while setting in motion a plan of updating historic customer records and getting their email addresses on to the database as well. This way they will build up their own email list very quickly, but make sure you follow the data privacy and opt-in regulations mentioned above.

2. **Commercial lists (cold or 'opt-in')**

   Many of the mailing list suppliers are now collecting email addresses along with their other respondent data. Therefore, while the numbers on an e-list are currently much smaller than on a similarly targeted mailing list, it is now possible to email lifestyle clusters such as motor insurance renewals by month. Testing these lists now is definitely worthwhile, because they are going to grow in number very rapidly and the companies that understand how to work them will gain an advantage.

3. **Collection of new addresses**

   Via online advertising campaigns, data capture banners, questionnaires or microsites using competition or games mechanics.

Once data has been collated it needs to be formatted, cleaned and de-duplicated just as you would with any other list.

Viral marketing

Viral marketing has become popular due to its innately efficient marketing potential. It is the least precise of the available digital media, but if the idea is good it can be very impactful and cost-efficient. Many organisations use it to stimulate awareness and drive response. Nike used it to extend its campaign for its 10 kilometre run, so that was a good example of a company using it to extend its brand awareness.

Viral marketing is the creation of an impactful vehicle, usually a game or competition emailed to a small, but targeted base. The marketer then relies on that base forwarding the game etc. on to other like prospects because they think it will be of interest or, usually, amusement. In this way, the marketing message is transmitted to a wide audience at no further cost to the marketer. This is the electronic equivalent to word of mouth, and is very good for member-get-member schemes.

The other side of viral marketing is that even though an organisation can start it, they cannot control it, so it can stimulate counter action by disgruntled customers.

Indeed, many viral communications these days are not even started by marketers but by customers. Many of these are set up to criticise an organisation and a good example of this is the 'United breaks guitars' videos on YouTube. When this happens all that an organisation can do is to respond openly and fairly in an attempt to limit the damage to their brand. A new departure in early 2010 is the brand critical video produced by an environmental organisation. Search YouTube for 'Nestle Greenpeace' to see this in action.

Even when a consumer generated video is put up on the Web, say, on YouTube, an organisation has very few options. They can ignore it and hope it goes away but this can backfire. When consumers first posted the fact that Mentos react with Coca-Cola, the two organisations reacted differently. Mentos rapidly embraced the idea seeing that it could cause a major uplift in sales. Coke on the other hand attempted to distance itself from it, but when the story became so popular on YouTube they were forced to change their stance.

Not all consumer comment is true or fair but the studies mentioned earlier show that consumers, and especially those who frequent the Web, tend to trust social networking comment from other consumers before trusting big name brands, even those that are generally considered to be trustworthy.

Mobile Internet and SMS/MMS

The mobile network can be used in all aspects of direct marketing from acquisition to retention and customer service. Mobiles for public use have been around since Vodafone introduced them to the UK in 1985 but they were very much less mobile then. Today there are approximately 50 million mobiles in the UK and their popularity is due to the fact that they have multiple uses. Phone calls obviously but the other statistics are very impressive.

SMS (text) messaging

In the UK 95 per cent of text messages are opened compared to 25 per cent of emails (IAB).

The Mobile Data Association tells us that in the UK in 2008 more than 6.5 billion text messages were being sent every month – this is twice as many as there are Google searches, and that was a year on year growth of 30 per cent over 2007. Latest industry estimates say that a total of 97 billion texts were sent in UK in 2009.

For some sections of the marketplace it can be the prime choice.

---

48 per cent of 15 to 24-year-olds in UK say SMS is their preferred written communication method *IPA TouchPoints*

Over New Year's Eve and January 1st 2010 there were almost 900 million texts transmitted in the UK.

MMS (video and picture) messaging Industry estimates are that 601 million MMS messages were sent in UK in 2009.

Mobile Internet

23 per cent of mobile users (17.6 million people) accessed the Internet on their phones in 2007 (Mobile Data Association) 3G penetration was estimated to be 50 per cent in 2009. It is claimed that 80 per cent of iPhone users access the Web on their phones. This does not yet have a huge impact on the overall figures because iPhone penetration is still quite a small percentage of the overall population. Mobile Internet usage in 2009 was skewed towards men (59 per cent men; 41 per cent women).

Research by O2 tells us that we use mobiles to:

Request a brochure	74 per cent
Access company information	70 per cent
Check product availability	70 per cent
Locate a retail store	64 per cent
Make a booking	50 per cent
Respond to an offline ad	51 per cent (30 per cent of mobile users have used a short code to respond to an ad)

Example of a short code

Bookstart – a government initiative to encourage **parents** and carers to enjoy books with **children** from an early age by offering them a **free** book per household.

TV ads featuring a **prominent text call to action** ran on 34 channels.

By texting **BOOK** along with their **name, house no.** and **postcode** to the short code 80800, viewers could receive a free book from Bookstart.

Mobile was the **only response medium** used. Texts were **free** to viewers.

Almost 80,000 responded (8% * of UK households with pre-school age children)
*Source: ONS

Short codes can also be used to find a cab, book an appointment, donate to a charity and so on.

According to Orange – mobile is the most accessed communications medium between mid morning and late afternoon, only being overtaken (marginally) by TV and online access by computer after 6 p.m.

SUMMARY

In this chapter we endeavoured to cover the entire digital communications landscape, but this is very difficult as the situation is constantly changing.

We discussed the continuing shift of marketing budgets from offline to online and we noted the powerful impact that social networking has had on traditional marketing strategies.

Today's consumers are far more likely to trust friends and social networking recommendations than the promises of advertisers.

Even in 2004 consumers were expressing their preference for search engines and personal recommendations against advertising claims, and when asked which information sources are most honest and fair 90 per cent opted for 'personal recommendation' with comparison sites coming second at 73 per cent. (Source: Henley Centre/AOL, 2004).

Since then Web 2.0 has arrived and social networking sites have proliferated, which means that consumer interaction has grown dramatically, thus increasing the likelihood of consumers seeking news and advice from friends online.

By mid-2009 70 per cent of UK households had Internet access and 90 per cent of these had broadband; more than 53 per cent of UK adults had bought something online in the three-month research period.

We considered the main options for delivering marketing messages online and saw that search engine optimisation (SEO), although theoretically very powerful, was extremely difficult to achieve. Experts who claim to be able to get your site to the top of the listings are to be avoided.

We saw that pay-per-click is a quick and easy way of testing keywords and simple marketing propositions; that affiliates can help in generating site visitors but also in improving a site's position in search listings. But the affiliations have to be relevant or the search networks will downgrade the site.

We discussed the value of building an information bank by setting up RSS feeds with relevant newsletters and blogs. We outlined the various types of banner advertisements and detailed the various ways of buying and measuring these.

We pointed out that most social networks now take advertising and recommended readers to keep up to date with developments by carrying out their own research into this area.

We discussed email and the problem of overuse that is leading business people to complain that they receive too many. Consumers too are increasingly using Outlook's preview pane to decide whether to open an email or not.

We saw the potential benefits and the possible dangers of viral marketing.

Finally, we considered the immense growth of mobile marketing and the fact that already many millions of people use their mobiles to respond to advertisements, log on to social networking sites, search the Web and so on.

No book can keep you up to date with the rapidly changing online situation; this can only be done by carrying your own research, subscribing to newsletters and blogs and setting up RSS feeds with relevant websites.

You'll find a list of useful links in the Appendix.

CHAPTER 11
INTEGRATED MARKETING COMMUNICATIONS – BRAND MANAGEMENT IN THE DIGITAL AGE

IN THIS CHAPTER

We consider perhaps the core asset of any company, its brands. John Stewart, the former CEO of Quaker, put it very well:

'If this company were split up, I would give you the property, plant and equipment and I would take the brands – and I would fare better than you.'

After reading this chapter you should be able to:

- Define the brand and understand key elements of brand management
- Understand and apply the concept of integrated marketing communications
- Plan for the integration of direct and digital marketing communications across channels
- Understand how to recruit and manage agencies to deliver integrated marketing
- Measure integration and the media multiplier effect

Specific topics include:

- Integrating online and off line communications
- The brand and attitude formation
- Media Neutral Planning (MNP)
- Integrated Marketing Communications (IMC)
- Planning tools for IMC
- Integration and the media multiplier effect
- Agency issues
- Measuring integrated effects
- Summary

INTRODUCTION

In Chapter 2 we looked at the value of brands and saw that the leading global brands were worth many billions of dollars. In its latest study on brand valuation published in 2009 Interbrand, one of the world's largest branding agencies, valued Coca-Cola at $68.7 billion followed by IBM at just over $60.2 billion. Not only are these brands worth more than twice the GDP of Kenya ($30 billion) they are also apparently immortal. Some of the world's best known brands are senior citizens at least.

The table below shows the year that the brands were launched in the UK.

Brand	Launched in the UK
Coca-Cola	1900
Heinz	1901
Kellogg's	1922
Kit Kat	1935

The advertising and marketing agencies that served them have also had a long and interesting life. The origins of J. Walter Thompson (JWT) one of the world's largest such agencies, lie in the 60s – the 1860s, around 1868 in fact. Publicis, another global agency, was founded in Paris in 1926. The first brand manager role was created in around 1929 for a Procter & Gamble brand, Camay soap, and a brand-based marketing organisation was developed in 1931. Only nine of the top 50 brands in the UK were launched after 1995.

The point is that brands are extremely valuable: managed well they are long lived and vigorous, but they are also vulnerable. The list below is an example of once high-profile brands that have had to adapt significantly to changes in their marketplace or have failed.

- Woolworths
- Kodak
- Encyclopaedia Britannica
- Bebo
- Boo.com
- Ratner's, the high street jewellers

For marketers, management of the brand is one of the most important tasks they undertake and this chapter explores how direct and digital marketing contributes to this area. We will also look at the process of managing the brand through multiple channels to market, and how the concept of integrated marketing communications can be planned, delivered and measured.

Proliferation of routes to market

For many marketing professionals one of the most pressing challenges is the fragmentation of media and the proliferation of routes or channels to market.

Look at the retail banking sector. The days of the old school, Captain Mainwaring-type bank manager in charge of his solidly built high street branch are long gone. We are no longer dependent on the physical location of a bank for banking services. We can access our accounts, and information about those accounts, via the telephone, the Internet or using smart phones and other mobile devices. This means that we can effectively manage our money from anywhere in the world. Costs of entry have reduced and now we can buy our groceries and do our banking in the same place; from the sofa, in the comfort of our own home. For consumers this is perhaps a great benefit. For the owners and directors of the banks it has meant a huge investment in technology and change in order to stay competitive and effectively manage rapidly changing customer expectations.

Equally banks can advertise using the vast range of media that are available to them: online, offline, face-to-face and at the tills. All this has to be managed to produce the consistent and coherent communication that customers and prospects demand. It is not easy. The principle of the integration of marketing communications around the relationship between the customer and the brands they buy is a way of making sense of this complex situation.

What is a brand?

The word brand was originally associated with the branding of cattle. Its wider commercial use began as a result of industrial production and the increasing physical distance between producers and consumers of products. The brand mark, once referred to as a 'trust mark', was a guarantee of product quality. Indeed 'Made in Germany' used to be stamped on goods imported into the UK from Germany as a warning of potentially inferior product quality. The use of logos, images and pictures in commercial branding strategies was originally due to high levels of illiteracy. Although the association of brands with their logos remains today, the logo is now only a small part of what branding is about.

However, the role of imagery persists in brand strategy and it is very important as it links to consumer perceptions of what a brand represents and how it is perceived and understood. When you read the word Guinness you do not see the word Guinness as it is typed across a page or screen or as a bare word imprinted on your brain. Instead, you almost certainly see in your mind's eye a series of fleeting but real images that you associate with and relate to the word. If you like Guinness, you may see your favourite pub, friends that you have shared a pint with, you may think of St Patrick's Day or a game of rugby, you may even see a pint of Guinness or recall some of the great advertising that Guinness has produced over the years. The Guinness 'Surfer' advertisement is regularly voted the best ever TV commercial. Take a look at it at the Campaign magazine website: http://www.campaignlive.co.uk/thework/news/930129/Guinness-surfer-Abbott-Mead-Vickers-BBDO.

Brands are therefore not just a name or a symbol but a collection of perceptions about a product or organisation based on our experience of the brand: how we use the brand, how we come across the brand and how we see the brand being consumed.

There are three key elements to successful branding:

- the product or service must work – the brand must deliver consistently tangible, functional benefits to brand users;
- customers must believe in the brand – there must be a rational reason to choose one brand over another;
- it must feel right– there must be an emotional connection with the brand, i.e. 'this brand is right for me now' and over time the brand must be presented consistently.

If this is managed correctly then a variety of positive outcomes emerge.

- We create a sustainable point of difference in our chosen market segments which is hard to copy and is legally enforceable. The core differences between one brand and another are at the heart of brand identity. This can assist in creating loyalty and out of this we can possibly charge higher prices and implement other ways of improving profitability.

- For our customers and prospects we define clearly the value that they expect from the brand. The brand is a guarantee of a consistent unchanging experience.
- Above all the customer decision process is simplified and often subconsciously processed. You may have had the experience of going to your favourite supermarket for bread and milk and emerging with £50 of groceries. Much of the decision-making that we undertake is subconsciously processed and we lapse easily into pre-programmed patterns of behaviour. We believe that a brand is right for us because we have been educated over time via our various experiences of the brand that this is the case. The brand becomes part of our personal identity.

Attitude formation

Jeremy Bullmore, former Chairman of both JWT and The Advertising Association, said: 'Consumers build brands the way birds build nests; from the sticks and straws they chance upon.' When Archibald Ingall Stretton, the successful London-based direct marketing agency, did some work looking at how customers come across the BMW brand they identified over a hundred different interactions some of which were carefully managed – others which were not.

What is consistent across all these touch points is the brand. Whether we are online, calling a contact centre, using the product or looking at an advertisement, the brand is a constant and is a shorthand device for our understanding of what the brand stands for and what it will do for us. Indeed, we could say that everything connected with a brand communicates something about that brand. In the last few years much more effort has been expended in the area of brand communication. The rise of experiential and sensory marketing is an example of this. Marketers are beginning to understand that words and pictures are not the only way we can deliver and receive messages. We develop attitudes from the full range of stimuli to which we are exposed and these include sounds, colours, smells, body language and design and form – to list just a few.

Estate agents have recognised this for many years advising clients to put on a pot of fresh coffee before prospective purchasers view a property to create a feeling of intimacy and belonging. Supermarkets 'bake off' industrially prepared dough in the in-store bakery to create a homely feel and car dealers spray used or 'previously enjoyed' cars with a scent that replicates the smell of a new car. Intel and Direct Line have a unique sonic brand and the use of music to support brands from Orange to Coca-Cola is widespread.

The formation of attitudes is a complex area of psychology and it forms an important part of the study of consumer behaviour. Put simply, there are three basic elements to attitude formation these are:

1. thoughts, perceptions, images and ideas;
2. feelings and emotions for example, excitement, happiness, love and affection;
3. habits, intention and behaviours.

You may also see these written as:

1. the Cognitive domain
2. the Affective domain
3. the Conative domain

The basic and important outcome of attitude formation is that thoughts are always moderated by emotion to create belief and belief drives behaviour. If those beliefs are positive, then it follows that customers are more likely to display loyalty and this can drive profitable relationships.

If we remember that marketing involves the mutual exchange of value, then the brand acts as the vehicle by which value is transferred from the producer to the consumer. Crucially the delivery of value through the brand should be consistent. Anything that compromises the brand's positioning in the mind of the consumer, i.e. anything that affects attitudes in a negative way, can cause problems. We would not expect Heinz to be sold 'exclusively to Harrods' and we would not expect to buy Paul Smith at Asda. Consumers will not necessarily do our work for us.

The brand needs to be communicated in a way that is honest and true; personally relevant; sufficient to meet objectives without overburdening consumers with unnecessary communication; interesting and consistent. This process needs to be managed across multiple channels. How many times has a bad experience online or in store compromised the promise made in advertising messages or mission statements? Every communication and every experience adds a deposit or removes capital at the bank of brand equity depending on the quality of that experience.

These experiences impact on perceived product quality and value and on the overall image of the company. Dissatisfied customers trust the brand less and are less committed. Ultimately the quality of brand experiences affects the loyalty of customers, and loyal customers tend to cost less to serve, spend more, recommend more and stay longer. These are key drivers of organisational profitability.

If the brand is delivered in an inconsistent way customers typically will turn away from it rather than try to reconcile these contradictions. If we are lucky they may complain but often the first we hear of this is when they move to the competition. This applies equally in business to business and consumer markets.

So now we can begin to determine what makes a successful brand.

What makes a successful brand?

First we need to understand what the brand stands for and how it is differentiated from the competition. This means understanding our customers' perceptions of the brand, their attitudes to the brand and the benefits that the brand delivers to them, both tangible and intangible.

If advertising is a truth told in an interesting way then what links advertising with branding is an attempt to locate and communicate essential truths about products and services. The development of most advertising creative work starts with an attempt to understand the core differentiated benefit delivered by the product or the unique selling proposition (USP). Typically this is something that is tangible in the product or that is believable about the product or service or often a combination of the two.

So, for example, the idea that Gillette is 'the best a man can get' or that Stella Artois is 'reassuringly expensive' are, if examined outside their commercial context, ridiculous. However, in the context of the category and the brand we willingly suspend belief and buy into the promise. The key thing is that the claim is based on, and tested through, consumer research and insight.

The brand also has to work for all stakeholders. For example, if staff do not believe the brand promise then it will not be delivered with passion and energy. Internal marketing is important and the brand must be communicated using clear and consistent messages to all audiences including those within the organisation, and working on behalf of the organisations, such as channel intermediaries and agencies. This must work to join up the promises made with the delivery of those promises, so systems and processes must also support the brand promise. So if BMW is the ultimate driving machine, its website needs to reflect this engineering excellence perhaps as much as the car itself.

Media Neutral Planning (MNP)

Media Neutral Planning has been very important in marketing over the last decade. The concept emerged as a response to the limited approach to media buying that was practised by advertising agencies in the late twentieth century.

Advertising agencies are so named because they originally acted as agents on behalf of media owners and took a commission based on a percentage of the value of the media spend placed, typically around 15 per cent of the value. Unsurprisingly, this meant that agencies tended to advise their clients to place their advertising in the media that attracted the highest levels of commission – very often this was television.

Related to this are the concepts of 'above the line' and 'below the line' communications. It is surprising how often these terms are still used and yet they reveal an approach to the communications task that is outdated and inadequate. These terms refer to the fact that advertising agencies drew a line in their accounts above which was revenue from media commission, and below which were the agency fees charged directly to clients. The client did not pay for the agency's work on media advertising as those costs were covered by the commission from media owners. So 'below the line' related to activities for which the client had to pay. Advertising agencies therefore encouraged clients to advertise in commissionable media and clients preferred this because it reduced the fees they had to pay. This approach to marketing was of course supposed to be customer-focused was in fact driven by an accounting procedure.

The term 'below the line' has consistently been misused and confused with direct marketing. Direct marketing is not below the line. Much of direct marketing is carried out in commissionable media such as press and television advertising. If 'below the line' were applied to direct marketing it would only be correct to use it for non-commissionable media such as direct mail, email and telemarketing.

Several things have changed in the past two or three decades. The media has been fragmented and the effectiveness of mass media has to some extent declined. Whereas 30 years ago an exciting episode of Coronation Street would attract 20 million plus viewers, today the audience is lower and rarely exceeds ten million viewers. In 1984 there was just one commercial TV station in the UK, now there are hundreds all battling for a share of advertising budgets. According to the Broadcaster's Audience Research Board (BARB) although, we are watching more TV than ever before, 28 hours and 15 minutes each week in the year to June 20101; and we are watching more channels and accessing TV via the Internet using 'on demand' services. The ability to fast-forward through advertising breaks is easier than ever. Whilst we can now reach niche audiences the ability to reach large audiences has declined.

The same is true in almost every medium. Radio stations have blossomed as the digital space has opened up new opportunities. Newspapers are no longer print bound but can be accessed via iPhone, iPad and the hundreds of smart phones and mobile devices that are available.

The pace of change in the media market has been matched by changes in the way that we market to customers. We are no longer seeking mass markets but using databases and research to target smaller segments using approaches that are more personal and relevant and therefore more effective whilst reducing the costs per contact in order to make our activities more efficient. This idea sits at the very heart of this book.

The media-buying function has also changed and the structure of the industry is slightly different; most advertising agencies either outsource their media buying or have specialist subsidiaries with their own profit targets; also the commission structures are different.

Media Neutral Planning (MNP) is a simple concept made complicated by the history of client agency relationships. It simply reflects the fact that media and channels should be selected on the basis of insight into consumers and the objectives of the company rather than on the basis of what is good for the agency. The Media Neutral Planning Best Practice Group, supported by the Centre for Integrated Marketing, defined MNP as:

'a rigorous process for the selection of communication options which combines facts and imagination in order to drive continual improvement to overall ROI.'

The Media Neutral Planning Best Practice Group, www.cfim.co.uk

The Centre for Integrated Marketing can be found at www.cfim.co.uk. This site contains some very useful material and case studies and is well worth a visit.

The Media Neutral Planning Best Practice Group identified five essential characteristics of MNP. According to the group, companies need to:

1. Adopt a broader concept of media. 'Media' is whatever conveys a brand experience to a customer, prospective customer or other audience, and should not therefore be restricted to commercial media.

2. Aim for an optimised mix of communication media and activities conceived as a creative, harmonious and efficient whole, rather than a series of isolated or even parallel communication activities. (Just occasionally, the mix might be one brilliant and innovative solution). Thinking widely about the mix options one is more likely to discover such strokes of genius.

3. Marketing managers should review their assumptions about what works and how, recognising that historic attitudes to planning have included significant dysfunctional biases and barriers to excellence.

4. Develop clear communication objectives using a common framework across all communication channels. By doing this, marketers replace the historic practice of

disconnected and often weak communication objectives with a single coherent framework. This also establishes a common currency for evaluation.

5. Ensure a competent, organised and committed client, working with agencies as a team through an integrated media/creative process. The Media Neutral Planning Best Practice Group recommends that this team process should be led by a communication planning team which includes five core skills:
   1. branding
   2. communication
   3. the customer
   4. media
   5. social skills and logistics/project management

   These principles are then translated into implementation.

Source: www.cfm.co.uk

MNP is designed to optimise communications effectiveness and efficiency using a variety of research approaches including database analysis and qualitative and quantitative research. It forces clients to understand that communications take place every time a customer or prospect comes into contact with the brand and therefore the whole organisation is involved in communicating to clients. This may mean a new approach to evaluation and a new approach to measuring and rewarding the performance of agencies.

The MNP Best Practice Group also identifies 12 core benefits from the implementation of MNP. These are:

1. improved business cost (efficiency);
2. improved employee motivation and alignment (psychological effects);
3. improved business performance (effectiveness);
4. improved customer value proposition (creative design, mission);
5. better media-mix selection (budget efficiency);
6. improved touchpoint management (CRM effects);
7. media-multiplier effect (harmonisation);
8. improved communication relevance;
9. improved customer bonding post acquisition, share of wallet, and retention (satisfaction, psychological effects);
10. improved customer brand equity (social pressure, market equity, price differentials);
11. lifetime financial effects (time effects);
12. improved analyst perceptions (shareholders equity).

Source: www.cfm.co.uk

What is Integrated Marketing Communication?

IMC takes the benefits of MNP and places them in the broader communications context. It is based on several core beliefs.

- The communication of differentiated value happens in many and various channels and media.
- Certain dimensions of value can be better communicated to certain customers in certain media.
- Media are more effective and efficient working together – known as the media multiplier effect.
- A single medium will decline in effectiveness over time.
- Repetition across media is not integration.

Although much of this is common sense, until recently the problem for marketers was that the tools to deliver and evaluate IMC strategies did not exist. The development of database marketing and CRM strategies and systems has improved our ability to track and measure response across media. This has given us the evidence to support and justify the approach. A study in Europe, carried out by Behaviour Scan, identified that the use of direct marketing, alongside TV marketing, boosted response by around 40 per cent. This confirms studies carried out in the 1980s by Brian Thomas and Drayton Bird for Reader's Digest which showed that TV in combination with Direct Mail boosted response by up to 40 per cent.

Equally, customers now expect their information to be used effectively across the multiple points of contact that are available to them.

IMC is defined by the IDM as:

'...the coordinated planning of communication for each customer community or public to achieve creative harmony of messages, customer interest and marketing objectives across media at each touchpoint and over time.' Institute for Direct Marketing

This contrasts with Schultz and Schultz's definition who define IMC in a much broader way.

'IMC is a strategic business process used to plan, develop, execute, and evaluate coordinated, measurable, persuasive brand communications programs over time with consumers, customers, prospects, and other targeted relevant external and internal audiences.' Schultz, D.E. & Schultz, H.F. (1998)

'Transitioning marketing communication into the twenty-first century'.
Journal of Marketing Communications, 4(1), pp. 9–26

A combination of the two definitions appears to cover the bases quite well. The broader business process is important as the whole organisation needs to commit to an IMC approach. The need to reconcile the interests of a variety of internal and external stakeholders and functions, manage the creation and distribution of content through multiple channels and track and evaluate the results of this activity is an organisation-wide task.

Historically, effective implementation of IMC has been a difficult task and there are several barriers to overcome. Part of the problem is that managers have been trained in a specific way and the approach to IMC lies outside their competence. The way we describe the communications task also limits an approach to IMC. Typically, we talk about what we do as marketers; advertising, PR etc. rather that what these things do to customers and the outputs they produce for the business. Often the way we are organised reflects this task-based environment. The politics of organisations can also be a barrier, power and influence tends to follow budget. Strong leadership at director level is needed to reconcile the fact that whilst most of the budget might go to the brands agency the output in terms of sales is the result of the activities of all areas of the business.

If these barriers can be overcome, then the benefits can be significant. In its course on IMC the IDM identifies some of these benefits.

- Improvements in customer attitudes and behaviours arising from improved and more consistent experiences of brand value.
- Synergy and multiplier effects on profitability from improvements in customer attitudes and behaviours.
- More efficient (and effective) media choices and mixes as well as better deployment of communication disciplines.
- More flowing, efficient (and effective) business processes, creating higher added value.
- Substantially enhanced evaluation and improved applied learning across the brand organisation.
- Improvements in staff morale, work rate, cohesion, stress and creativity.
- Reduced employee replacement costs, employee cost/benefit synergies and an enhanced employee cost/customer value ratio.
- Reduction in internal fragmentation and cost holes.
- More cost-effective use of agencies and business partners with better team results.
- Cost-effective synergies.

Source: The IDM

Planning for IMC

The strategic approach to IMC links with the chapters in this book on strategic planning, campaign planning and implementation, testing and measurement. However, there are some specific models that have been developed to help with this process. Professor Angus Jenkinson's Four Needs planning approach is a useful framework. Professor Jenkinson is Director of the Centre for Integrated Marketing, (www.cfim.co.uk) his approach covers four key areas:

1. **Market Insight**
   - Defines the communication challenge
   - Customer insights: who are they? What are their needs?
   - Brand insights
   - Market insights
   - Value proposition

2. **Communications challenge**
   - Attitude equity objectives and communications brief
   - Creative brief
   - Creative concepts
   - Media brief
   - Contact/media strategy.
   - Budget
3. **Optimisation and execution**
   - Optimised budget
   - Plan/optimise execution logistics and schedule
   - Execute plan
4. **Evaluation and Learning**
   - Did you reach the people and did you communicate effectively and efficiently?
   - How well did each element work?
   - And how well did the overall plan work?
   - How did marketing communications link to business objectives?
   - How did people work together?

This approach can be bedded down within a structured method. There are several different planning models but Angus Jenkinson's nine stage work flow process is useful.

IMC COMMUNICATION PLANNING PROCESS

- **Customer/market insights:** Who are we talking to? How do they make decisions? Where do they go for information? What are their attitudes?, Are they loyal? This insight can be obtained through database analysis and qualitative and quantitative research.
- **Brand insights:** What does the brand stand for? What is its positioning relative to the competition? This area typically involves qualitative research.
- **Value proposition:** What is the core benefit delivered to customers? Is the USP relative to the competition?
- **Communications brief:** A central communications brief which covers core outputs across media and channels. This is based on insight and research and is core to the IMC process; it is a single point of reference for all parties to the communications plan.
- **Creative plan:** Identifies the core creative platform that is delivered through multiple channels.
- **Contact strategy, touchpoint or media plan:** This covers media and channel integration across all touchpoints, when and how do we talk to our target market how do we develop the relationship over time.
- **Budget optimisation:** This is the allocation of funds based on objectives and tasks.
- **Execution logistics:** Implementation timetable and project plan.
- **Evaluation and learning:** Closing the loop against objectives. This is dealt with in more detail below.

Figure 11.1: The IMC planning process

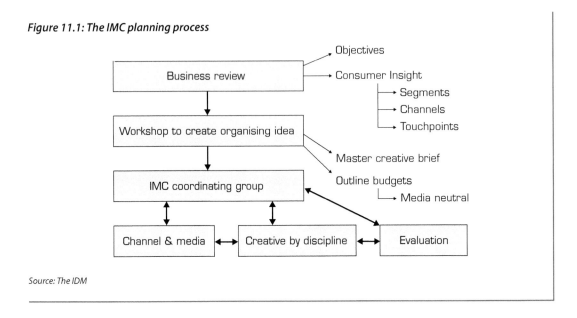

Source: The IDM

The IDM's approach highlights two important areas. The first is the enhanced requirement to manage the process. This means the IMC workshop and coordinating group have an extended role in overseeing the range of partners in the delivery of the plan. Also the master creative brief determines the feel of the creative across multiple channels rather than the precise execution. This does not mean that everything should look the same, rather, that the output of the plan meets the objectives set.

In order to deliver the plan effectively there is a need to:

- clearly understand the core brand proposition and values;
- agree on the problem and objective;
- gather and analyse core insights from each key customer segment;
- attitudes, buying behaviour, etc.;
- understand which channels each segment uses:
- when? In what circumstances?;
- develop the core organising idea internally and for consumers;
- understand what different media and disciplines can do;
- take an unbiased view on the capabilities of different media and disciplines;
- understand the preferences of different segments at different touchpoints;
- optimise media combinations over time and across touchpoints;
- create a collaborative team of Internal and External partners;
- appoint a senior level management champion.

Measuring IMC

The measurement of IMC has always been a major stumbling block to implementations – however, direct marketing methods coupled with traditional approaches to brand tracking can help. The key output of course is incremental sales so a basic evaluation technique is the measurement of outputs against inputs; i.e. the return on marketing investment. If the research is correct, integration should deliver incremental return on marketing spend. This can also be linked to customer value over time and the measurement of customer lifetime value (LTV) is also important. LTV is covered in Chapter 16.

We should also be tracking a range of brand metrics. For example, brand recall – both prompted and unprompted – relevance and salience, likeability and consideration should all be tracked over time and against the competition. We should also be looking at tracking response rates for individual media as well as measuring the multiplier effect. The management of this task may mean multiple control groups and sophisticated testing strategies will be required to determine the optimum media mix that will achieve the maximum output from an integrated strategy. Chapter 14 on testing and Chapter 16 on measurement cover this in more detail.

Evaluation should cover the following areas.

- Sales analyses and return on investment.
  - How effective at building immediate sales?
  - How effective at building long term relationship/value?
- Customer lifetime value by source of acquisition.
- Customer satisfaction at each touchpoint.
- Analysis of the customer journey and decision-making process.
- Complaints and critical incident analysis.
- Brand awareness, recall, salience and likeability.
- Individual medium and channel metrics, response rates, conversion, cost per sale etc.
- Media multiplier measurement:
  - track effect of combinations, e.g. region/time period v. control.
- Traditional single discipline measurements and tests:
  - Awareness, cost per sale, value of PR coverage etc.
- Econometric analysis.
  - Computer models showing the value of all different variables.

Managing agencies to deliver IMC

So we have considered the nature of IMC. Its delivery is another matter and is much more difficult to manage. If we are trying to produce an integrated output, then we need to reconcile the different disciplines and different specialisms that exist within and outside the organisation.

We have already discussed the process of internal marketing and communication but typically we are trying to manage a range of different individuals and departments. Externally too we are managing a wide range of suppliers and agencies.

Managing integration – internal and external audiences

Internal audiences
- Other marketing staff
- Production
- Research

- IT
- Finance
- Logistics
- HR
- Sales and other intermediaries
- Shareholders
- Trade unions

External audiences
- Agencies
  - Direct marketing
  - Events and exhibitions
  - Experiential
  - Advertising
  - Public relations
  - Sales promotion
  - Logistics
  - Digital
  - Database
  - Design and new product
  - Branding
  - Research
  - Media buyers
  - Marketing and business consultants
- Intermediaries wholesalers retailers, agents
- Suppliers

Despite the recent claims that agencies are offering integrated solutions the reality remains that most agencies are specialised in certain communications disciplines and even after large-scale investment in personnel and signage this remains the case. Integrated agencies with one profit and loss account and a full range of in-house services are rare. Typically, larger organisations will be managing a broad and wide-ranging network of agencies each of which makes a contribution to the overall objectives for the planning period.

The agency community is diverse and if you consider the outlook, skills and training of those working in a digital agency with those working in sales promotion you will see two very different sets of people with very different views on how businesses should be run, and on the key performance measures that should drive success.

There is a range of things that can be done to try to reconcile the tensions that may exist between agencies and that can sometimes emerge between agencies and clients.

The first depends largely on the client. Strong management of the agency network is required so that each knows their role in delivering overall marketing and communications objectives and the dependencies and milestones that exist within any plan. This means strong and effective communication and experience shows that this should be done face-to-face wherever possible. The idea of the client managing a meeting at which all involved agencies present progress and credentials seems to work quite well, extranets and intranets can be set up for the day-to-day management of activity but the development of chemistry between partners is important and this meeting needs to be personal.

The other key area is remuneration. It is true for the most part that measurement drives behaviour and if the right things are measured and rewarded, then a commitment to IMC can be achieved. However, this can cause some issues. For example, if we are measuring an integrated effect how do we isolate the role of the branding agency versus a digital agency?

One way that can work is to leave some budget to be allocated as a collective reward for certain overarching targets being met and this can be allocated proportionately to total fees charged, or equally between partners. This approach to performance-related reward is more accepted today and can work to drive IMC across agency partners.

So how do we make IMC happen successfully?

First of all we need to understand the brand intimately, what does the brand stand for and what are we trying to achieve?

We need to create a unified approach to the task through a multidisciplinary planning meeting and the approach overall needs to be collaborative and open, both internally and between external partners. We must recognise that everything we do says something about the brand and creates or damages loyalty. Finally we need to measure, test and evaluate and share learning throughout the team.

SUMMARY

In this chapter we looked at one of the core assets of any business; its brands. We looked at the history of branding. We saw that brands are different from branding and that the brand logo is only a small part of the branding process. We saw that brands are valuable and long-lasting but need careful management.

We looked at the role of attitude formation and explored how thoughts and feelings drive behaviour. Managing perceptions, therefore, becomes a very important part of brand management. These perceptions are created from the range of stimuli that consumers encounter, only some of which can be managed. We looked at the development of Media Neutral Planning and the associated concept of Integrated Marketing Communications. Finally we outlined benefits of, and barriers to, IMC implementation and examined approaches to planning and evaluation of IMC strategy.

REVIEW QUESTIONS

1. When was the world's first brand manager appointed?
2. What are the three components of attitudes?
3. According to Interbrand what is the world's most valuable brand?
4. Define touchpoints and outline an approach to touchpoint analysis for a brand of your choice.

5. What is MNP?
6. Define 'above the line' and 'below the line' communications. Why are these concepts outdated and damaging to communications planning.
7. Define IMC.
8. List five benefits of IMC.
9. List five barriers to the implementation of IMC and outline how these can be overcome.
10. Outline an approach to agency remuneration that may facilitate the delivery of IMC.

CHAPTER 12
DEVELOPING COMPELLING PROPOSITIONS

IN THIS CHAPTER

We will consider the process of building a compelling end-user proposition.

After reading this chapter you will:

- Understand the differences between propositions, offers and promotional offers
- Know the value of varying the proposition for each individual segment
- Understand positioning and how to express it
- Appreciate the different types of proposition and how they are used

Specific topics include:

- Understanding the confusing terminology
- The importance of relevance – how to vary the proposition for each segment
- The many different types of proposition
- The benefits and risks of using a promotional offer
- Prize draws and competitions
- The power of the testimonial
- Examples of positioning
- The use of hard sell techniques and the inevitable trade off
- Case study – RSPCA 'Home for Life'

INTRODUCTION

In this chapter we will discuss the importance of developing attractive propositions, and the often confusing terminology used to describe them.

Proposition and offer – what's the difference?

The confusion really arises because the proposition and the offer are the same thing, whereas a promotional offer is totally different.

In marketing your proposition (or offer) is basically the end user benefit, i.e. what your prospect will get in return for buying your product or service. This may be something highly tangible such as a consumable, perhaps a case of wine, a book or an item of clothing. On the other hand your customer may not be buying a tangible product at all but something which gives the buyer a feeling of security, such as an insurance policy.

Whatever you are selling you have to find a way of presenting the end user benefits in a clear and persuasive way.

Vary the proposition by segment

One major benefit of direct marketing is that we can vary the proposition according to the specific characteristics or interests of each group of prospects. It has been said that the difference between direct and traditional marketing is that traditional advertisers start with the product and look for a market to sell it to; direct marketers start with the prospect and match product and offer to the individual.

Sometimes it is not possible to make a direct 'one-stage' offer because of the complexity of the product, or perhaps the breadth of your range. In such cases you need to develop an offer, which will generate a 'lead' or enquiry.

Let us suppose you sell energy-saving systems for large companies – automatic light switches which turn off after a period of time with no movement in the room; insulated windows and walls to preserve heat and thus reduce power consumption and so on.

It would be quite difficult for you to sell such a product through a one-stage approach, even if you were able to quote lots of happy customers. In this case you may decide to advertise or mail prospects the offer of a FREE energy audit.

This would be attractive to prospects as the audit would tell them the various ways they could save money and precisely what this would cost to achieve. It would also be attractive to the vendor as it would identify, from a wide 'suspect' audience, those likely to be good prospects.

Although price and 'free gift' offers are very common, an offer does not have to include a discount nor is it even necessary to be 'promotional'. A free energy audit may sound like a promotional offer, and it could perhaps be classed as such, but in my mind it qualifies as a proposition. In two-stage marketing the objective is to get the prospect to take the first step so all we would offer in the initial communication (ad, mailing, email or whatever) would be the free audit. Those who respond would then be placed into a lead development or nurturing programme.

Your offer can be comprised of any combination of elements e.g.:

■ **The promise of a solution to a problem**
If you have the solution to a specific problem, and you do not have lots of competitors offering similar solutions, you may merely need to tell people they can buy this from you.

For example, let us suppose you offer a will-writing service

A high percentage of people do not make a will, although many realise they should. Your research shows you that the two most common obstacles are:

■ **Apathy** – people just cannot be bothered to get started with their will, mainly because of...

■ **The apparent size of the task** – there seems to be a huge amount of work involved in listing and valuing one's assets

What if you offered a trouble-free service where you visit the prospects in their homes, and which included a free valuation of assets, saving the prospect the trouble. That offer would clearly solve the two major problems and could be quite successful, without the need for discounting.

- **A specific (sometimes timed), promotional offer, e.g. an incentive or discount**
  Example: some companies make 'Early Bird' offers where the prospect is offered a discount or free gift if they order by a certain date.
- **A variation on the promotional offer might be quantity based, e.g. 'buy one get one free' (sometimes called a BOGOF) or a typical magazine subscription offer where a publisher offers a special discount if the subscriber signs up for two or even three years.**
  This sort of offer can be attractive to customers and it is very attractive to the publisher, who gains in three ways:
  1. Cash flow is improved.
  2. The margin available for discount is higher as there is no marketing cost for the second (and perhaps third) year's subscription.
  3. The extended commitment from the customer makes longer-term planning easier.

Another way of retaining subscribers is to take advantage of the apathy of the average person. Most people signing up with a standing order such as a Direct Debit Mandate or a Continuous Credit Card Authority, just cannot be bothered to take the necessary action to cancel their arrangements, even where they are no longer bothered about taking the magazine.

This is why many publishers and membership organisations offer an added incentive for a signed standing order form. Even a deferred standing order works well for many companies. You may well have seen an offer which is phrased in the following way:

"Buy 15 months issues for the price of 12, simply complete and return the attached direct debit form and we will send you your first three months' issues absolutely free. In this period you are free to cancel your arrangement without having to pay anything at all. After three months we will process your standing instruction and commence deducting the agreed amounts from your account (or 'charging them to your credit card')."

This offer clearly puts the customer in control but a very few actually bother to cancel the standing order and thus carry on paying for months or even years after the initial interest in the product has worn off.

- **Quality – the best available**
  If you use this claim make sure that quality is important to your prospects. It would not be worth making such an offer to a group of prospects who buy solely on price. It is therefore necessary to consider segmenting your customers and varying your offers according to their buying behaviour.
- **Value – best at this price**
  This works well for many marketers, just make sure you can sustain your price, or even reduce it further when the competition reacts.
- **Availability – 'only from ourselves'**
  If you have exclusivity on a product which is in demand, you may not need to make any more detailed offer than 'Now available from...'

■ **Reassurance**

Every advertiser tries to persuade you that theirs is the best product on the market. As a result advertisers' claims are devalued by prospects. However, if you can quote a credible third party endorsing your claims it is much more believable.

You should always make the strongest guarantee you can; a small number of people will take advantage of you, but many more will be reassured at the point of making a purchase decision.

EXAMPLE

Some years ago a company selling duvets 'off-the-page' was seeking a way of increasing response to their ads in Sunday supplements.

Peter Donoghue, who was then Chairman of their Advertising Agency, suggested they should offer a 10-year, unconditional, replacement or full money back guarantee on every duvet they sold. The manufacturer was appalled, saying: 'A duvet is only expected to last for about 10 years, your guarantee will make me bankrupt.'

Peter explained that, while the guarantee must be honoured, most customers would be very happy with the reassurance that they could return it if they wished. A small number of customers may be sufficiently zealous to take advantage of the guarantee if their duvet started to wear out after nine and a half years, but the majority would not.

Eventually Peter persuaded them to test this new offer and sales doubled.

The company realised a fortune due to Peter's suggestion and a careful study over the 14 years since the offer started showed no measurable increase in guarantee claims.

■ **Added value**

Customers also respond well to offers of help, so telephone help lines, free advisory booklets, etc. can be very successful.

■ **Better performance or technical superiority**

This is another area where testimonials help you achieve greater credibility. Everyone expects you to say yours is the best, and to a certain extent your statements are discounted. But if one of your customers, for example, the CEO of a well-known company, says your product is the best, that is a more powerful and believable statement to other customers. Such statements are especially persuasive if they quote some sort of performance improvement e.g. 'Since we changed to XYZ we have noted a 15 per cent reduction in machine downtime.'

If you have not got any testimonials do not despair. Assuming your product is as good as you say it is testimonials are not hard to get.

Do not do what a well-known consultant once recommended on a public platform 'Write your own!' Not only is this highly unethical it is also foolish; you have no need to resort to such dirty tricks.

The best way to get testimonials is to ask for them. Not in so many words, perhaps, but in the following way. When you send a customer satisfaction questionnaire to your customers ask a final question with an open response. You might say something like:

'Is there anything else you would like to say about our products or services? Please tell us whether it is good or bad.'

Some will say you are absolutely useless and you must respond to such comments immediately with remedial action.

Some will say yours is the most wonderful product they have ever encountered, and to these you respond with a request that they let you use their statement in promotional material. Occasionally your request will be refused but most customers will not object. Some will offer to say something even nicer if you wish, though it is usually better to leave the quotation unedited. This technique never fails to produce powerful, believable testimonials.

Many seminar delegates ask why business-to-business advertisers quote names and companies of people who give testimonials, while consumer advertisers rarely do. 'Is this because many consumer testimonials are false?' they ask. The truth is reassuring and depressing at the same time.

When a company quotes the name and address of a consumer who recommends their product, the subject often receives 'hate' mail from cranks. This does not often happen with business addresses – it is a sad comment on modern life!

> Remember: offers do not always have to be 'promotional'. Simply describing an appropriate benefit in the right way to the right person will often be sufficient.

Whatever you decide about your own offer, remember that it must also link to your longer term positioning.

What is positioning?

For many people, positioning can be a difficult concept to grasp; positioning is not something you do to your product although it may well require you to make changes to your services.

Positioning is the overall impression you wish to place in the mind of your prospect once they have read your advertisement or mailing. Your copy will describe the benefits which your product will bring to the prospect but something more is needed – what is there you can say which states very succinctly what this product *means to the prospect?*

Let's move away from the theoretical approach and look some examples.

EXAMPLE

Rolls-Royce is positioned as the top-quality car marque – other cars may be as well engineered, but they are still not Rolls and the difference is positioning. Rolls-Royce has pre-empted the top-quality position to the extent that the name 'Rolls-Royce' has become a colloquial description of quality for all sorts of products and services. Even Bentley, which is in many ways the same as Rolls, has not achieved that cachet.

American Express is positioned as the prestigious financial instrument – the company makes sure its communications reflect this positioning.

Rolls-Royce's positioning is largely to do with the excellence of the product. American Express is primarily selling a service; the product is similar to other charge cards but the way it is described gives it a cachet of better quality.

Rolls-Royce would clearly need to be particularly careful about any incentives offered to prospective buyers. A cheap free gift would be out of context with their positioning. So would a special weekend sale. On the other hand, free membership of a motoring organisation such as the RAC or AA would be quite appropriate.

Similarly, a free baby safety seat would be appropriate to the positioning of a Ford or Volvo; less so for a high-powered sports car.

What can you do to sustain a positioning? Perhaps you could offer a telephone advice line or a series of leaflets explaining changes in legislation as they happen. Perhaps you simply need to make a promise of availability whenever your customer has a problem.

Before they can start writing, copywriters are likely to ask clients the question 'What impression do we want to leave in the mind of the reader'. The copywriter is looking for a positioning statement and in answering this question it can be helpful to use an analogy. The two most popular in the advertising agency business are:

- 'If this product were an animal what would it be?'
- 'If it were a motor car what would it be?'

Such a simple analogy enables the copywriter to get a good feeling for what is required in terms of image, reliability, efficiency, etc.

Whatever positioning you choose must be appropriate for your product. It is easy to say, for example, 'I offer the Rolls-Royce of home catering services', but if your customers perceive your service as less than perfect you leave yourself open to criticism.

Your offer will vary according to what you want the customer to do. It may be quite acceptable to offer a helpful free booklet to business people in return for an enquiry about your product but a free booklet will not in itself persuade a prospect to order a £5,000 product.

A free technical helpline may, on the other hand, be enough to give your product the edge over a competitor.

You can vary your offer to pre-select the quality of enquiries you attract. The way you phrase your offer in your initial advertisement will have a major bearing on the quality of enquiries you receive. The less specific you are, the 'looser' your leads will be. For example you could simply say 'Return this coupon to rid your house of flies for ever'. This may attract thousands of 'loose' leads (enquiries) but when the prospects discover they have to spend hundreds of pounds having screens fitted to all doors and windows your conversion to sale ratio would be very small.

On the other hand, an advertisement which said 'A single investment of £1,000 would rid your home of flying insects for ever' would attract very few leads but the conversion rate would be much higher. These would be 'tight' leads.

As we can see, loose leads do not convert as well as tight leads but you get more of them. Your decision about which to go for can be complicated, taking into account the cost of servicing a lead, the amount of sales or telemarketing resource you have available, and even the competitive situation.

You may well have to carry out a series of tests to determine the ideal method for your business. See Chapter 14 for details of testing procedures.

You must make sure your offer is relevant to your prospects. People rarely buy products because of their technical superiority, but because of what the product delivers in terms of user benefits. For instance, someone wouldn't buy a lubricating oil because it is a technological marvel, they'd buy it because it stops a door squeaking. People do not buy features but benefits. A lecturer's pocket pointer is a nicely engineered telescopic device but the end user benefit is that it helps to demonstrate details on a screen and fits easily in the pocket.

Promotional offers

When discussing offers many people think only of discounts and 'buy one get one free' approaches. These are certainly offers but as we have seen not the only ones.

There is no doubt that price and volume offers attract increased response but we must also consider the effect on our conversion ratios and long term sales potential. Generating a high volume of low grade enquiries may not be the ideal way to build your business.

Also a 'buy one get one free' offer will not be appropriate for all products or audiences. Consider the relevance for your own market. There are many products which do not lend themselves to a 'two for the price of one' approach.

However, if you have enough information about your prospects you may be able to make highly selective offers of this sort. For example, perhaps your customer has a daughter who will be 18 next month, that could be an opportunity for a 'two for one' offer on a variety of products.

Offers do not have to be the same for all prospects, they can be varied by segment. If you hold detailed information about prospects you can communicate with them directly, varying your offer according to your knowledge of their circumstances.

EXAMPLE

A company that sells bulk supplies of foods to people in the catering industry, built a sizeable database by offering free product samples through press and direct mail.

It did not specify the amount of free product a respondent would get and on the sample request card it asked 'How many meals do you serve each day?' This information enabled it to deal with each enquiry according to potential:

- An establishment serving 500 lunches every day would receive a 1,000-portion sample. One serving 25 lunches would receive a 100-portion sample. The buying incentives would also vary. The 500-lunch prospect would be offered, say, an electric food mixer in return for an order for a 10,000 portion pack, this would be a totally unrealistic offer for the smaller prospect.

  The smaller prospect would be offered perhaps a set of ladles as an incentive to order a

500-portion pack. This incentive would have no stimulating effect on the larger prospect, and would simply be giving away free gifts without attracting any additional orders.
■ The information on the enquiry form also enabled the company to determine the ideal contact strategy for each type of prospect; the larger prospects would have their samples delivered in person by a member of the sales force. Smaller prospects may have their samples mailed to them.

There is often scope for selective marketing of such offers, once you have the information to enable you to segment your prospects.

Prize competitions and lotteries

The subject of promotional competitions and prize draws used to be fairly simple. Until the Gambling Act 2005 was enacted marketers had a simple choice between running a competition or a prize draw. The two major differences between a prize draw and a competition were:

1. A competition required the entrant to satisfy some test of skill, often requiring minimal intelligence – e.g. 'In which city would you find the Eiffel Tower?'
2. Unlike a prize draw entry, a competition entry could be tied to a purchase, e.g. 'Only open to customers placing an order of more than £50.'

As can be seen from the previous description, there were many anomalies and much uncertainty about what was legal and what was not; and precisely what constitutes a test of skill.

The Gambling Act 2005 defines the differences between prize competitions, free draws and lotteries, but like all legislation is highly complex in parts. To fully understand what can and cannot be done marketers need legal advice.

There is an excellent e-newsletter called Out-Law published by solicitors Pinsent Masons LLP, and if you wish to find out more about the Gambling Act or simply wish to keep up to date with the various forms of legislation affecting marketers you should subscribe to this at www.out-law.com. In addition to their regular newsletters, their site contains more than 10,000 pages of legal information.

Using incentives in marketing

There are two main ways of using incentives: in return for a purchase; and in return for a trial. Offering a free gift will usually increase the number of responses to a consumer advertisement or mailing. In marketing to businesses however, it will be less effective.

Many businesses, and all public offices and government departments will flatly refuse to accept any form of consideration in return for placing orders, and whilst this can be understood, a sensible seller can often find a way of offering an inducement which does not contravene the regulations in force.

■ You could try offering an incentive for a free trial, perhaps a free gift that might benefit the business as a whole, or a day's free consultancy. This would not compromise the company executive but the free gift technique is still frowned upon by many large corporations.

- You could offer an incentive in the form of free merchandise. Assuming they are interested in the product, some additional supplies could be quite acceptable. A laser printer could be supplied with some spare toner or several reams of paper. This would be more acceptable to many organisations.

You must decide what is right and also permissible in your marketplace. Remember that your promotional strategy will affect what customers and prospects think of you. As we said earlier, cheap free gifts are not advisable when you are selling top-quality products.

Balancing response, conversion and long-term positioning

Every business would like to improve the cost-efficiency of their marketing budget, and, as we shall see in Chapter 13, there are numerous devices that can increase response.

In your quest for more cost-efficiency, be aware that although making powerful offers will increase the response you attract:

- generating response is only the first step, even if you sell direct and a response is an order;
- the eventual profitability of a direct marketing business depends on total customer satisfaction with your product and your promises. Repeat sales are generally a highly important factor given the cost of acquiring new business;
- it is therefore highly dangerous to over-stimulate prospects and indeed to over-promise regarding the quality and benefits of your product;
- unless your product lives up to the claims you will suffer in three ways: you will have a higher than expected level of returned orders; you will not be able to sell additional products to disappointed customers in the future; and dissatisfied customers may spread the word. And if they choose to do so on the Internet you could rapidly be facing a huge problem.

As mentioned earlier, offering incentives in return for enquiries will increase your enquiry levels but may reduce your conversion ratio. There is no set rule about this. You need to test in your own market and find an offer that produces the best balance for your own business.

The trade-off from hard sell

You can usually increase your response by using aggressive techniques but remember that your response is likely to be simply the tip of the iceberg. If 2 per cent of people mailed, or 0.2 per cent of those who read a newspaper responded to your offer it is probable that around five or 10 times as many actually noticed and read at least part of your message.

What do they now think of you? Some will not change their attitudes but some will find your aggressive approach off-putting and may even think less of your company as a result.

One of the most powerful selling techniques is door-to-door selling, but this also attracts the most disfavour.

Next on the 'hate' list comes telephone selling – the more powerful the technique the more people resent it being used against them.

This same principle applies in advertising, direct mail and email. Some of the world's most successful marketing organisations use very hard sell techniques, attracting huge responses but also much criticism. Achieving the correct balance requires careful judgement. You have a duty to both your customers and your company. If a hard sell works it is generally because your offer meets your customers' needs better than your competitors'. As long as companies abide by the industry codes of conduct and use the mailing preference service (MPS) and related services there should not be a problem. The key is trust and this is what brands ultimately promise. Fail to deliver on this promise and you will ultimately fail in business.

CASE STUDY – DEVELOPING A COMPELLING PROPOSITION
RSPCA CAMPAIGN: 'HOME FOR LIFE'

BACKGROUND

In 2006, legacies contributed 55 per cent of the RSPCA's total annual income, equating to £58m. The charity is heavily dependent on legacy income to fund its ongoing work, and needed to find a new generation of legacy donors. Above all, the RSPCA had to find a way to make cold legator recruitment cost-effective in order for it to remain a sustainable source of charity fundraising. The Home for Life campaign was developed to fulfil this need.

Like other major charities, the RSPCA has a finely tuned programme to develop current donor relationships and encourage loyal supporters to pledge a legacy to the RSPCA in their wills.

A SENSITIVE APPROACH

The relationship building process and its economics are well understood by the charity. However, the scope of legacy fundraising activity had largely been confined to the RSPCA's existing supporter base, as recruiting new legacy donors is both expensive and challenging.

The subject of will-making and legacies requires a careful approach, as it inevitably broaches the subject of the recipient's own mortality. Fundraising response rates usually plummet at the mere mention of it.

The unpredictability of legacy income is another issue. The charity is rarely informed at the moment a bequest is made, usually only learning of the gift after the donor's death, but it is greatly to the charity's advantage to receive immediate notification of a 'pledge'. Knowledge about a future bequest allows the charity to reinforce the relationship through a bespoke marketing communications programme.

The RSPCA takes an integrated approach in its communications planning. Therefore, any cold recruitment of legacy donors needs to reinforce existing RSPCA brand attributes by demonstrating the additional value that the organisation delivers to its supporters.

CAMPAIGN OBJECTIVES

The primary campaign objective was to persuade significant numbers of animal lovers, who were *not existing RSPCA supporters*, to leave money to the RSPCA in their wills. It is also important that the RSPCA is informed of a bequest at the time it is made. The secondary objective was to demonstrate the value that the organisation brings to its supporters and to the wider animal-loving community, to reinforce the RSPCA brand.

TARGETING STRATEGY

From their extensive experience of their own legacy donors, the RSPCA and their agencies already possessed in-depth knowledge about the target market that was most likely to respond to a legacy campaign. A combination of experience, profiling and research indicated that the most receptive audience was likely to be found amongst a large group of ABC1 animal owners aged over 55 years. Research revealed that 10,000 elderly animal lovers die each year and leave an animal behind. Thus, elderly animal lovers were a key sub-segment within the broader targeting approach.

The targeting research identified two important secondary audiences whose opinions were likely to influence the primary target audience:

- Relatives and carers who might become responsible for pets if the pet owner dies.
- Solicitors and probate lawyers who offer trusted advice concerning will-making and bequests.

PRODUCT AND PROPOSITION STRATEGY – 'HOME FOR LIFE'

In order to meet the communication challenge, the RSPCA and their agencies, Mike Colling & Company and Whitewater, needed a fresh creative approach to deliver the necessary stand-out and engagement.

A BIG UNIFYING IDEA

The team began by reviewing customer and donor research and insights, seeking a 'big' unifying idea on which to base the campaign. A significant percentage of the 70,000 animals the RSPCA rehomes each year need a new home because their owner has died. This knowledge provided a crucial link between an issue of genuine concern to pet owners, an existing RSPCA service and the campaign objectives.

This insight led directly to the RSPCA's existing re-homing service being re-framed to form a new unique product and proposition that was strong enough to appeal to a cold target audience, whilst being in perfect harmony with the caring attributes of the RSPCA brand.

DONOR INSIGHT-LED PROPOSITION

The proposition 'If you die, who better than the RSPCA to look after your pet?' and product 'We will care for your pet if you die' together formed an emotive and motivational message to strike a chord with elderly pet owners.

Crucially, the campaign offered pet owners the chance to be proactive about planning for their pet's future by signing up to the pet rehoming service. Owners were offered this valuable service and peace of mind about their pet's future, in exchange for signing a pledge to support the RSPCA. Pet owners were asked to leave their pets to the RSPCA in their will, creating a 'home for life' for their pet(s) and giving themselves peace of mind. Legacy donors also had the option to place a copy of their will with the RSPCA. This was a novel and natural way to introduce the idea of leaving a legacy to the RSPCA.

DELIVERING VALUE BUILDS THE BRAND

'Who would you rather rely on to care for your pet?' reinforced the RSPCA's work with all animals. On a strategic level, Home for Life builds the RSPCA brand by delivering value to donors and differentiating the RSPCA from its competitors.

A further research-based insight concerning general donor attitudes was that a new generation of legacy donors want something back from the charities they support, something that reflects their commitment and concern and is more meaningful than promotional gimmicks. In a market where simply requesting a legacy pledge is the normal approach, the campaign proposition is innovative and appealing.

CREATIVE STRATEGY

With such delicate subject matter it was felt that a straightforward approach would be most effective. The message had to optimise response from a limited audience, demonstrating the value the RSPCA is offering to the potential donor before 'the ask'. Although the strength of the campaign's core idea would ensure that it stood out from the crowd, any communication on the subject of will-making and death still poses a significant creative challenge. The campaign's tone of voice had to convey the proposition in an appealing way to harmonise with the RSPCA's brand.

A PRAGMATIC APPROACH TO A TRICKY SUBJECT

A 'matter of fact' tone was selected to support the proposition that leaving the RSPCA a bequest is a natural step for owners to take for the sake of their pet and their own peace of mind.

'Ultimately, you don't want to think about it – but if it affects your pet, then you'll be glad that the RSPCA is thinking about it by providing this free service.'

CREATIVE TAILORED TO EACH MEDIUM

The strength of the campaign's unifying idea allowed a tailored creative approach to be employed in each medium. The DRTV ad conveyed the importance of owner's emotional connections to their pets, using 'You've Been Framed' – style video footage featuring pets getting up to mischief to make viewers laugh. The actress delivering the message about the benefits of the service adopted the style of a trusted friend.

The press ads, inserts and door drops focused on a visual representation of the relationship between animal and human, and the reward that an animal's love brings. These media were used to demonstrate how pet owners can make a return for the pets' loyalty and devotion, and enjoy peace of mind, by ensuring that their pets have a secure future.

Figure 12.1: Home for Life door drop leaflet

The RSPCA is here to look after your clients' pets.

It just needs to be confirmed in their Will.

Home for Life is a free service offered by the RSPCA, ensuring the welfare of your clients' pets after their death. All that's required is the inclusion of the relevant clause in their Will, and a telephone call from your client to the RSPCA to register.

For details of the appropriate wording to use in a Will, or for more information about **Home for Life**, please call Joanna Curtis on:

0870 7540 239

or email **jcurtis@rspca.org.uk**

The RSPCA is a charity registered in England and Wales.

£ **We receive no government funding**

H⊙me for Life

RSPCA

Registered charity no. 219099

Figure 12.2: Home for Life door drop leaflet

Peace of mind
– a *Home for Life* from the RSPCA

"We're using Home for Life because we know we can rely on the RSPCA to treat our pets with kindness. Making a provision in our Wills for our pets has given us relief from the worry of what would happen to them on our deaths."

Mr and Mrs Frisby, Notts

A new love for Benji

When Benji's owner passed away, we took over his care until we could find him a new home. Miss Staff, visiting a friend who worked at the kennels where this delightful little dog was staying, took a shine to the little chap. A couple of visits convinced Miss Staff that she and Benji were perfect for each other, so she offered to give him a permanent, loving home.

After going through the RSPCA's rehoming checks successfully she was able to take the little blonde Chihuahua to his new home, where he's lived happily now for two years. Of course he must have missed his previous owner, but he settled in well, and was soon getting on with her other pets: a dog and a cat. In fact, he's taken quite a shine to the cat – he follows her around everywhere! He's also learned to combat his fear of children and gets on with his new owner's nieces splendidly.

When Benji lost his owner, life must have seemed very bleak. But thanks to the RSPCA he's enjoying a new life, and the love of a new owner. A treat of a piece of cheese each evening, regular tummy tickles from his loving new owner... life is looking good for this happy little dog.

For more information call
0870 7540 239

We receive no government funding

Registered charity no. 219099

Peace of Mind
with Home for Life from the RSPCA

Online communications concentrated on providing practical support, discussing both the benefits to the animals and the steps that the owner, or relative, must take.

MEDIA STRATEGY - MIRRORING THE CUSTOMER JOURNEY

The media schedule was informed by recognition of the fact that the decision to join Home for Life is both a rational and emotional one. The media schedule mirrored a typical customer journey, moving from emotional through rational decision-making to the moment of commitment, in this case, making a bequest.

There were a good many reasons for the campaign launch to take place in broadcast media. One of the principal reasons was the charity's pressing need to find new legators. Another equally important point was that the delicacy of the subject matter meant that a personalised communication was not an appropriate choice as the initial contact method. The schedule reflected the media consumption of the target audience, and was refined using profiling and research information from existing donors.

DIFFERENTIATION FROM COMPETITORS

The media launch firmly established Home for Life as a unique service owned by the RSPCA, strongly differentiating it from its legacy-hunting competitors. Public media also reached the relatives and friends of the primary target audience, serving to reassure and inform them.

Finally, public media gives potential legators the opportunity to opt-in. It puts them firmly in the decision-making driving seat for this most intrusive and deeply personal of decisions.

Once someone had indicated either interest or commitment by responding to the public media messages, a personalised communication programme was designed to develop the ongoing relationship.

TESTING THE PROPOSITION

Prior to the launch, the proposition was tested with the RSPCA's existing supporters through a newsletter and direct mail. The strength of the results confirmed the power of the proposition, providing the charity with important reassurance about the likely return on the substantial investment required for a cold campaign.

A FULLY INTEGRATED APPROACH

An integrated approach to the mixed-media schedule ensured that each medium was allowed to play to its strengths. For example, DRTV was used to convey the core emotional message, as a response generator, and also contributed to the media-multiplier effect in other media.

Public relations (PR) communications leveraged the existing relationship between the target audience, their families and key media, using the editorial integrity of key publications to reinforce the credibility of the proposition. Press advertising was timed to coincide with PR activity in the national press to generate cost-effective responses by making the most of the uplift from PR.

Inserts were placed in niche and regional titles and at events, such as Crufts, to maximise responses from the finite core audience. In keeping with a fully integrated approach, inserts were distributed approximately two weeks after the DRTV advertising began, to allow the emotional messages time to build before introducing a rational approach.

Online search was optimised to support all offline media. (See Chapter 10 for details of search engine optimisation (SEO).)

Solicitors and probate lawyers were targeted through press, direct mail and outbound telephone. This key influencer audience was given detailed information about Home for Life and asked to display leaflets.

Three response channels were provided to allow for all donor preferences: phone, coupon and online.

BESPOKE RELATIONSHIP DEVELOPMENT PROGRAMME

Once donors or potential donors had opted-in through the broadcast media, direct mail and telephone were used to develop the ongoing donor relationship.

Legacy donors who signed up immediately were entered into a bespoke legacy donor care programme. They receive four communications a year: two legacy donor newsletters, a Christmas mailing and an April appeal mailing.

The RSPCA encouraged donors to discuss their plans with their family to avoid surprises at the will reading. The donor welcome mailing also included a wallet card (a bit like an organ donor card) to tell friends and family to contact the RSPCA in the event of the donor's death.

Figure 12.3: Home for Life advertisement to solicitors

INFORMING AND REASSURING DONORS

Regular communication from the RSPCA reassures donors that the Home for Life service is professionally managed, engaging the donor with the process and reassuring them that their animal companion will be well cared for in the event of their death. People who indicated an interest in Home for Life but who did not immediately sign up for the service were put in a donor development programme. There was a follow-up mailing six months after their first response, and selected individuals also received a telephone call.

CAMPAIGN RESULTS – RAISING THE BAR

This campaign was created around an entirely new product and proposition, so there were no targets to beat. However, all industry norms for legacy fundraising were outstripped:

The £79 cost per response was well below market norms, and much lower than the traditional cost per 'ask'.

The high volume of respondents included general and legacy enquirers and those not interested in the Home for Life proposition. Total response was 170 times greater than for the previous legacy campaign.

Overall, the campaign has produced an ROI of 10:1. Legacy donation value stands at a potential £10m in identified legacy pledges, accounting for 15 per cent of annual legacy income. This figure is an estimate, as the income has yet to be received. However, given the current average amount pledged, the RSPCA is confident that the campaign will generate this level of income. These are still very early days for the total campaign result.

In the long term it is likely that the campaign will continue to generate legacy income.

Registrations and updated wills were still being received in 2008 from the test work in 2006. Response from 2007 matured and converted following the same pattern, raising the total ROI to the extent of potentially doubling or even tripling the current 10:1 estimate. Inevitably, any legacy campaign is a 'slow burner'.

Strategically, there is initial evidence that Home for Life activity is uplifting the results of other fundraising activity. This effect is being further investigated to fully understand how Home for Life can be integrated with all other RSPCA communications.

LESSONS LEARNED

From conception to execution, a fully integrated donor-led approach was adopted. As befits a leading UK charity, the communications planning showed great sensitivity to its audience, in terms of both proposition and creative development, and media selection.

The RSPCA and their agencies incorporated key insights from donor research into how donor attitudes are evolving in a mature charity marketplace. Offering donors a valuable service before asking them for money radically changed attitudes and response rates. Not surprisingly, the donors loved it and responded enthusiastically.

However, the principal lesson from this case is the importance of finding a genuine donor insight-based idea to unify the campaign to give it real resonance with its target audience.

The RSPCA and its agencies recognised that there was a genuine unanswered need among older animal lovers, and had the imagination to link this insight with an existing product and their own requirement for a new source of legacy income. The power of this approach is borne out by the impressive campaign results, and the promise of more to come.

This imaginative campaign was devised by:

Media agency: Mike Colling & Company Ltd
Creative agency: Whitewater Ltd
RSPCA: Sharon Gearing. Marketing manager – Legacy products

SUMMARY

In this chapter we defined the terms proposition and offer and explored the use of offers in direct marketing. We saw that a marketing offer, or proposition is the end user benefit – what this product or service will give to the customer. The key factor in making a marketing offer, especially in direct communications, is relevance.

We differentiated the marketing offer from the promotional offer, and pointed out that whilst incentives can be very effective in stimulating response and orders, especially in consumer marketing, they will not work unless the underlying proposition is relevant to the prospect. We saw that offers will vary in terms of what we would like our customers to do and the nature of the offer will pre-select the quality of the enquiries gained.

We examined the possible elements of a proposition and pointed out that all types of offer must support the positioning of the product and we went on to examine positioning through a definition and the use of examples.

We saw that positioning happens in the mind of your consumers through a range of inputs, including advertising. The key question is 'What impression do we wish to leave in the minds of our consumers?'

We then looked at the types of promotional offers available to direct marketers including prize draws and competitions and incentives. These need to be used in an appropriate way, recognising that in certain markets the use of incentives to purchase may compromise our customers.

The need is to develop an offer that will balance response, conversion and longer term retention of customers to maximise value to the organisation.

REVIEW QUESTIONS

1. What is the difference between a marketing offer and a promotional offer?
2. What are the benefits to a publisher of getting a subscriber to sign up to a direct debit mandate or continuous credit card authority?
3. What is a BOGOF?
4. What is the value of testimonials?
5. Define positioning: how is positioning used in direct marketing?
6. What is the role of testing in the use of offers?

EXERCISE

For a company of your choice select an advertisement that offers an incentive to respond.

- How does the offer reinforce the positioning of the product?
- Would the offer cause you to respond?
- Is the offer appropriate to the target market?
- What other incentives could have been used?
- How would you improve this advertisement?

CHAPTER 13
PRODUCING EFFECTIVE CREATIVE WORK

IN THIS CHAPTER

This chapter is all about planning, producing and critiquing creative work.

After reading this chapter you should be able to:

- Understand where creative fits into the communications priority list, and how it varies according to the chosen medium;
- Set clear objectives to ensure satisfactory creative solutions;
- Decide when to use long copy and when short is better.

Specific topics include:

- When creative is the most important, and why it usually is not
- Long copy or short? The old argument and how to resolve the issue
- Writing is the easy part – how creatives divide their time
- Examples of creative development
- Managing response effectively
- Different approaches to copywriting – offline and online
- Direct response advertising – guidelines and key success factors; layout techniques to increase legibility and comprehension
- Popular misconceptions about mailing letters
- Good and bad personalisation
- How different typefaces can affect comprehension and response
- The importance of picture captions
- Tactical integration of media – how follow up works
- Creating for online advertising
- Case study: The Swinton Insurance 'Mystery Tipper'

INTRODUCTION

Why don't my ads and mailings work?

Judging by the number of seminar delegates who raise this issue, many advertisements and mailings fail to achieve their targets, even though the advertiser thought they were very well written and designed.

It is clear that, despite numerous disclaimers by many very experienced practitioners, many people still think that if you produce a good 'creative' you are bound to succeed.

> In fact creative is probably the least important of the various elements in a promotion.

In earlier chapters we have stressed that the three most important factors in the success of an advertisement or mailing are targeting the right person (by selecting the right medium or list); saying the right thing (developing an attractive and relevant offer); and delivering your message at the right time.

If you target the wrong person, or the benefit you claim does not match the needs of the prospect, your promotion is likely to fail because, no matter how well you have sold your proposition, it is simply not relevant to the reader.

On the other hand, if you get the three major factors right, you have a chance of achieving great things. If you achieve the above three objectives your results are likely to be reasonably acceptable, almost regardless of the quality of your creative work. Almost, for two reasons:

1. Many good, well targeted messages have been destroyed by poor design and typography.
2. If you have been able to identify the right prospect, and the benefits that will be most relevant, your competitors are likely to have done the same amount of research. In a worst case scenario your ad, mailing or email may be competing head to head with a competitive offer. In this case the one that is most clearly and attractively presented will win the order.

So the purpose of this chapter is to show you how to win those head to head battles and turn an acceptable response into a good or even exceptional response, by using the right creative techniques.

The first step – define your objective

You must be quite clear about what you want to achieve. Do you want to:

- sell your product or service direct, i.e. ask for an order now?
- persuade prospects to send for more information?
- ask for a salesperson to visit?
- encourage prospects to visit your shop or office?
- invite them to a demonstration or other event?

Defining a clear objective at the start will help you decide how much information you need to convey.

A one-stage promotion usually requires lots of detail because you are intending to move the prospect through all the stages of buying in a single communication. They have to be given everything they need to know in order to make a purchase decision.

With two-stage promotions you can usually use less copy, all you have to do is persuade prospects to call or send for more information.

Another factor governing the amount of information necessary is the knowledge already held by your prospect. Your product may be one that everyone will know about, such as toner or copier paper, or perhaps one that requires lots of detailed explanation like enterprise wide CRM software. You will clearly need to say a lot more about the software than the printer supplies.

Do they already deal with you?

Another consideration is whether your prospects have bought from you before. Regular buyers need less information about your products and your company.

Long copy or short?

We will tackle this topic in detail later but let's just start here by addressing those critics of long copy whose objection is simply 'No one will read long copy.' *This is complete drivel.*

People read for as long as they are interested and no longer. Thus long copy is appropriate in some circumstances and not for others. In a one-stage situation, long copy will often be needed if:

- you are addressing a new prospect who has never heard of your company nor your product;
- your product is a complex one and there are many factors which the prospect must consider;
- your product is totally new and therefore not known, even to established customers;
- your audience likes to read long copy – this may sound unlikely but charities often find that established donors like to know what is being done with their money. Their letters are often three or four pages long and, far from being unacceptable to recipients, they actually generate many replies from people saying how much they appreciate hearing all the news.

Generally, established customers will not need such long copy, even in a one-stage situation because they already know quite a lot about you and your products.

In a two-stage situation you are less likely to need long copy because the prospect has a second chance of getting the information they need. Bear in mind that the more you tell them up-front, the fewer wasted enquiries you will receive.

Writing copy is easy – preparing for it is very difficult

In the past 20 years the authors have run many seminars to teach people how to write effective mailings, advertisements and newsletter articles. The objective is not to turn beginners into star copywriters – that takes years not hours, and also requires a considerable degree of talent. But anyone with a reasonable grasp of English grammar can learn how to write convincing copy or to critique someone else's copy in a constructive way. The assessment scores indicate that delegates find these seminars very useful.

There is one element in these seminars that is the key to writing effective copy. The secret is that the writer must think carefully about the prospect and imagine a face-to-face discussion. 'What do you need to tell them to persuade them to buy your product? What questions will they ask?'

Ideally the writer will actually speak to some customers or prospects and find out the questions because there is no substitute for sound research. When top copywriters are asked how they divide their time when tackling a writing job they invariably come up with something like:

Research   **30 per cent**
Idea generation   **20 per cent**
First draft copy   **20 per cent**
Review and rewriting **30 per cent**

So a large amount of time is spent in advance research – this is when you identify the questions you have to answer. If you can list the key questions your copy will almost write itself because it is simply a series of answers to these questions. This is not to say that great writing is easy. This process will enable you to write accurate, relevant copy – it will not necessarily be great copy. Great writers like Bird, Harrison, Watson, Hunt, Barraclough et al, use the same process and perhaps even simply answer the questions in their first draft. Hence the 30 per cent allocation for review and rewriting. That's when professional writers turn adequate copy into great copy.

Bear in mind here that not all prospects will have the same questions, or even if they do, they will not always have them in the same order of importance. And certainly when you are writing copy for one-to-one communications you should start with the most important question for that specific segment of your audience.

It is clear that copy length and complexity will vary according to several factors. The natural corollary to this is that we should not write the same copy to everyone.

The key difference between what used to be called 'mail-shots' and effective targeted communications is that the former assume that all prospects are exactly the same, whereas the latter aim to address the information needs of each individual.

EXAMPLE
Situation one – Existing subscriber renewal programme

Let's imagine you are the publisher of a management magazine wanting to persuade existing subscribers to renew. As they are already regular readers your copy may be quite short. The subscriber will want to know any price change, and any new or special features which you are planning to introduce which may increase their perception of the value of your magazine.

You may be planning a new online helpdesk for subscribers and a regular European update e-newsletter, and you will want to explain the benefits to them. **But you will not need to explain what your magazine is about. To do so simply underlines the fact that you are treating all prospects in the same way.**

You have two broad categories of subscriber:

1. Those who set up a continuous direct debit mandate for their subscription – these will simply need a brief confirmation that you are planning to take the subscription from their

bank account on the due date. To reduce cancellations you will need to tell them all about the new features.

2. Those that did not take up your previous offer of a continuous direct debit and paid by cheque or credit card. In this case you will have to set up a more comprehensive renewal sequence, starting with a low-cost email. The email may be sent six weeks before renewal date and followed up two weeks later with a mailing pack to those that did not respond. Two weeks before expiry a further low-cost mailing and/or email may be sent offering an additional incentive – perhaps a desktop accessory.

Situation two – New subscriber acquisition plan

Alternatively, if you are planning to mail or email a rented list of people who match your subscriber profile but have, as far as you know, never read your publication you will need to tell them more. You may tell them what regular features they will find and perhaps send them details of contents over the past six months. You should also tell them of the special reports you are planning for the next few months. In this situation you will obviously need longer copy. Incidentally, one thing not to do is send a single previous copy of the magazine – if there is nothing in that one issue that appeals you may lose them forever.

Developing a creative outline

Once you have established your objective you can develop your creative outline:

- **Objective** A clear statement of your aim for each of your targeted segments
- **Target audience** A precise definition of your audience is needed here.
- **Offer** What will make prospects respond in the way you wish? Should you use a one-stage or two-promotion?
- **Timing** When are prospects likely to be interested?
- **Medium** This will depend on who the prospects are. Existing customers will generally be approached using email, mail and telephone. New prospects using one or more of:
  - Direct mail or email
  - Online advertising and search marketing
  - Magazine or newspaper advertising
  - Loose or bound-in insert
  - Affinity sites
- **Creative approach** Your message and how this can be delivered, e.g.
  - Copy approach, i.e. long or short – this will vary according to your objective, target audience, offer, existing relationships, and the complexity of the product.
  - It will also depend on your chosen medium – advertising tends to dictate shorter copy; mail longer copy; email shorter copy with links for interested prospects to read in more detail.
- **Implementation** Production of copy, artwork and so on. Selection of suppliers, including printers and Web specialists.
- **Response forecasts** Your estimates of volume and plans for efficient handling and despatch of material, orders etc.
- **Follow-up** To stimulate response or perhaps to acknowledge enquiries and orders.

EXAMPLES

Let's work through this outline for the two situations mentioned above:

Situation one – Renewal campaign

Target:	Existing subscribers due for renewal.
Offer:	Renew within 30 days and receive a free desktop appointments planner. Details of online helpdesk and of new European update e-newsletter. Renew online in next 10 days and save 10 per cent.
Timing:	To arrive approximately 6 weeks before existing subscription expires – sent in batches according to renewal dates.
Medium:	Email.
Creative:	Message – renewal offer, details of free gift and new features.
Implementation:	Copy written and pdf brochures uploaded to website one week in advance of first batch of emails being sent.
Response handling:	Estimates of responses to receiving department. Plans for response handling (data capture and updating of database subscription records, despatch of free gift).
Follow-up:	Mailing pack to be sent to non-respondents after two weeks. Further mail or email follow-up two weeks before expiry – new incentive offered at this point.

Situation two

Target:	Rented names – people who match the profile of existing subscribers, e.g. business people (generally managers and above) aged 30 to 45; readers of serious dailies and weeklies (*Financial Times, Time*); subscribers to online business newsletters.
Offer:	Special introductory discount offer of 30 per cent off full price; 40 per cent discount for two-year subscription. Special free gift for an annual direct debit mandate or continuous credit card authority – this tends to increase retention/renewal dramatically.
Timing:	No specific timing constraints – start testing asap.
Media:	Loose inserts in press; email to subscriber lists; online ads in relevant newsletters and websites.
Creative:	Message – Subscribe now, it will enable you to do your job better and enhance your career prospects. Details of introductory offers, and free gifts. Sample contents and testimonials. Creative executions will vary in the different media. Reply methods – all relevant methods but always including drive to web for the online special offer.
Follow-up:	Follow-up emails to Web visitors who registered but failed to subscribe.

Note that these outlines are not intended as creative briefs but are simply to help you devise a brief without forgetting any major feature.

Briefing is tackled in detail in Chapter 15.

Managing response

Businesses need a constant supply of new leads, but with limited resources it is important not to generate enquiries you cannot handle quickly and efficiently. You therefore need to estimate response very carefully and, if necessary, to phase your acquisition programme so that the flow of leads is easily manageable, without you having to resort to expensive overtime or external resources.

By sending out a controlled number of mailings each week a business gains two advantages:

1. The quantity of leads received is manageable.
2. Each lead can be followed up quickly ensuring maximum conversion.

A badly handled enquiry can do more than lose you a single sale – it may have been your first contact with a potentially important customer.

Planning your communication

Many people find it useful to devise a checklist when planning the design of a communication. Let's consider the desired sequence of events. The first task is to:

Attract attention

– In an advertisement, apart from any considerations of size, timing and position, you will do this through a combination of headline size and wording, and a picture.

When writing headlines and designing ads it can be useful to get someone to look at your work and tell you what they 'take out' of it. It is all too easy to attract attention with a 'stopper' whilst leaving totally the wrong impression in the mind of your reader, as the following example shows.

The government of New South Wales, Australia, planned to run a campaign aimed at young drivers to try to reduce the incidence of drinking and driving in this group.

The advertiser had some striking photographs of youngsters blowing into breathalysers, and asked two agencies to present ideas using one of these. One was a traditional advertising agency, the other a direct marketing agency.

The traditional agency, exponents of short snappy copy, wrote this headline:

'Don't blow it!'

above a picture of a young man blowing into the bag.

The client liked this headline but fortunately it was subjected to comprehension research before being run. Only 4 per cent of the people shown this ad understood it. Many thought it was a protest ad from a civil liberties group!

The direct marketing agency came up with:

'Don't blow your licence!'

which was used over the same photograph as above.

All the people shown this version understood it instantly.

David Ogilvy discovered many years ago that long explicit headlines containing news always out-pull short, snappy, non-specific headlines.

Writing copy for emails

The two most important elements in getting an email opened are the subject line and the 'From' field. With email the subject line does the job of the headline. But with email we have to be aware of spam filters – if your subject line contains things such as FREE, or any WORDS ALL IN CAPITALS, ££, !!, it is unlikely to get past the filters. There are also many words that are better not used in email body copy, even phrases such as 'risk free'; 'money back guarantee' can raise your spam rating. Obvious ones like Viagra will alert the filters, but even innocent words such as 'quality' and 'enhanced' can trigger an alert. One man in London emailed his friend at work to ask for help preparing for his young daughter's birthday party. He asked 'could you come along and help me erect the marquee'? The intended recipient did not get the message.

The 'From' field is also important. If you have already established a relationship, by getting the recipient to subscribe to your newsletters, or even to have designated your emails as 'not spam' you will not have a problem here. But when using email lists, tests have shown that personalisation in the 'From' field works well. For example 'James@bizrate.co.uk' is more likely to be opened than 'Bizrate.co.uk'.

There are also several technical things relating to coding so it pays to use expert help, at least if you are planning an email campaign for the first time. You should also run your copy through a spam checker. If you use an external email consolidator they will usually be able to organise this for you. If you are on your own, simply Google 'spam checkers' and you will be offered thousands, many of which are either free or offer a free trial.

Body copy for emails

The key here is to keep it as short as you can without leaving out any important point. Rather than attempting long copy emails you should use a sort of verbal shorthand with plenty of click though links for those who want to read more. The same rule applies to website copy. In his excellent book *Don't Make Me Think!* (New Riders, 2005) Steve Krug says '...having drafted your copy, get rid of half the words on each page, then get rid of half of what's left.'

The following is a good example of a newsletter that contains a huge amount of information but the list at the start gives the reader the opportunity of quickly reaching the items of interest. Each of the six items can be clicked on to open up the full text.

Figure 13.1: Sample email newsletter

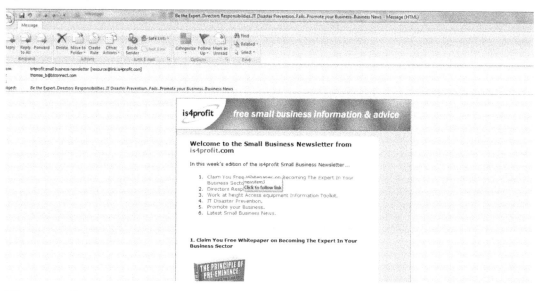

Direct mail copy

With a mailing there are two opportunities for headlines, one on the outer envelope and the other at the top of the letter. There is considerable resistance to envelope messages from those not experienced in direct response but more often than not such a message increases response. More on this later.

◾ **Establish the relevance of your offer**

Where possible you should try to vary this for individual customer segments – if you have the necessary personal information this will be fairly easy to achieve with a targeted one-to-one communication. It is more difficult in broadscale advertising. It is possible to vary copy in different publications but not to various segments of the same readership – except to a certain extent with loose inserts (see pages 236–8 in Chapter 9) .

◾ **Convince the prospect of the benefits**

Again you should vary this where possible. It will be more convincing if you back it up with credible testimonial statements.

◾ **Close the sale**

With a powerful 'call-to-action' and, in a letter, a postscript reminding readers of the major benefits of replying, and perhaps the penalties for not doing so.

◾ **Confirm the action required and take the order**

A clear statement of 'how to take advantage of this offer' will generally increase the number of responses. This is probably because it just makes things easier for your reader. In a mailing or advertisement a well-designed coupon or reply form, pre-printed where possible with the prospect's name and address, will make sure you maximise your response. With email where response is achieved through a link to a mini-site, make sure that the action required is made crystal clear – too many Web pages leave the prospect uncertain what to do next – so they leave your site. To make sure this doesn't happen, read *Don't Make Me Think!* by Steve Krug.

Make sure you give all the possible response options – freepost, Freephone, email, website URL and even fax – whatever is appropriate to your audience. Most of the consumers you would want to attract and virtually every UK business has Internet access and more than 70 per cent of these have broadband. Although fax is considered by many to be out of date, in mid-2009 one UK office products supplier was getting higher responses from fax than from email – perhaps because of the novelty value, or maybe because of 'email overload'. Whatever the reason this may be worth trying, especially as business people receive so may emails.

Now, having looked at the process of developing a sales argument by email, mail or advertisement let's take a closer look at direct response press advertising.

What are the essential elements of a direct response advertisement?

Firstly we need to define direct response advertising. There are broadly three types of advertising:

1. **Awareness advertising**

   The objective here is to increase awareness or influence opinions. This form of advertising does not invite a response and will often not even carry a response address, though most will include a Web address.

2. **Direct response advertising**

   The objective is to generate a response or lead by use of an 'offer'. Direct response ads include response addresses, telephone/fax numbers, and of course the Web address. In one study advertisements that included a coupon attracted more attention, see below.

3. **Dual-purpose advertising**

   Where there is a primary and a secondary objective, for example an awareness advertisement which carries a Web or email address, phone number or postal address will often attract large numbers of responses, requests for further information, etc.

Equally, an advertisement whose principal objective is to generate enquiries, can have a measurable effect on attitudes and awareness of a product or service.

Awareness advertising

This type of advertising is still widely used although companies who have tested and researched type three (dual-purpose advertising) have found that their brand and image objectives can be achieved whilst their advertisements simultaneously generate significant website traffic producing potentially valuable responses from interested readers.

It is therefore recommended that, where awareness is required, you consider the use of dual-purpose advertising as a first option. Even if you do not wish to supply customers direct, the resulting enquiry data can be very useful for research purposes - satisfaction surveys, customer profiles and so on. And encouraging regular website visits can significantly benefit your brand.

As in most cases direct marketers are primarily seeking response we will now concentrate on type two: direct response advertising.

Direct response advertising – the key factors

The critical success factors for a direct response advertisement are largely the same as those for direct mail, but the way they interact and the precise emphasis of each varies slightly;

Targeting	As with all forms of advertising the message can only work if it reaches the right person, so the first step is to select the right publication.
Offer	The main benefit message, terms, and promotional factors, e.g. discounts etc.
Timing & frequency	This is an issue which is very different for advertisements as opposed to mailings, mainly because we cannot vary the exposure of the message according to our prospect's ideal timing. We therefore time our insertions to fit times of peak interest or demand.
Creative	Although creative is correctly placed in relationship to the other factors, such a simple listing is not really appropriate for press advertising.
	In a newspaper or magazine, the creative treatment is often a crucial factor in targeting the reader. Without the correct headline, displayed in the correct manner, the prospect may not even see the advertisement. So in this case creative becomes part of targeting. This is also true of online and broadcast advertising.
Response mechanics	The main purpose of response devices is to make it easy for the prospect to reply. We cannot in this case fill in the prospect's name and address, but we must do all we can to facilitate the process. All ads should carry the Web address and email if appropriate; but don't forget that, if 70 or 80 per cent of your prospects have Web access, 20 or 30 per cent don't. So make sure you also include the postal address and telephone number.

Let us look a little closer at some of these factors:

Targeting

Selection of the right publication is vital and there are several ways you can approach this:

1. You should know which publications are read by your existing customers (from satisfaction surveys). You can then match prospect segments against your customer profile and identify the most appropriate media.
2. If customer data is not available or not clear you may have to do some telephone or postal questionnaire research to find the information you need.
3. Newspapers and magazines also have detailed readership data that can tell you the type and quantity of prospects you can reach through their publication.
4. The main lifestyle database companies (such as Acxiom) can link their data to the Target Group Index (TGI – the largest continuous media readership survey in UK) so if they profile your existing customers they can tell you which newspapers and magazines are likely to reach your best prospects.

5. If none of these gives you the answers, the next step is to watch which media your main competitors are using – if they consistently use a certain publication you can be pretty sure it works well for them, so it should work for you too.

6. Finally, although the above steps may well give you a good idea of your best targeting options it will still be worth considering some tests to discover which publications and creative approaches produce the best results.

In fact you will probably use a combination of all the above methods – if you do decide to test several publications, remember that where loose inserts are available they can be a very cost-effective test method (see Chapter 14).

Timing and frequency

Timing is very important but, unlike in direct communications, we cannot vary this for individual segments of the audience. This means that we may need to run the same advertisement several times to be sure that a large proportion of our prospects have an opportunity to see the offer at a time appropriate to them.

Alternatively we may try to deal with this problem by breaking down the communications process into stages, e.g.:

With a targeted and appropriately timed email or mailing we may attempt, in one stage, to move the reader to taking action; with an advertisement, we cannot be confident of getting the timing exactly right. So, unless our offer is one which is likely to appeal to a sizeable proportion of the audience at any time, we may well consider a two-stage approach.

Here we will ask readers to send for more details and, at the same time, try to discover when the timing will be ideal for each respondent. In these circumstances we need some sort of attractive but inexpensive offer, perhaps a free booklet which those in the market will find appealing.

Let's assume we make household security systems, these are expensive and may be bought at any time of year. We could produce a booklet called '20 things every householder should know about security'.

People who send for this booklet are singling themselves out as prospects for the product. We can then use follow-up techniques to convert prospects into buyers.

An alternative to this approach is that used by direct insurance companies whose message in broadscale media is: 'Do you want cheaper insurance? Call this number now.' Anyone who responds is clearly in the market right now. This can be more economical but it requires a very simple proposition for success.

Creative

As mentioned above, the creative aspects of a direct response advertisement interact with each of the other issues, and creative is in some ways the most vital consideration.

Ten guidelines for successful direct response advertising

A direct response advertisement is an action-oriented communication calling for a response from the prospect. There are some principles that while not 'golden rules' have been proven many times over the years. Unless you are very experienced you will find these guidelines improve your chances of success.

There are many examples of successful advertisements that broke all the rules but these have generally been produced through careful and thorough testing, and until you are thoroughly familiar with the basics it's best not to start experimenting.

Here is a summary of the guidelines:

1. **Readers generally scan an advertisement in the order: picture, headline, copy**
   The layout should therefore be arranged in the same sequence. In tests of headline position some advertisers have experienced response increases of more than 100 per cent by simply placing the line below the picture, rather than above it.

2. **The picture should be striking and 'action-oriented'**
   Easier said than done you may think but again tests have shown that simply showing a pair of hands on a computer keyboard produced more response than when the keyboard was shown on its own. On another occasion the addition of a hand filling in a form caused a double figure increase in response to a subscription offer. So, where possible, show your product in use.

3. **80 to 90 per cent of 'readers' will not read further than the headline**
   The headline and main illustration must therefore put across the entire proposition in clear simple terms. Only very rarely do people buy a publication to read the advertisements, and even then they generally scan the headlines first. The headline must therefore be informative. Remember David Ogilvy's research showing that long, informative headlines usually out-pull short, witty versions.

4. **Body copy length is not critical**
   Ensure the picture and headline attract interested prospects – clear layout is essential and it must not look hard to read. Some advertisers have had huge success with very long copy in direct response newspaper and magazine advertisements. However, in this case they break up the type with some indented paragraphs making it look easier to read.

5. **Compare the following two pieces of writing by David Ogilvy:**
   Version 1

   Repeat your winners. We don't run our best print advertisements often enough. God knows, it is hard enough to create a good advertisement. When we succeed, it is downright asinine to run it only once. Starch has demonstrated that readership holds up wonderfully when you re-run good ads. Ditto Gallup & Robinson. In the early days of Instant Maxwell House, when the brand was climbing at a steep angle, Benton & Bowles repeated the same ad without change for five years. A profitable time was had by all. Mail-order people, who know their results, repeat their winners. The Sherman Cody School of English repeated the same ad at intervals over forty years; it continued to pull.

   The audiences of magazines rotate – like TV audiences. We repeat commercials. We should repeat our ads. Some agency people worry that their clients will think them lazy if they recommend re-running ads. But most clients are savvy enough to understand that it takes more work to produce one superb ad than to crank out dozens of lesser ones. Re-running the best ads can give our clients more advertising power for their money – and as a bonus it can save them thousands of pounds in production costs. Waste not, want not.

Version 2
Repeat your winners.

We don't run our best print advertisements often enough.

God knows, it is hard enough to create a good advertisement. When we succeed, it is downright **asinine** to run it only once.

Starch has demonstrated that readership holds up wonderfully when you re-run good ads. Ditto Gallup & Robinson.

In the early days of Instant Maxwell House, when the brand was climbing at a steep angle, Benton & Bowles repeated the same ad without change for five years. **A profitable time was had by all**.

Mail order people, who know their results, repeat their winners. The Sherman Cody School of English repeated the same ad at intervals over 40 years; it continued to pull.

The audiences of magazines rotate, like TV audiences. We repeat our commercials. **We should repeat our ads.**

Some agency people worry that their clients will think them lazy if they recommend re-running ads. But most clients are savvy enough to understand that it takes more work to produce one superb ad than to crank out dozens of lesser ones.

Re-running the best ads give our clients more advertising power for their money – and as a bonus it can save them thousands of pounds in production.

Waste not, want not.

Which version looks easier to read? Length of copy will depend on the objective; longer copy for direct orders, shorter to generate enquiries for more information.

6. **Turn features into benefits.** Features and attributes of the product must be expressed as 'end-user' benefits; customers are only interested in the relevance of this product to their own needs.
   Include a prominent, easy to understand 'call to action' directing readers to the various response routes. Ask someone not directly involved to read the advertisement and then to tell you if they understand what is required. **Make it obvious that a response is called for.**

Some years ago, a UK national newspaper study reported that the inclusion of a clear, obvious coupon not only increased response but also awareness scores. The researchers thought that this may be because the coupon 'flagged' that prospects could send for something. So far as I know this has not been tested in recent years and perhaps a mouse icon with a clear URL might do the same job today?

7. **Repeat the main points near the call to action.** If your picture and headline have done their job properly, some readers will skip directly to the action section, by-passing the body copy, therefore it pays to restate your proposition at that point.

8. **The smaller the space the more cost-effective will be the result.** (See Chapter 9, pages 234–5 for a summary of the relevant research.)

   If cost-effective response is your main objective, the smaller the space you use the better. Three caveats, however:

   a) Make sure you use enough space to tell the whole story in a good readable typeface and size.

   b) Small spaces will not impress your channel partners nor your sales force.

   c) It is easier to negotiate discounts on larger spaces.

9. **Avoid sans-serif type for body copy** Reader comprehension is dramatically reduced. See the research data on pages 326–8 of this chapter.

This paragraph is set in **sans serif type** and several researches have shown that adults reading several lines of copy in this sort of face, cannot answer as many questions about what they have just read as those reading the same text in a Roman or serif face. To demonstrate the difference we will now show a similar paragraph set in a classic Roman typeface.

This paragraph is set in **Roman type** and several researches have shown that adults reading copy in this sort of face achieve much higher comprehension scores than those reading the same text in a sans serif face. This does not look obvious, in fact the above paragraph actually looks clearer. This is why we must read the research rather than rely on personal opinion.

10. **Don't reverse out body copy.** The same research tells us that we must never use 'reversed out' type for body copy - in this case the decline in comprehension is even more dramatic. See the following example, then read the comprehension statistics on pages 326–8.

> This paragraph is set in Roman type but is **'reversed-out'** i.e. printed in white on a black background. Research shows that adults reading copy in this style score very badly in comprehension tests compared to those reading the same text and type style printed black on a white background.
>
> Designers like reversed-out type because it looks dramatic and stylish – but far fewer people read it so it does not get your message across effectively.

Do not permit inexperienced designers to reduce your responses in this way.

Note that as with all 'rules' there are many exceptions, some advertisements which 'do everything right' fail to work and others which break all rules may work.

Now, let's have a look at direct mailings

It is often said by online specialists that direct mail, or 'snail mail' is finished as a direct marketing medium, but this is far from the truth.

It is true that total volumes in UK have declined by around 11 per cent since 2000, but there are three very good reasons for this:

1. Email has replaced some of the volume, especially in B2B markets.
2. All direct marketers are trying to reduce volumes by better use of data. If we really are getting better at targeting and segmentation volumes should be reducing.
3. In the past 20 years a large percentage of consumer direct mail has been sent by financial services companies; volumes in this sector have declined dramatically in the past few years as a result of the current recession.

Mail is still a major medium for direct marketers with a total of more than 4.3 billion pieces mailed in 2008. The declining volume of mail from the financial sector has masked increases in the travel, health and utilities sectors. We can safely assume that mail will be a dominant direct marketing medium for many years to come.

One crucial difference between a mailing and an advertisement is targeting. If you have done your research thoroughly you should be able to vary your mailing copy for different segments of your audience. So in planning a mailing give some thought as to how you may be able to make these variations cost-efficiently.

It may be useful to run though the elements in a typical pack and consider at the same time, which could be varied without excessive cost:

Outer envelope If you opt to use plain envelopes, or even to have a generalised message or a simple logo, there is no need to dwell on this element further.

However, as many advertisers have discovered that printing messages on envelopes can increase responses, we should consider how we might print relevant envelope messages to each prospect segment.

If we are planning a very large mailing with segments in excess of 50,000, the economics are such that we could consider making printing plate changes to give a different envelope message to various audience segments.

Whatever the print quantity, it will generally be more economical to restrict message changes to a single colour.

With smaller lists (and smaller budgets) there are still a few options:

1. **A second window** Print a large batch of envelopes (perhaps a full year's supply) with, say, your company logo, and with a second window like this:

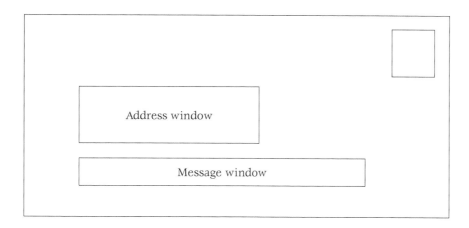

You can then plan your letter to carry a headline which will show through the lower window; in theory you can change this as often as you wish. You will need to shop around for such envelopes as they can be quite expensive. The second window could easily add £10 to £15 per thousand to your envelope costs.

2. **Stickers** One direct marketer had great success by buying small stickers and affixing these to the appropriate batches of envelopes. This can be quite an inexpensive option. He paid £7 per thousand for the stickers but he is an excellent negotiator!

3. **Print** them yourself Most desktop printers can address envelopes although this is usually a very slow process. It is however, very cheap, and you can vary the message as often as you like.

4. **See-through envelopes** Plastic envelopes can be used to show all or part of your enclosures. With a bit of care you could show a letter headline in the same way as option 1.

Other things to consider about envelopes

- Remember that your envelope is the first thing your prospect sees, so be sure to make a good impression.
- Is your message truly relevant to your prospect? This is very important. Put yourself in the place of your prospect, sifting through a pile of mail deciding which are worth opening. An envelope that indicates through a very general message, that it is a mailing but which does not say anything of interest to the reader, may be the first into the bin. So, a message which is too general may well be worse than no message at all.

Some people like envelope messages because they save time – the message tells them whether they will be interested in the contents. Many business people say the envelope message helps them to sort out their mail before deciding what to open.

Now, having got the prospect to look at and open the envelope, we want them to read our letter.

The letter – the key to success in direct mail

If you get your reader inside through an interesting envelope message it is only logical to start your letter with the same thought. Once again we should start by tackling a few of the common misunderstandings about direct mail letters:

Five popular myths about direct mail letters
1. They should never be longer than a single page of A4.
2. They are not really necessary if you have a good brochure.
3. Personalisation does not increase response.
4. The letter should start with a gentle, generalised introduction.
5. Using a postscript is old fashioned and does not work.

Let's tackle these myths one by one:

Myth number 1

■ **The letter should never be longer than a single page** 'No one will read more than a single page.' This is held to be especially important when writing to business people. **And it is entirely wrong**. People continue to read for as long as they are interested.

Over the past 15 years many companies have had great success with mailing letters of three, four and even five pages to business people, often directors and CEOs.

Of course, there is the odd fanatic who will not read anything longer than a single page 'on principle' but people who are so dedicated to learning nothing can be considered in the same category as that person so beautifully described in the Abbot Mead Vickers posters:

'I never read the Economist'
Management trainee, aged 42.

Myth number 2

■ **A letter is not necessary in a mailing** 'If you have a colourful brochure you do not need a letter in a mailing.' **Another fallacy**. Testing over many years shows that 99 times out of 100, a letter will increase response.

■ **The brochure should demonstrate the product – the letter should explain what it would do for the prospect.** Another important point because if we are trying to increase the relevance of our mailings we will want to vary our copy for different segments – and this is much easier and cheaper to do in a letter than a colour brochure.

Myth number 3

■ **Personalisation doesn't work** Many people think it is not important to personalise letters but again, tests show this is not true. However, let's be clear what we mean by personalisation. Simply saying 'Dear Mrs Smith', while a good way to start a letter, will not increase response significantly. Referring to some recent event, transaction or query often does increase response.

■ **Take care not to overdo personalisation.** I received a letter, airmailed from a 'medium' in Gibraltar, which started with the headline:

> Were you born on 3rd March 1950?
> Then I have some very important news for you.
> In exactly 7 weeks and 2 days you are going to be very lucky!

Unfortunately for this company, I was not born on that date and thus the entire mailing was a waste of time.

> The more you use personalisation the more important it is to have totally accurate information.

Ideally you will be using data that you know is up to date and you can then proceed with confidence. If you are not sure it is wiser to be safe by avoiding such closely personalised factors as birth date, and adopting a general salutation such as 'Dear Manager', rather than addressing someone by the wrong name, gender or even title.

You should take every opportunity to gather data and to verify existing information but you must always think through your procedures to make sure you don't do something like this:

As you probably know, many business publications offer free subscriptions to selected business people – all you have to do is confirm your status with an online questionnaire.

One of the authors was recently registering online for a subscription to a direct marketing magazine and came to a box that said 'Name of company' – not having a company, being self employed, he left this blank. The system would not accept it and eventually in desperation he entered NONE – I AM SELF EMPLOYED. Now he gets mailings like the following:

Not content with this, the publishers wanted to show how sophisticated marketers can use personal data, so on their next edition they produced a fully personalised wrap around which included the following gems:

> 'I RECEIVED A PERSONAL LETTER FROM NONE - I AM SELF EMPLOYED THE MORNING AFTER I CALLED THEM. THAT'S FAST.'

> 'NONE - I AM SELF EMPLOYED'S NEW CATALOGUE SHOWED ME EXACTLY THE RIGHT OFFERS. NO WAFFLE, THAT'S WHAT I LIKE.'

How did this happen? Simply because the person who designed the online questionnaire forgot rule one of direct marketing – 'think about your audience'.

There are a large number of marketing consultants in the UK and many will be self employed. All that was necessary here was to add a box alongside the 'Name of company' field saying 'Self employed – tick here'.

This would have prevented the problem and would also have provided a useful additional piece of data.

Myth number 4

■ You should start with a little gentle introduction such as:

'Dear Mr Thomas,

You as a marketing manager will know that social networking is high on the agenda of every marketing director.

We at B & M Direct Marketing have been helping companies build relationships with their customers since 1992.'

This is another common error in direct mail. Readers cannot be bored into accepting your proposition, yet this opening tells them one thing they already know – **'you, as a marketing manager'**, and another that they do not need to know, certainly not at this stage – **'we have been doing it since 1992'.** Neither of these sentences is relevant to the prospect. Siegfried Vögele's research shows that many readers will not read further than the first couple of sentences unless they encounter something of true relevance.

The third sentence of this notional letter contains the first item of interest.

'Now an entirely new marketing event SOCNET 2011 "Building Brands through Social Networking" is about to be launched. In the words of Derek Holder, Managing Director of the Institute of Direct Marketing this event is:

"Quote about how this event will cover every aspect of the topic"

Now, although this may be an interesting paragraph, if it is run after those two opening paragraphs, the reader may never get this far. Business people get many mailings and if yours does not get to the point quickly it will be discarded for something more relevant or interesting. If the copy had been displayed differently the advertiser may have been able to hold attention and get the reader through to the third paragraph containing your key benefit.

'Visit our stand at SOCNET 2011 and you will have the opportunity of gaining a FREE two hour consultancy with one of our senior partners.'

Now, if you have got them through to this point, they may well be asking themselves: 'What is a two-hour consultation with this company worth to me?'

Now you can start to tell them about your experience in this field.

This letter could have been made more interesting and compelling in the following way:

Envelope message

Social networking and brands – the facts and where to find them – see inside

Letter Headline

'Social networking is changing the face of marketing. No professional marketer can afford to miss SOCNET2011'

Derek Holder, Managing Director of the IDM

Dear Mr Thomas

Recent research by the DMA shows that more than 80 per cent of senior marketers now feel that adding social networking to their mix is critical to their future success. **But most are not sure how to do this without risking alienating their customers.**

Now an entirely new marketing event SOCNET 2011 'Building Brands through Social Networking' is about to be launched. In the words of Derek Holder, Managing Director of the Institute of Direct Marketing:

'SOCNET 2011 is the only event which focuses on the integration of social networking with traditional marketing methods, in order to develop strategies for adding truly relevant value to brands'

SOCNET 2011 has been devised to answer all their questions. **Put these dates in your diary now (details of dates and venue).**

Make sure you don't miss the B & M stand

'Visit our stand at SOCNET 2011 and you will have the opportunity of gaining a FREE two hour Consultancy with one of our senior partners.'

This paragraph can then go on to discuss the credentials of B & M and close with a call for online registration.

When the letter is displayed in this sequence it exposes the elements in the correct order for easy assimilation by the prospect.

Myth number 5

The PS is old fashioned and does not work Tell that to the many experienced mailers who always use a PS. Siegfried Vögele, the German marketing researcher carried out a 25-year study into the way people read mailing letters. In his book *Handbook of Direct Mail* (see appendix) Vögele reported that nine out of every 10 people he studied read the postscript **first** and that they read it more slowly and carefully than the rest of the letter.

Why should this be so? Maybe people have come to realise that the postscript is a quick reference to the gist of the offer contained in the letter? Whatever the reason you should experiment with the postscript – it just may make the crucial difference to your letter.

Incidentally Professor Vögele says that the postscript is less important in very short or in original (i.e. truly individual) letters.

Vogele tells us that readers 'scan' letters before they read them. This starts to explain why longer copy letters tend to generate more response; the scanning process 'burns off' the casual reader very quickly, but real prospects will read as much as is relevant to their needs.

Your prospects are reading your letter to see whether it contains any news or other information pertinent to their needs. They wish to spend the least amount of time possible in establishing this. **You must get to the point very quickly.**

So, while short copy is not important rapid explanation is. People rarely select reading material according to how long it is, they are more concerned with how interesting it is.

Techniques to make your letters more effective

Let's summarise some techniques that generally work:

Long copy This often works because it answers all the questions that a real prospect might raise in a face to face discussion. It will be too long for the casual scanner, and of course for the established customer who knows all about you and your products.

Headings Some of the most successful letters start with a strong headline – a statement of the key benefit or perhaps a startling statistic. These are sometimes run above the salutation in bold face like this:

'60 per cent of UK businesses are gathering sophisticated web analytical data but many do not have the resources to benefit from it'
2009 Research Survey by IMDA

Dear Mr Jones…

Headlines sometimes stand out better in a box like this one:

Free Energy Audit of your business **Telephone 0800 24 24 24** **No charge and no obligation**

Dear Mr Jones…
This is called a Johnson Box, named after an American direct marketer who first gave a name to this technique.

Not all letters start with a heading but the technique works because this immediately tells prospects whether the letter is relevant to them.

Sub-headings like this help to get the gist of your message across

If you do use long copy you must make sure that it is broken up into short paragraphs with a liberal use of sub-headings. Remember Vögele's findings – prospects scan before they read – sub-heads enable scanners to see the key points quickly.

Other successful letter techniques include:

> **Indented paragraphs** These give long copy an 'easy to read' appearance. The indentation does not need to be large; a single 'tab' position like this is sufficient to make a paragraph stand out and lighten the whole appearance.

Displayed selling points Where you have a lot of points to get across it can be easier for the reader if these are displayed as numbered or bulleted points like this:

Three good reasons why you should choose James' 2011 Directory of Engineering Accessories

1. **James' is more comprehensive** – it carries 50 per cent more references than any comparable directory
2. **It uses high quality illustrations to demonstrate key products** – most comparable publications are in text only
3. **It is also available on CD-ROM or pdf that can be downloaded from www... etc.**

Note how where necessary, each point can be extended to qualify the stated benefit.

Using the correct type style

One thing that many marketers find hardest to accept is that letters produced in an old-fashioned typeface can sometimes produce more response.

Many say that this contravenes their house style (which is usually Univers or Helvetica, of which more later), which is a fair comment and also that they would never read anything that looked so outdated (not a fair comment and one we'll return to in a little while).

```
This is the face which many highly respected marketing companies use -
it's called Courier and, for some reason it seems to increase response
to many mailings.
   Perhaps it is because it is large and clear; other studies have shown
that comprehension drops as the number of characters in a line of text
increases.
   Whereas an average line in this book with the normal typeface contains
approximately 100 characters and spaces, in this typeface a line contains
no more than 70.
```

If you study the mailings of many major direct marketers, who test their responses regularly you will find that they continue to use Courier. Among the most test conscious direct marketers are publishers and many of have stuck firmly to Courier to this day. This must be because it still works better for them than Roman faces, like this one, which is ITC Veljovic, **or sans serif faces like this one, which is Univers.**

There have been numerous studies into the efficiency of typefaces over the past 50 years, the most recent being a lengthy study carried out by Australian journalist Colin Wheildon between 1984 and 1991. Wheildon issued a report of this study but subsequently repeated many of his tests in conjunction with another researcher Geoffrey Heard and they published the results in 2005 in *Type & Layout* (ISBN 1 8757 50 22 3). This book has been roundly applauded by many of the world's foremost writers and designers.

Much of the previous research into typefaces has been less than robust in its methodology. Simply asking people which style they prefer does not tackle the basic issue. The important thing about printed text is not how pretty it is, but how well it communicates.

Wheildon set out to test how well panels of readers comprehended body text printed in a variety of type styles, faces and colours. He asked people to read an article and then to answer 10 questions about what they had just read. Before showing the results we will again show what each typeface looks like.

Roman or 'serif' type

This paragraph is printed in Times New Roman, a popular serif or Roman face. Many advertisements and newspapers are printed in faces like this one, although some magazines tend to ignore the rules, and print in 'fashion' type styles. Experienced direct response designers use Roman or serif faces for all body copy, except where they use Courier for letter text.

Sans serif type

This paragraph is printed in Univers, a popular sans serif face, used by many designers in the advertising industry. It is interesting to note that sans serif faces are used much more frequently by designers of traditional (non-response) ads. Most experienced direct marketing designers know that using sans serif faces can reduce their response, despite the fact that this face actually looks clearer than the Roman type.

The next example shows another style popular with designers, but not with experienced direct marketers.

Reversed-out type

Another form of display to avoid for body copy is this which is 'reversed-out' – we can reverse-out any typeface – this is Times New Roman whereas the next paragraph is in Univers
– some people feel that when reversing out, sans serif faces work better than Roman but there is very little evidence to support this

Let's look at Wheildon's statistics. Groups of adults and college students were each given a magazine article to read.

The tests were repeated at intervals, with groups being switched from serif to sans serif type, and articles varying from those of general interest to those of direct interest to the reader.

Participants were supervised while reading and were then given a printed questionnaire asking ten questions about what they had read. In the tests mentioned here one group was given the articles set in Corona (8 point on 9 point body), a serif face similar to Times New Roman; the other group read the same article set in Helvetica (8 point on 9 point body) a sans serif face similar to Univers.

Comprehension was judged on the following basis:

Seven to 10 questions answered correctly = **good comprehension**
Four to six correct answers = **fair comprehension**
Zero to three correct answers = **poor comprehension**

Here are the results of this section of the test:

Type style	Comprehension level		
	Good	Fair	Poor
Serif type for body copy	67%	19%	14%
Sans serif type for body copy	12%	23%	65%

After the tests and questionnaires were completed, readers were asked if they had any comments on what they had just experienced. These too are very interesting. Here is an extract from Colin Wheildon's report:

'Comments made by the readers who showed poor comprehension of articles set in sans serif type had a common theme – the difficulty in holding concentration.'

An analysis of the comments offered by one group of 112 readers **who had read an article of direct interest to them, set in sans serif type revealed:**

'Of the 112 readers, 67 showed poor comprehension, and of these:
- 53 complained strongly about the difficulty of reading the type;
- 11 said the task caused them physical discomfort (eye tiredness);
- 10 said they had to backtrack continually to try to maintain concentration;
- five said when they had to backtrack they gave up trying to concentrate;
- 22 said they had difficulty in focusing after having read a dozen or so lines.

Some readers made two or more of the above comments.

Yet when this same group was asked immediately afterwards to read another article with a domestic theme, but set in Corona, they reported no physical difficulties, and no necessity to recapitulate to maintain concentration.

The conclusion must be that body type must be set in serif type if the designer intends it to be read and understood.'

Tests on reversed-out type

In another series of tests Wheildon examined the effect of reversing out the text people were asked to read. The format of the tests was the same. One group read the article printed in black on white paper; other groups were asked to read the same article in white on a black background; white on a purple background; and white on a deep blue background. In all cases the typeface was a Roman (serif) face. Here are the comprehension scores:

Type style	Comprehension level		
	Good	Fair	Poor
Text printed Black on white*	70%	19%	11%
Text printed White on black	0%	12%	88%
Text printed White on purple	2%	16%	82%
Text printed White on deep blue	0%	4%	96%
* Very similar to the serif scores in the previous tests (same type style)			

To complete this series and to test the school of thought which contends that reversed-out type is only a problem with Roman or serif faces, a final set of groups was tested on reversed-out type but this time set in Helvetica.

The results were:

Type style	Comprehension level		
	Good	Fair	Poor
Black on white**	14%	25%	61%
White on black	4%	13%	83%
** Very similar to the sans serif scores in the earlier tests (same type style)			

Note that the above tests and the comments relate to body copy only. It is not suggested that you should avoid sans serif or reversed-out type for short headings or occasional emphasis, in some cases this can make things stand out well against the rest of the text.

Additional enclosures

Leaflets and brochures As we said earlier the job of the letter is to sell the proposition while the brochure's role is to demonstrate it. Pictures, showing the product in use, with captions emphasising the benefits can ensure that the brochure is a valuable addition to the pack.

Don't ignore the value of captions. Most people read them so make sure they tell benefits and are not just throwaway lines. A major charity once found it could increase the effectiveness of a fundraising leaflet simply by rewriting the captions. The left-hand caption was the one they originally used; the right-hand one was much more effective:

Picture of Brazilian rain forest	Picture of Brazilian rain forest

The Brazilian Rain Forest

The Brazilian Rain Forest –
an area the size of Reading
disappears every week

Which of these conjures up a realistic picture for you? Incidentally this would be a good example of how you could vary your text to suit segments of the audience. The example of Reading could be used for donors with a Berkshire postcode, whereas Preston may be substituted for those living in Lancashire.

Supporting pieces

Sometimes, when mailing a general list you may not have enough data (or enough budget) to enable you to separate your audience into discrete segments. Yet you want to make sure that you leave no question unanswered for those who have not heard about you.

Additional leaflets

In this case you may opt for a multi-piece mailing, so instead of putting everything into the letter and perhaps 'overselling' to someone who is already convinced, you could introduce a couple of additional leaflets e.g.:

- **About Belgrave Supplies** – a leaflet giving some background for those who like the sound of your services but have reservations because they are not familiar with you.
- **What our customers say about us** – an additional leaflet carrying testimonial statements from well known or credible customers to reassure those who like the sound of your offer but are not quite sure whether they can trust a company they do not know.

Testimonials have worked reliably for many years, despite the comments of some cynics who say no one believes them. Do such people really think that companies like IBM or Hewlett Packard would stand idly by while an advertiser made up a statement and credited it to them?

Newspaper and magazine reprints

If you have been lucky enough to get a good review in a newspaper or magazine you should use it for all it is worth.

The publication is assumed to have an independent point of view, and if they say your product is good, it carries much more weight than the same claim made by you. You are expected to say yours is the greatest product ever so the reader discounts your claims a little. Newspaper reprints are sometimes even more powerful than testimonials. Don't forget that in each of the above cases you need to get the permission of the authors before reproducing their comments.

Now you have done all you can to 'sell' your proposition and reassure your prospect that you are a worthy supplier, you need to think about closing the sale, or in a two-stage situation, generating a response.

What are the essentials of a good response device?

1. **First and foremost, make it easy for the respondent. Here's how:**
   - **Give a choice of reply options** – website URL, email, phone, post, and perhaps even fax – **let them decide which is most convenient**. One commentator recently said that offering a choice of response methods can confuse respondents but again test results do not bear this out. Tests do not prove that prospects are not confused, but they do show that responses tend to increase when a choice is offered.

     Put yourself in your respondent's place How would you like to respond? A large number of people, perhaps 60 per cent or more, responding to advertisements for financial products such as loans do so on the telephone. That means that 40 per cent do not use the phone. Why not? There could be several reasons:
     - they have a speech problem
     - they have a hearing problem
     - they have a name which no one can spell or pronounce
     - they just don't like using the phone

     There are probably another three or four reasons but the point is made. Most of these people would prefer to go online or return a coupon by mail or fax.
   - **Do as much of the work as you can** – where relevant you should try to fill in the prospect's name and address on the response form. There are several good reasons for doing this:

     You get more replies – you have removed one of the barriers to response.

     You will be able to read and process all the coupons you receive. A surprising number of people fail to include their post town and postcode and when the item they sent for doesn't arrive, you get the blame!

     You can print a customer reference number or barcode on the form so you only have to scan or key in a few digits and your system will automatically pull up the full address. This could save around 60 per cent of your order-input time.

2. **Repeat your address and the main details of the offer on the order form** Some people will keep just the order form until they have time to send it, so if the details are not repeated those who cannot remember will not return it. Others may pass it on to a friend or colleague, who will not always see the full mailing.

3. **Pay for the reply** When inviting phone or postal response make sure you pay for the reply, it's a small extra amount to pay for a warm lead.

Designing for online advertising

Like all online topics, the situation is constantly changing and you are recommended to keep in touch by subscribing to some of the many newsletters and blogs that are published. Unless you are planning to use external specialists a good place to start may be by signing up to Google AdSense.

If you go to their AdSense location at www.google.com/images/adsense/en_us/support/general_en.jpg you will find the following graphic:

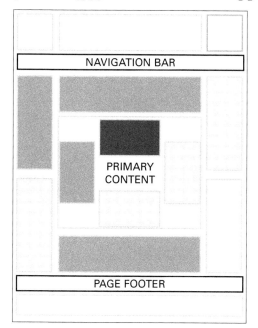

As in offline, some advertisements that seem to break all the rules are highly successful. However, until you have gained experience it makes sense to improve the odds by following expert advice.

Google tells us that certain locations offer a better chance of success – in the diagram the darker tinted positions are considered to be better i.e:

Those closer to the centre of the page

Left hand better than right hand
Close to site navigation

Above the fold – though those at the end of an article also seem to do well

Google also tell us that large rectangles tend to perform best, although this clearly depends on your product, your creative design, and the content of the Web page it is served on.

This latter point can be quite important. In general advertising and in PR, some practitioners have found that writing or designing advertisements and press releases to match the style of a specific publication can be very effective. So this is also likely to be true for online advertisements. If you have chosen a specific website on which to advertise this is worth considering. There also seems to be some evidence that removing borders from around a banner makes it blend into the page better, and may therefore increase readership.

Copy for online

A good starting point might be copy length. Whereas long copy can be very effective in offline ads and mailings it is not recommended for online. The general rule seems to be that copy should be no more than half as long as for offline, and Steve Krug goes even further saying 'reduce your text by 50 per cent, then reduce it by a further 50 per cent.' This may seem a bit drastic but the general principle is certainly correct.

Action words, such as 'Free', 'Save' and so on are frowned upon for email subject lines but are not detrimental to achieving click-throughs on Web pages.

As in offline, the best advice is that you should test to find out what works for you.

Here are a few pointers to help you make the most of your online budget:

1. **Take expert advice** – this does not mean you have to pay large fees to specialist agencies. There are literally hundreds of newsletters and blogs that will give you advice. There is a lengthy list in the Appendix but among the best are: ClickZ Experts – www. clickz.com; Sherpa – www.marketingsherpa.com; and Marketing Experiments www. marketingexperiments.com. These sites offer lots of valuable, downloadable reports which will be very helpful to you

2. **Use a professional designer** – if you do not want to hire an agency there are many excellent freelance designers – just check that they understand direct marketing and online advertising

3. **Test as much as you can** – remember, you can test simple propositions with email subject lines and pay-per-click advertising before committing to a large scale banner campaign. And don't stop testing once you have developed your propositions. Now it's time to test online sizes and formats; position on the page; copy variations; static or animated executions and so on

4. **Collect testimonials** – another idea in common with offline. Prospects expect you to say your product is the best – a third party confirmation can work in your favour

5. **Make sure your landing page 'fits' with the click through instruction**. Read Steve Krug again – don't make me think! If a prospect has clicked through they are looking for what you promised in the ad. If you want to start collecting additional data offer some form of bonus to encourage this – and don't let this get in the way of the main purpose of the click-through

And finally a general creative checklist

A summary of the things to remember when designing your promotion. These are based on the well proven AIDCA formula – **Attention, Interest, Desire, Conviction, Action**.

Gain attention

Remember that a high percentage of emails don't get past the preview pane; most mailings are binned unopened; 80 per cent of people who see an advertisement don't read beyond the headline, and many website visitors leave your site within 20 seconds if they don't immediately see something that attracts them.

So the first thing to consider is how can you gain attention. If it doesn't state a clear end-user benefit your headline must promise something very relevant to achieve this. Traditional advertisers search for a USP, a unique selling proposition, and this is then carried through every medium they use in the campaign.

Direct marketers also use USPs but in a different way. Of course when using broadscale media to acquire new prospects we too have to use general benefit statements, but when we can target individuals we adapt the selling proposition for each customer segment so it becomes more customer focused and thus more relevant.

Start with your strongest benefit statement or main item of news. Don't save it – they may not get to the end unless you have excited their interest. News or benefit headlines are invariably more successful than humour, curiosity or other gimmicks.

Maintain interest

Create visual interest by intelligent use of pictures and captions. Remember that pictures of people always attract the eye.

Use real numbers – £294.70 sounds more 'real' than £300.

Do not assume others share your tastes, this is especially important when considering humour. If in doubt, err on the side of good taste.

Tell the full story – don't be afraid of using long copy if necessary. There is no merit in long copy, nor short; copy should be long enough to answer all the likely questions, and it will vary according to your objective.

Use subheadings, especially if the copy is long. Many readers will scan these first before deciding whether to read the whole thing.

Note that with email your main copy is often better short with click-through links for readers to go further if they want to. If there are lots of questions to answer then a link to something like: *The 10 questions most of our customers ask* can do the trick.

Make it easy for the reader with careful layout and display of key points.

Keep to a logical sequence – a good final check on a piece of copy is to write a one line summary of each paragraph and then check to see if the sequence is correct.

Use short words, short sentences and short paragraphs. There are around 1,000,000 words in the English language but few adults have more than 30,000 in their vocabulary. Make sure you use words that everyone knows, and use them in a way that makes your copy easy to read.

Generate desire

Confirm the relevance of your offer – link your claims to the reader's situation where possible.

Demonstrate the product benefits – show how it will improve the customer's life.

Use active rather than passive language. Avoid 'will be delivered in 6 days' and instead use 'in less than a week you could be using this to...'

Involve your reader – enclosures or links that get the reader to do something often work well.

Convince

Sell the benefits not the attributes. People buy products because of what they do for them, not for what they are.

Use testimonials – they are always more believable than your own claims.

Quote research data – it carries greater authority.

Provide reassurance – no obligation; strong guarantee.

Ask for action

Don't forget to take the order, and make sure your copy closes with a powerful final paragraph, summarising the benefits and the action required.

Test a time close, e.g. 'Offer closes in seven days.'

Summarise what you want them to do. Don't be vague and give clear, concise instructions.

Give alternative response options – it makes it easier for the respondent and removes another barrier.

Using a follow-up

If you want to maximise response consider a follow-up by email, phone or mail.

Escalating your offer – some experienced direct marketers, especially publishers, use follow-ups extensively and they often increase the value of the offer as the series progresses without success.

This is a technique that requires careful testing and evaluation but the simple rule is to continue to send follow-ups until the latest one loses money. The loss on the last will generally be well covered by the additional gains from earlier follow-ups.

Escalating discount follow-ups must be approached with extreme caution when asking existing customers to renew. You may 'train' them to wait for the best deal, and the net result is often a reduction in your margins.

EXAMPLE

One large international company selling business equipment, measured the performance of its entire staff on their quarterly sales figures. If they reached or beat their targets they got a bonus; if they failed heads would roll – people would actually be fired if they missed their targets for two successive quarters.

This of course led to a bizarre situation where, in the final three weeks of every quarter the salespeople would offer the most amazing discounts to make sure they got the order in before the end of the quarter.

Within a few months customers got the message. Sales in the first ten weeks of every quarter reduced and there was always a boom in the final three weeks. Unfortunately the margins were being decimated and the European management was soon facing another head office purge.

Following up by telephone

Many companies have had great success by using the telephone to follow up mailings and, to a lesser extent emails. The approach varies from the classic direct mail follow-up:

- **The follow-up is made earlier, ideally within three days of the mailing arriving.** In a mailed follow-up you can repeat the details in hard copy so a week to 10 days delay is not detrimental. But how much of the mail you received last week is still on your desk?
- **The telephone follow-up is not a sales call,** it is more of a service call, e.g.
  'I sent you some information. Do you have any questions about it? Is there any further information you would like? Should I send it to one of your colleagues?'

When this technique was first introduced in the 1980s the results were highly impressive:

1. A major international software company found that using a rapid telephone follow up (within three days) increased the number of leads generated from 2 per cent to 19 per cent.
2. Using the same technique a UK charity changed a 2 per cent into a 72 per cent response.
3. A charge card company mailing retailers to persuade them to accept the card as payment had a 4 per cent sign-up to their proposal. Of the sample which received the rapid telephone follow-up 26 per cent accepted.

Today, however, the technique is widely used and the uplifts are not so large. Nevertheless it still works in both business and consumer marketing. Some companies have found that a mailing followed by an email reminder a week later can also have a major impact.

A final reminder – in this case the follow-up should not use a hard sell approach but be simply a friendly customer service enquiry. This can be an advantage as the calls can often be made by office staff rather than highly trained (and more expensive) telemarketers.

CASE STUDY
SWINTON INSURANCE:
'Mystery Tipper' drives sales in Swinton's Taxi Insurance Division

INTRODUCTION
Swinton is one of the UK's leading insurance brokers, offering its private and business customers a one-stop shop for insurance and related cover for homes, cars, caravans, businesses, holidays, motorbikes and other specialist areas. Swinton price-checks the UK's top insurers to find the most appropriate cover for its customers at the best price.

CONGESTED CHANNELS
In 2007, Swinton Taxi Division recognised that its traditional communication channels had become congested, with too many similar-seeming products and advertisements, making it very hard for consumers to distinguish one brand from another. Too many competitors were chasing fewer policies in a shrinking pool of customers, and everyone was under financial pressure. Swinton Taxi Division had watched its sales plateau over the preceding five years.

Swinton Taxi Division and its agency Red C launched the 'Mystery Tipper' campaign to kick-start its sales recovery in 2008.

This campaign demonstrates just how effective a great creative idea can be in re-invigorating an existing product in a mature and difficult market. The 12-month campaign broke all Swinton Taxi Division's previous sales records. This case explores how these impressive results were achieved by this straightforward, yet highly original and slightly quirky, campaign.

BACKGROUND
Insurance intermediaries, or brokers, play an important role in the UK's insurance industry. They provide a professional advice service to businesses and individuals, and assist in the identification, measurement, management, control and transfer of risk. They are responsible for the distribution of almost two-thirds of all UK general insurance, generating £1.5bn in invisible earnings in 2007.

THE ROLE AND CONTRIBUTION OF INSURANCE BROKERS
According to recent research by the British Insurance Brokers' Association (BIBA), 'insurance brokers regularly help consumers achieve better results when pursuing a claim. The majority of brokers surveyed have secured increased payments for clients in the past year, following an initial lower offer from insurers, and 58 per cent of brokers said that they had to fight harder to

get claims paid during the recession.' According to Eric Galbraith, BIBA's Chief Executive, 'Many consumers do not have the experience or knowledge to negotiate claims themselves. Brokers know how to evidence and support negotiations through their understanding of policy wording, relevant case law and their relationship with the insurer.'

The insurance broking sector has proved itself to be fairly resilient, and is still seeing growth in terms of both profit and new business start-ups in some areas. However, insurance brokers are not immune to the economic downturn, as their clients' revenue determines the size and scope of insurance premiums. BIBA's members have reported an overall drop in income due to reductions in their clients' revenue, stock and payroll. Brokers are also facing higher trading costs, mainly due to the growing cost of regulation.

CONSUMER PRESSURE TO REDUCE PREMIUMS

As in any market experiencing economic turmoil, customers are trying to reduce their premiums where possible, sometimes cutting back on their insurance cover altogether. Competition among insurance brokers has become fierce, as cash-strapped customers shop around for the best deal. In addition to a wide choice of generalist and specialist brokers, there are numerous online price comparison aggregators, increasing the downward pressure on brokers' profit margins. Some aggregator sites are owned by brokers or underwriters, and there are clear indications that all such sites are going to be more tightly regulated by the Financial Services Authority in the near future.

As a result of all these market pressures, brokers are working harder than before to secure lower returns, leading to some consolidation within the sector. However, the market remains dynamic, as the growing recruitment pool of skilled workers has prompted some of the more successful intermediaries, and new businesses, to seize the opportunity for cost-effective growth.

Swinton was founded in Salford in the north-west of England more than 50 years ago. The business has grown steadily, mainly due to customer recommendations and the acquisition of other insurance brokers in the UK and Europe. Today, it is the largest high street insurance broker chain in the UK. In 2008, Swinton announced record profits of £ 50.1m, a 4 per cent increase year on year, generated by selling 25 per cent more policies than in 2007; a total of 3.25 million policies. The year 2008 marked Swinton's seventh consecutive year of growth.

Peter Halpin, Swinton's Chief Executive, believes Swinton has been successful because it has gone 'against the received wisdom that the majority of modern consumers are totally price-driven and promiscuous when it comes to their insurance renewal.' He expects continued growth over the next five to 10 years, 'through a combination of organic growth, both on and offline, and more acquisitions.' A recent announcement revealed plans to double the size of its commercial business by 2012.

FULLY INTEGRATED SERVICE

Swinton offers its customers a fully integrated service across on and offline channels, with more than 550 high street shops covering 90 per cent of the UK, five call centres and a well-established online presence. Swinton is seeing an increasing proportion of its policies sold online. In 2008, the Swinton Group was named Personal Lines Broker of the Year at The British Insurance Awards.

RESPONDING TO CONSUMER DEMAND

At the award ceremony, Swinton was praised for its personal approach to customer service and the success of its integrated communications and customer service strategy across its online, call centre and extensive high street shop channels. The award also recognised Swinton's success in developing its products in response to customer demand for more products relevant to their needs. (Source: Insurance Daily Magazine.)

Swinton Taxi Division is a specialist division within the Swinton group, with a well-established independent reputation as a trusted taxi insurer. However, since 2002, increasing on and offline competition and a reduction in premiums has seen the taxi division's sales plateau.

Taxi insurance providers traditionally advertise predominantly in the trade press and magazines. Six years ago, taxi drivers would have found adverts for an average of four different taxi insurers in the back pages of their magazines. In 2008, more than 30 insurers were competing for the same volume of business, all using virtually indistinguishable advertisements telling prospective customers that their taxi insurance offered the best value.

LIMITED BUDGET

Swinton, and its agency Red C, had a limited budget with which to create the year-long campaign it urgently needed, to generate immediate sales and create a good foundation for healthy growth in the future.

OBJECTIVES

The specific acquisition objective for the campaign was to achieve a 10 per cent quotation enquiry uplift year on year in 2008. Swinton knew from its database that many customers choose to stay with the same insurer for an average of three to four years, so a 10 per cent uplift was sufficient to recover its competitive advantage in the commoditised taxi insurance market.

MARKETING STRATEGY – AN INSIGHT-BASED CAMPAIGN

Swinton Taxi Division's 2008 campaign strategy was based on two very important insights. The first insight arose from recognising that the rapid increase in similar-seeming adverts in traditional taxi insurance advertising channels made it very difficult for Swinton to distinguish its product from those of competitors and attract new business. Swinton Taxi Division knew that it had to find a novel way to get its message across to potential customers. This thought prompted Swinton to introduce a face-to-face element into its communications strategy; it would create a precedent in its sector by taking the campaign directly to its target customers on the taxi ranks.

UNDERSTANDING CUSTOMERS' NEEDS

The second key insight came from Swinton Taxi Division's understanding of its customers' needs. Taxi drivers are hard working, hard-done-by no-nonsense characters. They are at work much of the time because if they are not at the wheel of their cabs, they are not earning money. Buying insurance of any kind is a rather dull business, and busy taxi drivers have little time to expend on this activity. Shortage of time being a key characteristic of the target audience, the creative needed to be simple, hard-hitting and attention-grabbing in order to get its message across quickly, minimise potential objections and prompt the necessary action.

A STRONG CALL-TO-ACTION WAS NEEDED

Getting a taxi driver's attention can be tough, but if you succeed in capturing their interest, word of mouth can give the campaign a powerful boost. Taxi rank conversation can produce a rapid viral effect. The campaign sought to exploit this great opportunity for free PR by creating a strong call-to-action that was engaging and fun. The main campaign objective was to get taxi drivers to contact Swinton for a quote or policy renewal, so the creative solution had to give them a thoroughly compelling reason to act promptly.

The creative solution was a quirky, highly original theme for the campaign that offered taxi drivers a handsome reward in return for very little effort. No matter how busy they are, almost every cab driver you'll ever meet will thank you for a tip; and the bigger the tip the better. Enter the 'Swinton Mystery Tipper' – a sassy cartoon character inspired by Dick Tracey with just a dash of Jessica Rabbit. The Mystery Tipper had at least one £1,000 tip to give away to UK cabbies every month, but only if she spotted a Mystery Tipper sticker in their window. The only way for non-Swinton customers to get the sticker was to get a quote.

CAMPAIGN EXECUTION

The Mystery Tipper campaign ran throughout 2008, visiting a different UK city each month. The Mystery Tipper's touring schedule included a wide selection of large and small cities in areas where Swinton Taxi Division already had a good proportion of its existing customer base.

Not every local authority allowed the Tipper into their town, which, sadly, excluded London from the campaign. The Mystery Tipper was a Swinton or Red C employee appropriately disguised in a trilby and mackintosh, but her true identity was kept a closely guarded secret.

THE CAMPAIGN LAUNCH INVOLVED LOYAL CUSTOMERS

Swinton knew it was essential to involve its current customers in the campaign, both to acknowledge their loyalty and as the basis for cost-effective growth. Mystery Tipper stickers were sent to the existing database, giving loyal customers an opportunity to win the prize money and quickly raising awareness of the campaign launch. Lapsed customers also received a direct mail pack, inviting them to request a quote and sticker.

CAREFULLY INTEGRATED MEDIA

The campaign was carefully coordinated to ensure media were fully integrated to support the campaign objective. Each medium had to work individually and in concert, to achieve the synergistic media-multiplier effect.

Taxi drivers typically read newspapers and trade magazines and listen to the radio. The campaign launched through a wide range of media including direct mail, trade press advertisements and advertorials, flyers, letters and phone calls to local fleet offices and monthly shout-outs on local radio.

Figure 13.2: Swinton Mystery Tipper – integrated communications

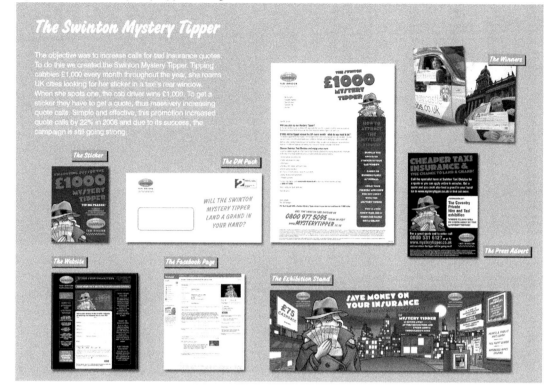

Advertisements and editorials appeared monthly in the most popular trade titles, such as *Taxi Talk, Taxi Today,* and *Private Hire* and *Taxi Monthly.* The strong and rather surprising image of the Mystery Tipper brandishing a fist full of cash really stood out from the typically serious and newsy editorial and traditional insurance advertising. A microsite was created especially for the campaign, featuring a shadowy 'Tipper' figure ambling across the screen accompanied by Sam Spade-style music to add an extra touch of mystery.

The first tip took place in Liverpool, a slightly anxious moment for the campaign team. However, the campaign's launch communications had been effective and several taxis were spotted sporting the sticker.

The Mystery Tipper was able to give prize money to the first lucky winner, getting the campaign off to a flying start.

ENTHUSIASTIC RESPONSE

Before and after every tip, news of the Tipper's next visit and the latest winner appeared in trade press, flyers, trade shows, direct response ads and advertorials, the campaign microsite, Facebook and emails, all written in 'detective speak'. All cab offices and hackney cab drivers in the next area to be visited were informed about the Tipper before her arrival, raising awareness of the campaign and the Swinton brand. The campaign also achieved great success at trade exhibitions, such as the Coventry Private Hire and Taxi exhibition. The Tipper had a field day, with thousands of taxi drivers together in one place and £4,000 to give away. More renewal dates were collected at this event than in any previous year; results were 75 per cent up compared to the 2007 exhibition.

The Mystery Tipper campaign generated enough excitement to get itself talked about on taxi ranks, as cabbies speculated where she would appear next and encouraged each other to get a sticker. Data collection was an important aim of the campaign, especially insurance renewal dates; an extremely valuable piece of data in this market. Whether cabbies called to get a quote, or registered their details on the mystery tipper microsite, good-quality data capture was a priority for the campaign.

The meticulously planned integrated communications triggered a sense of anticipation and ensured that the campaign continued to gather momentum as it developed. As the campaign built, a record number of calls were received from taxi drivers across the country, including Leeds, Sheffield, Derby, Chester, Bristol, Newcastle, Norwich, Liverpool, Cambridge, Blackpool and Manchester; they called in their thousands to get a sticker.

The final tip of the campaign took place in Norwich. The Norwich cabbies responded to news of the Mystery Tipper's imminent arrival by lining up enthusiastically, with their bright orange 'Tipper' stickers proudly displayed. The palpable sense of expectation and excitement on the ranks contrasted with the relatively subdued atmosphere surrounding the first tip, clearly showing the high impact achieved by the campaign's communication strategy.

DRAMATIC SALES UPLIFT

The Mystery Tipper campaign was a complete success, and increased Swinton Taxi Division's business by 30 per cent in 2008. In a tough marketplace, this deceptively simple campaign produced record-breaking results with a limited budget over the 12 months that it ran.

The campaign began with a clear objective and a solid understanding of the key issues in its target market. From this starting point, the campaign team developed a quirky, original creative and communications solution that was strong enough to achieve an instant and long-lasting impact in its target market, without any need to alter its core product.

The campaign succeeded because the creative was relevant and engaging and the rich communications mix was meticulously planned and coordinated. The Mystery Tipper's fresh and straightforward approach, combined with attention to detail and a great call to action, proved to be an irresistible combination for its target audience.

This campaign allowed Swinton's Taxi Division to exceed its annual sales target and establish a firm foundation, both in terms of renewal and prospect data and brand awareness, for sustained cost-effective growth in the future.

Since the beginning of the Mystery Tipper campaign there has been a significant increase in the number of calls received by the division: 10,741 more than in 2007 against a backdrop of increasing competition and five years of stagnation. Response rates have improved by 130 per cent year on year, with individual media, direct mail (£9 per quote), inserts (£14 per quote) and press (£12 per quote) performing very cost-effectively.

The Mystery Tipper campaign has contributed greatly to building general awareness of Swinton Taxi Division's brand in the target market; taxis sporting Mystery Tipper stickers are likely to be seen for many years to come. Due to the campaign's success since its launch in 2007, the Mystery Tipper is now in its third year. She is still prowling the UK's taxi ranks looking for new 2010 stickers. It looks as though the campaign will continue to have a positive effect on enquiry, quotation and sales performance, and benefit the division's business as a whole, for many years to come.

With many thanks to Swinton Taxi Division and its agency Red C for permission to include this case study.

SUMMARY

The most important factor in direct marketing communications is targeting. This means that in one-to-one communications creative work is quite low down the list of priorities.

The point is that, unless we get the right message, to the right person, at the right time, it doesn't matter how wonderful the creative execution is, it will not work.

This is not to suggest that creative is unimportant – quite the contrary. It is prudent to assume that if we have taken the trouble to identify the first three factors (right message, right person, right time) our competitors may also have made the effort. So in a worst case situation our mailing or email may be in a head to head comparison with a competitive offer.

> In this situation the message that is described most clearly and attractively will win the order.

Furthermore the above situation only really applies in one-to-one media. Where we are advertising in broadscale media such as press, TV or online banners, creative has a broader role. Its first job is to attract the prospect's attention so in this case it becomes part of targeting and moves to be joint top of the priority list.

We stressed the importance of giving clear briefs with clear objectives to enable our creative partners to concentrate on producing an effective result.

We saw how the creative development process works through the use of examples.

The long copy/short copy issue was explained in detail. The main point is that copy should be long enough to answer all the questions that a prospect may have – **at this stage**. If we are expecting the communication to do the entire job in one stage there will be more questions and thus copy will be longer. When we are lead generating (i.e. in a two stage situation) shorter copy may work very well. **So the argument is not for long copy but for complete copy.**

We saw how creative people divide their time when producing a job, which generally works out approximately as follows:

Research	**30%**
Thinking up initial ideas	**20%**
First draft copy	**20%**
Revising and reworking	**30%**

We saw the need to manage any response generated and that successful implementation generated a regular and manageable supply of leads.

We saw that when designing any direct marketing communication the desired sequence of events is as follows:
- Attract attention
- Establish relevance
- Convince the prospect of benefits
- Close the sale
- Confirm the action to be taken and take the order

We looked at the three types of advertising and distinguished between awareness advertising, direct response advertising and dual-purpose advertising.

We considered the differences between writing copy for direct mail and for emails. Whereas a direct mailing letter can be quite long, several pages in many cases, email copy must be shorter with the additional information available through click-through links.

We went on to explore ten guidelines for the creation of a successful direct response advertisement.
1. Readers generally scan an advertisement in the order: picture, headline, copy. Place the headline below the picture.
2. The picture should be striking and action-oriented.
3. Ensure the headline works hard – 80 to 90 per cent of 'readers' will not read further than the headline.
4. Body copy length is not critical but clear layout is.
5. Promote benefits not features.
6. Include a prominent, easy to use 'call-to-action'.
7. Repeat the benefits near the response device.
8. Smaller space is cost-effective.
9. Avoid sans serif type for body copy.
10. Avoid reversed-out type for body copy.

We went on to look in detail at the construction of the mail pack looking first at the outer envelope. We saw that the envelope should make an impression and if an envelope message is used it must be highly relevant.

We exposed five popular myths about direct mail letters:
1. Letter should be no longer than one page.
2. A letter is not always necessary in a mailing.
3. Personalisation does not work.
4. The letter should start with a gentle introduction.
5. The postscript doesn't work.

We summarised techniques that work in letter writing:

- the use of headings and subheadings;
- the right typeface – Roman at least but Courier is also worth a test;
- no reversed-out copy.

We saw that the response device should make it easy for the respondent to reply. They should be offered a choice of reply options, i.e. website URL, email and postal addresses, telephone, and also fax numbers where relevant.

REVIEW QUESTIONS

1. What are the key success factors in creative execution?
2. What are the benefits of long copy and when should long copy be used?
3. Outline the communications planning process; what is the desired sequence of events in any direct communication?
4. What is the best type style to use for body copy?
5. Why should reversed-out body copy not be used?
6. What is the role of the subheading in a letter?
7. How do additional enclosures help build response?
8. What are the characteristics of a good response device?

EXERCISE

Go to a website of your choice. Look at the banner advertisements and click on those that offer some interaction. Choose one of these and click through to the landing page. Did this fit seamlessly with the advertisement? Were you able to find what was promised within a few seconds?

CHAPTER 14
THE POWER OF TESTING

IN THIS CHAPTER

This chapter explores the important role that testing plays in direct marketing planning and management.

After reading this chapter you will be able to:

- Understand how testing can be deployed to reduce risk and generate more effective campaigns
- Select from the various test alternatives the most appropriate method for your requirements
- Evaluate test results and predict future outcomes within reasonable parameters
- Plan and execute substantial test campaigns
- Understand the vital role of statistics in judging test results

Specific topics include:

- The special problems of precise measurement today
- The purpose of testing
- What can be tested
- Size matters
- The hierarchy of testing – Bob Stone's five big things
- How testing works
- The value of online testing
- Developing your test strategy
- Can I trust a test result? Samples and statistical significance
- Testing with very low response rates

INTRODUCTION

The special problems of precise measurement in the twenty-first century

Direct marketers today face a conundrum. Our entire marketing philosophy of direct communication with individuals, which has often meant that our cost per contact has been much higher than traditional broadscale media costings, has always been justified by the precise measurement tools peculiar to direct marketing. Hitherto we have been able to prove through our precise response analysis that direct marketing can be hugely cost-efficient.

Today, however, we have two problems:

1. We have established beyond doubt that multimedia campaigns are more effective than single medium approaches – but this means that we cannot measure individual media with our previous precision. We can get close through the use of complicated regional testing –

e.g. omitting one medium from the mix in one area and measuring the effect, but it is not as precise as before. And in any case we are really only measuring the response route that the customer finally settled on – there is no way of measuring precisely which and how many of our communications the customer saw before responding. **And that is the simpler of the two problems.**

2. More complicated is the involvement of the Internet. Most offline ads and mailings, even if they ask respondents to respond by phone or mail, include a URL – not a problem in one sense as it can only increase response but a real problem when it comes to attributing the response to a specific stimulus. Yes we can design specific landing pages so that we can measure the final decision point but again, we will never know what other messages they saw before deciding to contact us. And that's the offline problem. With online ads it is even more difficult. If someone sees an online banner we know for sure that they are online, so that means they have several options available at the click of a mouse.

So here's an example of the problem, a research study by Neilson/Netratings and commissioned by Harvest Digital asked 'If you see an online ad for flights or holidays, which of the following actions do you usually take?' Here are the responses:

Click on the ad i.e. directly attributable response   **26 per cent**

Go directly to the advertiser's site – i.e. attributable if the
ad carries the URL for a unique landing page   **29 per cent**

Go to a travel agent or other route – not attributable   **8 per cent**

Use a search engine – i.e. 'Google it' – totally unattributable   **57 per cent**

What this tells us is if, even in the best case, more than 60 per cent of responses cannot be correctly attributed, that measurement of online advertising is inherently unreliable. It could be argued that if we can judge an online campaign as successful from the attributable responses, the true situation can only be much better, and that seems a reasonable argument. But it does not offer us our usual precision; and in any case without much further research we will never know whether travel advertising stimulates different behaviour to that for other product areas. And unless we carry out a similar study into offline advertising we will never know how far this effect carries into offline.

Two options for the future of precision testing

If in the future, we want to use testing as a precision measurement tool we will have to adopt one of two strategies for each test:

1. We may have to test individual elements in a standalone situation, so that whatever our longer-term plans for integration across media we run the test in total isolation. This will be possible to a certain extent, so long as we select times when we have no other advertising

running on other channels, and where we always use unique attribution codes. Thus we would have a unique telephone number; a unique Web landing page and email address if relevant; and a uniquely coded address for postal response.

Unfortunately this will not be totally watertight and there will still be leakage to the website, because people today are generally aware that companies tend to offer better deals for online orders. Thus, whatever unique URL we run in the ad, some respondents will simply make a note of the offer and then do a general search for the Web address when they decide to take it further.

This, in my opinion, is likely to be a factor in the many stories we are hearing of declining responses in offline advertising, mailings, inserts and so on. In many cases these media will have played a part in persuading the prospect to visit the website. **A research study into this situation is overdue I feel.**

2. The second alternative will be to adopt the strategy followed by traditional broadscale advertisers in the past, where one factor is added or dropped from the mix, by region. The campaign could be run in one area without TV; another area may have direct mail, press or email added or dropped.

This can be very complicated to set up and to evaluate, and unfortunately it can set up other biases. Perhaps this offer does not appeal so much to people in the north east, or there may be stronger competition in the south west. So such results are not totally reliable.

Historically direct marketers have therefore tended to use testing first, whereas traditional marketers have had to rely on broader research to help them track attitudinal changes, and campaign wide sales.

Direct marketers use research too but generally to answer the question 'why?' rather than 'what?' The first issue for direct marketers is cost-effectiveness, so tests will be built to answer such questions as:

- Is direct mail more or less cost-effective than email?
- Do online banner ads work better than national press?
- Is the *Daily Mail* as cost-effective in gaining new customers as the *Daily Express*?
- Is the cost per reply from television higher or lower than that from press?
- Will long copy produce more replies than short?
- Which pay-per-click headline and text works best for me?
- Is the long-term buying performance of customers recruited through loose inserts better or worse than that of television respondents?
- Does our new creative idea produce more or less response than the previous treatment?

Testing is a crucial part of any major direct marketing campaign, though of course not all tests will produce a positive result. However, a well-planned test programme will generally produce enough information to enable you to more than recover your investment over the longer term. Typically one test in four produces a new 'winner'.

So if you have a mailing list of 200,000 and try four new approaches against your control as follows:

Five samples of 10,000 = 50,000 names used. You will receive a different result from each test but normally one will be better than the others. You roll this out to the balance of 150,000 names and a total of 160,000 of the 200,000 get your best pack.

And even if several new ideas do not produce better results than your old faithful at least you have the satisfaction of knowing that your existing advertising is as effective as you can make it.

A word of caution

Testing is not an exact science but deals in probabilities. The rules of statistics are not exact so it is necessary to understand how to read a test result and how confident you can be in applying your findings to future activities. We will return to this point later in this chapter.

Test objectives

The purpose of testing is to enable the direct marketer to reduce risk by restricting the amount of budget exposed until alternatives have been evaluated. Many companies manage to trade very profitably without testing but this does not disprove the case.

Who is to say that they could not produce even better results? It is not unusual for one variant in a test to produce dramatically more response than another, which appears to be equally good.

EXAMPLE

A UK publisher offered the same subscription incentive for five years and was quite satisfied with the results of his advertising.

His marketing consultant eventually persuaded him to test an alternative incentive that produced 100 per cent more subscriptions.

If he had done this test five years earlier and got the same result his advertising would have been twice as effective – and he would have been even richer!

What can we test?
- Media type
- Medium
- Position
- Timing and frequency
- Size
- Offer
- Creative treatment
- Response methods

Testing media types

Here we will be evaluating the use of offline advertising versus online; press advertising against DRTV; email versus direct mail and so on. To get a definitive result we may need to run several advertisements and accumulate the data. We will typically be looking to judge the amount of business generated by each media type for a fixed budget. We will try to keep the messages as similar as possible to reduce the amount of bias inherent in such test.

Testing an individual medium

In this case we will have decided on our broad media type and now need to decide between, for example, the *Daily Mail* and the *Daily Express*, daily papers versus Sundays, terrestrial TV versus satellite, two or more rented mailing or email lists and so on. Or we may wish to test alternative sites for banners or some form of behavioural placement.

This sort of testing is quite common and although we will not always obtain a totally reliable comparison from a single test*, we can easily compare the cost per enquiry; conversion rate; cost per order and so on.

Supposing our press advertisement produces customers more cost effectively than our DRTV. Does this mean we should in future place our entire budget in press? It may do, but before we make such a decision we should examine the test scenario very carefully.

We may then find that on the day we ran our test, advertising an investment product, the newspaper ran an article commenting very favourably on such products, while the television station ran a programme 'exposing' a company for misleading customers while selling a similar product. These would certainly affect response in both media and could present us with a highly misleading result.

If in any doubt about a bias affecting one or both halves of the test it is advisable to re-test at a later date. If both results show the same pattern you can feel more confident in making your decision.

This is less of a problem when testing two alternative rented mailing lists as your mailing will be in a 'semi-solus' position. You cannot guarantee that the individual mailed will not receive a competitive mailing on the same day but you can be fairly certain that the same mailing list will not have been mailed with a competitive product. A good list owner or broker will make sure this does not happen.

Testing position

In newspapers and magazines this relates to whether we go early (front of publication) or late (back of publication); or perhaps to evaluation of special positions such as front page, football results page, television programmes, alongside the crossword, readers' letters page and so on.

Testing positions within the same publication can be quite complicated, as it generally requires a 'partner'. We cannot simply run an ad on the front cover this week and the same ad on the sports page next week and expect the comparison to be meaningful. There could be a number of factors affecting the validity of such a test:

- **Competition** A major competitor may advertise in the same paper on one of our test days, which could seriously affect our response.
- **Importance of the news** If a major crisis breaks on the day our ad appears this is likely to affect response.

Nor can we simply run both ads in the same paper on the same day; this would produce another set of problems. Even though we could put different response codes on each we could not be sure

---

* The reason for this is that we do not have control over the surrounding material, i.e. other advertisers appearing at the same time; gravity of news appearing at the same time and so on. Thus we must be careful not to make major decisions based on a single test result, especially where we are testing two different media.

that a response was solely attributable to the particular ad carrying the reply code.

What if someone saw both ads and of course only responded to one? What if seeing both ads stimulated more people than normal to respond - this would be quite probable.

How can we avoid these problems? The first thing we need to do is make sure that the publication in question takes A/B split-runs. (Split-runs are explained in detail on pages 352–3)

We could then set up a split-run 'cross-over' test with a 'partner' advertiser who takes the other half of the test. It works like this:

We buy two split-runs on the same day, one on the front page and the other on the sports page. On the front-page split we may take the A half with our partner taking B. On the later page we will run our same advertisement in the B half with our partner placing his in the A position. In this way we can test each position without any bias creeping in from people seeing both ads in the same copy of the paper.

A word of warning – with this technique, only half of the newspaper readers will see each advertisement. This will reduce the response to each half of the test by around 50 per cent, which is no problem if the responses are large but you must be sure that the response figures are statistically significant i.e. large enough to enable a valid comparison between the two advertisements. (Statistical validity is explained on pages 360–9.)

Testing timing   Many advertisers find that results from daily newspapers vary according to the day of the week on which their advertisement appears. Others find that advertisements which run in March, say, are more cost-effective than those appearing in May.

There are additional timing considerations in broadcast advertising. Here we may also be selecting breaks within specific programmes or at least time segments which promise to deliver a certain type of audience. We could for example set up a test to compare off-peak versus peak time, running the same commercial in the middle of the afternoon and during 'Coronation Street'.

The cost and response calculations will then be done to identify the most-cost-efficient time for future exposure. Remember statistical validity may require you to run this test more than once, especially to get a reliable reading on the off-peak slot.

Testing frequency   The traditional awareness advertiser seeks to maximise impact by running multiple insertions in a very short space of time. Based on readership data and 'opportunities to see', this theoretically optimises the media spend.

The objective of the traditional media planners is thus to achieve maximum coverage as rapidly as possible. This means that high audience duplication across media, and rapid repetition in the same medium are considered to be beneficial.

A direct marketer has a totally different approach, mainly driven by knowledge of what happens to responses if there is too much duplication or too rapid repetition.

When, through our direct response mechanisms, we are able to measure the effectiveness of **each individual appearance** of an advertisement we find that, if we run an ad too frequently, each successive insertion is slightly less efficient that its predecessor.

The time gap between insertions is critical. If we repeat the same advertisement in the same publication with too short a gap our response will decline rapidly. The optimum length of gap can only be determined by testing but it would typically be a minimum of three weeks in a national daily paper.

We also see a marked fall-off in response when the same advertisement appears at the same time in two publications that have a high cross-over of readership. For example if we ran an advertisement on a Saturday in the *Daily Mail* and then repeated the same ad the following day in the *Mail on Sunday* it would not be surprising to see a lower than expected response from the Sunday insertion.

Testing size   Although traditional media planners try to dominate a page or publication with large advertisements, the precise measurability of direct marketing tells us that cost-efficient response is easier to achieve with small spaces.

You may remember Sainsbury's Square Root Principle from Chapter 9. Some years ago Philip Sainsbury of the London School of Economics, analysed the results of hundreds of direct response advertisements and came up with his 'Square Root Principle'. Sainsbury identified that advertisement response does not increase in proportion to an increase in size but merely by the square root of the increase.

Thus, if an advertisement is doubled in size (x2) the increase in response will be approximately 41 per cent (the square root of 2 is 1.41).

Theoretically, if a full page produces 100 replies a half page should produce 50, a quarter 25 and of course a double page spread 200 replies.

What Sainsbury's research showed was that **smaller spaces were progressively more cost-efficient and larger spaces progressively less cost-efficient.**

The actual numbers were: ¼ page: 41 replies
                            ½ page: 71 replies
                            Full page: 100 replies
                            Double Page: 141 replies

> So if cost-efficient response is your main consideration the smaller the space you can fit the whole story into, the more effectively you are spending your budget.

The problem of size tests

Testing the size of advertisements can be even more complicated than testing position. In order to test a full page against a half page for instance one would have to buy a full page split run and make up, or persuade the publication to find, some additional editorial, running the test as follows:

```
┌─────────────────┐      ┌─────────────────┐
│                 │      │ Special editorial │
│   Full-page     │      │      here        │
│ advertisement   │      ├─────────────────┤
│    here in      │      │                  │
│   the A half    │      │  Half-page ad    │
│  of the split   │      │  here in B half  │
│                 │      │                  │
└─────────────────┘      └─────────────────┘
```

As an alternative to producing special editorial some companies trying this test find a partner advertiser, often a sister brand, to take up the spare half page.

Having pointed out the difficulty of such a test, it may well be worthwhile. According to Philip Sainsbury's research we would expect to achieve 71 replies from the half page for every 100 we received from the full page. Therefore if we can buy a half page for less than 70 per cent of the cost of a full page we should find the half page more cost-efficient.

This same technique could be used to test any combination of sizes, though the smaller the size the more difficult, or expensive, it would be to persuade the publisher to cooperate. Remember that there will come a point when the space is too small to contain your entire message comfortably – changing the content of the message is highly likely to invalidate the test.

Testing offers and creative – these aspects have been covered in Chapters 12 and 13.

Testing response methods – tests can be set up to measure the effectiveness of reply coupons versus telephone numbers versus fax numbers versus email and web addresses. You can measure the effect of paying the reply postage or telephone charges, and, in direct mail where a form has to be returned, such as when applying for a credit card, the effectiveness of pre-printing the addressee's name on the response form.

The hierarchy of testing

There is no use spending time on tuning up our creative treatment, nor the mechanics of obtaining a reply, until we have targeted the right person; decided on the most relevant offer or message for that person; and identified the right time to approach them.

Once we have these elements in place we can start to tune up the performance of our advertisements and mailings through creative development and response devices.

While considering hierarchy we should heed the advice of the late, great direct marketing guru Bob Stone, who recommended 'Test only the big things'. So what are the 'big things'?

Testing Bob Stone's 'big things'

There have been many studies over the past 60 years and whilst relative weightings have varied they have generally agreed on the ideal hierarchy:

1. Targeting – medium or list – to repeat, once the product is as good as we can make it the main requirements are to contact the right person, with the right message, at the right time.

2. Offer or key benefit statement – this key benefit message can be reinforced with promotional offers where relevant. Offers were discussed in detail in Chapter 12. And remember, this benefit may vary for different segments of your target audience.

3. Timing – understanding the decision-making and buying processes of your prospects is a crucial part of marketing planning.

4. Creative approach – although only fourth in the list this does not mean creative work is not important; simply that until the first three elements are in place creative is irrelevant. No matter how good or exciting your creative may be, it will not work unless it reaches a genuine prospect. However, once you have made the effort to identify the three elements it is prudent to assume that your competitors have done the same. So in the worst case your prospect could be comparing two similar approaches at the same time. In these circumstances the one that is explained most clearly and presented most attractively will win the order. **At this point creative becomes all-important.**

5. Response devices – some marketers tend to offer only one or two response methods but experienced direct response advertisers offer as many as they can. Although today many respondents use the website there are still lots of people out there who prefer to telephone, email, post or even fax their replies. Some feel that posted coupon response is not worth including but recent experience is that the percentage of response coming by post is increasing. We are not sure why this is so but perhaps with the increasing concerns over identity theft, some people are nervous or suspicious of giving their details online or by telephone.

How does testing work?

Let's start with A/B split-runs in newspapers and magazines

A number of publications offer the facility of split-run testing. Many newspapers and magazines are printed on very large cylinders, so large in fact that two copies of the publication are printed simultaneously side by side.

If an advertiser wishes to test two alternative creative treatments these can be placed one on either side of the printing drum as in the example below.

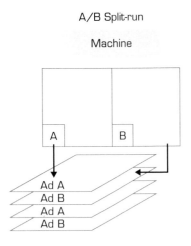

A/B Split-run

Machine

A   B

Ad A
Ad B
Ad A
Ad B

As the printed paper comes off the end of the press it is cut in half so that the individual copies can be folded and assembled. This process finishes with alternative copies being stacked one above the other on a pile.

The finished 'ream' thus contains precisely the same number of copies carrying each alternative advertisement, so that in a pile of 500 papers every alternate copy would carry either advertisement A or advertisement B.

This process is called an A/B split-run (or A/B split).

> What if our test does not produce a 'winner' but merely another advertisement that produced the same response as control?

In one sense such an advertisement could be termed a 'winner', despite only producing the same response as our existing ad. We said earlier that if we run the same advertisement too frequently our response will show a marked decline. Having an alternative but equally strong ad enables us to shorten the gap without paying such a high penalty in lost responses.

Furthermore, having a second equally good advertisement is like an insurance policy. No advertisement continues to work indefinitely, sooner or later it will become 'tired' and response will fall. Our second, newer advertisement will often continue to pull responses at the original level for some time to come, giving us time to run another test programme to find another reliable alternative. We may also find that the original advertisement will start to work well again after a rest.

What we can learn from studying A/B splits

Even when they are not running their own tests, all serious direct marketers should check newspapers regularly to find A/B splits. They are easy to find because at the top of the page there will be a very small letter A or B. You then have to look through the next few papers on the stack to find the alternative ad. What can this tell you? Well firstly that this advertiser is testing something. Comparison of the ads will quickly make the variable clear. But that's just the start.

If you check that newspaper for the next couple of weeks you will find either:

1. One of the two tested ads is now being run on its own – that was the winner, or
2. The same test is repeated – in which case either the responses were too small to give a statistically significant result, or something went wrong with the test.

In the first case you have learned something that may be very useful. In the second you have to persevere until the result becomes clear.

Testing with loose inserts

One thing we may wish to evaluate is the performance of display advertising compared to loose inserts. Note that we would not simply compare on a single measure such as cost per reply as this could lead us to some dangerous conclusions.

For example, it is generally accepted amongst direct marketers that loose inserts produce considerably more response than display advertisements in the same medium. However, it is also quite common for conversion rates to be lower with inserts. We must therefore continue to measure performance after the initial enquiry is generated.

> Apart from comparing inserts with display advertising, loose inserts offer a number of benefits for testing offers, creative approaches and even individual media.

Some benefits of testing with inserts

Although there are some variations in response patterns compared to display advertising, loose inserts are a very valuable test medium. Among the benefits we find:

- **Power** – an insert can easily produce three or five times as much response as a colour page advertisement in the same publication.
- **Flexibility** – the big advantage of inserts is that they are loose. This means firstly, that they do not all have to be the same, and secondly that you do not have to place one in every copy of the publication. This gives you flexibility in several ways:
  - **Design** – you could vary your design thus testing a variety of creative and offer treatments simultaneously. For example, in a magazine with a circulation of 1,000,000, you could try four alternative inserts, each to 250,000. These could be randomised across the circulation to avoid geographical bias.
  - **Distribution** – you could insert in only a proportion of the circulation. So you could place your inserts in only the subscription copies, or only the newsstand copies enabling a targeted message, such as a subscription offer to that segment of the readership for whom it would be relevant.

Another use of this facility would be with a multinational publication, so you could choose to insert in only the UK editions, or perhaps vary the language of your message for each country.

- **Targeting** – many local newspapers and freesheets take loose inserts at quite low rates, and this enables you to target even local promotions. Some national newspapers allow you to insert down to the level of a local wholesaler. This could be very interesting for a local business as the leaflet would carry the cachet of arriving inside a national newspaper whilst you would only have to pay for a local campaign. You would need to get your media buyers to identify which papers offer this as inserting contracts are renewed periodically and so precise arrangements may change.

Note: please refer to the section on statistical significance before attempting to evaluate tests with such local campaigns.

- **Size** – there are few limits on space. You can insert anything from a single A5 leaflet to a 64-page catalogue. The greater the weight the more you pay but even an 8 page leaflet can carry a lot more copy than a single-page advertisement.

Note – each publication has its own rules regarding weight, size, folds etc. You or your media specialists must talk to each before finalising your design. Remember that not all publications will accept loose inserts.

Direct mail and email testing

This can be very reliable because you can:

- select precisely matched test cells from a list;
- ensure that the quantities and the timing are precisely controlled;
- vary the length, size, design, etc. of your communications.

You can also vary your message:

- by segment (perhaps making one offer to people living in detached houses and another to those living in flats);
- by individual (by, say, varying the copy according to whether you are communicating with a company chairman or a shop assistant). This is not a matter of snobbery or discrimination, it simply makes sense to talk to people in the language they would use themselves.

How online testing can help

There are two online methods that can save time and money in advance of carrying out a major test.

Email subject lines

One of the best and quickest ways of testing a simple headline statement is to run a test of emails with alternative subject lines. This must be run under normal test conditions, i.e. both halves of the test must be sent simultaneously and the samples must be randomised to avoid any bias. Within hours of the emails being sent we can compare the response rates in terms of opening or click-through statistics. If all we are testing is which headline most attracts prospects we can proceed rapidly with an email roll out or finalise a larger test with a press ad or a direct mailing.

We may want to measure in a little more detail by waiting to measure quality through conversion rates or perhaps length of time spent on our website. Nevertheless this is a very good and quick way to measure a simple proposition.

Pay-per-click advertising (PPC) such as Google AdWords

This is another excellent test bed before campaigns are extended into more expensive channels. We can test offer, price, copy (tone of voice), whether featuring the brand name makes a difference and so on. Many major marketers use this technique and again it delivers very quick answers to important pre-test questions. PPC can also be useful in identifying the ideal keywords to improve your natural search listings.

Tracking the response

Electronic media gives you the ability to track an immense amount of information, and integrated techniques can be added to the core message to gain more detail on respondents. This might be done by inviting respondents to visit a unique entry page and then calculating the response rate. For instance, prospects could be given the opportunity to enter a competition based around the organisation's products. Alternatively you can use trackable email broadcasting systems or ad-tracking systems.

Legislation in 2003 shaped the context within which e-marketers can speak to customers and prospects. This has been mirrored by a growing receptiveness of consumers and business professionals to email messaging, and house email files continue to grow at great pace. The costs of managing email communications has dropped and sophisticated Web-based technologies bring advanced email techniques within reach of all marketers. Indeed, with its relatively low costs of production and high levels of personalisation, email is recognised by many as one of the most powerful direct marketing techniques.

However, because it is so inexpensive it is in danger of being overused. Indeed, in 2009, one office products company found they were getting higher responses to fax than to email. As with all communications, relevance is the key and if customers and prospects are receiving communications they find interesting the problem will not be too serious.

Traditional direct marketers find testing through email offers numerous advantages: testing is fast – the testing phase can be as short as a few days, or even a few hours for specific kinds of testing. Immediate response and real-time reporting tools make this pace of activity possible.

Roll-out is very fast – once a winning element has been identified this can be used swiftly, (many platforms broadcasting at over one million messages per hour) with none of the production lead times associated with offline campaigns.

Testing is cheap – the complexities of constructing test matrices and message design may be the same as offline, but the 'make-ready' and broadcast costs run to a few pence per message.

As the table below shows, email marketers are now able to set up a range of tests to deliver greater performance at every stage of an email marketing campaign:

Issue	Possible reason	Options
High 'hard bounce' rates	Broadcaster blacklisted with ISPs	Use alternative broadcasters
High 'soft bounce' rates	HTML formats?	Test text only versions to high bounce domains
Low open rate	Lack of engagement	Test alternative subject lines and 'from' fields
Low click-through rate	Offer not sufficiently compelling	Test new offers
High unsubscribe rate	Over-mailing?	Test lower frequency despatches
Low conversion rates	Over-promise of benefits?	Test less promotional copy

Note: although many test programmes concentrate on new business activities, e.g. lead generation and conversion activities, they are not restricted to these areas. It is just as important to test alternative approaches to existing customers. In many cases the payback from a successful test to customers will be much higher.

An important reminder

When we first get involved in the excitement of running and evaluating tests it is easy to become 'test-happy'. We can get carried away by raw response statistics and take our eye off the main aim which is to develop profitable long term business. Response evaluation is only the beginning – the true measure is the long-term quality of the business generated by the activity.

Developing a test programme

Let's now examine the procedure for designing, implementing and measuring tests.

1. **Establish your control** (the base or 'yardstick' against which your new ideas will be measured). A control is your best-performing existing package, insert or advertisement (or at the least, one that you know has worked previously to this market segment). It is the approach you would choose to run if you were unable to test alternatives. If you are new to the market and simply trying to find a cost-efficient way of attracting business, you will not have a control.

2. **Decide what to test**

   There are numerous possibilities but as discussed earlier your test priorities should be worked out according to the hierarchy on pages 351–2.

   Analysis of previous results (if applicable) will help you decide which of the potential new tests look the most promising.

   It helps to verbalise your test strategy like the one below. This will have many uses including briefing, (creative people, mailing houses and internal colleagues), estimating costs and obtaining quotations. It is also a useful matrix for developing an evaluation report.

   Here's an example of a test strategy for a direct mail campaign.

ACQUISITION TEST STRATEGY

Project: Spring 2011 new customer recruitment mailing campaign
Issued: 4 August 2010
Control: C5 window envelope, two-page letter, standard brochure – phone, post and website response options.

Test	Objectives	Method
1. Format test: DL vs C5 envelope	Achieve same response at lower cost	Internal elements same as control, folded to DL size
2. Free gift offer included, low-key presentation	Improve response by offering free gift. No change to basic tone and structure of control pack	Mention free gift in the letter copy and the PS
3. Free gift offer included, with heavy emphasis	Improve response by featuring free gift heavily throughout pack	Separate four-colour gift 'flyer'; refer to gift in letter copy and PS; show in order section
4. New creative approach – larger (C4) envelope	Achieve a 'breakthrough' against control	New design to be briefed and discussed

Testing mailing and email lists

Where several are available, your test strategy should also include the testing of lists. Equally sized randomised samples of each list should be mailed **with the identical pack or email**. This is very important, because mixing alternative creative themes or presentations within a list test would leave you without a readable result.

Isolate the variables

Any segment of a test can incorporate any number of variables but **if we want to measure a specific factor we must make sure that no more than one variable appears in any single test cell.**

For example, let's refer back to our Acquisition Test Strategy. In evaluating tests 1, 2 and 3, assuming that our list cells have been produced correctly, we will know that any changes in response are the results of the individual changes made to the packs. The objective for Test 1 is not an increase in response of course, but if we can attain the same response with the cheaper pack this will in itself make a significant contribution to the cost-efficiency of future campaigns.

Tests 2 and 3 are intended to increase response over control and if this happens we can say with confidence that it is due to the free gift. Comparing Tests 2 and 3 will enable us to judge the desirable level of promotion of free gifts in future.

However, when we compare the results of Test 4 with Control, we will know only the performance of the overall pack and not which element of the pack is responsible for the change. Was it the larger envelope, the fact that we had a message on it, the longer letter, or a more effective free gift? We will not be able to judge this and thus cannot apply this detailed learning to our other packs. It is still a worthwhile test as many breakthroughs in results have come about through trying totally new approaches. If such a test works well for you can start to fine tune the individual elements in future tests.

Testing requires common sense as well as science

A good general rule is to isolate variables where you can, bearing in mind your budget and the facilities available. You cannot carry out multi-cell testing if the total universe numbers 5,000 names. Nor can you use split-runs if the publications you want to test do not accept them.

The statistics of testing

Note the formulae demonstrated in following section on evaluating statistical significance apply only when we know the precise sample size and when the response rate (per cent) is greater than 0.1 per cent. So they are really only used with targeted addressed communications such as mailings and emails.

There is another method used for press, TV, online advertising and door-to-door distributions and this will be explained later.

Sample sizes

As mentioned earlier, testing is designed to help you make sound judgments, but it is not an exact science. Test results will help you reduce risk by following the route that offers the **greatest probability of success**.

The word 'probability' is very important – no test result can offer a guarantee that when repeated the same activity will produce the same result. It is therefore necessary for you to understand a little about statistics. This is so that:

- **You will know how many people you need to mail in order for a test result to be 'significant', and thus be a reliable predictor of what will happen when you 'roll-out' the chosen mailing to the full list.**
- **You will be able to decide, after the event, whether a particular test result can be relied upon i.e. if it is a 'significant' result.**

Direct mail and email tests are conducted on samples from the various lists available. For comparative tests to be reliable you must ensure that you are testing like with like, in other words the samples used for each test cell must be:

- **Matched with each other in terms of composition and characteristics.**
- **The same size, or at least each of a known size so that you can allow for size variances in evaluation.**
- **Randomised, so that they are entirely typical of the universe they represent, and so that you can predict the eventual performance of a roll-out from the test data.**
- **Large enough to give a statistically significant number of responses.**

Randomisation

To ensure that samples are truly representative of their total 'universe', they would typically be chosen on a systematic basis, i.e. 1 in 'n' samples. (For example, to select a sample of 10,000 names from a list of 300,000 you would instruct the computer to select every 30th name to ensure randomisation across the list and eliminating bias caused by keeping the list in chronological or geographical order.)

Note: Randomisation is a very important point. The simplest and quickest way of extracting 10,000 names from a list of 300,000 would be to take the first 10,000 records. If you used this method with a list held in chronological order, you would extract the 10,000 newest or oldest names, which would not be typical of the list as a whole.

There are three basic statistical concepts involved in planning tests:

1. **Confidence level** This is the number of times out of 100 that one could expect the test result to be repeated in a 'roll-out' – the levels commonly used in direct marketing testing are between 80 per cent and 95 per cent.
2. **Limit of error** Statistics is not an exact science and every test result is subject to a plus or minus correction according to sample size and response level.

3. **Significance** This means simply, is the difference observed sufficiently large for it to be outside the variances expected due to the limits of error? If the answer is 'yes' the result is significant, if 'no' it is not significant.

Selecting samples for testing

The minimum sample size will vary according to how precise you want the results to be.

As we said above, testing relies on the laws of statistics and these are not exact. In order to be able to 'read' a test result with confidence we need at least a basic knowledge of how statistics work.

Our first consideration is **confidence level** (also called **reliability**), i.e. how confident do we need to be in the answer. We generally work to a confidence level of between 80 per cent and 95 per cent. In other words, what we have experienced in the test is likely to happen when we roll out to the larger list eight times out of 10 (80 per cent confidence level) or 19 times out of 20 (95 per cent confidence level).

Note the use of the phrase 'likely to happen'. Even after our test we are only able to say what is **probable**, thus confidence level is sometimes also referred to as probability or **significance level,** e.g. 80 per cent or 95 per cent probability or significance.

Next we have to consider **error tolerance**. This is the allowable error – a plus or minus amount we have to allow when reading our test results. In other words, again because of the imprecision of statistical laws, a 2 per cent response to a test cannot be taken as exactly 2 per cent, but as 2 per cent + or –, an amount which is determined by the number of responses we have received. This is a simple function of the number of names we have mailed multiplied by the response rate.

What this means in general is that the more names we mail in our test sample, the more we can rely on the result.

Before we look at a few examples we need to consider the formula for calculating sample size, error tolerance and reliability of results.

Let's start with sample size and this will lead into the other things. First of all, let's dispel a couple of myths. It is not unusual to hear experienced marketers say statements such as:

'You should always test 10 per cent of the list.'

'I never use test cells of fewer than 15,000 names.'

The first statement is clearly nonsense; the second can often be wasteful – though as we shall see, such an approach may sometimes be prudent.

There is a formula for calculating sample size, or if we know the sample sizes and the response rate, for determining the error tolerance we need to apply for any given degree of reliability.

It enables us to:
1. **Decide on an appropriate sample size for our test.**
2. **Evaluate a result in retrospect and decide how reliable a test actually is.**
3. **Predict the range of response we can expect if we roll out the test to the larger list of which our test sample is truly representative.**

To use the formula for calculating sample size you need to have an idea of the likely response you are expecting and the degree of error allowance you are prepared to tolerate. While this may seem onerous, you would not really wish to embark on a mailing, even a test mailing, without some idea of what sort of response you expected.

The formula is:

$$\textit{Sample size} \quad = \quad \frac{\textit{(confidence level)}^2 \textit{ x expected response x non-response}}{\textit{(error tolerance)}^2}$$

Confidence level is expressed in standard deviations, e.g.

99 per cent confidence = 2.58 standard deviations
95 per cent confidence = 1.96
90 per cent confidence = 1.65
85 per cent confidence = 1.44
80 per cent confidence = 1.28

Expected response and non-response are simple percentages, e.g. 2.5 per cent expressed as 2.5; 97.5 per cent expressed as 97.5.

Error tolerance is the +/- amount you are prepared to accept – e.g. 0.5 per cent (0.5).

We must remember that the formula gives us error tolerance2 (ET2) so having arrived at this figure we hit the square root button on the calculator to find the final error tolerance figure.

In marketing we normally work to either 90 per cent or 80 per cent confidence, though statisticians like to be more precise preferring 95 per cent or even 99 per cent confidence – they do not have to pay for the names, of course!

Now we will demonstrate how this process works

Let's take a sample size of 5,000 names and a response rate of 2 per cent. What does the formula tell us about this result? Well if we want to be confident that the result will be repeated nine times out of 10 (90 per cent confidence level) the formula gives us:

$$5{,}000 \quad = \quad \frac{(1.65 \text{ x } 1.65) \text{ x } 2 \text{ x } 98}{(\text{error tolerance})^2}$$

1.65 x 1.65 x 2 x 98 = 533.61

Thus, reversing our equation:
(error tolerance)^2 = 533.61 / 5,000 = 0.106722

The square root of 0.106722 is 0.3266833

Thus our error tolerance in this case is 0.33 per cent

This means that our test that produced a 2 per cent response, can be relied upon to deliver somewhere between 1.67 per cent and 2.33 per cent when rolled out – 90 per cent of the time.

If we wanted to have 95 per cent confidence then the calculation would be:

$$ET2 \quad = \quad \frac{(1.96 \times 1.96) \times 2 \times 98}{5,000}$$

Thus: ET2 is 0.1505907 so ET is 0.39 (0.3880601)

As we can see, the requirement for greater confidence increases the possible range of responses on roll out to: 1.61 per cent at worst to 2.39 per cent at best, but we can feel confident that our roll-out will be within this wider range 19 times out of 20.

So far, so good. If 1.61 per cent is sufficient to give us an acceptable business result we can confidently proceed with the roll-out.

Now let's use the same formula to select an appropriate sample size.

We estimate the likely response we are expecting and the degree of error allowance we are prepared to tolerate. So here we say 'expected response' as we are guessing in this case.

Just to repeat, the formula is:

$$Sample\ size = \frac{(confidence\ level)2 \times expected\ response \times non\text{-}response}{(error\ tolerance)^2}$$

So, allowing for **90 per cent probability**, if we anticipate a **response of 2.5 per cent** and we want to try to keep the **error tolerance** fairly small, let's say no more than **0.25 per cent**, we see the following:

$$\frac{(1.65 \times 1.65) \times 2.5 \times 97.5}{(0.25 \times 0.25)} \quad = Sample\ size$$

This gives: 663.609375 divided by 0.0625 = 10,617.75 – a required sample size of, say, 10,625. Clearly, with such stringent requirements, if we want to test several things we will soon run up a very large bill.

What can we do to reduce the sample sizes and the cost?

We can consider our significance level. We have worked to 90 per cent (nine times out of 10); what would happen if we were prepared to accept an 80 per cent probability level? Let's work out the numbers:

80 per cent significance level

$$\frac{1.28 \times 1.28 \times 2.5 \times 97.5}{0.25 \times 0.25}$$

This reduces the sample size to 6,389.76, or rounded up to 6,400.

What else could we do? Let's say we are prepared to go to a 0.5 per cent error tolerance. What difference does this make to the sample size?

$$\frac{1.28 \times 1.28 \times 2.5 \times 97.5}{0.5 \times 0.5}$$

That's better; our sample size now reduces to a mere 1,597.44, rounded up to 1,600. Bear in mind here that all we would be able to predict from a 2.5 per cent response from a sample of 1,600 names is that the roll-out will produce somewhere between 2.0 per cent and 3.0 per cent, eight times out of 10.

The law of averages

Some marketers (though not qualified statisticians) argue that allowing for the 'law of averages', an 80 per cent confidence level could be taken as 90 per cent given the following scenario:

80 per cent confidence means that during roll-out:

Eight times out of 10 the response rate will be within the range defined by the +/- error limit.

Once out of 10 there will be a lower response rate.

Once out of 10 there will be a higher response rate.

In fact there is no 'law of averages' – the 'law of the inertia of large numbers' means that the above is possible but by no means a statistical probability, and we would need to carry out very many tests to expect an even spread above and below the expected range.

However, given that eight out of 10 probability is not bad odds and it is at least likely that some of the outliers will be above the range, eight out of 10 could reasonably be considered as eight +. So, if budgets are tight, or available numbers are small, you might be prepared to accept 80 per cent confidence for some of your test programmes.

Had enough of stats yet? Sorry, we have hardly started. All we have done so far is to show how confident we can be in evaluating or predicting a roll-out from a single test cell.

In many cases (probably most cases) we will want to compare two or more results against a control. And when comparing results with each other we use a different formula.

Here we may want to see whether a 2.5 per cent test result is actually significantly better than a 2.0 per cent control. On the face of it, the test has out-performed the control by 25 per cent, which sounds great. But it really does depend on whether the samples are large enough to allow the result to stand once we have taken allowable error into account.

In this case we use a formula that predicts the *probable difference* between two results according to the expected variation brought about by the imprecision of the laws of statistics. The formula predicts a 'normal' variation (or spread of responses) and we then see whether the gap between our two test cells exceeds this, if so the result can be relied upon, but if not – no result!

This formula is as follows:

$$\text{Expected difference} = \text{confidence level} \times \sqrt{\frac{r1\,(100 - r1)}{n1} + \frac{r2\,(100 - r2)}{n2}}$$

Where – confidence level is expressed as standard deviations (as before)
$r1$ = response to test cell 1 (per cent in decimal format)
$r2$ = response to test cell 2 (per cent in decimal format)
$n1$ = number mailed in test cell 1
$n2$ = number mailed in test cell 2

Now let's try this with the above test result, using samples of 5,000 per cell at a 90 per cent confidence level.

Sample 1 gets 2 per cent response
Sample 2 gets 2.5 per cent response

Expected difference is:

$$1.65 \times \sqrt{\frac{2 \times 98}{5,000} + \frac{2.5 \times 97.5}{5,000}}$$

So: 1.65 x square root of: (0.0392 + 0.04875)
i.e. 1.65 x square root of 0.08795 which is 0.2965636
So expected difference is: 1.65 x 0.2965636 = 0.4893299

Our expected difference is say 0.49
Our observed difference is 0.5 (2.0 per cent compared to 2.5 per cent)

The result is significant – **but only just.**

Another quick example:
Sample 1 gives 1 per cent response
Sample 2 gives 1.2 per cent
Sample size was 7,000 for each cell

So, expected difference is 1.65 x square root of

$$(1 \times 99 / 7,000) + (1.2 \times 98.8 / 7,000)$$

$$(0.0141428) + (0.0169371) = 0.0310799$$

Square root of this is 0.1762949 x 1.65 = 0.2908865

So, expected difference is 0.29
Observed (actual) difference is 0.2
This result is not significant

Alternatives to working with formulae

The easiest way to use these formulae is to input them into Excel. However, in order to give a simple demonstration the following tables are included:

Note: the tables are constructed using the formula shown earlier but if you work out some of these on your calculator you will find there are small differences in the numbers of sample sizes. This is simply because of rounding and does not affect their usability.

This first table is based on 90 per cent confidence level and shows required minimum sample sizes for range of responses from 0.5 per cent to 10 per cent, and a range of +/- error limits from 0.1 per cent to 1 per cent.

The key factor is that minimum sample size increases when we want smaller tolerances. For example, if we expect a 5 per cent response and are prepared to accept a result of 5 per cent + or – 0.5 per cent (i.e. our test can only be relied upon to produce between 4.5 per cent and 5.5 per cent when re-mailed) a sample size of 5,141 will be adequate. On the other hand, if we want the error limit to be halved to 0.25 per cent the minimum sample size must be four times as large (20,566).

Response %	Error tolerances @ 90% confidence level				
	0.1%	0.25%	0.50%	0.75%	1%
0.5%	13462	2154			
1.0%	26790	4286			
1.5%	39982	6397	1599		
2.0%	53038	8486	2122		
2.5%	65959	10553	2638	1173	660
3.0%	78745	12599	3150	1400	787
4.0%	103911	16626	4156	1847	1039
5.0%	128536	20566	5141	2285	1285
7.5%	187730	30037	7509	3337	1877
10.0%	243542	38967	9742	4330	2435

This second table is based on 80 per cent confidence

Response %	Error tolerances @ 80% confidence level				
	0.10%	0.25%	0.50%	0.75%	1%
0.5%	8151	1304			
1.0%	16220	2595			
1.5%	24207	3873	968		
2.0%	32113	5138	1285		
2.5%	39936	6390	1597		
3.0%	47677	7628	1907	848	
4.0%	62915	10066	2517	1118	
5.0%	77824	12452	3113	1384	
7.5%	113664	18186	4547	2021	1137
10.0%	147456	23593	5898	2621	1475

As we can see, being prepared to accept a lower confidence level makes required minimum sample sizes much smaller.

Let's look at a couple of examples to see how these tables can be used. For simplicity we will work these examples using only the 80 per cent confidence table.

Let's take a sample size of 5,000 names and a response rate of 2 per cent. What can we predict from this? Looking this up in the 80 per cent confidence table we see that a response rate of 2 per cent from a sample of 5,138 (the nearest number quoted to our sample size) means we have to allow for error tolerance of 0.25 per cent. **This means that our test that produced a 2 per cent response, can only be relied upon to deliver somewhere between 1.75 per cent and 2.25 per cent when repeated (or rolled out).**

Allowing for our 80 per cent confidence level we can say that when rolled out to the larger list (of which our sample was truly representative) we can expect a response rate of between 1.75 per cent to 2.25 per cent, eight times out of 10.

So far, so good. If 1.75 per cent is sufficient to give us an acceptable business result, we can confidently proceed with the roll-out. Now let's put some of this into practice with a few examples of test campaigns. Here's an example of a test matrix we might construct:

	Control Offer	Offer 2	Offer 3	Total
Control list	3,500	3,500	3,500	10,500
List B	3,500	3,500	3,500	10,500
List C	3,500	3,500	3,500	10,500
Total	10,500	10,500	10,500	31,500

What can we learn from such a test?

As we have seen, the sample sizes used here would enable us to compare list with list (across all offers) and offer with offer (across all lists) with a fair degree of confidence. Our total sample for each of these is 10,500 and at 2.5 per cent response this gives us an error tolerance of 0.25 per cent at 90 per cent confidence level, or 0.20 per cent at 80 per cent confidence level.

What we would really like to do is to compare what happened in each of the individual cells and if we do this we will find that the error tolerance will change because the sample sizes are smaller.

A response rate of 2.5 per cent to a sample of 3,500 requires an error tolerance of +/- 0.43 per cent at 90 per cent or 0.34 per cent at 80 per cent confidence level. This is not a problem in itself, but, as we have seen, it means that differences have to be larger to be significant.

Can we reduce test costs still further?

If we are prepared to take a slightly increased chance of our results not being totally reliable the easiest thing is to use a lower confidence (or significance) level. Let's take a look at another text matrix, this time using smaller samples:

	Control Offer	Offer 2	Offer 3	Total
Control list	1,300	1,300	1,300	3,900
List B	1.300	1.300	1.300	3,900
List C	1.300	1.300	1.300	3,900
Total	3.900	3.900	3.900	11,700

As before, this will probably tell us which list and which offer were more successful overall (2.5 per cent response from a sample size of 3,900 gives an error tolerance of 0.41 per cent at 90 per cent and 0.32 per cent at 80 per cent confidence level). Trying to compare individual cells at this level is not recommended. The error tolerance for samples of 1,300 at 2.5 per cent is huge (0.71 per cent at 90 per cent confidence, and 0.55 per cent at 80 per cent), making reliable comparisons difficult.

A few final comments
1. Test sample sizes are a matter for statistical calculation rather than guess work.
2. We can use the formula to select a suitable sample size and, in reverse, to assess the degree of reliability of any given test.
3. It is often easier to find a friendly marketing statistician than spend too much time learning and practising with formulae, although using the formulae in Excel makes it very easy.

Statistical significance with very small response rates or uncertain sample sizes
The formula for confidence level and error tolerance based on sample sizes does not work when we do not know the exact sample size nor any tests where response rate is lower than 0.1 per cent. So it is not used to evaluate split-runs in press advertising or inserts.

To evaluate a newspaper split-run test for example we use the chi-squared test. To apply this test we add up the total responses to both halves of the test (A + B). Then we take the larger of the two response numbers (A or B) and calculate what percentage that is of the total.

Significance factors in split-run testing – 90 per cent confidence level

Total Response i.e. A + B	Significance Factor (% for result to be significant	Winner	Loser	% Gain
100	60%	60	40	50%
200	57%	114	86	33%
400	55%	220	180	22%
600	54%	324	276	17%
1,000	53%	530	470	13%

First of all we can see that the greater the number of replies in total, the closer the difference can be between winner and loser. The numbers column 2 are the percentage of the total response that the more successful half of the split-run has to reach before we can be confident that the same ad would win nine times out of 10.

If our total response is 400, in order for us to be sure we have a 'winner' nine times out of 10 the winning ad must have achieved at least 220 replies (55 per cent of 400). These are not small differences; if the winner generates 220 of a total of 400 replies the loser must have achieved only 180. **Thus the winner shows a gain of 40 over 180 – a percentage increase of 22.2 per cent.**

With a total of only 100 responses the winner must receive at least 60 against 40 – an increase of 50 per cent.

A final word of caution
The numbers above represent the absolute minimum that a 'winner' must receive. Prudent marketers would re-run any split-run test where a marginal result occurred. A sensible rule of

thumb might be that unless you have a large number of responses, say at least 600, you should disregard (or at least repeat) any split-run tests where the difference between winner and loser is less than 25 per cent.

Don't stop monitoring

Measurement of response is only the start. You must continue to monitor the ongoing behaviour of respondents to ensure that an apparently successful new idea is not simply producing a large volume of poorly qualified enquiries.

SUMMARY

This chapter explored the central role of testing in direct marketing. While testing is carried on in mass marketing, the key strengths of direct marketing testing have always been that response can be tracked an individual event and that a far greater range of variables can be evaluated.

Today, however, we are finding that, unless a test is carried out in total isolation, it is increasingly difficult to attribute a response to its precise source. There are two main reasons why this is so.

Firstly we have found that multimedia campaigns are generally more productive and cost-effective than those confined to a single medium – hence although we can still track which medium has been used for the final response, we have no way of knowing how many of our other campaign elements have been seen by the respondent, nor indeed which triggered the final action. The choice of response medium might simply be convenience or personal preference.

The second reason is that however hard we try to get people to use our tracking codes, unique telephone numbers, specific Web landing pages and so on, many people on seeing our promotion go immediately to the website, using a search engine rather than the quoted URL, a) because they find that the most convenient way to gather further information, and b) because many Web users have come to expect special 'Web only' offers.

This means that to get a clear test result we have to ensure that any test must be isolated to a single medium.

Ongoing measurement of multimedia campaigns requires more complicated methods where we add or remove a single element from a region and then measure any change in the cumulative effect.

Despite the above, direct marketers still use testing as often as possible to help in creating cost effective campaigns. Testing does not eliminate risk but will reduce risk through the evaluation of alternatives. We saw that we can test a range of key variables these included:

- Media type
- Medium
- Position
- Timing
- Size
- Frequency
- Offer
- Creative treatment
- Response methods

We explored each of these in detail we saw that there is a standard hierarchy in testing and that this allows a logical sequence of testing activity.

We went on to explore the methods of testing in various media looking at:

- A/B split-runs in newspapers and magazines;
- testing with loose inserts – the several benefits here are that inserts are generally more responsive than advertisements; they are highly flexible in terms of design, distribution, targeting and size, part circulations can be bought enabling several media to be tested on a limited budget, and so on;
- we saw that testing in direct mail was also reliable due to the fact that we can select matched test cells for a list, quantity and timing can be controlled, and there is flexibility in length design and size of mailings;
- various online methods including testing of headlines using email subject lines, and simple copy variations using pay-per-click advertising.

We looked at the hierarchy of testing looking at the relative importance in order of testing:

- targeting – (the list or medium)
- the offer – (key benefit statement)
- timing
- creative
- response mechanics

We went on to explore the process of developing a test programme:

- Establish the control
- Decide what to test
- Set objectives
- Isolate variables
- Decide what methods
- Evaluate the test results

When managing the process we ensure that we are testing like with like. Samples must be:

- Matched in characteristics
- Of a known size
- Taken at random across a list through a 1 in 'n' selection
- Large enough to ensure statistical validity

We went on to explore the statistical basis of testing and looked at confidence levels, limits of error and significance.

The process of selecting a sample was explored in detail. We saw that sample size depended on the level of confidence and the limits of error acceptable in any results. We saw that it is not correct to say you should always test a certain percentage of a list or a certain number of names.

We looked at the formula required to calculate sample size. We saw that there were three key decisions to make:

1. What is the likely response?
2. What confidence level do we wish to work at?
3. What are the acceptable limits of error?

A worked example was provided for us that showed the impact on sample sizes of changing the tolerances we work to.

This section concluded with the use of tables to help us select a sample size and we worked through the implications for our business.

We went on to look at the measurement of difference between a two-cell test, and again a worked example was provided.

We finished the section with some important observations:

- test sample sizes must be statistically based;
- if we know likely response we can assess the suitable sample size and once we have response data we can assess the degree of reliability of any test;
- use a statistician if you are unsure;
- work with tables rather than formulae.

REVIEW QUESTIONS

1. Why is testing in direct marketing so important?
2. What is the most important factor to test?
3. At what level is media type testing evaluated?
4. What is the hierarchy of testing?
5. Name two types of online testing that give very quick results
6. Why are loose inserts a powerful testing medium?
7. Why are direct mail tests reliable?
8. What is a control?
9. What are the four requirements of a statistically valid test?
10. What are the three statistical concepts involved in planning tests?

EXERCISE

What is the formula for calculating sample size?

What is the sample size required when we anticipate 2 per cent response the acceptable limit of error is 0.5 per cent at a 95 per cent confidence level?

How does this change at 80 per cent confidence level?

See the appendix for details of how to download a useful Excel spreadsheet that will do these calculations for you.

CHAPTER 15
CLOSING THE LOOP – CUSTOMER SERVICE AND FULFILMENT OPERATIONS

IN THIS CHAPTER

We will examine the role of customer service and fulfilment operations, and consider the risks and rewards of outsourcing.

After reading this chapter you will:

- Understand the 'customer satisfaction trap'
- See why a customer's reasons for ending a relationship are often misunderstood
- Appreciate the value of customer complaints
- Be confident in finding and choosing external suppliers
- Be able to produce and deliver professional briefs for your suppliers

Specific topics include:

- Why customers leave – the corporate view and the customer view
- Why complaints should be welcomed
- The benefits of customer satisfaction surveys
- Hate sites and how to cope with them
- The vital role of customer service
- Outsourcing – risks and rewards
- Finding and choosing reliable suppliers
- When to use a consultant
- Effective briefing

INTRODUCTION

However good your product or service, and however effective your customer acquisition plans, your business will not survive today unless your fulfilment and customer service operations live up to your promises.

We have said a lot in earlier chapters about customer power, but it is worth repeating here because this is usually the point where the whole thing falls apart. It is no good striving to achieve 'customer satisfaction'. Customers expect that and a lot more:

The customer satisfaction trap – studies have shown:

Automotive – 85 per cent of customers said they were 'satisfied', but only 40 per cent of them re-purchased

Packaged goods – 66 per cent of people who identified a 'favourite brand' admitted to having bought a 'different brand' most recently

Business-to-business – 65 to 85 per cent of 'defectors' were found to be 'satisfied' or 'very satisfied' with their former supplier

> **'Customer delight' would not be too high an objective.**

Why do customers leave?

This study by the DMA and Future Foundation shows wide differences between the company view and the customer view.

Figure 15.1: Benefits – why customers leave

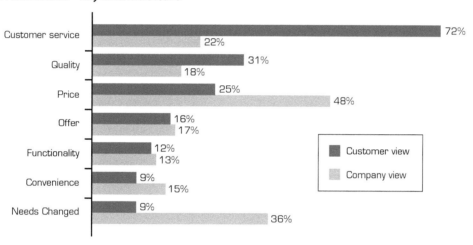

The two most important reasons in the view of the company were price and the fact that customers' needs had changed. **The most important factor to customers was customer service, followed by quality.**

Complaints – a source of free consultancy

One of the most successful customer service operations in recent years has been that of First Direct – the UK's first totally direct bank. Several years ago, the bank's marketing director said:

'We welcome complaints, they are a source of free consultancy, telling us where we are going wrong...'

First Direct is reported to have the highest percentage of new business through existing customer recommendations of any UK business.

Amazingly, some companies still try to make it difficult for customers to complain. If customers can't get satisfaction with an organisation, what do they do?

Before we answer that, let's consider how things used to be until we all had Internet access. Research in the 1990s told us:

91 per cent of unhappy customers will never return – resolve the problem fast and 85 per cent will buy again. (IBM)

Only one in 25 unhappy customers registers a complaint with the supplier – yet each unhappy customer will tell up to 17 others. Happy customers tell an average of only four people. (Nynex)

> Today the number of people who will hear of dissatisfaction is limitless – if a company offers poor customer service, and does not make it easy for customers to complain, they can face a nightmare scenario.

Companies must be aware of the growth of 'hate sites'. To experience a hate site simply search the Web with 'I hate (brand name)' and you will instantly find hundreds of sites and blogs telling all manner of horror stories from unhappy customers.

So today, forget the idea that an unhappy customer will tell 17 friends – how about eight million? To see this in action search YouTube for 'United Breaks Guitars', by May 2010 this customer-produced video and the several subsequent postings had been viewed on YouTube more than nine million times. It has also been featured on the Letterman show, thus reaching several million more viewers. By the time you read this, the total views will probably approach 20 million.

So, the first thing a company must do is listen. And listening can be very effective as the following example shows:

How Amazon went from hate to great

Launched in 1994, Amazon struggled to make money and in fact did not make a trading profit for ten years. In the battle for survival, especially through the dot.com burst of 2001, the organisation did not have customer service at the top of its priority list. Instead it was forced to focus on keeping its investors motivated.

If you search the Web for 'I hate Amazon' you will find many highly critical customer comments about appalling customer service, lost orders, payment problems, **and the difficulty of using the website.**

However, if you check the dates you'll find that most of these bad reviews are five or six years old. Clearly, once Amazon achieved stability they started listening closely to their customers and upped their game dramatically.

> Today if someone blogs a critical comment, their claims are immediately countered by messages of support from happy customers – this says a lot about Amazon's commitment to customers and its very well-designed website.

One common complaint among those old postings was that Amazon kept the customer service number hidden, so customers found it very difficult to make a phone complaint.

Today, after logging in a simple click on **'Help'** takes you to a page full of options, but the most prominent button is **Contact Us** – click on that and you are offered:

1. Email us with your query using this box, or click here...
2. ...enter your phone number and we will call you in the next few minutes. Alternatively, if you prefer to call us...
3. ...here's our toll free phone number – or, if you are out of the country here is an alternative number for you to call.

It would be very hard to fault this procedure.

Ask online shoppers what they like best about being an Amazon customer and you get a wide variety of answers such as:

'It's so easy to find what you want and then to order it with a single click.'

'Customer service is excellent and fast.'

'It's easy to return any product and they refund your payment quickly.'

'Even though you can sometimes find the same product a little cheaper elsewhere, Amazon shopping is so quick and easy I hardly ever comparison shop any more.'

'I recently ordered and paid for a pre-release DVD. The film duly arrived and then a week later I received an email from Amazon saying "We have discovered that this DVD is being sold in the high street for £5 less so we have today refunded your card account with £5".'

Don't make me think

In his excellent book *Don't Make Me Think!* Steve Krug cites Amazon.com as one of the easiest of all sites to use and to navigate through. (See the reading list in the appendix.) With the combination of their 'customer first' philosophy and their very easy and intuitive web site it is no wonder that Amazon customers stay loyal.

The role of the customer satisfaction survey

Many companies use customer satisfaction surveys (CSS) on a 'dipstick' basis, i.e. they sample only a small percentage of their customers and then construct tables showing trends in satisfaction levels.

This has its uses but is no substitute for asking every customer to complete one. They will not all do so but you can be sure that virtually all those who are unhappy will do so, and often before they had fired themselves up to make a complaint.

So the CSS is actually a powerful customer service weapon and a catch-all for dissatisfaction.

It is also an excellent source of testimonials. You should always include an open-ended question such as: 'Is there anything else you would like to say about us? Please tell us whether it is good or bad.' This will of course attract numerous complaints, but you need to know about those anyway. It will also (hopefully) produce some compliments. All you have to do then is ask for permission to use the quote as a testimonial. Most customers are happy to agree.

Note that such comments cannot be dealt with automatically so if you are planning to use automated analysis you will need to have any questionnaires with text in that field flagged for personal scrutiny.

Outsourcing – risks and rewards

There are numerous reasons why a company might consider outsourcing:

Volume – having insufficient resources to handle a one-off or occasional task – the response to a high-volume lead generation campaign for example.

Time – when a deadline is too short to permit the set-up of an internal resource.

Campaign-driven – when it would not be cost-effective to maintain a full-time unit for occasional activities.

Testing – establishing the case for an internal resource by running pilot schemes and measuring demand; or perhaps establishing demand in a new market before major investment.

Lack of specialist experience or knowledge – for example, sophisticated data mining and modelling are often best done by external specialists.

Free up internal resources – perhaps for a new development.

To save costs – it is often cheaper to use outside suppliers, but not always better!

What can be outsourced?

The simple answer is that almost anything can be outsourced, but some elements can only be outsourced with an element of risk.

Basic campaign tasks such as print, creative design, media buying and mailing house operations are outsourced safely and effectively by many organisations. Highly specialised functions such as market research, website design and sophisticated data analysis are often best managed by external suppliers.

These activities are typically project specific, start with a brief and can be monitored as they develop.

The problems generally arise when more sensitive areas such as call centres, customer services, delivery and distribution are concerned.

How easy to manage?

One useful check is to ask yourself how easy it will be to manage this process if it is remotely located.

Many organisations have been tempted to use offshore call centres because of the attractive costs. But costs have to be carefully balanced against quality of service and the potential loss of customers if satisfaction levels fall. It must be said that some of the complaints about overseas call centres were probably caused by xenophobia, but *perceptions* of poor quality still have to be dealt with.

It is no coincidence that many of the UK financial institutions that rushed to use offshore call centres have brought these back after experiencing problems. In fact this became such an issue that some banks started to feature that they used UK call centres as a major point in their advertisements.

Sometimes more complex functions survive better offshore

In contrast to some customer service experiences, technical help centres have operated effectively in this mode and this may well be because technical knowledge can easily be trained into highly educated people of any nationality whereas customer service operations require much broader knowledge of local conditions and idioms.

Furthermore, a technical help call is typically self-contained and does not require much involvement of other departments.

Where someone in a remote country is trying to sort out a problem of late or damaged delivery many more things can go wrong.

BPO and cloud computing

Although business services such as call centres, order processing and fulfilment and so on, have been outsourced for many years, a more recent development has been the outsourcing of entire IT requirements.

There are various names for these services such as:

- Business Process Outsourcing (BPO)
- Software as a Service (SaaS)
- Platform as a Service (PaaS)

Many of these services can be delivered over the Internet via Web browsers and in this context the Internet is known as the 'cloud'.

Be a mystery shopper

Every business tries to reduce its costs, but it is very important that the cost cutting does not result in a reduction in quality. As mentioned above, many outsourced customer service operations have been brought back in-house after generating a high level of complaints.

So, with any outsourced function, the internal manager must carry out regular anonymous checks to ensure quality of service.

Finding and choosing suppliers

We will now start to discuss some of the specialist resources that you may need and how you can go about finding them. Once you have found them you have to explain your needs very clearly – the more care given to this the better the job will turn out. Over many years of using specialist suppliers I have found that more often than not, when a job goes badly wrong, a good proportion of the blame lies with lax briefing.

Start outside, go in-house later

By using outside suppliers in the early stages of building a business you can learn many things, including how to avoid some costly mistakes. Once you have experienced a few campaigns you will be better able to estimate the cost and implications of providing such facilities in-house.

One advantage of using outside suppliers is that you can expect them to keep their equipment and expertise up to date. This may not be so vital in the case of an envelope-filling machine but can be crucial in the case of data analysis and modelling techniques.

What sort of suppliers are available?

There are many specialists but those most frequently required include:

- **Mailing and email list suppliers** – brokers/owners – discussed in Chapter 9
- **Mailing and fulfilment houses**
- **Email consolidators**
- **Data specialists**
- **Web consultants and site designers**
- **Online advertising and search specialists**
- **Printers and laser print specialists**
- **Direct marketing agencies, or freelance design and creative teams**
- **Marketing consultants**

Mailing house

An organisation that can carry out most or all of the functions involved in assembling and despatching a mailing. These typically include:

- receipt and storage of materials;
- assembly: folding, filling, sealing, sorting and bagging mail;
- addressing in a variety of ways: sticky labels to laser printing;
- letter and order form printing: often with laser addressing;
- liaison with and despatch to Royal Mail and other delivery services.

Fulfilment house

An organisation that can carry out all or most functions of a mail order company, such as:

- receipt of responses to promotions and mailings;
- despatch of ordered goods or information packs;
- receipt and storage of goods (including valuables);
- receipt and processing of mail orders;
- banking of customer remittances;
- picking, packing and despatch of goods;
- customer service functions often including helplines;
- reporting of orders, despatches, stock, banking etc.

Many companies offer all of the above facilities and several specialised add-ons such as database development, printing, plastic card embossing and so on.

It is important to shop around using the process described on pages 382 to 384. Once a short list is identified it is worth visiting a few to get a feel for their capabilities. Are they tidy or untidy? Is their security impressive? Can you speak to some of their existing clients?

The next step is to get a couple of quotations to help you choose. As with all suppliers beware of choosing solely on price. A few hundred pounds saved will not seem very good business if a vital part of the job is carried out badly.

Email consolidators

Do a similar job to a mailing house although none of the physical handling tasks are required. They will typically offer sophisticated online tracking tools as part of their service.

Data specialists

As mentioned in Chapter 5, external data specialists can take away a lot of the uncertainty of database development, especially for first timers. They are generally aware of state-of-the-art software and hardware and of the latest techniques in data processing, analysis and management.

And, because they have a range of clients with a variety of problems they have wider experience and can often develop a practical solution more quickly.

Some years ago, when computers were very expensive and difficult to manage, many companies outsourced their databases to computer bureaux. Although there are still some bureaux providing this service, the majority of databases are now held in-house.

However, data analysis specialists are still much in demand. They usually have up-to-date experience in sophisticated data analysis techniques. Such techniques develop almost daily and no in-house IT department could hope to stay totally up to date, so external specialists are often more capable of doing the job.

Web consultants and site designers

As we discussed in Chapter 2, the Internet has brought about many changes in the marketing landscape. And the changes continue. To keep up to date in this highly specialised field it is vital to find the right advice.

What you need is someone who understands the business applications of the Internet and can give you sound commercial advice. In this new field it is even more important to shop around and take up references before committing yourself to a major development.

A measure of the complexity of Web matters today is given by the 21 specialisms represented by the membership of the UK Internet Advertising Bureau (IAB) (www.iabuk.net), and the list of members of the Internet Service Providers Association (ISBA) (www.ispa.org.uk).

Website design is a topic in itself and apart from the advice in Chapter 2 you are again recommended to read *Don't Make Me Think!* by Steve Krug – see appendix for more details.

Online advertising and search specialists

We have discussed these experts in Chapter 2 and again in Chapter 10. A good place to start looking for one of these experts would be the IAB website, www.iabuk.net

Printing firms

If your only requirements are for simple colour leaflets, plain envelopes and single page non-personalised letters, you could choose almost any printer from the 'Yellow Pages' and get a good workmanlike job.

If, however, you want to take advantage of, or even simply find out about, the many specialised formats which have been developed by today's direct marketers, you must search a little more carefully.

There are thousands of printers in the UK but not all of them understand direct marketing. There are many with the right experience however and it will usually pay to seek out the good ones. A good starting place would be the DMA membership list. Being a member does not guarantee they will get everything right first time but it proves they have some knowledge of the special requirements of direct marketers; it also means that they subscribe to the DMA code of practice.

It is a major mistake to wait until a job is fully designed before talking to printers. Like other specialists, printers have experience that can help you to get a better job more cost-efficiently.

Getting the printer to talk to the designer can pay huge dividends – it is often possible to make major savings on print by getting printer and designer together at the start of the job. In some cases simply moving a fold can make a major difference to the cost. Very few designers have such detailed knowledge, so it makes good sense to take advantage of the skills and knowledge of a print specialist.

Printers can also advise on paper quality and availability, suitable weights, cost-efficient sizes and formats, artwork requirements and so on.

Direct marketing agencies

There are many agencies available, ranging from small 'hot-shops' to huge multinationals with offices all over the world. Your choice should be guided by a number of factors. It is important to find an agency that understands and can empathise with your needs and aspirations.

Many small companies seeking rapid success feel they should start at the top and hire the best known international agencies. There are two dangers in doing this:

Large agencies have large overheads – therefore their charges are likely to be high. An agency with a salary bill of £1 million a month cannot afford to charge small fees.

Large clients are very demanding – it is difficult for a very small client to command a high level of service, against the demands of large multinational companies.

On the positive side, large agencies:

Generally offer a wide range of services – apart from the normal media, creative and account management services many large direct marketing agencies can offer sophisticated planning, research, database and other skills.

Have more clients – and are therefore likely to have a wider range of experience across many product fields.

Choosing an agency is a rather different proposition to choosing a mailing house or a list broker. Although both may hopefully be the start of a long relationship the level of involvement expected with a mailing house or broker will be much less. These latter activities tend to be project-focused. An agency appointment is generally a much more complex relationship.

When choosing an agency it is important to be very frank – many agencies have taken on new clients on a loss-making or break-even basis on the promise of large billings to come. When this does not happen the entire relationship can go sour very quickly.

Many prospective clients find difficulty with the concept that an agency should act like a normal business. Yet, would you ask Tesco to give you your first week's groceries free as a gesture of their desire to have you as a customer? Do you give your own new customers free goods and services as a welcoming gesture?

When I ran Ogilvy & Mather Direct in London we were often asked for, but almost never produced, speculative work. In fact we would only agree to do so when my colleagues and I felt we were strong favourites to win a major account.

It is reasonable to expect some time and free advice about your business but not finished ideas and creative work. When I was a client and was offered free services from an advertising agency I used to wonder how they had time to do this if they were very busy. And if they weren't busy, why not? If they were producing free work for me, who was paying for it? If it was their other clients, would they use the time I paid for to do the same?

A lot of the other considerations about choosing an agency are the same for most suppliers so we will cover these collectively in the next section.

Freelance design and creative teams

If you run or work for a small business, don't overlook the possibility of using freelance designers and creative teams. Many of these people are ex-agency professionals who simply got fed up of city commuting and opted to work from home. And because of this their fees tend to be smaller and their concentration better.

Some of these work through collectives or freelance agencies so you could start by 'Googling' freelance advertising designers or something similar.

Marketing consultants

It may be worth considering the use of a specialist consultant such as a general direct marketer, a data specialist or a Web practitioner. Good consultants can be expensive but they can sometimes help to avoid costly or embarrassing mistakes.

Your decision should hinge on the overall advantage to the business and this is not a simple judgement to make. A consultant's charges could easily be more than the cost of hiring a full-time assistant so the first thing to do is to make an objective decision about your existing resources and experience.

If you have plenty of experience but are simply short of time, a good assistant may well be a better investment. On the other hand, if your experience is limited it can be very helpful to have a seasoned adviser available 'on tap'.

What will a consultant do for your business?

Here is a list of some services you could reasonably expect an experienced consultant to provide. You could receive help with:

- market analysis and strategic planning;
- targeting of prospects and sales forecasting;
- online advertising and search marketing;
- selection of mailing and email lists;
- location and selection of the specialist suppliers listed above;
- production of, and/or evaluation of creative work;
- recruitment of staff;
- specialised training for yourself and your staff;
- product design and development.

There are many consultants available; subject them to the same careful selection procedure as you would an agency or database bureau.

Where to find specialist suppliers

As mentioned earlier, a good starting point is the Direct Marketing Association (DMA) whose address you will find in the appendix. Membership of the DMA does not guarantee that a supplier will have a greater knowledge of direct marketing than a non-member will but there is a better chance that this will be so.

Your first step should be to ask the DMA for a list of member suppliers in your required area. Among their members are direct marketing agencies, online specialists, mailing and fulfilment houses, list brokers, database and computer services and printers.

Among the advantages of choosing DMA member companies are:

- they subscribe to the DMA Code of Conduct so you can be assured of certain minimum standards;
- they are likely to know more about the special requirements of direct marketers than non-members.

Choosing the right supplier

Once you have assembled your list of potential suppliers you have to start evaluating them. This task can be broken down into stages to reduce your involvement at the start.

I have developed the following process over the years and it has always worked well for me:

1. **Build a list of potential suppliers from trade press, membership lists and online research. You can make some basic judgements from their websites or advertisements.**
2. **Write or email those which look interesting asking them to tell you:**

- **What they can do for you** – i.e. what experience they have in your field.
- **Who their clients are** – this is one of the most revealing answers you can get. It is useful to know they have experience in your field and at the same time you can make sure they are not dealing with one of your major competitors.
- **Their basis for charging** – where possible you should look for project or 'menu' fees rather than hourly or daily rates.
- **Why they should be given the job** – their answers will tell you how keen they are to get your business.

This preliminary process can be completed without major time input on your behalf. The responses to your basic 'questionnaire' will give you enough information to draw up a 'long' list.

The long list

This is an intermediate stage that you may or may not use. It will vary according to whether you are placing a single project or looking for a long-term relationship with a supplier. Briefly decide on the six or eight most interesting candidates and telephone them for a detailed discussion. This is again an economical use of your time; there is no sense in travelling all over the country to ask questions which can just as easily be raised by telephone. The responses and perceived level of interest from each candidate simplify the job of producing your shortlist.

The shortlist

Now comes the labour intensive bit. You cannot complete this stage by phone. However, as your list should contain no more than three or four 'probables' it is not an impossible task.

The first task is to arrange to visit these *at their premises*. Many marketing executives insist on suppliers coming to them but I always visited my suppliers in the early stages, and especially during the initial selection process. How can you possibly get a feel for a business by meeting their sales people on your own or neutral ground?

You need to get a feel for the place, to look around and see if it looks efficient, and talk to the workers to judge whether they seem happy and cooperative.

Meet the account handlers

During your visit you should ask to meet the people who would be responsible for handling your business on a day-to-day basis. Senior management and sales people will impress you with their knowledge and experience, but if they will not be personally involved in managing your business this may be irrelevant, or even misleading.

Tell them exactly what you want them to do

Many suppliers make mistakes because they have not understood precisely what their clients' want. Of course they should tell you they don't understand but, unless you have actively encouraged this, they are often too embarrassed to admit it.

Once a mistake is made many suppliers will try to cover it up even though this can add to the problem in many cases. This is human nature and quite understandable. The best way to avoid this is to make sure that your brief is clear, complete, and totally understood. And the best way to make sure is to ask them to help you write your brief.

Your suppliers are the best people to tell you what they need to know. They have been at the receiving end of many briefs, good and bad, and can help you avoid the worst pitfalls, but only if you encourage their input. Far from it being unprofessional to ask a supplier for help, it is in fact highly professional. By doing so you are encouraging your suppliers to give of their best, and encouraging ownership of the project.

Asking for quotations

Once you have agreed on the brief you can invite quotations; let those you approach know you have asked for other quotations but don't overdo it. The best agencies do not mind quoting or pitching against a couple of others but will rarely be prepared to get into major bidding contests.

Expect a rapid acknowledgement

The best suppliers are the busiest so don't be surprised if they ask for a few days before they send you a full quotation. They should acknowledge your brief very quickly, either by phone or mail. If they are too busy to pick up the phone what will happen when they have a problem on your job?

Take up business and credit references

No reputable supplier will hesitate to give you the names of existing customers. They will naturally put you in touch with their favourite clients – you can choose to contact those or you could 'go it alone' and ask some of their other clients. Whichever option you choose this is an important part of the process.

It is also, sadly, important to run a credit check on a potential supplier. I once had a large mailing for IBM ready to be posted, when the mailing house, the UK subsidiary of a major international group, went into receivership. The receiver would not release our mailing and the whole programme had to be abandoned. That taught my colleagues and me two valuable lessons, one about references and the other about insurance!

Comparing quotations

When comparing quotations make sure you are comparing like with like. Suppliers will try to bend your requirements to fit their skills. This is fine to a point but if you do not want that extra report which only their unique system can deliver then why pay for it. If you are not happy with 'extras' like these, simply tell the supplier to quote again without the trimmings.

Some will, some won't, but the time to argue about it is before you give them your business.

Once you have the quotations in a form that makes comparison possible you can start to make decisions. But remember that price should not be your only consideration. As with many other things you tend to get what you pay for, and that £500 you saved will not be worth much if you have to spend several days sorting things out later.

You need to balance the price quoted with your assessment of their capabilities. Do they impress you with their systems and their staff? Do they seem the sort of people to take problems off your hands or to present you with new ones?

Writing a clear and effective brief

Because your brief will vary according to the type of job and the type of supplier, the following is an example of a creative brief only. A mailing brief will be somewhat different; a data analysis brief totally different. Don't forget to make use of the supplier's experience too.

As an example of the depth of detail required, here is a list of elements you should include in a creative brief to an agency:

1. **Information**

   You cannot usually overdo this. The top line summary should be brief. But most inadequate briefs are short on vital facts and figures. Tell them everything: about your product; your market; the sort of people who buy your product; the number of competitors you have. These are usually better as separate sections so they can easily be referred to when questions arise. If you don't feel you can trust them with your secrets, you have probably chosen the wrong partners.

   One major direct marketing company actually produces totally spurious briefs for new suppliers to see how they handle them and to check whether any of the 'confidential' information hits the streets. You may feel this is going a bit far but it depends on how confidential you feel your data is.

2. **Brief the right people – make sure you talk to at least one of the actual people who will do the job**

   In a creative brief this means either the copywriter or art director, preferably both. The questions asked by creative people are very different to those asked by account managers. The creatives write the copy. The account manager's job is to make sure it is developed into the finished job accurately and on time.

   Ideally both creative and account managers should be involved in the meeting. You will probably find this is easier to arrange when you go to the agency rather than asking them to come to you.

   Apart from the improvement in briefing there is an additional bonus. When you visit the agency you can have five minutes with the research manager, a quick chat with the print buyer, call in the chairman for a bit of extra advice and so on. Unless you are a huge client you will rarely get such a large team visiting your office.

3. **State a clear objective**

   A creative team, however brilliant, cannot generate a convincing advertisement or mailing unless they know what you want them to achieve. Do you want to attract orders or enquiries? If enquiries do you want 'loose' or 'tight' enquiries? You get loose leads when you mention benefits but not price. Tight leads are told more in the copy. Tight leads are easier to convert to sales but you do not get so many.

   Which should you go for? How good a salesperson are you? How easy is it to tell a full and convincing story in the advertisement or mailing? As with so many questions, the answer depends on your own business circumstances.

4. **Prepare a positioning statement** – this is an area that causes great concern but again, without clear guidance your creative team cannot hit the target. They need to know whether you are selling a Rolls-Royce or a Lada. Positioning is discussed in Chapter 12 – pages 289–91.

5. **Give an idea as to budget**

   It's up to you whether you specify the exact amount you have available, but they will not be able to give you what you want unless they know whether you want a low budget execution or a high quality prestige presentation.

6. **Set a timetable**

   Suppliers tend to operate to the 'just in time' principle. So do you and so do I. Once you have fixed the timetable, stick to it, from your own side too.

   If you have provided all the necessary information on time, you are entitled to expect the finished job to be on schedule. If your materials were provided late don't be surprised to find your job is also running behind schedule because there may be a knock-on effect. If you return the typescript copy two days late, the agency may have missed the appointed 'slot' they had at the studio. This could cause another couple of days delay. This makes the artwork late, which causes a problem for the printer. A small delay of two days on your part could easily escalate into a delivery hold-up of more than a week.

   Prudent suppliers build in time for 'slippage' but the key message is don't hold things up yourself and then expect everyone else to stick to the original timetable.

7. **Describe your prospect clearly**

   There is an old saying in direct marketing: 'You cannot write to a list, only to a person.' One of my most effective copywriters at Saatchi's used to spend the first half hour of any job thinking up a description of the person to whom she was about to write. This description is hypothetical but it helped her write believable, convincing copy. Compare the following prospect descriptions:

   a) Parent

   b) **Parent, owner of a fairly expensive detached house, professional, aged 35 + . Has two children at fee-paying schools, and a sizeable mortgage. Is concerned about school fees. Wishes to maintain a good standard of living. Needs convincing that further investment is worthwhile and affordable. Would probably listen to arguments supported by credible testimonial statements.**

   Would you find it easier to write to parent 'a' or parent 'b'?

8. **Define the benefits of your product**

   Only a small number of people buy products because of their technical excellence, most buy because they deliver better end user benefits. Make sure you tell the creative people how the attributes of your product deliver benefits to users. It will be helpful to explain how benefits vary for different types of prospect. Take electric central heating. Someone who travels a lot likes it because she can switch it on or off by telephone from anywhere in the world. Her father, who is 78, likes it because it is so easy to turn on and adjust.

   If you don't know what the end-user benefits of your product are, seen from the point of view of your customers, you need to do some research before delivering your brief.

9. **Explain your offer**

   We discussed offers in Chapter 12. Now you have to explain yours to the creative team. Expect them to question the power of your offer; listen to their arguments. They will not always be typical of your target audience but they will often produce good ideas that can improve your results.

10. **Put your brief in writing**

This seems obvious but many important briefs are not confirmed in writing. When something goes wrong who's to blame? When you are not available who can answer the questions?

It helps to produce a briefing form

A jointly designed briefing form serves several useful functions:

- it forces you and your supplier to think through the job very carefully, in advance of work starting;
- it reminds you to cover every aspect;
- it is a valuable checklist when no-one is around to answer questions;
- it helps when briefing other areas of the business, your call centre for example.

The following is a typical form for a creative brief:

Creative Briefing Form	
Name of job: For example, Spring mailing campaign	
Date:	
Product/service description to which this brief relates: For example, new spring models	
Background: Market situation, competitive situation, any other similar relevant comments	
Positioning: A brief statement describing the overall impression you wish to leave in the mind of the reader	
Communications objective: What you are trying to achieve, for example to attract enquiries, change attitudes, encourage trial, visit to dealer	
Target audience: Who are you talking to? Large or small customers, prospects, decision-makers, influencers, purchasing departments etc.	
Media to be used: Is this a standalone communication or will the same theme be used across several media	
Response mechanism: Telephone, email, website URL, mailed coupon?	
Proposition (offer): What customer benefit does this product offer? This should be expressed very briefly – if all else fails it may be used as the headline	
Rationale: Why will this product provide these benefits?	
Secondary benefits: Are there any other benefits which should be included?	
Tone of voice: Authoritative, questioning, advisory?	
Executional guidelines: Any wider issues to be conformed to? Corporate design elements, terminology, etc.	
Promotional aspects: Is there a promotional offer, such as price, prize draw, incentive?	

SUMMARY

We started this chapter by discussing why customers break relationships and comparing the corporate view with that of the customer. The two most important reasons in the view of the company were price and the fact that customers' needs had changed. **The most important factor for customers was customer service, followed by quality.**

We saw that 'customer satisfaction' should not be our objective; many customers who claim to be satisfied change suppliers readily. Only those who find real value in the relationship choose to continue dealing with us.

We looked at the importance of complaints in understanding what our customers really think of us; and the value of regular customer satisfaction surveys – sent to all customers rather than just a sample. It has always been important to deal promptly and fairly with complaints but never more so than today. With the power of the Internet behind them, customers now have a real voice and if their complaints are not properly dealt with they can quickly resort to airing their views to millions of customers and prospects.

To get a feel for the importance of customer service, readers are recommended to search the web for 'I hate (company name)' – they will find blogs, 'hate sites' and YouTube videos that amply demonstrate the potential disasters of poor customer service.

It is not possible for any large company to avoid criticism altogether; some complaints are inevitable. The important thing is to have a mechanism for dealing with them – ideally before they reach the level of Web exposure. If it is too late for that, it is still vital to engage with the complainant and to resolve the issue as quickly as possible.

In today's world of customer power the role of customer service has never been more important.

We considered the risks and rewards of outsourcing and pointed out that while many business processes can be successfully outsourced, companies should think very hard before outsourcing customer service. In fact some UK financial services companies that outsourced this vital function to save costs, have brought it back in house due to a rapid rise in customer dissatisfaction.

The process of finding and choosing reliable suppliers was covered in detail. The range of possible suppliers is significant and includes:

- mailing list suppliers – brokers/owners
- mailing and fulfilment houses
- email consolidators
- data specialists
- website designers and consultants
- search and online advertising specialists
- printers
- direct marketing agencies, or freelance design and creative teams
- consultants

Each of these suppliers was discussed in turn. We saw the need to take up references.

We developed a checklist for choosing suppliers:

- build a list of potential suppliers

- write to them with a detailed questionnaire
- create a long list and interview them by telephone or email
- drill down to the shortlist of three or four
- visit them
- meet the people
- write the brief
- ask for quotations
- take up business and credit references
- make your decision

We provided a framework to help write a good brief and this included:
- provide as much information as possible
- brief all concerned with the project
- give clear quantified objectives
- prepare a positioning statement
- give an indication of budget
- set a timetable
- describe the prospect clearly
- define the end-user benefits of your product
- explain the offer
- put it in writing

We saw that a briefing form forces a supplier to think through the job in detail, and is a valuable checklist if there are any problems. We closed the chapter with a specimen briefing pro-forma.

REVIEW QUESTIONS

1. What are the two main reasons why customers break off a supplier relationship?
2. What are the main benefits of making it easy for customers to complain?
3. Why should customer satisfaction surveys be sent to all customers?
4. What is a hate site?
5. What business process should never be outsourced?
6. What is the process of choosing an external supplier?
7. What are the key stages in the briefing process?
8. What are the benefits of a good brief?

EXERCISE

Select a newspaper advertisement and try to work backwards from that to complete the creative briefing form. Then approach it from the other direction and decide how you would improve the brief, and thus the advertisement.

CHAPTER 16
DIRECT AND DIGITAL MARKETING METRICS

IN THIS CHAPTER

We will review the main evaluation methods used both offline and online.

After reading this chapter you will:

- Understand the vital importance of measurement and evaluation
- Select the most appropriate measurement tools for any campaign
- Be able to build and explain the key features of a direct marketing budget
- Understand the importance and key success factors for lifetime value analysis (LTV)
- Be aware of the basic layers of Web metrics

Specific topics include:

- Acquisition or retention? Finding the correct balance
- The main measurement techniques, including:
  - allowable cost per sale
  - campaign based budgeting
  - the contribution method of campaign budgeting and evaluation
- How to deal with costs
- The processes and benefits of budgeting
- Example campaigns
- How lifetime value is calculated and applied
- Basic Web analytics – the four layers

INTRODUCTION
Why we need evaluation

As we have seen, direct marketers can evaluate many activities before making major investments.

Evaluation is the continuous measurement of marketing activities with a view to deciding whether they should be continued, amended or abandoned. Every marketing activity can be budgeted for, measured as it proceeds and evaluated. This high level of control means that by studying the results of our activities we can continually improve our performance, even while the campaign is in progress.

Measurability

Unlike general advertising, most direct marketing communications are designed to elicit a response from the recipient, and they can thus be measured very precisely. As we saw in Chapter

14, this enables us to identify good and bad publications, mailing lists, creative treatments and indeed types of prospect very quickly and without spending large amounts of money.

Acquisition or retention – finding the balance

As we know, developing relationships is one of the key concepts of direct marketing – some of the elements of direct marketing, developing websites and databases for example, require serious investment before any sort of payback is possible. It is only through developing longer-term relationships and thus ensuring a continuing flow of repeat business that such investment becomes viable.

Companies are mainly in business to make money and it is important to find the correct balance between investing in new customers who will become profitable later and getting a satisfactory return on our expenditure in time to stay in business.

This balance is a critical success factor and the point of balance will vary according to the nature of the business.

Let's look at an example:

EXAMPLE

Company A

Company A has a small range of products that it features in single product advertisements in national newspapers. Customers can buy direct 'off the page' or visit the website where the company's entire range of products is displayed. If a customer buys direct from the advertisement they are sent a catalogue carrying details of the other products in the range. If they order or even register online, they can choose to have a catalogue sent to them, or to download a pdf version immediately. The company will also hope to get site visitors to subscribe to its regular e-newsletter.

Primary objective: To make a profit from the orders received from each advertisement.
Secondary objective: To build a 'list' and make subsequent sales (and profit) from future offers to these customers.

Question: Should this company stick to its policy of making profit from the first transaction or could it do better in the long term by breaking even or making a small loss on the first sale and thus generating more customers for its database?

Answer: We don't know! It is likely that in most markets the investment route will eventually yield more profit, but only a carefully planned programme of testing and evaluation will enable the right balance to be found.

If a business has not been running very long it is likely to have only limited funding so it will not be able to afford to go flat out for later payback. However, some element of investment is probably advisable. In order to reach sensible and affordable decisions it is necessary to make constant comparisons between these options.

Marketing measurement techniques – comparing numbers

In direct marketing, although it is not necessary to be a statistician some familiarity with numbers is very helpful. It is all too easy when we are under pressure to hit the wrong key on a calculator and, if we are not able to do an approximate calculation in our heads, we will not know until it is too late that the result shown on the calculator is wrong.

In marketing we deal with a wide range of numbers from television audiences or newspaper readerships that are expressed in millions, to response rates which are often expressed in fractions of 1 per cent. We therefore have to be comfortable with both very large and very small numbers.

Standard measures used in marketing evaluation

Much of our analysis is involved in making comparisons between two or more results or response rates. To make such comparisons easier we use standard measures and some of the most common include:

Cost per thousand

We use this for a variety of comparisons:

- **Media rates** – these are usually expressed in 'cost per thousand' readers, site visitors, names, viewers and so on.
- **Print quotes** – we compare the cost per thousand of two or more quotations for leaflets or brochures.

It is all too easy to make basic errors when comparing costs on a cost per thousand basis. Take postage, for example. Second class postage is currently 32 pence and when building this into a total mailing budget many people cost in £32 per thousand. Of course, 32 pence is actually £32 per hundred or £320 per thousand. This simple error occurs time and again and makes a nonsense out of many mailing budgets.

NOTE: in real life the postage cost of most mailings, when the volume is more than 4,000, will be considerably less than £320 per thousand. Bulk mailings attract a discount from the postal authorities and depending on volume this can be as much as 30 per cent.

Cost per response/reply/enquiry/lead

Most direct marketing activities can be measured by activity generated and the results expressed in terms of cost per something.

Cost per order/per sale

This goes a stage further and measures the actual amount of business produced by the activity. The ultimate short-term activity measurement is cost per pound turnover, which gives us one version of return on investment (ROI).

Response rate

There are two common expressions of response; cost per response as mentioned above, and response percentage. We tend to use response percentage when dealing with mailings and emails, and cost per response when evaluating broadscale media such as press and television. However, for a full comparison of activities both are helpful. Response percentages are used when forecasting demand and comparing results from test cells, and cost per response when evaluating results over a longer period.

Evaluating campaigns

One of the simplest measures used to evaluate direct marketing activity is allowable cost-per-order, an approach which has been around for many years. This originated when most direct marketing activity was concerned with selling direct by mail order and is a very conservative approach to building business.

Allowable cost-per-order is reached by building a mini profit and loss account for an average sale including the desired profit but excluding promotional costs.

The calculation shows the amount we can afford to spend to secure a sale: our allowable cost-per-order. This is also sometimes called allowable cost-per-sale.

Table 16.1: Allowable cost-per-order

Calculating the allowable cost-per-order		
Order value – gross revenue		£90
Manufacturing costs	£25	
Order processing, packaging and despatch costs	£10	
Total costs	**£35**	£35
Contribution		£55
Profit required		£30
Allowable cost-per-order		**£25**

This calculation shows that we can afford to spend £25 to sell this product, and that each sale will give us a profit of £30 to help fund business management and growth.

We can use the allowable cost-per-order to calculate the required response rate from a mailing. For example, a mailing to 30,000 prospects might cost £650 per thousand including design, print and postage, which is a total of £19,500.

Dividing the £19,500 cost by our £25 'allowable cost' shows that 780 orders will be needed, i.e. a 2.6 per cent response from our 30,000 prospects, to give us our required payback of £30 profit per order.

We can take this costing a stage further by calculating how many orders we will need to break even, i.e. to get the investment back without any profit. In the above model we simply divide the £19,500 cost by the £55 'contribution' to show that 355 (354.55) orders would recover our investment. This represents 1.18 per cent of the total mailed.

If we were mailing for the first time we would need to use our judgement to decide whether this looks achievable. Alternatively we may run a test but without any previous experience we would have to take a chance on achieving a statistically valid number of responses (see Chapter 14).

Two-stage selling

Although much traditional mail order is 'direct sell' or one-stage selling there are many occasions when this is not appropriate. For example, when selling more expensive items or when advertising a large catalogue with many available choices for the prospective buyer.

The process of advertising to attract enquiries for a catalogue or brochure, or to drive prospects to a website is called two-stage (or two-step) selling and when using this method there are some additional costs to be built into the model.

If we expect to receive one order from every four people who enquire (a 25 per cent 'conversion rate') and it costs £1.50 (including despatch postage) for every information pack we send, and 33 pence postage for every reply we receive. The costings would now be:

Table 16.2: Allowable costs in two-stage selling

Calculating the allowable cost-per-sale		
Order value – gross revenue		£90.00
Manufacturing costs	£25.00	
Order processing, packaging and despatch costs	£10.00	
Cost of information packs 4 per order @ £1.50	£6.00	
Freepost on replies, say 4 × 33p	£1.32	
Total costs	**£42.32**	£42.32
Contribution		£47.68
Profit required		£30.00
Allowable cost-per-order		**£17.68**

We also need to build the conversion calculations into the estimate of response required to hit the target and to break even.

Firstly to see what is required to hit the profit target, we divide the £19,500 cost by the £17.68 'allowable' giving a target of 1,103 orders. At one order per four enquiries this means we need to attract 4,412 replies, which is a response rate of 14.7 per cent. This is considerably higher than the one stage route and it does not look particularly viable.

However, experienced mail order operators know that order values from two-stage selling are often considerably higher than from one-stage so it may be worth testing this method. Some mail order companies find that average orders from two-stage advertising are almost double those from direct selling or 'off-the-page' advertising.

Now let us rework the two-stage numbers on the assumption that average order values will increase to £150, an increase of 66.66 per cent over the one-stage average.

Table 16.3: Increased order values

Calculating the allowable cost-per-sale		
Order value – gross revenue		£150.00
Manufacturing costs	£41.50	
Order processing, packaging and despatch costs, say	£13.00	
Cost of information packs 4 × £1.50	£6.00	
Postage on replies 4 × 33p	£1.32	
Total costs	£61.82	£61.82
Contribution		£88.18
Profit required		£50.00
Allowable cost-per-order		**£38.18**

Dividing the £19,500 cost by the new 'allowable' of £38.18 gives a requirement of 511 orders and a response requirement of 2,044 enquiries; this is 6.8 per cent of the total mailed and looks more achievable.

Next we see what our base requirement is, i.e. what do we need to break even.

Dividing the £19,500 by the £88.18 contribution shows that 221 orders are required to get our money back. At the expected conversion rate of 25 per cent we need 884 enquiries, i.e. 2.95 per cent response.

Again, we must use our judgement to decide whether this looks achievable. We will return to this point later when we consider again the issue of whether it is essential to make a profit on our first transaction with a new customer.

The above demonstration has deliberately been kept very simple. Don't forget to reduce your sales revenue to allow for such things as products being returned, replacements for items damaged in transit, bad debts and so on. Remember to allow for all costs including, where relevant, design, photography, artwork, printers charges, any response costs (postage, telephone etc.).

Although the allowable cost approach is very simplistic, it does help to give a better feel for the point of balance between acquisition and retention. If you feel confident your new customers will buy further products in the future, *and you have sufficient funding to enable you to wait for profit,* you can be more relaxed about the amount of profit you achieve from your first transaction. You may aim for a simple break even or be prepared to accept a small loss.

The allowable cost approach is very useful but it has limitations too:

1. It requires sales, returns, damages and bad debts to be estimated in advance to enable realistic forecasting of net sales revenue.
2. It assumes that costs are fixed, i.e. they will not change with volume of sales.

3. It leads to decisions being based not on profit maximisation but on profit satisfaction and can become a self-fulfilling prophecy. If our target is to achieve 20,000 orders and our calculations show an allowable cost of £50 we have £1 million to spend. However, if that were our own money would we think differently? It is all too easy to spend this budget when we should be trying to achieve our 20,000 orders for as little as possible.

And finally, the most important limitation of this process:

4. It does not take into account any future purchases by a new customer. 'Forcing' a fixed profit from the first transaction can bias our judgement towards quantity rather than long-term quality.

The first of these concerns cannot be avoided. We will have to estimate these items in advance in order to calculate and justify the budget requirements so the calculation is not an idle exercise.

Overcoming the assumption that costs are fixed

This problem is easily addressed. All that is required is to re-run the numbers based on different levels of cost.

It is assumed for the purposes of this example that we are planning to offer a free gift to make our advertisement more attractive.

All other things being equal, an incentivised offer will produce a higher response rate, and thus more sales from the same mailing or advertisement. It may also affect the conversion rate from enquiry to sale. If the gift is given for simply enquiring it will increase response dramatically but lower the conversion rate.

If the gift is given in return for an order only, it may increase the response rate a little but improve conversion quite substantially. Only testing will show precisely what effect the gift will have.

Let us assume that we have decided to offer a free gift to customers who place an order. This gift has a retail value of £30 but costs just £10 on a sale or return basis. It is reasonable to assume that the free gift will improve both response and conversion rates.

What will be the precise effect on response rate and costings? We will not really know without testing it, but what we can do at this stage is to calculate what it will need to do to be equally cost-effective with the existing offer.

We can then use our judgement to decide whether the investment looks worthwhile.

Note: to simplify this demonstration we have assumed that the net sales revenue per order is a standard £300.

Table 16.4: Comparing offers

Calculating allowable costs and required response using different offers		
Mailing quantity 30,000		
Mailing cost £19,500		
Cost per test segment	£9,750	£9,750
	basic offer	gift offer
Product Price	£300.00	£300.00
Costs	£140.00	£150.00 (incl gift)
Contribution	£160.00	£150.00
Required profit	£100.00	£100.00
Allowable cost	£60.00	£50.00
Sales needed to achieve profit targets	162.5	195
Conversion rate	1 in 4	1 in 3.5
Responses required	650	682
Response rate	4.33%	4.55%

This costing shows that if, based on previous experience, the response rate of 4.33 per cent and conversion ratio of one in four seem reasonable, we need only a 5 per cent gain in response rate (32/650 x 100) and an improvement in conversion of 14 per cent to make the free gift offer viable. And, if it works out, we shall gain 32 additional customers, some of whom will continue to buy in the future.

Note that these calculations do not tell us what will happen. Only what the profit and loss situation will be under various circumstances. We still need to use considerable judgement; these cost exercises simply enable us to make better-informed 'guesstimates'.

We could use similar calculations to examine the effects of say, selling a higher volume, or reducing the profit margin to enable us to make better offers.

Taking a wider view

The third limitation of allowable cost calculations is simply that they encourage complacency – they encourage us to stop when the calculation works out at our estimated profit. In real life we should be seeking to maximise profit rather than simply achieve our estimates.

This issue can be tackled by moving up a level in the evaluations. Rather than use a single sale as the base level let's move up to the campaign level.

And rather than judge a required response rate against experience, we will use our best estimate of response rate and judge whether to proceed or not on the profit likely to be generated. We can work out individual sales profitability from the overall campaign calculation as the following example shows:

Taking the same costs as in the previous example shows:

Table 16.5: Campaign-based budgeting

Campaign-based budgeting		
	Campaign A	Campaign B
Net revenue per order	£300.00	£300.00
Costs	£140.00	£150.00
Gross margin	£160.00	£150.00
Number mailed	15,000	15,000
Response	4.33 per cent	4.55 per cent
Responses	650	682
Conversion ratio	1 in 4	1 in 3.5
Sales	162.5	195
Gross profit	£26,000	£29,250
Cost of promotion	£9,750	£9,750
Campaign contribution	**£16,250**	**£19,500**
Contribution per sale	**£100**	**£100**

This analysis shows one of the problems of restricting our view to a profit and loss account of a single transaction (the basis of the allowable cost process). At that level there is nothing to choose between the two approaches – each would deliver a contribution per sale of £100. If we made our decision at this point we may well decide on campaign A because it saves us the trouble of sourcing and offering a gift.

However, when we base our decision on the overall campaign contribution we see that the gift offer delivers an additional £3,250 of profit and an additional 32 customers to whom we can sell again in the future.

Remember that the above calculations are hypothetical but if you run your campaign plans against these models you will get a much clearer view of your own costs and profitability. One thing we need to consider before switching our entire acquisition strategy to the free gift model is quality.

The free gift generated additional profit and more new customers, but we need to evaluate these customers over a considerable time before we can be sure this new model is the right way to go. It may be that campaign B has produced a different type of customer that will only buy when we offer a gift or a discount. It may still work out better but only time will tell.

How to calculate and deal with marketing costs

Before we look at budgeting and decision-making more closely, it is important to understand costs: what they are and how they affect budgeting and evaluation.

Costs in marketing, as in every area of business, fall into two basic groupings: fixed costs and variable costs. In building a budget we need to be concerned with the costs we will incur, whether these costs are fixed or variable, and if variable, on which elements they depend.

Variable costs, fixed costs and overheads

The definition of costs changes depending on the level being addressed. Some costs may be fixed when looking at an individual campaign, but variable in the context of a year's worth of campaigns.

Variable costs

Are defined as costs that vary with the amount of a given activity. For example, the cost of an advertisement will vary according to the newspaper we choose (rates are based on the number of copies the paper sells), and on the size and position of the space we buy.

The cost of a mailing list will vary according to the quantity of names we decide to rent and perhaps the quality too if we are intending to segment the list by profiling factors. Outward postage will be directly proportional to the number of items mailed; reply paid postal costs, charges for free telephone response numbers and the cost of data capture of responses will vary according to the number of people who respond.

Fixed costs

Are costs that are not influenced by changes in activity. For example, the cost of artwork for a mailing is fixed at the campaign level; the cost is the same whether we print 1,000 or 10,000. However, it could be seen as variable at the strategic level – for example, we can decide at the start of a year whether we are going to produce expensive glossy mailings, or low-cost ones.

Overheads (indirect fixed costs)

Are costs which are incurred whether or not an activity takes place. For example, property rental is likely to be a cost that is not only independent of the size of a campaign, but also independent of the number of campaigns in a given period (within reason).

How costs vary with quantity

In general, marketing costs increase with quantity. For example, overtime charges can result from an unexpectedly high response to a mailing or advertisement.

On the other hand some costs, such as the unit cost of printing, can be dramatically reduced with increases in quantity, as is demonstrated by the following example for a fairly standard mailing pack:

Table 16.6: Effect of quantity on costs

Effect of quantity on print costs (C5 mailing)		
Quantity	Total cost	Cost per pack
Test – 5,000	£3,250	65 pence
Roll-out – 100,000	£50,000	50 pence

From this example it can be seen that a straight extrapolation from test mailing costs would seriously distort the financial implications of a roll-out: the cost of the 100,000 roll-out mailings projected from the costs of the 5,000 test would be £65,000, rather than the £50,000 it would actually cost.

However, if we were to 'run on' a further 100,000 copies there might not be much further reduction for quantity, as we would already have amortised the set-up costs and used most of the economy of scale.

Understanding the effect of quantity is important if the correct inferences about the financial implications of a roll-out are to be drawn from a test campaign. The basic rule is to base the evaluation of a test campaign on the level of costings that would have been incurred if we had mailed the larger (roll-out) number.

One of the main reasons for spending so much time and energy on defining costs is that it is vital to have as clear a view as possible of the true profitability of each activity. The main aim is to attribute as many costs as possible to the activities for which they are incurred.

Most variable costs can easily be attributed to an activity. If we had not done the mailing we would not have rented the list, bought the envelopes and so on.

Many fixed costs can also be attributed to an activity, advertisement artwork being a good example. However, there is one category of fixed costs called indirect fixed costs or overheads, which can create many problems for marketers.

How to handle overheads

The handling of overheads is probably one of the most difficult areas of budgeting.

We can attempt to allocate overheads to products or campaigns, but there are problems. For example, say our assistants have planned 12 campaigns for the year, we could allocate one twelfth of their salaries to each campaign.

But what if two of the campaigns take twice as much time as the others? Or, what if one of the campaigns is cancelled (after most of the work has been done) or another campaign is added during the period?

One answer is to instigate a method of decision making that allows us to consider the success or otherwise of an activity (proposed or completed) before overheads are allocated, and then make decisions based on the level of overhead this activity would support. This is the contribution or relevant costing approach.

The contribution approach

The most useful level for decision making is the contribution level. This takes into account all the revenue and costs directly associated with an activity, including those costs and revenues which are only incurred/generated because the activity is being undertaken.

Let's look at an example:

Example of the contribution approach

This example considers whether or not to undertake a mailing to 7,500 businesses. Net sales revenue is £200 per order and expected response is 4 per cent.

Table 16.7: The contribution approach

Expected costs are:		
Cost of goods		£80
List rental		£150 per thousand
Artwork/agency fees		£12,500
Production and postage		£750 per thousand
Marketing staff handling		
12 campaigns per year		£100,000
Other overheads (management, rent, etc. allocated to this campaign by finance dept)		£5,500
In-house order processing		£20 per order
Putting this together we can calculate		
Mailing quantity		7,500
Response		300 orders
Revenue		£60,000
Cost of goods		£24,000
Gross profit		£36,000
Costs to be deducted		
List rental	£1,125	
Production/print/postage	£5,625	
Agency artwork/fees	£12,500	
Staff ($\frac{1}{12}$ of annual cost)	£8,333	
Office costs (allocated)	£5,500	
Order handling	£6,000	
	£39,083	£39,083
Profit/(loss)		**(£3,083)**

According to this calculation the above activity makes a loss. But there are two indirect costs (overheads) included which are going to have to be paid whether or not the campaign goes ahead. These are staff costs and office costs. Together these costs add up to £13,833.

The contribution approach would say that the campaign generates a net sales revenue of £60,000 and, as a result of undertaking the campaign, costs of £49,250 will be incurred (cost of goods + promotion costs + order handling charges). Taking these costs from the revenue generated leaves an income of £10,750 to contribute towards overheads, i.e. if we don't do the mailing we will be £10,750 worse off at the end of the period.

This contribution (or relevant costing) approach, based on identifying the relevant costs associated with a campaign, looks to see if undertaking the campaign contributes towards the overheads (which will be incurred whether or not the campaign goes ahead).

It is important to remember that, although the contribution approach does not rigidly allocate overheads to a specific activity, which can be very difficult, overheads cannot be ignored. The contributions from all the activities that the overhead supports must add up to more than the overheads if the business is to survive.

The benefit of the contribution approach is that it looks at what additional costs will be incurred, over and above those that will have to be paid anyway, and so helps to lead to decisions which maximise contribution to profit, as the above example illustrates.

Now let's look at budgeting

Budgeting is building a 'picture' of a business in numbers. It provides a framework in which to make decisions, and examine the impact of those decisions on the business. In building a picture or model, there are two major influences:

1. **External influences**

The effect of external influences on likely performance, e.g. 'How will the launch of my competitor's new model affect my sales in the next 12 months?'

2. **Internal influences**

The effect of internal procedures on each other, e.g. 'If we sell 5,000 units instead of 2,000 what effect will this have on our production and handling costs?'

Building up the budget

Building a picture of the business does not have to be an all-or-nothing process. It is usually an accumulation of smaller pieces put together by individual managers or departments.

In simple terms, the annual marketing budget is the sum of all the budgets for marketing campaigns proposed for the year plus a share of the overheads needed to run the business.

The benefits of budgeting

Budgeting should not be seen as simply a form of monetary control. Among the many non-financial benefits of proper budgeting are that it:

- **forces us to plan ahead and define our future objectives;**
- **gives us a useful overview and checklist of planned activities;**
- **makes us highlight key actions and responsibilities;**
- **forces us to define measurements of performance;**
- **helps us make decisions about trade-offs and priorities;**
- **gives early warning of problems enabling corrective action.**

Figure 16.1: The budgeting process

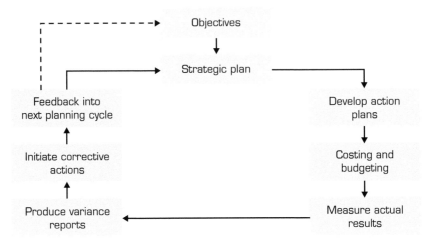

Budgeting – a continuous process

Budgeting should not be a one-off process. It is part of a cycle that helps manage a business and improve its performance. To make this happen results must be fed back into the budgeting process so that more accurate estimates (such as the likely response to our next offer) can be made.

The budget is a yardstick for performance measurement

The budget is a pre-event evaluation and should be the basis for continuous evaluation of actual performance during the budget period.

Providing the budget has been carefully constructed, we can use it to spot potential problems by comparing actual with expected performance.

What makes for successful budgeting?

Successful budgeting depends on a number of factors. Failure to observe any one will jeopardise its usefulness and reliability. The main factors are:

1. **Cooperation and communication between all the people concerned**

   Office politics should be outlawed. Energies devoted to 'politics' could more usefully be used to plan better campaigns.

2. **Realistic targets**

   Many plans fail because targets are unrealistically high or low; both of these are de-motivating to staff.

3. **Consistent objectives**

   A business cannot be run like a speedboat. Frequent short-term changes in policy leave staff with a 'who knows/who cares' attitude.

4. **An easily understood format**

   Budgeting is not just for accountants. If staff understand (and agree with) the business targets they will be better able to tackle the tasks required. Better still if they feel they have been consulted in fixing the targets they will 'own' them and work harder to help achieve them.

5. **Frequent reviews of progress and of the system itself**

A manager or director who is open to suggestion and comment deserves, and usually gets, more committed employees. One of the best ways of improving your budgeting, forecasting and eventual performance is to get those at the sharp end involved at the planning stage.

Creating a Campaign Budget

The first step in creating a campaign budget is to define the structure of the campaign. Are we approaching existing customers or new prospects? If new are we planning to go online or offline – or both?

Having broadly defined the campaign we can then identify the various costs we are likely to incur, and the inter-relationships between them.

Here is a typical structure for a new customer acquisition campaign. This layout could be used for consumer or business to business campaigns. A consumer campaign would not generally involve the sales force. A B2B campaign may not include social networking but may well include blogs:

Figure 16.2: Campaign diagram – new customer acquisition – B2B

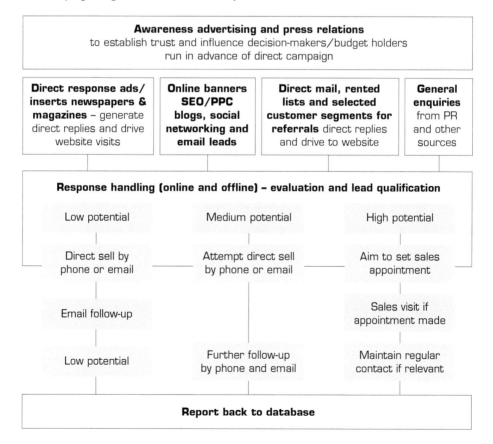

Finding the component costs

We can now look at each section of the campaign, start to build a detailed picture of what costs we are likely to incur and the various elements that influence the costs, and start to build budget models.

Figure 16.3: Typical costs

Typical cost components for an acquisition campaign	
Press/online advertising	— copy and design/artwork/media space
SEO/PPC	— specialists fees plus PPC costs
Public relations	— fees and expenses
Email	— lists, copy and design, consolidator's costs
Direct mail	— design/artwork/print/production etc. — list rental — filling and despatch/ postage
Response costs	— Freepost/telephone/business reply service — handling costs — data capture and de-duplication
Call centre	— fees plus time — reporting
Sales costs	— sales calls and expenses — telephone calls
Fulfilment material (enquiry packs etc.)	— design, artwork etc. — print and production for offline copies — stationery etc.
Other costs/ overheads	— premises, insurance etc. — allocated costs/internal charges etc.

Putting it all together

The final step is to draw up the individual campaign budgets and then to consolidate these into an overall annual marketing budget. Each budget will have its own requirements and the details will vary according to the type of work involved.

Table 16.8: Sample budget

SAMPLE BUDGET FOR AN ACQUISITION CAMPAIGN			
Press relations	Costs	£5,000	**£5,000**
Direct response advertising	Design fees/artwork etc.	£20,000	
Online and offline	Space costs	£350,000	
SEO	Consultancy fees	£15,000	
Pay per click	Estimated costs	£25,000	
Loose inserts	Artwork and print	£65,000	
	Inserting charges	£65,000	**£540,000**
Email (100,000 names)	Creative fees	£10,000	
Despatch and analysis	Consolidator's fees	£2,000	
Direct mail (50,000 names)	Creative fees/artwork	£10.000	
	Print	£20,000	
	List rental	£6,250	
	Assembly and enclosing	£750	
	Postage (@ £0.23 net)	£10,000	**£59,000**
Response costs (all media)	**Estimated 90,000 replies (70,000 online, 20,000 offline)**		
Website landing pages	Creative and implementation	£7,500	
	Postage (@ £0.28 x 7,500)	£2,100	
	Telephone costs (£1 x 12,500)	£12,500	
	Data capture and processing	£9,000	
	Order Handling @ £1.50	£45,000	**£76,100**
Follow-up costs	Telephone follow-up test (£5 x 2,000)	£10,000	
	Email follow up	£2,500	**£12,500**
Fulfilment materials (packs)	Complete – 10k (@ 50 pence)	£5,000	**£5,000**
Total costs of campaign			**£697,600**
Total sales value	**Est. 30,000 orders – average margin £28**		**£834,000**
Contribution Overheads			**£136,400**
Allocated proportion:	Staff costs	£38,000	
	Premises etc.	£16,000	**£54,000**
	Net Profit		**£82,400**

In this example, the expected net profit is considered good for an acquisition campaign, because while achieving that profit we will also:

- **cover £54,000 of overheads;**
- **have recruited 30,000 new customers, and 60,000 enquirers to follow up for future orders.**

If these estimates are realised this will be considered a successful campaign. Many acquisition campaigns register a loss when taking into account only the first transaction. A charity, when recruiting new donors, will not expect to recover its marketing costs from the initial donations, except in very special circumstances such as disaster relief. Their acquisition campaigns are intended to identify new donors who it is hoped will support the cause for many years.

Note that the above costings, while typical of those you may incur, are hypothetical. You must use numbers which relate to your own business, taking the above as a framework only. You will also have to make a judgement regarding the balance between short-term profit and investment in future sales.

There are three basic investment strategies when planning acquisition campaigns:

1. **Break even or better on first transaction** – this is the option with the lowest risk. But it also attracts fewer new customers, which means slower growth. This may be the safest option in high attrition (high churn) sectors. It is a very short-term strategy and ignores long-term customer quality.
2. **Short-term payback** – with this strategy costs are recovered in a short time – perhaps three to six months. An advantage is that it keeps the investment within the financial year with no ongoing liabilities. It relies on accurate forecasting of future sales. It offers faster growth than option 1 and lower risk than option 3.
3. **Lifetime value based** – in this model the investment is linked to predictions of future profits. It requires very accurate forecasting of future sales, sometimes over several years. It offers the best growth potential but also carries the highest risk. It maximises long-term revenue and profit – but only if you get it right.

We are now going to examine the process of customer lifetime value analysis.

Customer lifetime value analysis or LTV

One of the key questions in developing customer acquisition plans is:

'How much can I afford to invest in recruiting a new customer?'

This is a very simple question but not an easy one to answer. If our planning process stops at the 'allowable cost' level, i.e. we expect to make profit from the first transaction then the question answers itself. We are not prepared to invest anything, expecting all new customers to show profit from day one.

This may not be the best way to build a business. If we are confident that new customers will consider our products or services to be good value, and if we have the possibility of future orders we can expect to receive a continuing flow of business for some time to come.

If we have confidence in the probability of this future stream of business it makes sense to consider investing some proportion of future profits in order to maximise the number of new customers we recruit. So, now we can return to the question:

 'How much can I afford to invest in recruiting a new customer?'

In fact this question cannot be answered with any degree of confidence until we can answer this one:

 'How much will a new customer be worth to me in net profit over the time they continue to buy from me?'

Another difficult question, but this and the earlier one can at least be tackled using lifetime value analysis. This is a method of predicting the likely profitability of customers by modelling their future behaviour based on analysis of their (or other customers) previous actions.

We use LTV analysis in three main ways:

1. To answer the question 'What is a new customer worth over time?'. This enables us to justify an expenditure, say £80,000 on a new customer acquisition campaign;
2. To compare the long term quality of customers from different sources;
3. To evaluate the effects of a retention or customer development programme;

We will look at some examples shortly but first we need to discuss two financial terms:

1. **Discounted cash flow and net present value**
    If we invest today in a campaign that will only generate profit in the future we have to consider the cost to the company of funding that investment – commonly called the 'cost of money'. This is the element of lifetime value analysis that people have most trouble with. The reason we need to discount profits is simply that money has a cost – the value of £1 received in two, three or five years time is not the same as the value of £1 received today.

    Put simply, if I have £1 now I can invest it and it will appreciate by the interest rate I can achieve from my bank. If, instead of spending our money on the campaign we invested it in an interest-bearing activity it would gain in value year by year. If you owe me £10 and you do not return it for five years I have lost the potential earning power of that money and its value is therefore £10 minus the interest it would have earned had you given it to me now. This reduced amount is the net present value of my £10.

    To allow for that notional loss of interest we discount future earnings; the process is called discounted cash flow (DCF) and the discounted figure is called the net present value (NPV) of the amount. This is important because we will in many cases be considering investing money today (in customer recruitment campaigns, database developments and so on) to recruit customers whose sales will materialise over a period of years.

    Note that DCF has nothing to do with inflation. We allow for that by increasing (inflating) our sales estimates over the period of the model.

DCF – an example

To demonstrate this process, let's assume that I have just asked my financial director to invest £100,000 in a new suite of CRM software. She naturally asked me to show her how this investment would be recovered and I replied:

'I have already given you my five-year profit projection; with this new software I expect to be able to produce an additional £20,000 profit for each of those years.'

She would explain the concept of discounted cash flow and show me the following projection of net present value payback, assuming an interest rate of 5 per cent.

Net present value of £20,000 profit per year over five years
– discounted at 5 per cent per year

	Year 1	Year 2	Year 3	Year 4	Year 5
Net profit in year	£20,000	£20,000	£20,000	£20,000	£20,000
Discount rate	1	0.95	0.9025	0.8574	0.8145
NPV Profit	£20,000	£19,000	£18,050	£17,148	£16,290
Cum NPV Profit	£20,000	£39,000	£57,050	£74,198	£90,488

Things to note about the above table:

1. We do not normally discount if the earnings are achieved in the current financial period. So in Year 1 the discount factor is 1, i.e. we multiply by 1 and the net present value is the same.
2. The discount is compounded each year so a discount factor of 0.95 (5 per cent) in Year 2 (1 year of discounting) becomes 0.9025 in Year 3 (two years discount) and so on.
3. The £100,000 that I thought I would be paying back by the end of Year 5 actually only amounts to £90,488 at net present value.
4. I may still get my funding but the investment will not be fully paid back until the second half of Year 6.
5. We are currently in a period of exceptionally low interest rates. In more normal times the discount rate would have been considerably higher, and payback would have taken even longer.

What exactly do we mean by lifetime value?

Lifetime value is the net present value of the profit that a company will realise on a new customer during their 'lifetime' as a customer. 'Lifetime' is not to be taken literally – it really means over the length of time a customer stays with us. In forecasting LTV we typically run our models over five years for customers who can be expected to buy at least once a year. If we are dealing with more infrequent purchases such as cars or computers we may well model their expected behaviour over 10 years. A life insurance or mortgage company may choose to evaluate LTV over a longer period but, as we shall see, there are reasons why this is not only difficult but also unsafe.

How does LTV analysis work?

The best way of explaining the process is to take an example and work through it step by step. We will assume we have spent £80,000 on a direct mail customer acquisition campaign, and we recruited 1,000 new customers. In the first year our profit on sales (before allowing for the £80,000 investment) is £60,000. So we are £20,000 in the red at the end of Year 1.

Table 16.9: Five-year projected LTV

		Year 1	Year 2	Year 3	Year 4	Year 5
A	Customers	1000	700	507.5	385.7	308.6
B	Retention	70.0%	72.5%	76.0%	80.0%	85.0%
C	Sales p.a.	£300	£309	£318	£328	£338
D	Total Sales	£300,000	£216,300	£161,385	£126,510	£104,293
E	Net Profit 20%	£60,000	£43,260	£32,277	£25,302	£20,859
F	Discount Rate	1	0.95	0.9025	0.857	0.815
G	NPV Contribution	£60,000	£41,097	£29,130	£21,693	£16,990
H	Cum NPV Contribution	£60,000	£101,097	£130,227	£151,920	£168,910
I	Lifetime Value at Net Present Value	£60.00	£101.10	£130.23	£151.92	£168.91

This table shows the predicted net present value over the next five years. We have chosen 1,000 as an illustration; the actual number of customers can be more or less. The important point is that we need a sizeable group of customers to allow for attrition, i.e. the loss of those customers who do not continue to buy year after year.

Let us now work through this table row by row.

Row A – Customers

Row A shows how many of the 1,000 original customers we expect to continue to buy from us year after year. This expectation is based on an assumed retention rate (more of this below). Note that in Year 5 we show 308.6 customers; we cannot have part customers in real life but if we build these models on a spreadsheet such as Excel we will often encounter fractions of customers. If you are working these tables manually it is important to leave the unrounded numbers unchanged because when we multiply customer numbers by annual sales figures the differences caused by rounding can be quite significant. When presenting such a table in support of funding it is neater to set your spreadsheet to round to whole numbers, and of course the programme will still retain the decimals internally.

In the lower rows, rounding has a less dramatic effect so, apart from the customer row and the final Lifetime Value calculation the numbers have been rounded to the nearest pound.

Row B – Retention rate

Row B shows the retention rate we expect. At the end of the first year we only expect to retain 70 per cent because some new customers will be simply trying us out and will return to their regular supplier in future. However, the retention rate tends to increase year by year, as, by definition, customers who stay longer are more loyal.

Row C – Sales per year

Row C shows the average amount spent by each of these customers each year. In this projection it is estimated that sales will increase due to inflation by approximately 3 per cent each year.

Row D – Total sales

Row D shows the total revenue each year from customers who remain out of the original 1,000. It is simply the number of customers remaining (A) multiplied by the average yearly sales (C).

Row E – Net profit

Costs can include raw materials, processing costs, overheads, marketing and so on. Total costs are assumed to be 80 per cent, leaving a net profit of 20 per cent.

Note that these numbers have been selected arbitrarily as an example. When using this process you should use numbers that make sense in your own business. The only necessity is to keep this figure constant throughout the entire calculation. This is because one of the main uses of these calculations, apart from the basic one of showing how much a customer is worth over time, is to compare the effects of varying marketing strategies. For example, the difference caused to long-term (lifetime) value by adopting a new marketing approach. In this case there would be two or more cells of customers, one cell for each different programme.

So long as we keep to the same cost percentage throughout the evaluation we can be sure we are comparing like with like. In this context, the precise profit figure is not necessarily of crucial importance so long as it is approximately correct.

Row F – Discount rate

There are various ways of applying the discount but the easiest is simply to convert the rate to a decimal and multiply the net profit in Row E by that decimal. Thus, to discount by 5 per cent we multiply the profit figure by 0.95.

By how much should we discount future profits? The simple answer is to use the expected rate of interest – if we borrow £1,000 today and intend to repay it in one year's time the lender will expect some interest – for the purposes of this example I have assumed an interest rate of 3.4 per cent. Whatever rate we use the simple interest level will be sufficient for something so clear-cut as a loan. But when we are dealing with less tangible factors like predictions of future sales it will not be prudent to allow only today's interest rate.

Sensible marketers increase the discount rate to allow for the additional risks inherent in any long-term business relationship. Examples of such risks include:

- our product could be superseded by a revolutionary new development;
- interest rates may rise above our estimate of 3.4 per cent; only a few years ago UK interest rates were in double figures;
- our competitors may prove to be better at marketing than we are and thus take market share away from us;
- we may make mistakes – even with the most careful planning, mistakes can happen.

For these and other reasons it is sensible to base our discount rate on a higher figure, and in this example we have increased the expected interest rate of 3.4 per cent by 50 per cent to 5 per cent to reflect the additional risks.

This may seem conservative, but as one of the main purposes of this analysis is to justify investment to create future profits, it is safer to be conservative. As with net profit (Row E) you should base this on numbers that make sense in your own business. Your company's accountant or financial controller will tell you what rate they use.

Once we have settled on the discount rate we can apply it year by year. Each year will have a different discount rate, as the numbers compound year by year.

Note that in Year 1 we do not discount profits – this is deemed to be earned within the same accounting period and is thus retained at its full value. So let's see the process in action on Year 2.

If the discount rate is 5 per cent the decimal we use is 0.95 (100 minus 5) – we multiply our net profit (£43,260) by 0.95 to arrive at the NPV contribution of £41,097.

In subsequent years the discount rate is simply 0.95 compounded – thus in Year 3 the rate is 0.95 x 0.95 = 0.9025. Multiplying this figure by 0.95 again gives us 0.857375 (we have set Excel to show this as 0.857 but it actually calculates the NPV figure using the full decimal). A similar rounding can be seen with Year 5 – try it on your calculator.

Row G – Net present value (NPV) contribution

It is now a simple matter to calculate each year's NPV figure and then accumulate these year by year in Row H.

Row I – Lifetime value at net present value

The lifetime value row (Row I) is simply derived by dividing the cumulative NPV contribution in Row H by the original number of customers (1,000 in this model).

What this shows us is the NPV lifetime value for each of the customers we recruited, regardless of the fact that some of them have stopped being customers. As we can see, to divide by the number of customers remaining would not answer the difficult question we posed a few pages ago:

'How much is a new customer worth to us over time?'

In this example the lifetime value at NPV of those 1,000 customers we recruited in Year 1 is predicted to total £168,910. Dividing this by the original number of customers in the cell (1,000) means that each is predicted to be worth £168.91 over the five-year period.

It is worth repeating that the final calculation (Row I in each year) is always the cumulative NPV contribution for that year divided by the number of customers we started with at the beginning of the model, not for that year.

Before moving on to the next stage, which will show how LTV analysis can be used to predict, and eventually compare, the effectiveness of different marketing strategies, we will summarise the key elements of LTV modelling.

The entire success of these models depends on three factors:

- applying a sensible rate of discount;
- the accuracy of our estimated retention rate;
- how well we have predicted annual sales per customer.

The first, discount rate, is a matter of judgement but every company applies the principle of discounted cash flow so your financial director will be able to tell you what rate your company considers appropriate. You should simply use that figure.

The other two are more difficult to predict so most marketers, when using these models for the first time, base these factors on historical analysis of other customer groups.

The technique is simply to review the buying and retention patterns of a group of customers who started from a similar source to those you now wish to model, but who have been buying from the company for two years or more.

This analysis will enable you to calculate their retention rate and their average sales per year.

Where there are no previous customers we are forced to build our own historical file before we can start, we can thus only start with customers who have at least one year's history with us.

It is important to remember that this analysis will be used to make investment decisions so we must be conservative in our estimates, especially in the early days. As time goes on, we can measure the actual retention rates and sales and adjust our model accordingly.

Using LTV analysis with extended buying periods

This process is fairly simple when we are dealing with customers who buy at least once each year. When we are dealing with less frequent purchases, such as cars or computers, we use the same process but the discounting is more complicated. If we take cars as an example and assume that customers replace them every three years, then in place of Years 1, 2, 3, 4 and 5 we would see Years 1, 4, 7, 10 and 13. Because 13 years is rather too long in terms of estimating sales and interest rates we tend to restrict these models to three or at most four buying periods.

Here's a real-life example created for dealers selling £20,000 cars. The analysis was carried out on behalf of the car manufacturer, who was having difficulty persuading dealers to invest more than a small percentage of the profit from each individual sale. He pointed out that car buyers tend to stay with their favourite marque, and thus the profit from a new customer could be accumulated over say, four purchases in a 10-year period.

Table 16.10: 10-year projected LTV

		Year 1	Year 4	Year 7	Year 10
A	Customers	500	350	262.5	210
B	Retention	70%	75%	80%	85%
C	Sales p.a.	£20,000	£22,000	£24,000	£26,000
D	Total sales	£10,000,000	£7,700,000	£6,300,000	£5,460,000
E	Net profit 30%	£3,000,000	£2,310,000	£1,890,000	£1,638,000
F	Discount rate	1	0.857	0.735	0.630
G	NPV contribution	£3,000,000	£1,980,536	£1,389,324	£1,032,349
H	Cum NPV contribution	£3,000,000	£4,980,536	£6,369,860	£7,402,208
I	Lifetime value at net present value	£6,000.00	£9,961.07	£12,739.72	£14,804.42

The profit from a single sale is £6,000 and dealers were only willing to spend 15 per cent (£900) on achieving a conquest sale (sale to a new customer). Yet repeat sales cost very little to achieve. If they were prepared to spend 12.5 per cent of the 10 year NPV this would double their acquisition budget to more than £1,800.

Now let's look at the second use of LTV modelling – comparing customers recruited in different ways. This time we want to compare two sets of customers: one group was recruited from a direct mail campaign, the second from online banners.

What differences might we see? The online recruits might be younger and have more disposable income, which means their order values may be higher. However, being online shoppers they may also be more fickle and tend to shop around more. Here's a comparison of their five-year LTV projections:

We will use Table 16.9 from page 411 as the base as these were recruited by direct mail.

Repeat of Table 16.9: Customers recruited by direct mail

		Year 1	Year 2	Year 3	Year 4	Year 5
A	Customers	1,000	700	507.5	385.7	309
B	Retention	70%	72.5%	76%	80%	85%
C	Sales p.a.	£300	£309	£318	£328	£338
D	Total sales	£300,000	£216,300	£161,385	£126,510	£104,293
E	Net profit 20%	£60,000	£43,260	£32,277	£25,302	£20,859
F	Discount rate	1	0.95	0.9025	0.8574	0.8145
G	NPV contribution	£60,000	£41,097	£29,130	£21,693	£16,990
H	Cum NPV contribution	£60,000	£101,097	£130,227	£151,920	£168,910
I	Lifetime value at net present value	£60.00	£101.10	£130.23	£151.92	£168.91

Table 16.11: Customers recruited online

		Year 1	Year 2	Year 3	Year 4	Year 5
A	Customers	1,000	450	225	123.75	74.25
B	Retention	45%	50%	55%	60%	65%
C	Sales p.a.	£400	£412	£425	£440	£460
D	Total sales	£400,000	£185,400	£95,625	£54,450	£34,155
E	Net profit 20%	£80,000	£37,080	£19,125	£10,890	£6,831
F	Discount rate	1	0.95	0.9025	0.857	0.815
G	NPV contribution	£80,000	£35,226	£17,260	£9,337	£5,564
H	Cum NPV contribution	£80,000	£115,226	£132,486	£141,823	£147,387
I	Lifetime value at net present value	£80.00	£115.23	£132.49	£141.82	£147.39

This comparison shows that, although the online recruits spent more money, and we thus reached break even earlier, the higher attrition rate means that over the five-year period, the online recruits generated £21,523 less profit. Also, after five years there are only 74 customers remaining compared to 309 in the control group. Note that although the direct mail group performed better in this case it will not always work like this. However, many experienced direct marketers have found that customers who are recruited through a long copy application such as direct mail tend to be more committed in the long term.

Using lifetime value modelling to evaluate marketing strategies

We can also use LTV analysis as a measure of the relative effectiveness of alternative marketing strategies.

Let us assume we wish to test a new customer retention strategy. This strategy is to anticipate customers' needs by means of a sophisticated database system fed by information from detailed questionnaires. These questionnaires are gathered in various ways: via the sales force, through website registrations and email responses, telephone and by post.

The objective of this new strategy is to increase sales and retention rates by targeting our communications to increase their relevance and thus their acceptability and effectiveness.

The plan is to contact individual customers with relevant offers at appropriate times.

The information on which this strategy is based must be accurate and constantly updated, which requires a lot of effort from all customer facing employees.

Good database management is crucial. In each promotional cycle, the database identifies customers for whom a specific offer would be appropriate. In addition to identifying the individuals the system should:

- match products to customer types and buying patterns;
- indicate the potential value of each prospect enabling an appropriate offer to be made. For example, a firm selling catering foods to cafés and restaurants would make a different offer to a café selling 50 meals a day than it would to one selling 1,000 meals a day;
- produce the necessary personalised communications;
- monitor results, produce reports and update customer records.

We can produce some lifetime value models to evaluate the effects of the new strategy. The first step is to build a control (or base) table like the ones we have studied earlier. This is built on the basis that, apart from our normal advertising, no additional customer marketing is carried out.

Table 16.12, overleaf, is the control against which we compare our predictions in Table 16.13 – the one that allows for the extra expenditure and its likely effects on our customers.

Table 16.12: Control group, no additional marketing

		Year 1	Year 2	Year 3	Year 4	Year 5
A	Customers	1000	650	455	341.25	273
B	Retention	65%	70.0%	75%	80%	85%
C	Sales p.a.	£400	£420	£445	£475	£510
D	Total sales	£400,000	£273,000	£202,475	£162,094	£139,230
E	Net profit 20%	£80,000	£54,600	£40,495	£32,419	£27,846
F	Discount rate	1	0.95	0.9025	0.8574	0.8145
G	NPV contribution	£80,000	£51,870	£36,547	£27,795	£22,681
H	Cum NPV contribution	£80,000	£131,870	£168,417	£196,212	£218,893
I	Lifetime value at net present value	£80.00	£131.87	£168.42	£196.21	£218.89

We develop and test our marketing ideas and build the likely effects into Table 16.13 opposite – we then monitor closely to measure the actual effects of the new programme as it progresses.

We start with the assumption that if we treat our customers well they will respond better. If we only communicate with them when we have an offer or some useful information that is relevant to them, rather than simply mailing each customer with lots of offers, we will generate more sales at less cost. We will also retain more customers year to year.

Customer retention strategy (loyalty building) affects five things:

1. **Recommendations** Satisfied customers are more likely to recommend us to their friends and colleagues. We can also undertake positive marketing actions to encourage this.
2. **Retention** Building relationships by regular, relevant communication tends to increase customer retention.
3. **Sales** Targeted database activities can be expected to increase cross-selling, up-selling and frequency of purchase.
4. **Profits** Database activities can also help us reduce costs, in some cases, by changing distribution channels. Companies selling via resellers for example, find they can dramatically reduce their costs when they sell further products by direct mail to their database customers (i.e. those who return warranty cards or register in some other way). Great care must be exercised with such a strategy so as to avoid alienating existing profitable business channels.
5. **Marketing costs** Will increase because the estimated costs of running the new communications programmes have also to be built into the LTV model.

Well-planned marketing campaigns, targeting only those prospects more likely to be interested, can actually achieve the same or even more sales at less cost. Furthermore, if the funds invested are transferred from another less cost-efficient programme, they can actually reduce overall marketing costs.

The objective of a retention strategy is to increase the first four factors, recognising that costs will also increase, especially to the targeted segments.

EXAMPLE

A good example of better, more relevant targeting is the experience of a major British high street bank. Before the change they sent out around 80 promotional mailings a year, with little customer targeting. Now they send more than 400 mailings a year, each to a tightly targeted segment of their customer file. This new policy has increased their costs but the return on investment from the programme has grown by more than 300 per cent.

We now develop a second model using our best estimates of the changes the new programme will cause. Table 16.13 shows how these factors can affect our calculations.

Table 16.13: Showing the effects of the retention strategy

		Year 1	Year 2	Year 3	Year 4	Year 5
A	Recommends rate	5%	5%	5%	5%	5%
B	Customers gained		50	40	34	31
C	Customers	1000	800	680	612	569
D	Retention	75%	80%	85%	88%	90%
E	Sales p.a.	£480	£500	£550	£630	£700
F	Total sales	£480,000	£400,000	£374,000	£385,560	£398,412
G	Net profit 20%	£96,000	£80,000	£74,800	£77,112	£79,682
H	Retention activities £10	£10,000	£8,000	£6,800	£6,120	£5,692
I	Net contribution	£86,000	£72,000	£68,000	£70,992	£73,991
J	Discount rate	1	0.95	0.9025	0.8574	0.8145
K	NPV contribution	£86,000	£68,400	£61,370	£60,867	£60,266
L	Cum NPV contribution	£86,000	£154,400	£215,770	£276,637	£336,903
M	Lifetime value at NPV	£86.00	£154.40	£215.77	£276.64	£336.90

As before we will work through the table row by row.

Row A – Recommends rate

We have assumed that by developing better relationships through making more relevant offers, we can encourage 5 per cent of our customers to recommend someone to us. If this assumption is correct our customer base will increase by 5 per cent each year, partially offsetting the natural attrition.

Thus our Year 1 base of 1,000 customers will bring in 50 additional customers during the year and these can be added to our Year 2 customer strength.

Note: This is the only circumstance in which new customers can be added to the model during its life. Our objective is to track only the performance of the 1,000 customers recruited in Year 1. The recommended customers are with us only because we recruited those 1,000 in the first place so they can legitimately be added.

Row D – Retention rate

We are assuming that better customer communications will increase our retention rate in Year 1 from 65 per cent to 75 per cent with further small increases in the rate each year. This is a very conservative assumption because many programmes have produced much better gains than this.

How much control do we have over the retention rate?

We can control our marketing activities and, by careful testing, identify factors that increase or decrease the retention rate. We can also control the level of service we offer and our customers' perceptions of us as a supplier.

There are some things we cannot directly control:

- **Our competitors** – they may make better offers than we do
- **The economy** – recession can ruin many carefully constructed marketing plans
- **World news** – many well-planned marketing campaigns perform below expectations at times of world crisis when many customers have a lot more on their minds than making buying decisions

Row C – Customers

If we have estimated our recommends and retention rates correctly we will see a considerable increase in the number of customers remaining with us year on year.

This time in Year 5, instead of having only 273 of our original 1,000 customers we have 569 remaining. But there is more to come.

If we are going to spend more time and money communicating with our customers it is reasonable to assume that they will buy more from us – we do not yet know how much but some increase is highly likely. We have estimated this at approximately 20 per cent in Year 1 (£400 + 20% = £480), with similar increases in subsequent years.

This may not prove totally accurate but it is typical of what many retention programmes have achieved and careful monitoring will soon tell us how good our estimating is. We can adjust our model as time goes on to reflect actual achievements in the earlier years.

The improvements in customer strength and sales have a significant effect on our total sales shown in Row F.

Row H – Cost of retention activities

We have allowed £10 per customer per year for this programme, which should be enough for some database analysis, and four communications per customer.

Note that although based on fact, the figures in these models are hypothetical to demonstrate the process. You must calculate your own figures based on conditions in your own company and industry.

Rows I to M are calculated in the same way as rows E to I in Table 16.12.

Comparison of lifetime values with and without the retention programme

In Table 16.14 we compare the bottom lines of Tables 16.12 and 16.13 (lifetime value at net present value) and we can clearly see the difference between the values with and without the new communications programme (assuming our projections are correct).

Table 16.14: Comparison with and without database programme

	Year 1	Year 2	Year 3	Year 4	Year 5
Table 1	£80.00	£131.87	£168.42	£196.21	£218.89
Table 2	£86.00	£154.40	£215.77	£276.64	£336.90
Increase	£6.00	£22.53	£47.35	£80.43	£118.01
1,000 customers	£6,000	£22,530	£47,353	£80,425	£118,010
5,000 customers	£30,000	£112,650	£236,766	£402,125	£590,051

Table 16.14 shows that if our assumptions are correct, our customer retention programme will increase the average lifetime value of each customer recruited (not just those remaining) by £118.01.

This means that if we have a total of 1,000 customers, and we can increase their lifetime (five year) profit by an average of £118.01, we shall add £118,010 to the bottom line. With 5,000 customers the additional profit would amount to £590,051.

What if the analysis predicts a drop in profits?

Although the above example shows a worthwhile gain in net profit, not all retention building programmes will work so well. In effect we are seeking a positive balance between the extra expenditure we need to implement the programme and the additional profit it produces.

Sometimes the additional costs incurred in buying and implementing new software and office systems can cost more than the gains. Costs, especially those relating to systems development, must be carefully and fairly allocated especially if they can also contribute to future prosperity.

However, even if the predictions are negative, the LTV analysis will give us early warning and prevent us from pumping further money into a redundant strategy.

How long is 'lifetime'?

In most of the above examples we have used a period of five years, but is this correct? This is one of the questions most frequently asked by my students. The answer is that the period varies according to business circumstances.

A consumer mail order company for example, may use a period of five years, whereas a life insurance company may consider 20 years the minimum. A bank may use five years for a current account customer but 25 years for a mortgage customer. And as we have seen when customers buy only every two or three years a 10- or 13-year projection is sensible.

It is sensible to work out models for a number of periods in the light of prevailing conditions in your own marketplace, asking 'What is a sensible period for us?'

Why not run the model through until there are no customers left? This is another frequently asked question. The answer is that, as this is a predictive technique, it is full of assumptions. Therefore, to stop when there are still a good number of customers in the model gives us an additional margin of safety. Even if we have been a little optimistic in our sales estimates the fact that some customers remain means that we will probably reach our profit target eventually even if it takes a little longer than we predicted.

Predicting lifetime value by customer segment

LTV analysis is not just used to make investment decisions and compare retention strategies. Many companies also use it to compare the longer-term quality of customers recruited by different media or offers. We may be able to increase the number of new customers by offering a free gift with first purchase, but this offer may attract a less committed customer whose future buying behaviour may be markedly different from the customer who first bought without an inducement.

Lifetime value can vary according to the medium we used for recruitment, the product first purchased, the time of year that the first purchase was made and so on.

Where possible we should segment customers by type (perhaps taking account of geodemographic and lifestyle factors), product, source (e.g. online, offline, targeted and broadscale media), and by the type of offer that originally attracted them.

We may then see that differing levels of investment are appropriate for each segment, perhaps ranging from thousands of pounds to zero. If we do not segment down to this level we will be ignoring one of the key strategic benefits of direct marketing, which is the ability to vary programmes, timing, even copy according to the response and buying patterns we predict or observe for each segment.

How to develop LTV calculations

Lifetime value predictions are not as difficult as they may seem. The essential steps are:

1. Select the samples. Size is not critical so long as there are enough of them to leave a

significant sample in the final year of the model. They should have become customers at around the same time and, if this is the first LTV exercise in the company, more than one year ago. Unless there is at least one year's data we will not be able to make sensible estimates of annual sales and retention rates. Data from two years would be better.

2. Calculate the retention rate into Year 2 from Year 1. Estimate retention rates for the remaining years of the model. First year retention is likely to be lower than subsequent years.
3. Calculate annual sales.
4. Calculate costs and profit margins.
5. Decide on an appropriate discount rate. Be prudent and remember the risks.
6. Project the figures over the remaining years of the model. Build the model in a spreadsheet such as Excel, which will make it easy to make modifications and instantly see the results.
7. Plot the effects of various assumptions:
   — 'What if I can increase retention by a further 5 per cent.'
   — 'Let's see what will happen if I spend £15 a head on the retention programme.'
   — 'Suppose I cut my predicted gains in half.'
8. Keep practising the technique. Don't stop experimenting and checking actual results against predictions.

Conclusion

For many businesses, lifetime value analysis is a practical realistic technique for determining the effectiveness of various marketing strategies. It can be applied to a marketing plan to predict the likely outcome before a significant amount of money is spent.

Before acting on hunches and presumptions, we work hard to prove, at least in theory, whether any proposed programme has a chance of success, and if not, which factor needs improving.

The theory can be tested as the programme progresses, and the activity can be modified or even abandoned if the assumptions prove to be incorrect. The basic idea is to produce strategies that increase lifetime value by as much as possible. Once we have set up a model it is possible, using theoretical 'what if' analyses, to see what we can do to increase lifetime value. The effect of each possible action can be estimated to determine whether the result is likely to be worth the investment.

As mentioned earlier, not all customer development programmes will prove to be cost-effective. Constant rigorous evaluation is necessary so that non-productive programmes can be identified and abandoned quickly.

The special metrics of online marketing

The budgeting and campaign planning tools we have examined so far are equally applicable for both offline and online campaigns.

There are some additional tools available only to online marketers and we will now consider those.

What are the basic Web metrics?

This is an immensely complex area and one that has engendered several full-length textbooks.

This complexity is illustrated by some recent research by Forrester, published in 2010. They found:

1. In the USA and Europe alone, in 2009 around $50 billion was spent on interactive marketing, yet around 50 per cent of the organisations using it say that they struggle to justify the return on investment (ROI) of this expenditure.

2. And around 60 per cent of those struggling say this is because they do not have enough people to do the necessary analysis.

What this research is telling us is that there is a huge amount of data, but it takes many people hours to read it.

The first step

If a company wants to prove ROI from online marketing, the first thing is to decide what it wants to measure from the vast amount of data out there, and then either commit to hiring the necessary staff, or find an external partner that can do the metrics for them.

There are several 'layers' of measurement, from simple audience measurement through to highly sophisticated emerging metrics such as online sentiment towards a brand, so we will now summarise the options.

1. **Audience and activities**

    For example, how many people were exposed to an advertisement; number of click-throughs; unique site visitors; email delivery and bounce rates and so on. These data can usually be obtained from ad servers, online agencies, and email service providers as part of their normal service.

Many users permit this basic data to be shared and so organisations can compare their performance against current industry 'norms'. They can also compare these basic results with those obtained from offline media. A good source of this data is Neilson NetRatings.

Such basic audience data is easy to obtain and compare, but doesn't tell us anything about the people who are responding.

2. **Behavioural measures**

    Somewhat more sophisticated than simple audience data these tend to go further into the next stage, such as how quickly visitors leave a site. An important measure here is 'single-access ratio', which is the percentage of visitors who leave the site immediately; it is also important to identify further points at which an unusually large number of people leave a site, which can help in improving site navigation.

These measures also enable costs to be analysed: cost per 1,000 ad impressions served; cost per click; cost per order; and so improve the marketers ability to compare performance of different online activities and also with offline media actions.

Referrals can also be measured in this category and their volume can help to infer levels of satisfaction. A higher number of referrals implies customer satisfaction. At this stage we are still only measuring actions as opposed to attitudes and insight

3. **Attitudinal measures**

This is where we start to use more advanced direct marketing methods, because at this stage we start to gather information from individuals.

Using registration questionnaires, satisfaction surveys and similar response devices we can start to identify attitudes and purchase intentions, and this can lead us to developing much more customer-centric communications. A good example of this is the following online questionnaire from Direct Line.

Figure 16.4: Direct Line online questionnaire

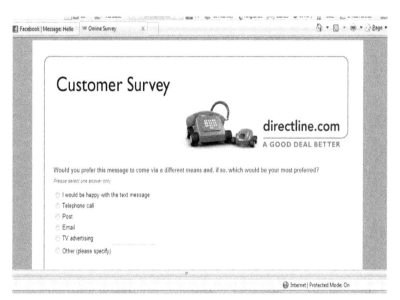

The two subsequent screens asked the following, each with multiple choice answers:

'To what extend would you be willing to receive messages like this again?'

'How often would like to receive these messages?'

Finally:

'Listed below are some ideas of the types of messages we could potentially send to you in the future. Please tell us which, if any, of the following topics appeal to you.'

This is excellent because it puts the customer in control of future communications. The epitome of permission marketing.

Gathering this type of data also enables us to identify those with a higher propensity to recommend their friends or colleagues, and also to start sophisticated segmentation, modelling and ultimately loyalty building campaigns

4. **Multimedia measures**
   Now we are entering the advanced stage, where we start to identify and measure the interaction between and across various online and offline media.

There are many tools and specialists offering immensely detailed reports in this area and at this stage an organisation needs to consider the involvement of professional external partners to gain the full benefit of such data.

5. **What's new?**
   Development in this field is never ending, in fact it is accelerating. There are organisations and tools to measure the content of the millions of blogs out there, to identify mentions of keywords, such as your brand name, on social media sites,

Many large brand advertisers now measure the 'buzz' surrounding their brand, a current campaign, or just some fact that has been in the news this week.

Again this requires specialist knowledge, and it is a full-time job for many analysts in large organisations.

Keeping in touch

If you simply want to keep in touch generally you should sign up for some of the many newsletters listed in the appendix.

In a field such as this, with new developments happening all the time understanding Web metrics can be a full time job. The following new book has received lavish praise from Web experts including the legendary Seth Godin who said:

'Analytics is vitally important and no one (no one) explains it more elegantly, more simply, or more powerfully than Avinash Kaushik. Consider buying up all the copies of this book before your competition gets a copy.' Web Analytics 2.0 by Avinash Kaushik

CASE STUDY
VISITSCOTLAND: THE IDM BUSINESS PERFORMANCE AWARDS
2009 Silver Award-Winner Campaign: Keep Discovering

INTRODUCTION

The Keep Discovering programme is a new approach for VisitScotland and its agencies, Union Direct and Fraoch Marketing — a shift from product-focused direct marketing to a more customer relationship-based strategy. This programme was able to capitalise on VisitScotland's successful 2005 Climbing the Ladder campaign, and many years of data collection and enhancement, including the introduction of a 'loyalty question' in 2003.

VisitScotland already had a good understanding of its visitors, but this programme signified a move to deepen its knowledge of their needs, motivations and revenue potential, in order that customer relationships could be strengthened and revenue increased. The Keep Discovering programme is believed to be the first of its kind undertaken by a tourist authority.

An enviable 68:1 return on investment is adequate proof that VisitScotland has successfully implemented a ground-breaking visitor relationship marketing programme, contributing £58m to the Scottish economy in 2007. The Keep Discovering programme exceeded its challenging targets in its first 12 months in a highly competitive marketplace. Programme reviews and refinement are ongoing, to build on the programme's early success and enable the marketing strategy to continue to meet VisitScotland's immediate and long-term business objectives.

MARKET BACKGROUND

VisitScotland is Scotland's official tourism agency. Its remit is the creation and nurturing of a strong 'Scotland' brand by producing high impact marketing communications targeting a diverse target audience to encourage first-time and repeat visits to Scotland. Eight out of 10 visitors to Scotland arrive from the UK and Ireland. As UK consumers represent 83 per cent of the volume and 68 per cent of the value of Scottish tourism, worth £2.84bn per annum (UKTS 2007), it is no surprise that increasing UK market share is of great strategic importance to VisitScotland.

VisitScotland's main aim is to increase Scotland's share of the UK holiday market by 50 per cent over the next 10 years. In order to achieve this ambitious objective, VisitScotland must demonstrate Scotland's richness and diversity as a holiday destination. It needs to balance the maintenance of long-term relationships with existing visitors with an effective strategy to attract new ones. As a holiday destination, Scotland faces stiff competition from the many choices in the global holiday market. The proliferation of budget airlines offering a good choice of flights from regional airports, has made far flung destinations accessible to even modest budgets.

Prior to the Keep Discovering programme, VisitScotland's marketing communications strategy had concentrated on marketing activities and destinations, segmenting visitors and potential visitors according to their known interests, largely based on database records of previous information requests. VisitScotland recognised that this product-led approach had created two key issues:

1. Individuals might receive a variety of mailings and emails about different products and destinations, potentially leaving recipients with the impression of a disconnected series of rather disparate communications.
2. As the marketing communication budget was being allocated on the basis of expressed interest rather than individual revenue potential, low-value visitors might receive multiple mailings, while high-value visitors could be ignored.

Research findings supported the view that, in most cases, multiple holiday interests needed to be addressed by VisitScotland's communications to both current and future visitors. VisitScotland recognized that it needed to shift the basis of its marketing communication planning from product to relationship marketing.

KEEP DISCOVERING PROGRAMME OBJECTIVES

It was imperative that the new loyalty programme supported VisitScotland's overall marketing objectives, to nurture a strong 'Scotland' destination brand. All Keep Discovering communications had to deliver the core brand proposition that Scotland offers a 'powerfully enriching personal experience' to visitors. Communications had to engage visitors on a personal level in order to ultimately achieve every visitor's full revenue potential.

The specific objectives for Keep Discovering were:

- To deliver a minimum return on investment of 25:1, a significant uplift on previous direct marketing campaign performance.
- To move 10 per cent of the visitor database from the 'Occasional' segment to the 'Regular' segment. These segments are VisitScotland's two top-performing database segments, classified according to its in-house segmentation system, the loyalty ladder.

SEGMENTATION AND TARGETING STRATEGY

In order to optimise the £500,000 direct marketing budget, it was imperative that the Keep Discovering programme selected the most promising of 3 million database records. VisitScotland has an impressive database as a result of the merger of all of Scotland's regional area tourist board databases in 2005, and its long-running data collection and enhancement strategy. It has been continuously improving its database profiling techniques since 1995.

The inclusion of a 'loyalty question' in 2003, provided a vital insight into a person's attitude to Scotland as a destination and the likelihood that they will visit. The loyalty question is asked at the first data-capture opportunity, allowing a person to be assigned to an appropriate rung on VisitScotland's loyalty ladder. The lowest rung on the ladder is 'Rejecter', moving up through 'Prospects', 'Lapsed' and 'Occasionals', and ending with the most loyal 'Regular' visitors who occupy the top rung.

The database provided the richest source of good prospects for the Keep Discovering programme, as many of them had already indicated a much stronger affinity for Scotland than the wider public. Research revealed the percentage of people on the database, and in the wider market, who could be allocated to VisitScotland's 'Regular' and 'Occasional' loyalty ladder segments (Table 16.16). Research also enabled VisitScotland to calculate 'Regular' and 'Occasional' visitors' potential annual value to the Scottish economy: £900 and £320, respectively. This finding quantified how much the Scottish economy could benefit from encouraging visitors to progress up the loyalty ladder by deepening their relationship with the Scotland brand.

Extensive database analysis and profiling, quantitative research and segmentation modelling, identified the five inter-related factors that best defined the most promising visitor segments for the Keep Discovering programme:

- Geodemographics;
- Location, that is, proximity to Scotland;
- Preferred holiday marketing channel, for example brochure or website;
- Existing relationship with Scotland defined by their status on the loyalty ladder; and
- General preference for holidaying in the UK or abroad.

This exercise created a classification of the UK population consisting of ten strategic segments, each with a defined potential value to the Scottish economy.

VisitScotland prioritised six segments, which were then overlaid onto existing database records to improve targeting, specify communication tone of voice and content, and highlight data gaps. This segmentation approach allowed spend to be targeted to the individuals who offered the greatest revenue potential, paving the way for two layers of personalisation, at individual and segment level. Now that the visitors with the highest revenue potential had been identified, VisitScotland could develop communications to encourage them to take more breaks and deepen their interaction with Scotland, strengthening their relationship with the brand and helping them ascend the loyalty ladder.

COMMUNICATIONS STRATEGY

VisitScotland's communication strategy has been developed to reflect well-established visitor holiday patterns. The Keep Discovering programme had to be fully integrated with this rolling 12-month seasonal communications plan to ensure that communications did not appear fragmented to recipients. Thus, within the existing communications framework, the programme aimed to deliver timely and relevant messages to maximise each recipient's engagement with the Scotland brand, ultimately leading to positive action by the recipient.

A product portfolio was developed in conjunction with each Keep Discovering communication. The product portfolio offered people a good range of options reflecting their areas of interest and expectations.

Table 16.15: VisitScotland segmentation

Loyalty ladder Segment	Database record %	Wider UK market %
Regular	45	10
Occasional	30	14

This directly supported the overall programme objective of realising each visitor's revenue potential. This new product development approach was informed by the insight that, if potentially high-value visitors are given relevant, inspirational ideas for 'things to do on a Scottish holiday', supported by related personalised offers from travel, accommodation and activity companies, then they are more likely to visit Scotland, and keep coming back.

PROGRAMME EXECUTION — THE FIVE 'Is'

Segment-based research indicated that migrating people from 'Occasional' to 'Regular' segments represented a potential annual revenue uplift of £580. Therefore, it made sense to initially concentrate the marketing budget and effort on the 'Occasionals' on the database.

This segment received four mailings during the year, whereas 'Regular' segment visitors were sent only one, relatively expensive, high-impact communication. 'Regulars' were already demonstrating a high degree of loyalty to Scotland as a holiday destination, and it was therefore more likely that they would be proactive about contacting VisitScotland for information or to arrange a trip. The 'Regulars' existing relationship with Scotland was recognised by allowing a more natural two-way dialogue to develop without further prompting. Communication content reflected each person's areas of interest from the database.

To achieve excellent implementation, the Keep Discovering team focused on the five 'Is' , as follows:

1. *Inspire* – Scotland's beautiful scenery is its strongest attraction for many visitors, so stunning photography was used in all programme communications to create and reinforce a desire to visit Scotland

Figure 16.5: Keep Discovering envelope

2. *Individual* – Communication content was personalised and tailored to correspond to each recipient's current level of engagement with Scotland, in addition to featuring content known to be of interest to them:

   'Regular' visitors received a handy glovebox-sized folder, with personalised 'off the beaten track' ideas in a glossy insert format, ideal for future reference and practical use. For example, a known 'foodie' who enjoys walking would receive inserts featuring walks in leafy glens culminating in a country pub or noteworthy restaurant.

'Occasional' visitors received personalised information featuring Scotland's better-known attractions, as non-regulars may not yet be familiar with all of Scotland's headline venues and experiences. 'Occasionals' received an invitation to request the folder, allowing VisitScotland to simultaneously gauge interest, encourage interaction and manage costs

3. *Incentives* — Digital printing techniques meant that personalised tailored offers could be compiled and delivered cost-effectively. For example, potential visitors travelling from Ireland received a travel discount offer from Stena Line ferries and known walking enthusiasts were sent a discount offer on walking maps, while those preferring to stay in bed and breakfasts were given an appropriate accommodation offer:

Figure 16.6: Keep Discovering personalised offers

Figure 16.7: e-zine Keep Discovering — visitscotland.com/keep discovering

4. *Interaction* — Relationship marketing programmes must encourage response and provide recipients with a range of options for interacting with the brand, including updating personal information. Every mailing incorporated a personalised incentivised survey. VisitScotland pre-printed any individual data it already held on its database in the survey, recognising its existing relationship with the recipient and saving them the trouble of re-supplying the data.

5. *Integration* — Keep Discovering was fully integrated with VisitScotland's other channels and promotions to ensure that all communications contribute towards a harmonious dialogue with visitors, for example, www.visitscotland.com/keep discovering — a sister website was created to enable visitors to develop their own online file, and a monthly e-zine keeps registered visitors up to date with new information and offers

Figure 16.8: Keep Discovering Autumn Gold mailing

National promotions — the rolling marketing communication plan incorporated several high-profile promotions to encourage tourism during the quieter times of year, notably the Autumn Gold and Winter White promotions.

The Keep Discovering programme maximised its synergy with these promotions by including related offers in its mailings and reflecting seasonal themes in its creative content and imagery.

RESULTS

Keep Discovering programme metrics show the positive impact of the new relationship marketing strategy. The programme will continue to deliver benefits in the future, helping to strengthen strategic partnerships with regional councils and business partners. Maintaining and developing these relationships is essential in ensuring the programme's ongoing success, enabling it to reach a wider audience with the most appropriate products, offers and communications to steadily increase the revenue from Scottish tourism in the longer term.

Key programme measures include the following:

Return on investment — Research results show that 127,529 Scottish breaks had been taken by 160,000 visitors in the Keep Discovering programme. This equated to a revenue contribution of £58m, of which £18m is considered to be directly attributable to the Keep Discovering programme. The programme budget was just under £265,000, meaning that Keep Discovering achieved an exceptionally high return on investment of 68:1, significantly exceeding the 25:1 target.

Progress up the loyalty ladder — Movement was measured using a telephone tracking study of mailed and non-mailed (control) visitor sample groups. Research conducted after phase three of the programme showed that 5 per cent more of the mailed group had become 'Regulars' and lapse rates in this segment had fallen by 10 per cent compared to the control — overall, a 15 per cent increase in loyalty compared to the control sample. Database analysis at the end of 2008 demonstrated that the number of visitors classifying themselves as 'Regulars' had increased by 19.75 per cent. Loyalty development continues to be a key success measure as the programme develops.

Response rates — The first four communication phases of the programme achieved good response rates, exceeding expectations and revealing a high level of engagement with the programme among the target segments.

Table 16.16: Mailing results

	Phase One Response	Phase Two Response	Phase Three Response	Phase Four Response
Mailed 'Regular'	17%	Not mailed	Not mailed	Not mailed
Mailed 'Occasional'	14%	11.8%	10.4%	14.8%
E-zine	6.5%	4.9%	5.0%	5.6%

Quantitative research confirms a high level of engagement:

80 per cent of 'Regulars' and 74 per cent of 'Occasionals' surveyed agreed that the communications made them 'feel that VisitScotland knows what interests me personally'.

84 per cent of 'Regulars' and 82p per cent of 'Occasionals' said they 'looked forward to receiving the literature'.

86 per cent of 'Regulars' and 75 per cent of 'Occasionals' agreed that the mailings 'made me want to take a break in Scotland'.

LESSONS LEARNED

The Keep Discovering customer relationship-building programme created a unifying focus for VisitScotland's communication strategy, helping to drive visitor communications that reflect the customer journey across channels. Improving the synergy between on- and offline communications strengthened VisitScotland's brand, contributing to its longer-term goal of establishing www.visitscotland.com as the principal portal for Scottish tourism. The objective to significantly increase the number of visitors classified as 'Regular' provided a clear aim for the Scotland programme in the short and long term, and created a useful springboard for continued revenue and market share growth.

VisitScotland's sophisticated segmentation, using rigorous data analysis and research, underpinned every aspect of the Keep Discovering programme. The carefully developed data strategy enabled the Keep Discovering team to define and implement tight targeting and deliver highly personalised content to generate an impressive and prompt return on investment. This approach also enabled it to deliver a positive and consistent brand experience, open dialogue and excellence throughout the programme's implementation.

The programme could not have succeeded without the data and insight legacy inherited from previous campaigns and strategies. VisitScotland has long recognised the value of collecting, analysing and enhancing good-quality visitor data, and this has enabled a culture of ongoing learning and improvement that allows it to capitalise and build on its constantly growing body of knowledge.

We are grateful to VisitScotland and its agencies Union Direct and Fraoch Marketing, for permission to reproduce this case study.

SUMMARY

In this chapter we looked at the process of evaluation, measurement and budgeting. We saw that measurement and accountability is a key advantage of response-driven direct marketing.

One of the benefits of measurement is the understanding of where revenue comes from; is it from existing or newly acquired customers? This allows the company to focus its marketing activity on the most profitable source of business.

We explored several key direct marketing measures including the use of cost per thousand as a way of comparing different quotes; cost per enquiry, lead, reply, response, order or sale as a way of evaluating campaigns and finally the simplest percentage, response rate.

We reviewed the strengths and weaknesses of the allowable cost approach and then moved up a level to see the more effective 'campaign based budgeting'.

We went on to consider how we should manage overheads and explored the contribution approach. This takes into account all the revenue and costs directly associated with an activity. We followed a detailed case study that showed the value of the contribution approach to costs in looking at the additional costs incurred in carrying out any activity.

We started the budgeting process by looking at fixed, variable and overheads or indirect fixed costs and defined each.

We looked at the behaviour of costs over large volumes and saw that generally up to a certain point they fell proportionately. However, we also saw that after a certain volume there were only limited savings available as the economies of scale had been used. The importance of understanding costs was stressed, as we need a clear view on the profit of each activity.

The internal and external influences on the budgeting process were explored and the benefits of budgeting were outlined:

- it forces us to plan ahead and define our future objectives;
- it gives us a useful overview and checklist of planned activities;
- it makes us highlight key actions and responsibilities;
- it forces us to define measurements of performance;
- it helps us make decisions about trade-offs and priorities;
- it gives early warning of problems enabling corrective action.

We saw that budgeting is a continuous process that helps to manage and improve business performance.

We reviewed the factors that ensure successful budgeting including:

- cooperation and communication between all the people concerned;
- the setting of realistic targets;
- consistent and sustained objectives;
- an easily understood format that is 'owned' by staff;
- frequent reviews of progress and of the system itself.

We saw how to create a campaign budget and this was developed through a worked example of an acquisition campaign.

We went on to explore the key problem for all companies of how much to invest in creating a new customer. This question is answered in part through the use of lifetime value calculations.

We looked at a definition of lifetime value as the net present value of the profit that a company will realise on a new customer during their time as a customer.

We saw that 'customer lifetime' for various companies will vary considerably. We explored the concept through a worked example. We explored each line in detail and saw that the key element in the calculation was of net present value and by how much should we discount future profits. In this example we used 5 per cent but the amount will vary according to the interest rates at the time and our assessment of the additional risk factors.

Lifetime value analysis depends for its success on three factors:

1. A sensible rate of discount.
2. The accuracy of the assumed retention rate.
3. The accuracy of the predicted annual sales per customer.

The importance of conservatism in estimates was stressed as we went on to consider the use of lifetime value analysis in evaluating marketing strategies.

We saw that feeding into the process is good database management to:

- identify individuals;
- match products to customer types and buying cycles;
- indicated potential value of each prospect;
- produce personalised communication;
- monitor results.

We can then produce a lifetime value analysis comparing the impact of alternative strategies.

A loyalty strategy will impact in five areas:

1. Recommendation rates
2. Retention rates
3. Sales
4. Profits
5. Costs

We saw how this worked in practice through an example that compared lifetime value with and without the new communications programme.

Lifetime value analysis allows the following advantages:
- It defines what we can afford to pay to recruit a new customer
- It enables the evaluation of expensive retention programmes
- It helps us focus on the long-term life of a customer and to answer the question, 'What is a sensible period for us to expect a customer to remain with us?'

The final section outlined the various levels of online measurement tools:
1. **Audience and activities** – basic audience data that is useful but does not tell us anything about the individuals that are responding.
2. **Behavioural measures** – these are more sophisticated and include measurements of the length of time visitors stay on the website. These measures also enable many costs to be analysed including cost per click; cost per order and so on.
3. **Attitudinal measures** – these are much more useful for direct marketers as they start to gather information about individuals. We can use registration questionnaires, satisfaction surveys and similar devices to identify attitudes and purchase intentions. You saw an example survey done by Direct Line.
4. **Multimedia measures** – this is the advanced stage where we can measure the interaction between and across online and offline media. This is a very complex field and most companies need to consider the use of external specialists to gain the full benefit of such data.
5. **New measures.** Development in this field is accelerating and there are tools and organisations to measure the millions of online blogs; to identify mentions of key words in searches and on social media sites. A popular measure is 'buzz', the amount of activity that is taking place across the whole Internet. However, the marketer must remember that 'buzz' is secondary to 'business' – the real measure of success is how much business is being gained from the online activity.

In such a rapidly developing field there is no substitute for active online research – so here are some things for you to do:
- Read Avinash Kaushik's book *Web Analytics 2.0.* (Indiana: John Wiley & Sons, 2009).
- **Start exploring – try everything**
  - Explore online videos   *YouTube*
  - Explore online photos   *Flickr*
  - Explore social networks   *Facebook, LinkedIn, My Space,Bebo and so on*
  - Subscribe to the trend-watching sites   *Future Foundation, Forrester, Gartner*
  - Use social media monitoring tools   *Google Alerts is FREE*

- **Start sharing**
  - Use instant messaging *Skype, MSN, Yahoo*
  - Find a blog about something you like *Technorati*
  - Start your own blog *Blogger.com*
  - Upload content and share *Facebook, YouTube*
  - Tag and share content *del.icio.us/digg*

REVIEW QUESTIONS

1. What is the benefit of measurability in direct marketing?
2. List three standard measures in direct marketing.
3. What are the three types of costs in business?
4. Define overheads.
5. What happens to costs with quantity?
6. Why is it important to understand costs and the way they behave?
7. Define the contribution approach to costs.
8. List six benefits of the budgeting process.
9. What are the stages of the budgeting process?
10. What are the requirements for a successful budget?
11. What is net present value?
12. What is the role of lifetime value analysis in direct marketing?
13. What are the three requirements for successful life time value calculations?
14. What are the five 'layers' of online measurement?

CHAPTER 17
ETHICS AND THE LAW

IN THIS CHAPTER

We will introduce the concepts relating to societal marketing, ethical practice, corporate social responsibility and regulation and the law.

After reading this chapter you should be able to:

- Understand the influence of ethics and corporate social responsibility on direct and digital marketing
- Define societal marketing
- Understand the role of corporate values and ethical auditing
- Discuss the concept of the good corporate citizen
- Understand the role of self regulation and codes of practice
- Understand core legal duties and responsibilities within the law relating to direct and digital marketing
- Understand where to go for further advice

Specific topics include:

- The nature of ethics in marketing
- Corporate social responsibility
- The role of self regulation
- The Code of Advertising Practice
- The DMA code of practice
- Direct and digital marketing and the law
- The Data Protection Act 1998
- The Freedom of Information Act 2010
- The Privacy and Electronic Communications (EC Directive) Regulations 2003
- Sources of further information
- Summary

INTRODUCTION

As we enter the second decade of the twenty-first century companies are realising the full extent of their influence on the society and culture that they reflect and contribute to. This influence is rarely neutral and companies can be a force for good or bad. The idea that companies can and should act in an ethical way has been an issue in certain areas for many years, but now, perhaps due to enlightened self interest, companies are taking an active approach to 'good' citizenship. They recognise that they can create 'value from values'. This may be expressed through their values and mission statements based on ethical auditing. It may be through an extended system of self-regulation or it may be forced on companies through the law. This chapter will briefly deal with these areas and in the latter case, outline the key legislation affecting the business and make recommendations on sources of advice.

It could be argued that marketing is not great at marketing itself. In the last decade marketing has been accused of contributing to childhood obesity, binge drinking in young adults and creating false needs in the population as a whole as well as the exploitation on a global scale of natural resources and labour. The direct marketing industry itself has been dealing with the 'junk mail' tag for many years as well as important issues around cold calling door-to-door and on the telephone, miss-selling of utilities and financial services and spam email.

At the heart of the debate around the ethical position of marketing lies the issue of whether we create needs or simply identify and satisfy existing needs, whether we are responsible for driving prices higher, issues on high-pressure sales techniques, whether consumer culture is in itself sustainable and marketing's role in creating built in obsolescence in products.

It would be foolish, naive and irresponsible to say that these issues are not important and should not be dealt with however it is clear that some of the problems placed at the door of marketing are more general in origin and need wider discussion and action in order for them to be resolved. Equally it is true that more and more companies are realising that marketing can be a force for good if it is accountable to its range of stakeholders and we understand that values or not necessarily divorced from creating value and profits.

Values, vision and ethics

Professional ethics can be defined as the standards that govern the behaviour of an individual or group of individuals within a professional context. Ethics generally relate to a moral code and as such they are informed by and influence in turn, the society and culture of which they form a part.

For example, the employment of child labour is now seen as unethical and is illegal whereas in the nineteenth century it was accepted practice. Establishing a code of conduct based on ethics is often subjective and has to adapt to the changing attitudes it draws on, reflects and to some extent reinforces or challenges.

The focus on ethics within the business community has increased dramatically over the last decade and today most major companies will have some sort of values statement or statement of ethical conduct.

The Institute of Business Ethics is a very useful source of information on this area and the website can be found at www.ibe.org.uk.

There are two key drivers behind this focus: a number of high profile corporate scandals and increasing scrutiny of businesses by a variety a stakeholders.

Within companies a range of high level corporate scandals, for example Enron, has created a far greater awareness of the need for a broader approach to corporate governance. Corporate governance concerns itself with who the organisation serves; how the purposes and priorities of that organisation should be decided and how it should function and how power and influence is managed and distributed amongst stakeholders. This is informed by the values, vision and ethical stance of the business.

For many small businesses these interrelationships are simple, personal and reconciled easily through discussion and conversation and they do not need to be formally codified. In larger companies the governance chain as it is known may be very complex and has to deal with a range of contradictory forces. Take, for example, the conflict between operational directors and shareholders. The former may desire to develop the business over time whilst the latter will want an ever increasing level of dividend payments.

The second reason for growth is the fact that marketing practices are open to ever more scrutiny and marketing is finally recognising the core position of trust in building longer term sustainable relationships. Sharp practice damages trust and in the long term can damage the profitability of organisations. These factors have contributed to the development of the societal marketing concept.

Societal marketing

The societal marketing concept is linked with the development of ideas relating to relationship marketing, which, as we have discussed, encourages businesses to think outside the transactional focus of traditional marketing. Societal marketing places the traditional definition of marketing (i.e. the identification satisfaction and anticipation of customer needs) into a broader context, it extends the idea of customer and stresses that exchanges must be in the long term interests of the customer, the company *and* the wider society in which they exist: in other words marketing as enlightened business practice.

This is all very well if we are working in an enlightened business environment but may present problems if competitors are not working in this way and our enlightened marketing means that we are more expensive than the competition.

There is clearly a balance to be achieved that reconciles the organisation, its customers and competitors and the legislative environment in which we work. The criticisms of marketing are often made in isolation and to some extent may invest the profession with more influence than it is capable of exerting. It could be argued that all marketing and marketers can do is comply with the law which is made for the most part by representatives elected by members of the society in which the profession exists.

Some would disagree with this point of view. However, there are many companies who are trying to deliver this principle for a variety of reasons.

Value from values

Here is a list of recent issues that have affected marketing and made headlines – and not just in the marketing press.

- Shock advertising
- False claims and the misuse of statistics
- Advertising to children
- Pester power placing confectionery next to checkouts
- Airbrushing of models in fashion and cosmetic shoots
- Stealth marketing through advertorials
- Intrusive marketing through spam emails and telemarketing
- Marketing of unhealthy products and promotion of obesity

- Data loss and identity issues
- Greenwashing or making false claims about the environmental impact of products
- Marketing of financial services products to vulnerable customers for example loans and credit products
- Marketing of redundant or unsafe products in the developing world, for example baby milk formula in Africa is mixed with unclean water and causes infant deaths, or the use of pesticides banned in Europe in the production of crops in developing countries

We also have accusations of the dumping of toxic waste in the developing world, exploitation of child labour, and the bullying and exploitation of workers in Chinese manufacturing facilities. The last accusations have been levelled at major global corporations and go beyond marketing to the way the business is set up, managed, controlled and scrutinised.

The perceived unethical practices of some marketers give opportunities for companies to exploit a new positioning and since the inception of the Body Shop there have been companies in sectors from cosmetics and beauty to food and drink and financial services that have attempted to promote an ethical positioning. Some examples include:

Green and Black's	www.greenandblacks.com
Ben and Jerry	www.benjerry.co.uk/caringdairy/index.php
Pret A Manger	www.pret.com
Body Shop	www.thebodyshop.co.uk
Innocent	www.innocentdrinks.co.uk

The ethical premium is such that today the ownership of these companies has changed:
- Cadbury (now Kraft) owns the Green and Black's brand
- Ben and Jerry is now owned by Unilever
- Pret A Manger is owned by a venture capital company
- Body shop is owned by L'Oreal
- Innocent is part-owned by Coca-Cola

For these major multinationals the acquisition of 'ethically' positioned companies is simply an approach to market segmentation. They are targeting customers who are willing to pay a premium for ethically positioned products and services aiming to create value from values.

Ethical audits

One area that has grown in influence recently is the role of ethical auditing. Ethical audits allow companies to assess the role and nature of ethics within their marketing plan. This process would take place within the situation analysis of the planning process.

An ethical audit attempts to establish the values that the organisation will live by and will cover a range of areas including:
- the nature of the business
- how it values and rewards employees and
- its policy to customer relationships

- its relationships with other key stakeholders including shareholders and the way it seeks to reward investment
- its relationship with suppliers
- its responsibilities and attitude to the environment and community of which it is a part

Ethical auditing

An ethical audit may cover the following areas:

- impact on the environment – carbon foot printing, sustainability and environmental impact
- impact on vulnerable groups, children, the elderly and disabled
- investment in training and staff development
- employee welfare and working conditions – for example family-friendly employment policies
- HR policies relating to equality and the rights of the individual and anti discrimination policies
- community engagement and impact, recognition of political diversity and trade unions
- leadership and management styles
- communication, whistle-blowing and feedback systems
- competitive stance, style of business, issues relating to gifts and entertainment, inducement and bribery
- management of conflicts of interest, use of company resources and confidentiality
- management of suppliers and channel intermediaries, fair trade
- product safety

Corporate social responsibility (CSR)

As companies have increasingly embraced ethical positioning, corporate social responsibility (CSR) has become an important factor in the development of business strategy. Johnson and Scholes in their book on corporate strategy, define CSR as:

> *'The ways in which an organisation exceeds its minimum obligations to shareholders specified through regulation.'* This implies that CSR goes beyond a simple approach to following the law and regulation and implies a proactive approach to corporate citizenship.' Johnson Scholes, *Exploring Corporate Strategy*. Essex: Pearson, 2008

There are many examples of good CSR practice and your own company maybe involved in a number of ways from sponsoring a sports team, to providing opportunities for work placements to encouraging and enabling staff to volunteer. However, what is important is the idea that we are trying to deal with a range of stakeholder interests and these may vary. This leads to the concept of stakeholder analysis which we touched on in earlier chapters.

Stakeholder expectations

Stakeholders exist inside and outside the organisation. Stakeholder groups include:

- pressure groups
- owners and shareholders

- the investor community
- competitors
- suppliers
- government – local and central
- unions
- customers
- trade bodies
- employees

Therefore, stakeholder analysis can determine the nature of the influence each group exerts and it means that a CSR strategy can attempt to reconcile some of the potentially conflicting areas of interest.

CSR standards

CSR is also being enshrined in international standards and ISO 26000 will be a voluntary standard for companies wanting to adopt procedures for social responsibility.

Whether all this is playing lip service to the rise of the ethical consumer and to quote Barack Obama 'you can put lipstick on a pig but it is still a pig' is open to debate. However, it is clear that the days of corporations being able to run roughshod over local communities and the law are numbered.

Whether this is a result of an enlightened approach to business or simply the need to adopt policies to preserve profitability perhaps does not matter so much as the fact that businesses are increasingly aware that they can be a force for good in the world and produce returns for all their stakeholders.

For a good example of CSR in action take a look at the Marshalls website at: www.marshalls.co.uk/sustainability.

MARSHALLS' CORPORATE RESPONSIBILITY POLICY

We manage our business with pride and integrity.

We are committed to full legal compliance in all that we do.

We aim to provide a safe, fulfilling and rewarding career for all our employees.

We will continue to develop community programmes which support our brand values and further promote our recognition as an active contributor to local community development.

We actively assess and manage the environmental impacts of all our operations.

We will further develop our standing as a responsible business in the community.

We will benchmark and evaluate what we do in order to constantly improve our competitive edge in the marketplace.

We will continually benchmark and evaluate what we do in order to improve our CSR performance.

Source: www.marshalls.co.uk/sustainability/publications/pdfs/CR%20Policy.pdf

---

Self-regulation and codes of conduct

Almost every professional body has a code of conduct some are more rigorous than others. Marketing and direct marketing in particular has a range of codes and regulations that regulate the activities of individuals and companies operating in the business.

The DMA code of practice

The DMA code sets out standards for its members and is enforced by the DMA compliance team and the independent direct marketing commission. The code can be read at: www.dma. org.uk/_attachments/resources/45_S4.pdf. To quote the DMA:

'All the emerging direct marketing channels, such as Bluetooth, SMS, MMS and other online commercial communications are included within the Code, as well as the traditional media such as direct mail, inserts and telemarketing.

The requirements of new and amended legislation, such as the Consumer Protection from Unfair Trading Regulations 2008, the Charities Act 2006 and the Gambling Act 2005 are fully reflected in the Code. The Code also includes a section on environmental responsibility, a full glossary of terms, an appendix on marketing to children and an update on Financial Service Authority (FSA) rules.

In addition to the Code, a number of Best Practice Guidelines set standards that are desirable to achieve. Best Practice Guidelines are supplementary to the Code and are not mandatory except where there is an overlap with the law or with the DM Code of Practice.' www.dma.org.uk

Direct marketing standards

The DMA also manages a range of standards.

- **PAS 2020**
  Produced by BSi British Standards, PAS 2020 is the first independently-accredited environmental standard to provide the direct marketing industry with the means for certifying the environmental performance of a direct marketing campaign.
- **DMA Field Marketing Best Practice Accreditation Scheme**
  The Field Marketing Accreditation Scheme provides an innovative benchmark for field marketing professionalism and establishes a response to the need by practitioners and clients for a high assurance standard.
- **Accredited Response Management Scheme**
  ARM is a rigorous and transparent industry standard that raises professional standards within the response management industry to secure commercial client and consumer satisfaction.
- **List Warranty Register**
  Inspired by the DMA Data Council, the List Warranty Register is designed to make compliance with industry codes of practice easier for both DMA and non-DMA members alike to benefit the industry and consumers.

The preference services

Also under the control of the DMA are the various preference services. The preference services enable businesses to register their wish to opt out of receiving unsolicited telephone calls, and consumers to register their wish to opt out of receiving unsolicited messages by mail, telephone, fax or email. Organisations are obliged either by law or by codes of practice to ensure that these wishes are adhered to.

Figure 17.1: The DMA preference services

The **Mailing Preference Service** allows consumers to register their wish not to receive unsolicited direct mail.
www.mpsonline.org.uk

Baby MPS is a service which allows parents who have suffered a miscarriage or bereavement of a baby in the first weeks of life to register their wish not to receive baby related mailings.
www.mpsonline.org.uk

The **Telephone Preference Service** allows businesses and consumers to register their telephone numbers in order to not receive unsolicited sales and marketing calls.
www.tpsonline.org.uk

Corporate Telephone Preference Service (CTPS) is the central opt out register whereby corporate subscribers can register their wish not to receive unsolicited sales and marketing telephone calls to either all their organisation's telephone numbers, or to certain numbers. It is a legal requirement that companies do not make such calls to numbers registered on the CTPS.
www.tpsonline.org.uk

The **Fax Preference Service** allows consumers and businesses to register their home or business fax number not to receive unsolicited sales and marketing faxes.
www.fpsonline.org.uk

The **Email Preference Service** is a global service managed by the DMA in the States which allows you to register your email address so as not to receive unsolicited sales and marketing email messages. Since December 2003, UK law (EU Privacy and Electronic Comms Dir) changed so that EMPS only needs to be used for email campaigns sent outside the European Union.
www.ims-dm.com/cgi/offemaillist.php

Your Choice allows consumers to register their wish not to receive most unaddressed mail.
www.dma.org.uk/sectors/d2d-choice.asp

The Committee of Advertising Practice (CAP) and the Broadcast Committee of Advertising Practice (BCAP)

CAP and BCAP between them cover all advertising media and they design the codes that are administered by the Advertising Standards Authority (ASA). The codes lay down the general principles for advertisers and media owners to follow and they cover specific areas such as advertising to children and controversial product categories such as alcohol and tobacco.

The CAP core content

- General sections
  - Compliance
  - Recognition of marketing communications
  - Misleading advertising
  - Harm and offence
  - Children
  - Privacy
  - Political advertisements
  - Sales promotions
  - Distance selling
  - Database practice
  - Environmental claims
- Specific category sections
  - Medicines, medical devices, health-related products and beauty products
  - Weight control and slimming
  - Financial products
  - Food, food supplements and associated health or nutrition claims
  - Gambling
  - Lotteries
  - Alcohol
  - Motoring
  - Employment, homework schemes and business opportunities
  - Tobacco, rolling papers and filters

Source: www.cap.org.uk/the-codes.aspx

The CAP and BCAP were updated on September 1 2010 and they can be downloaded at www.cap.org.uk/the-codes.aspx. Other areas of the marketing profession are also governed by codes of conduct and self-regulation.

The CAP provides a comprehensive list at: www.cap.org.uk/resource-centre/useful-links.aspx.

- **Advertising Standards Authority**
  The ASA regulates the content of advertisements, sales promotions and direct marketing in the UK. We make sure standards are kept high by applying the advertising standards codes.
  www.asa.org.uk

▪ **Copy advice service (CAP).**

Copy Advice is an essential service for advertisers, agencies and media owners who want to check how their non-broadcast ads or multimedia concepts measure up against the CAP Code. **www.copyadvice.org.uk**

▪ **Clearcast**

Clearcast, previously the Broadcast Advertising Clearance Centre, operates the clearance system for television commercials before they are screened. **www.clearcast.co.uk**

▪ **Dept for Business, Innovation & Skills**

The Department for Business, Innovation and Skills (BIS) is committed to building Britain's future economic strengths. Its mission is building a dynamic and competitive UK economy by: creating the conditions for business success; promoting innovation, enterprise and science; and giving everyone the skills and opportunities to succeed. **www.bis.gov.uk**

▪ **Financial Services Authority**

The FSA is an independent non-governmental body, given statutory powers by the Financial Services Act 1986, the Banking Act 1987 and the Financial Services and Markets Act 2000 (and other legislation). Its four main aims are to maintain confidence in the UK financial system; to promote public understanding of the financial system; to secure the right degree of protection for consumers; and to contribute to reducing financial crime. **www.fsa.gov.uk**

▪ **Information Commissioner**

The Information Commissioner's Office is an independent supervisory body responsible for enforcing the Data Protection Act and the Freedom of Information Act. It has a range of duties including the promotion of good information handling and the encouragement of codes of practice for data controllers, that is, anyone who decides how and why personal data, (information about identifiable, living individuals) are processed. **www.dataprotection.gov.uk**

▪ **PhonepayPlus**

PhonepayPlus is the organisation that regulates phone-paid services in the UK - the services and goods that can be bought by charging the cost to a mobile phone bill and pre-pay accounts. These include helplines, competitions, downloads, TV voting, news alerts, charitable donations and interactive games. **www.phonepayplus.org.uk**

▪ **Portman Group**

The Portman Group is supported by the UK's leading drinks producers. Their concern is solely with the social responsibility issues surrounding alcohol. **www.portmangroup.org.uk**

▪ **Press Complaints Commission**

The PCC is an independent organisation which deals with complaints from members of the public about the editorial content of newspapers and magazines. **www.pcc.org.uk**

▪ **Radio Advertising Clearance Centre**

RACC is the commercial radio's advertising clearance body. Administered by the industry's trade body, the Commercial Radio Companies' Association, and funded by the commercial radio stations. The RACC clears radio advertisements and sponsorship credits to provide easy use of an otherwise complex medium for both advertisers and agencies. **www.racc.co.uk**; **email: adclear@racc.co.uk**

Internet Advertising Bureau

IAB unifies members of the online advertising community to foster the growth and effectiveness of the industry. It supports ecommerce, interactive advertising and online marketing by establishing standards for the industry, developing innovative research projects and keeping members informed of developments in the sector. **www.iabuk.net**

Internet Service Providers Association

ISPA represents Internet Services Providers in the UK and promotes the interests of the UK Internet industry. **www.ispa.org.uk**

The Internet Watch Foundation

IWF is an independent body which is funded by the UK Internet industry to assist in the regulation of content, particularly child pornography. **www.iwf.org.uk**

Direct Selling Association

DSA is the trade association for direct selling companies. **www.dsa.org.uk**

Electronic Retailing Association

The European division of the Electronic Retailing Association, serving direct-to-consumer and distance retailers, who sell through TV, Internet and radio. **www.eraeurope.org**

Fax Preference Service

The FPS is available to businesses and individuals to register fax numbers on which they do not wish to receive fax marketing messages. **www.fpsonline.org.uk**

International Advertising Association

The IAA is a worldwide business association for all individuals and enterprises involved in the branding process. A global advocate for the freedom of commercial speech, the IAA represents 4,300 members in 95 countries. The UK is one of the largest and most active groups. **www.iaauk.com**

Institute of Direct Marketing

Founded in 1987, IDM is Europe's foremost professional development body for interactive and direct marketing. The Institute is a non-profit organisation, and educational trust and a registered charity. **www.theidm.com**

Institute of Practitioners in Advertising

The industry body and professional institute of UK advertising agencies, the IPA acts as spokesman for its members, representing them on issues of common concern and speaking on their behalf in negotiations with media bodies, government departments and unions and media owners. **www.ipa.co.uk**

Incorporated Society of British Advertisers

ISBA represents £6.5b of marketing communications spend and is the single body, within the UK, to represent advertisers' interests across all marketing communication disciplines. Founded almost 100 years ago, ISBA's fundamental remit is vigorous. **www.isba.org.uk**

Institute of Promotional Marketing

The IPM is dedicated to protecting and promoting the sales promotion industry. Members are promoters, promotional marketing agencies and companies in the marketing services sector. **www.theipm.org.uk**

Direct marketing and the law

Before starting this section of the book, the advice has to be: If in any doubt, consult a lawyer.

The law covers every aspect of commercial life. From employing staff, to appointing an agency, from advertising and promotions to online selling and branding, the law applies and it is always possible to trip up. Most of the time the result of our mistakes will be a problem, just occasionally it can be a disaster. The advice is that legal advice is invaluable and whilst the services of a good commercial lawyer may seem expensive, the cost of a fine and damage to personal and company reputation may be far more.

We have discussed relevant areas of the law previously in the book. However, here we will touch on the most important Acts of parliament relating to data and electronic communications and show how they impact the practice of direct and Internet marketing.

For other areas of the law we will refer again to www.out-law.com as an invaluable source of information on legal issues that affect marketing and business.

The Privacy and Electronic Communications (EC Directive) Regulations 2003

To help control the increased use of email for direct marketing, and in part to deal with the risk of spam the EU issued in 2002 a directive on privacy and electronic communications. This was put into English Law under the The Privacy and Electronic Communications (EC Directive) Regulations 2003. Again detailed advice should be obtained if there is any doubt. The site www. out-law.com is as we have said a valuable source of advice and the Information Commissioners Office (ICO) is also useful. The ICO is at www.ico.gov.uk.

This area relates to electronic communications and specifically deals with the fact that all Electronic communications need to be opted in. That is consumers need to actively state that they wish to receive these communications. Email and SMS/MMS messaging are the most likely media affected by this.

▪ Email and SMS/MMS messaging

To quote the ICO:

'Electronic mail is emails, SMS (text), picture, video and answer-phone messages. Electronic mail marketing messages should not be sent to individuals without their permission unless all these following criteria are met:
1. The marketer has obtained your details through a sale or negotiations for a sale.
2. The messages are about similar products or services offered by the sender.
3. You were given an opportunity to refuse the marketing when your details were collected and, if you did not refuse, you were given a simple way to opt out in every future communication.' Information Commissioners Office (ICO)

The regulations also cover telemarketing, automated calls and faxes.

▪ Telesales calls

Again quoting the ICO:

'Telesales calls are 'live' marketing calls, where you speak to a person. Telesales do not include genuine market-research calls, recorded messages or silent calls. Silent calls can occur where automated diallers call a range of numbers and there is no call-centre worker free to talk to the recipient.'

Silent calls are dealt with by Ofcom and their website is www.ofcom.org.uk.

Telephone sales calls should not be made to those registered with The Telephone Preference Service (TPS) or the Corporate Telephone Preference Service CTPS), or to those who have told the caller they do not want to be contacted in this way.

▪ Automated calls

Automated marketing calls are pre-recorded marketing messages and can only be used with the prior permission of an individual or organisation. They do not include 'live' sales calls (where you speak to a person), voicemail messages or 'silent calls'.

▪ Faxes

The same system applies to faxes through the Fax Preference Service.

The Data Protection Act (DPA) 1998.

According to the ICO the DPA 1998 works to give individuals rights to know what data is held on them and to ensure that this information is handled properly.

The DPA works in two ways. First, data controllers (i.e. those that process personal data) must comply with the Act's eight principles in managing data subject's personal information. Data subjects are those about who data is held.

Eight Data Protection Principles

1. Personal data shall be processed fairly and lawfully and, in particular, shall not be processed unless:
   a) at least one of the conditions in Schedule 2 is met, and
   b) in the case of sensitive personal data, at least one of the conditions in Schedule 3 is also met.
2. Personal data shall be obtained only for one or more specified and lawful purposes, and shall not be further processed in any manner incompatible with that purpose or those purposes.
3. Personal data shall be adequate, relevant and not excessive in relation to the purpose or purposes for which they are processed.
4. Personal data shall be accurate and, where necessary, kept up to date.
5. Personal data processed for any purpose or purposes shall not be kept for longer than is necessary for that purpose or those purposes.

6. Personal data shall be processed in accordance with the rights of data subjects under this Act.
7. Appropriate technical and organisational measures shall be taken against unauthorised or unlawful processing of personal data and against accidental loss or destruction of, or damage to, personal data.
8. Personal data shall not be transferred to a country or territory outside the European Economic Area unless that country or territory ensures an adequate level of protection for the rights and freedoms of data subjects in relation to the processing of personal data.

Secondly, the Act seeks to ensure the right to find out what data is held. A fee of £10 can be charged for this activity and the data must be provided within 40 days of the request being received.

The ICO publishes the following checklist to help companies establish if the comply with the Act. Can you answer 'Yes' to all the ICO's questions?

- Do I really need this information about an individual? Do I know what I'm going to use it for?
- Do the people whose information I hold know that I've got it, and are they likely to understand what it will be used for?
- If I'm asked to pass on personal information, would the people about whom I hold information expect me to do this?
- Am I satisfied the information is being held securely, whether it's on paper or on computer? And what about my website? Is it secure?
- Is access to personal information limited to those with a strict need to know?
- Am I sure the personal information is accurate and up to date?
- Do I delete or destroy personal information as soon as I have no more need for it?
- Have I trained my staff in their duties and responsibilities under the Data Protection Act, and are they putting them into practice?
- Do I need to notify the Information Commissioner and if so is my notification up to date?

Source: www.ico.gov.uk

The Freedom of Information Act 2000 and the Freedom of Information (Scotland) Act 2002

These Acts came into force in 2005 and they cover the right individual to access data held on them by public bodies. It also gives rights to third parties to access data, hence the *Daily Telegraph*'s ability to disclose MP's expenses claims. The Act provides individuals or organisations with the right to request information held by a public authority. They can do this by letter or email. The public authority must tell the applicant whether it holds the information, and must normally supply it within 20 working days, in the format requested.

SUMMARY

In this chapter we looked at the role of ethics, regulation and the law. We saw that ethical positioning and a societal approach to marketing are never incompatible with the idea of creating value for the organisation concerned. Indeed it should be considered as part of the strategic approach to customer relationship management. We also discussed the fact that this exists within a competitive market and that CSR strategy needs to align the interests of all stakeholders within the broader business context. In order to achieve this we discussed ethical auditing and reviewed the concept of stakeholder analysis.

We went on to cover the role of self regulation and looked in detail at the DMA Code of Conduct and the CAP codes. Links were proved to relevant websites.

We finally considered the legal environment of direct and digital marketing looking in some detail at the law relating to data and electronic communications and referring readers to a range of additional resources for further and detailed information.

REVIEW QUESTIONS

1. What is CSR?
2. Why does CSR work within a relationship marketing programme?
3. What's ethical auditing?
4. Outline the range of stakeholders for an organisation of your choice.
5. Visit www.group.barclays.com/sustainability and review the CSR activity of the bank. How consistent is the content with your view of the Barclays brand? You could do the same for any brand of your choice.
6. What is the CAP and what does it do?
7. What is the ASA?
8. What is the intention of the preference services?
9. List the eight principles of the Data Protection Act 1998.
10. What are the key implications of the Privacy and Electronic Communications (EC Directive) Regulations 2003 for direct marketers?

GLOSSARY

The following is a selection of key terms used in the book and the marketing industry – you'll find a larger glossary at www.theidm.com/resources/jargon-buster.

A/B split – A type of two-way test used for two variations of one element of the same mailing package, press ad or online execution to determine which version will bring in greater response.

Above the fold – The part of a web page that is visible once the page has loaded – normally the top part. It is a key section of the page because it should grab a casual visitor's attention. The term comes from the newspaper industry.

Above-the-line – Out-of-date jargon which is best avoided. Derived from traditional accounting practice that treated advertising through television, radio or published media as 'above-the-line' expenditure. Other advertising, such as direct marketing, was accounted for 'below-the-line'.

ACORN (A Classification Of Residential Neighbourhoods) – A consumer list selection and targeting system used, based its name suggests on the predominant property types within a Census enumeration district which comprises approximately 150 households.

Acquisition cost – The advertising cost of obtaining a customer or enquiry.

Ad server – A program or a type of server that manages and maintains ad banners for a website or collection of websites. These programs are capable of keeping track and reporting website usage statistics.

Affiliate marketing – A commission-based arrangement where referring sites (publishers) receive a commission on sales or leads by merchants (retailers).

Average order cost – The total cost of orders, divided by the total number of orders.

Banner – A horizontal or vertical graphic element on a web page used to title the page, head a new section, present a company's or advertiser's message or provide a link to another page.

Behavioural targeting – Dynamic serving of relevant online content, messaging and display ads that match the inferred interests of a website visitor or email recipient. The inferred relevance is based on data gathered from tracking the user's previous online behaviour.

Below-the-line – Opposite to above-the-line. An outdated and misused term originally based on whether agency remuneration was based on commission or fees. Misused because it is often applied to direct marketing which often uses commissionable media. Today there is no line.

Blog – Short for 'web log'. Personal online diary, journal or news source. The author is referred to as a 'blogger' and the act described as 'blogging'.

Bounce rate – The percentage of visitors who visit a site but access one page only.

Channel marketing strategy – A strategy that defines the specific objectives and methods an organisation sets for using a channel and how its proposition and communications for that channel will vary to suit the particular characteristics of the channel.

Chat (forum/rooms) – A group of Internet users exchanging messages on a subject of common interest. Unlike newsgroups all the participants are connected to the forum at the same time and the messages are displayed immediately for members of the forum to see.

Click stream data – This shows the which websites a user has visited in a session and their progress though the site. Additional information on the user can also be collected through the use of cookies.

Click-through rate – The percent of individuals viewing a web page who click on a specific banner ad appearing on the page.

Cluster analysis – A mathematical technique for grouping data into clusters with similar characteristics.

Cloud computing – Internet-based computing, whereby shared resources, software, and information are provided to computers and other devices on demand, like the electricity grid. *Source: Wikipedia*

Content management system – A software tool for creating, editing and updating documents accessed by intranet, extranet, or Internet.

Control – A control is normally the standard promotional presentation of a product against which tests are evaluated to see if any improvement can be made.

Conversion – A marketing term for where your prospects or website visitors become buyers, usually expressed in terms of percentage conversion. In TV parlance, this refers to the relative efficiency of a channel, programme or campaign in reaching a sub-audience compared to a broad audience, normally expressed as an index.

Cookie – A small bit of software placed on a user's web browser by a web server. The browser stores the software in a text file called cookie.txt. It sends a message back to the server each time the browser requests a page from the server. The main purpose of cookies is to identify returning users and to store browser session data.

Cost per acquisition (CPA)/Cost per customer (CPC) – How much you can afford to spend to acquire a customer.

Cost per click (CPC) – Cost of advertising based on the number of clicks received. (Source: www.iab.net)

Cost per enquiry (CPE)/Cost per lead (CPL) – The cost per enquiry is calculated by dividing the total cost of an activity by the number of enquiries or leads, it generates.

Cost per order (CPO) – Total cost of an activity divided by the number of orders it generates.

Cost per sale (CPS) – The advertising cost of generating a single sale.

Cost per thousand – Expressed as either CPT or CPM (cost per mille). Used in media planning to describe the cost of 'reaching' 1,000 people. Also used in print advertising, e.g. cost per thousand envelopes; mailing packs; rented names and so on.

Customer lifetime value (LTV) – The total value of all future contributions to profit and overhead you can expect from that customer.

Customer relationship management (CRM) – The discipline of organising business resources to enhance and personalise each customer encounter as part of a long-term strategy of profitable retention. *Source: Angus Jenkinson*

Customer segmentation – Customers are grouped according to their needs and value and different offerings delivered to each.

Data – A general term for information but particularly where used for input material for a computer. Also used for the trail left by surfers as they traverse the net.

Data mining – The analysis of data for relationships. With information supplied over the Internet already in digital format, details can be loaded into databases where software can search for similarities, differences and patterns that can feed into marketing initiatives or launches.

Data protection – The prevention of the passing of an individual's personal information from one computer system where the information legitimately resides to other computer systems without the consent of the individual.

Data subject – The legal term to refer to the individual whose data is held.

Data warehouse – Repository of subject-orientated, historical data designed to optimise analysis rather than transaction handling; used for regular extraction and analysis of data from large transaction databases.

Database – A collection of records retained permanently on computer, constantly updated and supporting a range of applications. Data may be added from other sources, e.g. questionnaires and telemarketing reports. *Source: www.jks.co.uk/mi*

Database Management System (DBMS) – A suite of programs which typically manage large structured sets of persistent data, offering ad hoc query facilities to many users. They are widely used in business applications.

Digital marketing – 'Digital marketing' has a similar meaning to 'electronic marketing' – both describe the management and execution of marketing using electronic media such as the Web, email, interactive TV, mobile phones, wireless media.

Direct mail – Postal mail sent through the letterbox either to advertise or to sell goods or services.

Direct response – Advertising or selling through any medium inviting the consumer to respond to the advertiser.

E-marketing – The use of the Internet and related digital information and communications technologies to achieve marketing objectives. Broadly equivalent to digital marketing.

Email – The grandfather of new media technologies and still the most widely used. Early commercial users often abandoned the technology for the brighter lights of the Web, only to return to the accessible simplicity of written communications.

Feed/RSS Feed – Blog, news or other content is published by an XML standard and syndicated for other sites or read by users in RSS reader services such as Google Reader, personalised home pages or email systems. RSS stands for rich site summary (or really simple syndication).

Fulfilment – The process of dealing with an order or enquiry, from its receipt to delivery. This includes opening, processing, administration, packing and transport.

Gains chart – Results of a multi-variant regression usually arranged in percentiles and quartiles etc.

Gap analysis – The study of the difference between the position an organisation holds currently, and where it would like to be. Also refers to gaps in a specific market.

Gone aways – Term used by direct mailers to indicate that the person at an address is no longer residing there. Royal Mail normally returns gone aways if a return address is printed on the envelope.

Guard book – A book that contains copies of all advertisements published for a client with relevant data, e.g. response rates. The electronic equivalent is a Guard file.

Hard bounce – Refers to an email message that has been returned as permanently undeliverable, meaning either the domain is invalid, the user does not exist, or the email had some errors that made it un-mailable.
House mailing – A mailing to your own house list.

Incentive – A promotional offer such as a free gift, competition etc. Aimed at encouraging potential customers to purchase.
Insert – Loose or bound-in leaflet within a magazine, newspaper, or other publication. To insert items into a mail pack.
Integrated marketing communications (IMC) – The co-ordination of communications to deliver a clear, consistent message.
Interactive advertising (IA) – All forms of online, wireless and interactive television advertising, including banners, sponsorships, email, keyword searches, classified ads and referrals. In the context of digital TV, refers to advertisements with an overlay prompting the viewer to press the red button on their remote control for more information, a competition, sample etc.
Interactive marketing – All types of advertising through the Web, wireless and interactive television. Interactive advertising can include banners, site sponsorships, email ads, PPC search engine ads and classified ads. A broader definition is 'direct marketing using electronic (digital) media'.
Internet – Global communications network that carries communications protocols including the world wide web, email and newsgroups.
Interstitial – A web page not requested by a user, usually containing an advertisement, which appears on the user's screen, often in an automatically opened new browser, when the user has clicked on a link to move from one web page to another.

Junk mail – Badly targeted, irrelevant mail.

Key word – The word (or words) a user types in when presented with a search box (for example the box in front of where it says 'Look It Up' near the upper right-hand corner on the homepage of NetLingo). On a search engine, for example, a keyword is the term or phrase that you type in to begin an online search.

Mailing List – A list of names and addresses for either postal direct mail or email.
Mailsort (1, 2, 3) – Schemes for pre-sorted mailings for which the Royal Mail offer discounts. There are three service standards: first class, second class and slower bulk rate.
Media neutral planning – A rigorous process for the selection of communication options which combines facts, imagination and impartiality in order to drive continual improvement to overall ROI through choosing the optimum mix of media.
Media-multiplier effect – When different types of media are used in combination as part of an integrated communication plan they work differently than when used alone.

Member-get-member (MGM) – A marketing technique whereby a member is asked to recommend a friend or colleague to become a member. Often but not always incentivised.

Merge and purge – The process of combining two or more mailing lists in order to build one larger one, but including the removal of duplicates.

Metcalfe's Law – The total value of a network to its users grows as the square of the total number of users. Bob Metcalfe's law shows that ratio of value to cost is disproportionate to rate of increase of the network, i.e. growth in numbers can give increasing returns.

Microsite – A small-scale separate website (or pages within a website) with a separate URL, providing specific information about a product or service (also called a minisite). Also refers to a designated area on digital cable or satellite TV platforms that can be owned by an advertiser that is used for information, data-capture, callback and branding.

Mosaic – Mosaic UK is a geodemographic targeting tool based on property types at the postcode level. There are 155 Mosaic person types aggregated into 67 household types and 15 groups, to create a three-tier classification that can be used at the individual, household or postcode level.

Mouseover – Refers to a JavaScript element that triggers a change on an item (usually a graphic) in a web page when the cursor passes over it. The change usually signifies that the item is a link to related or additional information. Also referred to as 'hovering'.

Multivariate testing – Techniques that enable two or more variables to be tested simultaneously in the one experiment. Commonly used multivariate approaches include CHAID and regression analysis.

Natural or organic listing – The page listing results from a search engine query that are displayed in a sequence according to relevance of match between the keyword phrase typed into the search engine and a web page according to a ranking algorithm used by the search engine.

Net names – The number of names used for a mailing, after duplicates have been eliminated.

Nth name – A way of identifying names to create a test file. This involves taking a percentage of the total number of names by selecting out every Nth name. For example, Of 100,000 names, where 10 per cent are required, N would be every 10th name throughout the list. It is a way of ensuring randomness to the test list.

Off-the-page (OTP) – Obtaining a sale directly from a press advert.

Off-the-screen – Obtaining sales directly from a television advertisement.

Online reputation management – Controlling the reputation of an organisation through monitoring and controlling messages placed about the organisation.

Opt-in – The action of a person giving a company permission to use data collected from or about the individual for a particular reason, such as for marketing.

Opt-out – A form of permission marketing whereby the customer is given the opportunity to reject further promotional messages from a marketer. Frequently this appears as a tick box as on a reply coupon or response email.

PAF – Royal Mail's postal address file.

Page View – A unit for measuring website readership which corresponds to one person viewing one page, or at least a portion of a page, at one time. If a person leaves a certain page and returns to it in the same visit to the website two page views are counted.

Pareto's principle – The so-called 80/20 rule. The general tendency is for the majority of revenue to come from a minority of customers.

Pay per click (PPC) – A type of search marketing where advertisers pay a set amount every time their ad is clicked on by a prospect (known as a 'click-through').

Permission-based marketing – The sending of marketing messages, typically email messages, to individuals who have given the marketer permission to send such messages.

Personicx – A marketing segmentation system, developed by Acxiom, that places UK households into different clusters based on specific consumer and demographic characteristics. Unlike segmentation systems based on property types Personicx has been built on recent lifestyle data.

Portal – A website that acts as a gateway to information and services available on the Internet by providing search engines, directories and other services such as personalised news or free email. A portal is intended to be the site its users first connect to whenever they log onto the Internet.

Probability tables – A set of statistical estimates which tabulate the confidence levels which can be achieved.

Profile – Description or picture of a customer typical to a company. The profile (composition of customers) is typically expressed in percentages of the total accounted for by each significant sub-demographic, e.g. age group.

Profiling – Collecting and analysing information that individuals have provided about themselves (see registration) and information about their online behaviour (e.g. sites visited and content viewed), for the purpose of targeting marketing campaigns.

Proposition – What the customer is being asked to accept; incorporates the offer.

Prospect – A person who has either expressed an interest in a company or its product, or whose profile suggests they would be likely potential customers.

Push advertising – Proactive, partial screen, dynamic advertisement which comes in various formats.

Qualified enquirer – A person who has acted in such a way as to indicate that he or she is a serious prospect for goods or services.

Rate card – A document or card which sets out the costs for advertisement space, together with production details and copy dates.

Reading and noting studies – Studies that measure the average proportion of readers of a newspaper or magazine who actually paid attention to separate pages and even individual advertisements. The method was invented by Dr George Gallup in the 1920s. A rival service was set up by Starch and reading and noting became an accepted method of testing advertising effectiveness. Individuals are tested on what elements of a newspaper or magazine they recall.

Regression – A mathematical technique which produces a functional relationship between two or more correlated variables. It is often used to predict values of one variable when the other values are known. ***Source: www.tedhaynes.com***

Regression analysis – Regression analysis compares two or more variables and determines the 'line of best fit'. This line is used to read off the characteristics of customers and thus seek out further customers whose profile falls on or near the line.

Relational Database – A relational database allows the definition of data structures, storage and retrieval operations and integrity constraints. In such a database the data and relations between them are organised in tables.

Respondent – A person being interviewed in a research study or one who replies to a mailing or other direct advertisement.

Response rate – The percentage of orders or enquiries received of the total number of people who received the promotion.

Search engine – On the world wide web, a website such as Google, that catalogues a vast number of web pages and other documents on the Internet and provides links to them and descriptions of them for users.

Search engine optimisation (SEO) – Using relevant keyword phrases to increase an organisation's position in what is known as the natural or organic listings on the search engine results pages.

Search query – Words or phrases input for the search engine to use to access relevant documents.

Seed names (or seeds) – Names and addresses inserted into a mailing list, to ascertain whether proper usage of the list has been maintained, or to measure speed of delivery etc.

Social media – The creation of useful, valuable and relevant content and applications by brands, or by consumers with specific reference to brands, that can be shared online, facilitated by Web 2.0 technology.

Soft bounce – An email message that has been returned as temporarily undeliverable or for an unspecified reason. Try re-sending it to see if it eventually gets through (e.g. once a crashed server has been restored)

Source code – A unique identification distinguishing one list or media source from another.

Split run – A test where one element of a promotion is tested against another or a control using alternate copies of the same issue of the same publication. These are also known as A/B splits in the press, and a 'head to head' in direct mail.

Superstitial – An interactive online advertisement.

Take one – Leaflets displayed at point-of-sale dispensers placed in areas where potential customers gather.

Television rating(s) (TVR, GRP) – Currency of the television industry, which measures popularity of a programme, daypart, commercial break or advertisement by comparing the audience to the population as a whole. 1 TVR = 1% of the potential audience (universe).

Test – A trial of two or more variants (lists, packages, offers, prices etc.).

Test market – A defined area which has characteristics representative of the entire market, which make it suitable for testing a product or campaign.

Uniform Resource Locator (URL) – Most often referring to a web address. A URL is the location and access method of a resource on the Internet. It identifies a particular Internet resource, for example a web page, a library catalogue, an image or a text file.

Unique Selling Proposition (USP) – The single most saleable feature of a product used in broadscale advertising to distinguish a particular product benefit/feature from competitive offers.

Viral marketing – Using powerful offers to stimulate proliferation of a message via online 'word of mouth' (through social networks, emails, blogs etc.) to reach large audiences rapidly and cost-effectively. Can be used to build response, sales, awareness and PR.

Web 2.0 – Describes a host of user-driven technologies such as blogs, wikis, social bookmarking tools, syndication services and podcasting. These are about creating and remixing content (i.e. user-driven content environments) not just consuming it.

Web analytics – The assessment of a variety of web data, including traffic, transactions, server performance and usability studies to help create an understanding of the visitor experience online.

Web page – A document that is stored in HTML format. It can contain text, images and hyperlinks. Web pages are usually grouped with other pages on the same theme to form a website.

White list – A list of accepted email addresses or domain names from which an email blocking program will allow messages to be received.

Wiki – Derived from the Hawaiian word for 'fast', an online encyclopaedia created by many web users. It is an open, public collaboration, authored and edited by users without the need for registration or subscription. A famous example is Wikipedia.org.

Zipf's Law – In a list ordered or ranked by popularity, the second item will be about half the popularity of the first and the third will be about a third of the popularity of the first. In general, the kth item is 1/k the popularity of the first.

FURTHER READING

The following have been drawn on throughout our careers they represent a small part of the literature available to help your professional development.

BOOKS

Bird D. *Commonsense Direct and Digital Marketing*. 5th Ed. London: Kogan Page, 2007.

Broderick, A. and D. Pickton. *Integrated Marketing Communications*. 2nd Ed. Harlow: Financial Times Prentice Hall, 2005.

Bruhn M. *E-business and E-commerce Management*. Harlow: Financial Times Prentice Hall, 2002.

Chaffey D. *Internet Marketing*. Harlow: Financial Times Prentice Hall, 2006.

Chaffey D. et al. *Internet Marketing: Strategy, Implementation and Practice*. 4th Ed. Harlow: Financial Times Prentice Hall, 2009.

Chaffey et al. *Total Email Marketing*. 2nd Ed. Oxford: Butterworth Heinemann, 2006

The Institute of Direct Marketing. *The IDM Marketing Guide: Best Practice Direct, Data, Digital Marketing*. Middlesex: The Institute of Direct Marketing, 2007.

Egan J. *Relationship Marketing: Exploring Relational Strategies in Marketing*. Harlow: Financial Times Prentice Hall, 2004.

Gamble P. et al. *Up Close and Personal?* 3rd Ed. London: Kogan Page, 2006.

Grappone J. *Search Engine Optimization: An Hour a Day*. Chichester: John Wiley & Sons, 2006.

Harrison S. *How to do Better Creative Work*. Essex: Pearson Education Limited, 2009.

Johnson G., K. Scholes and R Whittington. *Exploring Corporate Strategy*. 8th Edition. Essex: Prentice Hall, 2008.

Kaushik A. *Web Analytics 2.0: The Art of Online Accountability and Science of Customer Centricity*. Chichester: John Wiley and Sons, 2009.

Kaushik A. and J. Sterne. *Web Analytics: An Hour a Day*. Chichester: John Wiley & Sons, 2009.

Krug S. *Don't Make Me Think: A Common Sense Approach to Web Usability*. Berkeley, CA: New Riders, 2006.

McCorkell G. *Direct and Database Marketing*. London: Kogan Page, 1997.

McCorkell G. *Advertising that Pulls Response*. London: McGraw-Hill, 1990.

Nielsen J. and K, Pernice. *Eyetracking Web Usability*. Berkeley, CA: New Riders, 2009.

Nielsen J. and H. Loranger. *Web Usability*. Essex: Pearson Education Limited, 2008.

Peppers D. and M. Rogers. *Return on Customer: Creating and Maximizing Value from Your Scarcest Resource*. USA: Crown Business, 2005.

Porter M. *Competitive Strategy: Techniques for Analyzing Industries and Competitors*. New York: Free Press, 1998.

Schultz D. and H. Schultz . *IMC, The Next Generation: Five Steps for Delivering Value and Measuring Returns Using Marketing Communication*. London: McGraw-Hill Professional, 2004.

Stone B. and R. Jacobs. *Successful Direct Marketing Methods: Interactive, Database, and Customer-Based Marketing for Digital Age*. London: McGraw-Hill Professional, 2007.

Stone M. et al. *Foss Consumer Insight: How to Use Data and Market Research to Get Closer to Your Customer*. London: Kogan Page, 2004.

Tapp A. *Principles of Direct and Database Management: A Digital Perspective*. 4th Ed. Essex: Pearson Education Limited, 2008.

Vögele S. *Handbook of Direct Mail*. Harlow: Financial Times Prentice Hall, 1992.

Wheildon C. *Type and Layout*. Australia: Worsley Press, 2005.

JOURNALS AND MAGAZINES

Advertising

Campaign: www.campaignlive.co.uk

International Journal of Advertising: www.internationaljournalofadvertising.com

Journal of Advertising Research (US): www.journalofadvertisingresearch.com

Database Marketing

Database Marketing: www.dmarket.co.uk

Journal of Database Marketing and Customer Strategy Management :
www.palgrave-journals.com

Journal of Targeting, Measuring and Analysis for Marketing: www.palgrave-journals.com

The Journal of Direct, Data, and Digital Marketing Practice: www.palgrave-journals.com

Direct Marketing

Direct Marketing International: www.dmionline.net

Response Magazine: www.responsemagazine.com

Brand republic: www.brandrepublic.com

Interactive Marketing

New Media Age: www.nma.co.uk

Marketing

Journal of Brand Management: www.palgrave-journals.com

Journal of Marketing Management: www.informaworld.com/rjmm.

Marketing: www.marketingmagazine.co.uk

Marketing Week: www.marketingweek.co.uk

Relationship Marketing

Colloquy: www.colloquy.com

Destination CRM: www.destinationcrm.com/CRM_Magazine

Loyalty: www.loyaltymagazine.com

Journal of Relationship Marketing: www.tandf.co.uk/journals/WJRM

INDEX